# The Baltic Battle of Books

*Formation and Relocation of European Libraries in the Confessional Age (c. 1500–1650) and Their Afterlife*

*Edited by*

Jonas Nordin
Gustavs Strenga
Peter Sjökvist

BRILL

LEIDEN | BOSTON

This is an open access title distributed under the terms of the CC BY-NC-ND 4.0 license, which permits any non-commercial use, distribution, and reproduction in any medium, provided no alterations are made and the original author(s) and source are credited. Further information and the complete license text can be found at https://creativecommons.org/licenses/by-nc-nd/4.0/

The terms of the CC license apply only to the original material. The use of material from other sources (indicated by a reference) such as diagrams, illustrations, photos and text samples may require further permission from the respective copyright holder.

Open access funding provided by Lund University.

 Research funding provided by the Ministry of Education and Science of the Republic of Latvia, 'The Significance of Documentary Heritage in Creating Synergies between Research and Society', VPP-IZM-2018/1-0022.

Cover illustration: Part of the Riga Collection, Uppsala University Library. Photo: Magnus Hjalmarsson.

The Library of Congress Cataloging-in-Publication Data is available online at https://catalog.loc.gov
LC record available at https://lccn.loc.gov/2023025741

Typeface for the Latin, Greek, and Cyrillic scripts: "Brill". See and download: brill.com/brill-typeface.

ISSN 1874-4834
ISBN 978-90-04-44120-0 (hardback)
ISBN 978-90-04-44121-7 (e-book)

Copyright 2023 by Jonas Nordin, Gustavs Strenga and Peter Sjökvist. Published by Koninklijke Brill NV, Leiden, The Netherlands.
Koninklijke Brill NV incorporates the imprints Brill, Brill Nijhoff, Brill Hotei, Brill Schöningh, Brill Fink, Brill mentis, Vandenhoeck & Ruprecht, Böhlau, V&R unipress and Wageningen Academic
Koninklijke Brill NV reserves the right to protect this publication against unauthorized use.

This book is printed on acid-free paper and produced in a sustainable manner.

PRINTED BY DRUKKERIJ WILCO B.V. – AMERSFOORT, THE NETHERLANDS

The Baltic Battle of Books

# Library of the Written Word

VOLUME 116

---

# The Handpress World

*Editors-in-Chief*

Andrew Pettegree (*University of St Andrews*)
Arthur der Weduwen (*University of St Andrews*)

*Editorial Board*

Ann Blair (*Harvard University*)
Falk Eisermann (*Staatsbibliothek zu Berlin – Preußischer Kulturbesitz*)
Shanti Graheli (*University of Glasgow*)
Earle Havens (*Johns Hopkins University*)
Ian Maclean (*All Souls College, Oxford*)
Alicia Montoya (*Radboud University*)
Angela Nuovo (*University of Milan*)
Helen Smith (*University of York*)
Mark Towsey (*University of Liverpool*)
Malcolm Walsby (ENSSIB, *Lyon*)

VOLUME 94

The titles published in this series are listed at *brill.com/lww*

# Contents

Preface   IX
*Jonas Nordin, Peter Sjökvist and Gustavs Strenga*
List of Figures and List of Tables   X
Notes on Contributors   XIII

A Battle of Books through Five Centuries   1
*Jonas Nordin, Peter Sjökvist and Gustavs Strenga*

## PART 1
## *Creating Libraries*

1  Fifteenth-Century Manuscripts
   *The Liturgical and Musical Testimonies from the Cistercian Nunnery in Riga*   13
   Laine Tabora

2  Gradual Formation and Dramatic Transformation
   *Mendicant and Cistercian Book Collections in Late Medieval and Post-reformation Riga*   37
   Andris Levāns and Gustavs Strenga

3  The Printing of Missals and Breviaries as Ecclesiastical Authority in the Late-Medieval Baltic Region
   *A Battle between Printers or between Bishops?*   62
   Mattias Lundberg

4  A Game of Cities
   *Driving Forces in Early Modern Scandinavian Book History*   78
   Wolfgang Undorf

5  English and Scottish Jesuits and Print Culture of the Sixteenth-Century Grand Duchy of Lithuania   107
   Hanna Mazheika

6   Pre-suppression Jesuit Libraries
    *Patterns of Collection and Use in Northern, Central, and
    Eastern Europe*   126
        Kathleen M. Comerford

### PART 2
## *Relocating Libraries*

7   Building a Nation through Books
    *From Military to Cultural Armament in Seventeenth-Century Sweden*   151
        Jonas Nordin

8   War Booty of Books from Olomouc
    *Catholic Libraries in Lutheran Sweden*   179
        Lenka Veselá

9   Useful Literary Spoils of War from Riga at Uppsala University
    Library   197
        Peter Sjökvist

10  Battles of Books in Denmark from the Reformation to the Great
    Northern War   214
        Anders Toftgaard

11  'An Ornament for the Church and the Gymnasium'
    *The War Booty in Strängnäs Cathedral and Its Relation to the School*   242
        Elin Andersson

### PART 3
## *Reconstructing Libraries*

12  The Fragment of the Personal Library of Johannes Poliander in the
    National Library of Poland   267
        Fryderyk Rozen

CONTENTS

13  The Fate of the Riga Jesuit College Library (1583–1621)
    *Aspects of Research into a Historic and Unique Book Collection in the Digital Age*   300
        *Laura Kreigere-Liepiņa*

14  Dissonance and Consonance in the Early Modern Battle of Books   326
    *A Personal Reading*   326
        *Janis Kreslins*

    Colour Illustrations   337
    Index   343

# Preface

This book, like the book collections described and analysed in it, has been influenced and formed by historical events. Most of the chapters were originally intended to be presented at the conference 'Sacred Books, Looted Books: Formation, Transfiguration and Replacement of the Northern European Libraries in the Confessional Age (c.1500–c.1650) and their Afterlife' at the National Library of Latvia, Riga, in October of 2020. Due to the COVID-19 pandemic the conference had to be cancelled. Instead, an open online workshop was held in March of 2021, where the authors presented and discussed their chapter drafts. In putting the volume together, the editors noticed some conspicuous gaps and approached other authors to render the collection, if not complete, at least less wanting. We want to thank all contributors for their efforts in making this such a rich volume. We also want to thank the series editors Andrew Pettegree and Arthur der Weduwen for encouraging the editors to publish the book in the Library of the Written Word series. Finally, the editors want to express their gratitude to Lund University, which generously bestowed funding to make this an open-access publication, and the National Library of Latvia, which funded the copy-editing.[1] The language editing has been carried out by Professor Andrejs Plakans, whom the editors thank for a thoroughly performed work.

*Jonas Nordin, Peter Sjökvist and Gustavs Strenga*

---

1 The book has been partially funded from the project of the Ministry of Education and Science of the Republic of Latvia 'The Significance of Documentary Heritage in Creating Synergies between Research and Society', VPP-IZM-2018/1-0022.

# Figures

3.1 Dioceses with printed missals and breviaries 1478–1500: 1. Schwerin; 2. Lübeck; 3. Hamburg; 4. Bremen; 5. Ratzeburg; 6 Schleswig; 7. Odense; 8. Roskilde; 9. Viborg   67
3.2 Dioceses with printed missals and breviaries 1484–1500: 1. Uppsala; 2. Västerås; 3. Strängnäs; 4. Linköping; 5. Skara; 6. Turku   69
3.3 Missals and Breviaries printed for dioceses around the neck of Denmark   69
3.4 The final page of the *Missale Othoniense*, Brandis, 1483   71
3.5 Gilded initial in the second Missale Upsalense, Pforzheim: Basel, 1513   339
6.1a–b Geographical distribution of the Jesuit Libraries in the EJLPP and the identified subset   134
7.1 Swedish domestic and foreign print production 1478–1599: number of titles   154
7.2 Swedish domestic print production 1600–1719: number of titles   176
8.1 A record of the attack on Olomouc made by the imperial army in 1644. From: Helfrich Emmel, *Sylva Quadrilinguis* (Prague: Daniel Adam z Veleslavína, 1598), Universiteitsbibliotheek Leiden (721 C 15)   195
10.1 'Tout le monde est une farce, et se gouverne par opinion.' Corfitz Ulfeldt's motto in a copy of Martin Rinckart, *Circulorum memoriæ decas* (Leipzig: Elia Rehfeld und Joh. Grossen 1629)   234
11.1 Strängnäs Cathedral and Rogge Castle (school house) from Erik Dahlbergh's *Suecia antiqua et hodierna*   243
11.2 U 575 oct., possibly a war booty book from the Franciscan convent in Olomouc   340
11.3 A prospect for the disposition of rooms in Strängnäs Gymnasium 1807. Landsarkivet, Uppsala. Note that the cathedral library is to be kept separately in one of the smaller rooms (*För Domkyrkans Gamla Bibliothek*, 'For the Old Library of the Cathedral.')   253
11.4 Prospect by J.W. Geiss for turning the main auditorium in the school house into a library, 1835. Photo: National Library of Sweden   261
11.5 From Jan Łoś, 'Fotografier från den polska kommissionens besök i Sverige sommaren 1911' (Photographs from the Polish Commission's visit to Sweden in the summer of 1911), album kept at the National Library of Sweden   263
13.1 'Inventarium över Jesuitkollegiets i Riga bibliotek, uppgjort av hovpredikanten, sedermera biskopen i Linköping Johannes Bothvidi' (s. l.: [1683]), Uppsala University Library, U271, page 31. The last page of the

|      | inventory gives information about the church and household items listed in Swedish. Annotations about the origin and the date of the document below   306 |
|------|---|
| 13.2 | Madonna with child ('Our Lady of Vladimir'), sixteenth century, Uppsala University Museum Gustavianum, UU 749. Probably one of the five Russian icons brought from Riga and mentioned on the inventory list, now held by Uppsala University   341 |
| 13.3 | A title page of the Riga Jesuit college library's book bearing provenance inscription Bibliothecae Magnae of the former institution, Vilnius Jesuit college library, and a stamp of the Russian Academy of Sciences. John Fisher, *Opera, quae hactenus inveniri potuerunt omnia …*, (Würzburg: Georg Fleischmann, 1597), Vilnius University Library, BAV 7.2.10., CRJCBC No 392, USTC 689682   320 |
| 13.4 | The book binding representing the monogram D G and Riga city symbol: crossed keys. These features indicate to possibility that the book was bound in Riga or for an order from Riga's Jesuits. Noël Taillepied, *Summarische Historia Vnd Warhafftig Geschicht Von dem Leben* (Ingolstadt: Wolfgang Eder, Officina Weissenhorniana, 1582), Tallinn University Academic Library, I-851, CRJCBC No 747, USTC 694956   342 |

# Tables

| | | |
|---|---|---|
| 3.1 | Missals and breviaries printed for dioceses of the Baltic Sea region before 1500 | 65 |
| 4.1 | Religious books printed in Lübeck and Rostock för the Danish and Swedish markets | 97 |
| 4.2 | Religious books printed in Swedish or Danish in Sweden, Denmark and abroad in the sixteenth century | 103 |
| 6.1 | General subjects found in prescriptive materials and in Jesuit libraries in selected colleges in Europe prior to the suppression | 136 |
| 6.2 | Representation of selected religious orders among authors in the inventories and the EJLPP | 145 |
| 8.1 | Libraries confiscated in Olomouc in 1645 | 196 |
| 11.1 | Books in Roggebiblioteket with war booty provenance | 246 |

# Notes on Contributors

*Elin Andersson*
(b. 1977), PhD, is curator of special collections at the Rogge Library and the Cathedral Library in Strängnäs, and a specialist on medieval Latin manuscripts at Kungliga biblioteket/The National Library of Sweden. Her main research interests are book history and texts related to the medieval Birgittine order.

*Kathleen M. Comerford*
(b. 1966), PhD, is Professor of History at Georgia Southern University (Statesboro campus). Her main research interests are in the history of the book and libraries, Jesuit studies, and the history of Florence and Tuscany between the 1520s and 1630s.

*Laura Kreigere-Liepiņa*
(b. 1980), Mg. hum. in Classical Philology, chief bibliographer in the Rare Books and Manuscripts Collection at the National Library of Latvia. Her main academic interests are ideas of humanism, Neo-Latin literary heritage in sixteenth and seventeenth century Riga, and late medieval and early modern books.

*Janis Kreslins*
(b. 1955), PhD, is Senior Academic Librarian for Research Affairs at Kungliga biblioteket/The National Library of Sweden and the author of publications on identity formation, religious culture and the rise of indigenous language traditions in the early modern North European lands.

*Andris Levans*
(b. 1968), Dr. hist., is a Professor of Medieval history at the University of Latvia in Riga. His research interests include the history of medieval and early modern historiography and autobiographical texts, the history of concepts, memory phenomena and textual culture, as well as the history of the chancery practices of the Livonian bishops and Riga Cathedral chapter.

*Mattias Lundberg*
(b. 1976), PhD, is Professor of Musicology at Uppsala University. His research interests include late-medieval music and liturgy in Northern Europe, music of the Reformation movements, and historical music theory.

### Hanna Mazheika

(b. 1984), PhD, is Assistant Professor at the Faculty of History of the University of Warsaw. Her research interests lie in the field of cultural and religious exchange between Eastern and Western Europe in the early modern period.

### Jonas Nordin

(b. 1968), PhD, is Professor of Book and Library History at Lund University. His research is mainly focused on book culture and intellectual history of the sixteenth and seventeenth centuries.

### Fryderyk Rozen

(b. 1983), PhD, is librarian at the Department of the Early Printed Books, National Library of Poland, Warsaw. His research interests are incunabula and book culture of the Evangelical communities in the Polish-Lithuanian Commonwealth.

### Peter Sjökvist

(b. 1974), PhD, is Associate Professor of Latin at Uppsala University and Rare Books Librarian at Uppsala University Library. His research interests are early modern occasional poetry, dissertation culture and literary spoils of war.

### Gustavs Strenga

(b. 1981), PhD, is a Post-Doctoral Research Fellow at the University of Greifswald and has recently been a Senior Researcher at the National Library of Latvia. The history of medieval Livonia, memory studies, remembrance of medieval heroes, ethnicity in the Middle Ages, gift giving as a historical phenomenon, and book history are his main academic interests.

### Laine Tabora

(b. 1990), PhD candidate at the Pontifical Institute of Sacred Music in Rome. Her scientific interests include the liturgical and devotional culture of the Middle Ages with a focus on prayer practices of the late medieval nunneries. The area of particular interest concerns liturgical manuscripts and fragments from medieval Livonia and the Baltic region.

### Anders Toftgaard

(b. 1973), PhD, is Research Librarian at the Royal Danish Library, Copenhagen. He specializes in French and Italian Renaissance literature and book history.

*Wolfgang Undorf*
(b. 1964), PhD in book history, is Senior Librarian at Kungliga biblioteket/The National Library of Sweden. His main research interests are early Swedish and North European book history, especially the aspect of transnational history and cultural exchange from the fifteenth trough nineteenth centuries.

*Lenka Veselá*
(b. 1975), PhD, is a Senior Researcher at the Library of the Academy of Sciences in Prague. Her main academic research interests are Czech book culture before 1800, digital humanities, the history of early modern libraries in Central Europe, and Swedish literary spoils of war from the Czech lands.

# A Battle of Books through Five Centuries

*Jonas Nordin, Peter Sjökvist and Gustavs Strenga*

'*Habent sua fata libelli*' (Books have their destinies). This oft-repeated, even worn-out, phrase of Terentianus Maurus fits unusually well for opening this book. The chapters that follow do not study individual books as much as they study collections of books, and these have indeed had their different destinies and continue to have so today. This book is about the creation, relocation, and reconstruction of libraries between the late Middle Ages and the Age of Confessionalization, that is, the era of religious division and struggle in Northern Europe following the Reformation and Counter-Reformation in the sixteenth and seventeenth centuries. This was not only a time when different creeds clashed with each other, but also a period when the political and intellectual geography of Europe was redrawn. Centuries-old political, economic, and cultural networks fell apart and were replaced with new ones. The upheavals sundered old contacts and rendered established hierarchies and truths obsolete and unserviceable. A striking and forceful example of this is the destruction of monastic libraries and liturgical books in the new Protestant nations. What used to be revered objects and intellectual and spiritual tools of great value were suddenly reduced to binding materials for account books, tightening for organ pipes, or wadding for canons. Collections that had taken generations to assemble were dispersed, destroyed, or brought into new environments and made to serve new purposes. Were these relocations cultural disasters and abuses of international law, or were they part of a natural, although sometimes perhaps lamentable, lifecycle of book collections? The interpretations have shifted over time.

'Libraries abandoned or dispersed, burned down or looted, could be regenerated with astonishing speed', argues Andrew Pettegree and Arthur der Weduwen in a recent study.[1] A more common problem than losses through looting was that book collections were scattered through neglect and lack of interest in succeeding generations, but destruction of that kind have rarely become emblematic events. The fate of the most symbolically charged of all libraries throughout history, that of ancient Alexandria, has captivated peoples' imagination for centuries. The most widely held view among today's scholars

---

1 Andrew Pettegree and Arthur der Weduwen, *The Library: A Fragile History* (London: Profile Books, 2021), p. 100; see especially chapter 6, 'Reformations', for a discussion relevant to our subject.

is that this library slowly decayed due to lack of care, inadequate conservation techniques, and declining finances, yet stories of devastating fires or ravaging and culturally hostile conquerors, whether Romans or Muslims, live on in popular imagination.[2] The fact is that most libraries throughout history have dispersed or been destroyed one way or another, but generally it is only those whose demise was violent that has been regretted and lamented by posterity. Past disinterest, neglect, mismanagement or gradual decay has rarely entered the pages of the history books let alone attracted headlines in the newspapers.

Where does this argument put us with respect to the present book? Although four centuries or more have passed since the wars of religion, the plundering and abuses then committed by all sides occasionally stir up emotions among politicians and the public in many countries even today. The collections and books, once forcefully relocated during the seventeenth century wars, emerge in passionate political discussions and emotional social media disputes on restitution of the plundered cultural artefacts.

A rather tragicomic example unfolded in 2011. After many years of pressure from the national radical Danish People's Party (Dansk Folkeparti), the national libraries of Sweden and Denmark entered a bartered deal concerning a manuscript of Danish laws from the thirteenth century. In various contexts, this law code had been described both as a treasure of national importance for Denmark and Danish identity, and as a spoil of war that needed to be restored to correct an historical injustice. Until these claims were raised in the 1990s, no one had really investigated the provenance of the manuscript, but closer examination revealed that it was still owned by a Danish private collector in the early 1700s, several decades after the Swedes would have had the opportunity to snatch it. Most likely it was purchased legally by the Swedish Antiquities Archive later in the eighteenth century.[3] In spite of these discoveries a barter was made in early 2011, with the Royal Danish Library receiving the volume, Codex Holmiensis C 37, in exchange for a copy of the Swedish Law of Södermanland from 1327. The exchange was officially termed a mutual deposit of indefinite duration.

What makes this example especially bothersome is that even though new research could disprove the false historical claim, the authorities in both

---

[2] Myrto Hatzimichali, 'Ashes to Ashes? The Library of Alexandria after 48 BC', pp. 167–182, and Michael W. Handis, 'Myth and History: Galen and the Alexandrian library', pp. 373–4, both in Jason König, Katerina Oikonomopoulou and Greg Woolf (eds.), *Ancient Libraries* (Cambridge: Cambridge University Press, 2013).

[3] Cf. the thorough investigation made by Erland Kolding Nielsen, '"Jyske Lov" som krigsbytte: En mytes opståen, udnyttelse og fald', *Fund og forskning i det Kongelige Biblioteks samlinger*, 49 (2010), pp. 437–510.

countries chose to ignore both the research and the objections from the scholarly community to carry out the exchange, thus disregarding established principles on cooperation in the cultural heritage sector. For certain, the exchange took place with the expressed hope that the demand for both manuscripts would thereby increase. 'However, this was a subterfuge', as explained by professor in international law Ove Bring. 'It is largely the same group of legal history researchers who are studying both laws. The manuscripts have also long been digitised and freely available online.'[4] In other words, there was little historical and scientific reason for the exchange; what remains are the national symbolic ones.

In recent decades in Central Europe, from which many book collections had been taken as war booty during the wars of the seventeenth century, the public has on several occasions been reminded about the cultural artefacts removed in the distant past. In 2007, after centuries of absence, a Bohemian thirteenth-century manuscript, Codex Gigas, better known as the Devil's Bible, returned to Prague, the city from which it was taken to Sweden in 1648, at the end of the Thirty Years' War. The importance of the event, involving great uncertainty, was felt on both sides.[5] The owner of the book, the National Library of Sweden (or rather Royal Library) that had hosted this, the world's largest, manuscript for several hundred years, was concerned about the four-month loan and its return to Stockholm. The exhibitor, the Czech National Library, in order to host the book in Prague, had even involved the country's prime minister who approached his Swedish counterpart in the loan negotiation process.[6] Most likely in reaction to the public sentiment during the exhibition, the librarians of the Czech National Library emphasised that the return of the codex to Prague was impossible and that the Czech library itself has looted books in its collections.[7] The exhibition was an event of national importance, widely reported in the media and attracting great interest from the public; the spectators had to buy time-allotted tickets and were allowed to spend no

---

4 'Detta var emellertid ett svepskäl. Det är i stort sett samma grupp av rättshistoriska forskare som efterfrågar båda lagarna. Handskrifterna är dessutom sedan länge digitaliserade och fritt tillgängliga på nätet.' Ove Bring, *Parthenonsyndromet: Kampen om kulturskatterna* (Stockholm: Atlantis, 2015), p. 27.
5 Kamil Boldan (ed.), *Codex Gigas – the Devil's Bible: The Secrets of the World's Largest Book; Publication Issued on the Occasion of the Exhibition of the Same Name in the Klementinum Gallery* (Prague: National Library of the Czech Republic, 2007).
6 www.english.radio.cz/devils-bible-goes-display-prague-after-three-century-absence-8604007 (last accessed 20 November 2022), see Gunnar Sahlin's preface in the exhibition catalogue, *Codex Gigas – the Devil's Bible*, 13.
7 Brandon Swanson, 'Codex Gigas. The Devil's Bible', *The Prague Post*, 19 October 2022, www.praguepost.com/culture/codex-gigas (last accessed 1 November 2022).

more than ten minutes in front of the book. Before the departure to Prague, the manuscript had been digitised and made accessible over the Internet and the director of the National Library of Sweden, Gunnar Sahlin, in his preface of the exhibition catalogue emphasised the importance of a digital version by stating that:

> War booty taken during the 17th century will be readily appreciable not only in certain libraries or museums but almost everywhere. The original Codex will still be of great importance, but it now will be complemented by the digital version. This will enable us to better acquaint ourselves and identify with our common European heritage.[8]

Digital copies certainly make historical sources more easily accessible to users globally, and they may ease some of the tensions and complexities caused by claims for restoration. Yet they do not seem to alleviate the phantom pains of those who harbour essentialist notions about the 'true' homes of the books, whatever these are considered to be.

In the summer of 2022, Swedish Member of Parliament Björn Söder posed a written question to Foreign Minister Ann Linde about returning to Poland a copy of *Commune incliti Polonie Regni privilegium*, or Łaski's Statute, a collection of Polish laws, as an 'act of goodwill' in recognition of the country's ratification of Sweden's NATO application and of 'how quickly Poland acted for our country's security'. According to Söder only two copies remain of the original twelve printed on parchment in 1505. 'One copy is in The Central Archives of Historical Records in Warsaw. The second copy is found in Sweden after it was looted by the Swedes in the seventeenth century along with other priceless items treasures of Polish culture.'[9]

In actual fact there are eight copies printed on vellum and no fewer than 59 printed on paper preserved in Polish public collections.[10] It is certainly an important book, but there is nothing particularly unique about the Swedish copy. Furthermore, Söder's claim that Łaski's Statutes were registered on

---

8   *Codex Gigas – the Devil's Bible*, 13.
9   Written question 2021/22:1800 by Björn Söder (Sweden Democrats), 12 July 2022; Foreign Minister Ann Linde's (Social Democrats) answer, Foreign Ministry UD2022/ 10742, 26 July 2022: www.riksdagen.se/sv/dokument-lagar/dokument/skriftlig-fraga/aterlamnande-av-laskis-stadgar-till-polen_H9111800 (last accessed 21 November 2022).
10  Information provided by Fryderyk Rozen at the National Library of Poland. The relevant entries of the national union catalogue of Polish sixteenth-century prints can be accessed here: www.polona.pl/item/centralny-katalog-polonikow-xvi-w-las-mad,NjIyODg3MjQ/69/#item (last accessed 23 November 2022).

'UNESCO's World Heritage List' (probably a mix-up with UNESCO's Memory of the World Register, which lists documentary heritage) in 2016 is incorrect. It is, however, included on the *national* list established by the Polish committee for the memory of the world program, which is not sanctioned by UNESCO in Paris.[11] In this case it is the specific copy, which once belonged to the Polish King Alexander (1461–1506), that is considered significant, not the print as such.

No less incorrect was Söder's contention that the copy in Uppsala was looted by the Swedes during their wars of aggression in Poland. A quick examination by librarians at Uppsala University Library revealed that the book carried the signature of Gustavus Adolphus (1594–1632) and the year 1616, that is half a decade before Sweden's earliest book plunder.[12] The year might nevertheless be significant for other reasons. In 1615–1616 the deposed Swedish King Sigismund (1566–1632), now king of Poland as Zygmunt III, made a last serious attempt to regain the Swedish crown through negotiations and sabre-rattling. In this context it made sense for Gustavus Adolphus to keep himself informed on Polish laws and politics.

What Björn Söder thus proposed is that cultural objects, based on incorrect information, false claims and an unfounded narrative, should be used as tokens in international security policy. Foreign Minister Ann Linde rejected the request with reference to established international law and practice. Söder nevertheless repeated his question to the new foreign minister, Tobias Billström, in November 2022. This time he claimed that the new information that the book was *not* war booty should make return even less complicated, adding that the book was kept in 'the library's secured stacks underground and is consequently not an easily accessible document for the Swedish people, but must be specially ordered to the special collections reading room on the entrance floor'. As his predecessor, Billström remained unconvinced by Söder's arguments, stating that it is 'hardly appropriate in diplomatic contexts to thank for a ratification with a gift'.[13]

---

11   Pamięć Polski, 'Pierwszy w Polsce wydany drukiem urzędowy zbiór prawa': www.pamiecpolski.archiwa.gov.pl/statut-laskiego-z-1506-r/ (last accessed 23 November 2022).

12   *Commune incliti Polonie Regni privilegium constitutionum et indultuum ...* (Kraków: Haller, [1506]), Uppsala University Library, Sv. Rar. fol. 10:31, The disputed copy has been digitised by the Uppsala University Library and can be accessed here: urn.kb.se/resolve?urn=urn:nbn:se:alvin:portal:record-481618 (last accessed 22 November 2022).

13   Written question 2022/23:40 by Björn Söder, 4 November 2022; Foreign Minister Tobias Billström's (Moderate Party) answer, Foreign Ministry UD2022/ 15984, 16 November 2022; www.riksdagen.se/sv/dokument-lagar/dokument/svar-pa-skriftlig-fraga/aterlamnande-av-laskis-stadgar-till-polen_HA1240 (last accessed 22 November 2022).

In her reply to the original request, Ann Linde had rightly pointed to the fact that 'issues relating to the return of cultural-historical objects can generally be complex and it can also in some cases be difficult to determine which state or natural person the object would be handed over to'. In fact, in most instances the institutions from which books were looted four hundred years ago no longer exist, while the libraries that host the books today have continuity. Uppsala University Library, founded by Gustavus Adolphus in 1620/1621, stores numerous looted collections. Some of them are of high cultural significance in the countries they were taken from, and are frequently on loan for exhibitions. In 2023 the 550th anniversary of the birth of the well-known astronomer Nicolaus Copernicus (1473–1543) will be celebrated. The major portion of the extant books from his personal library are today at Uppsala. They were kept in the Frombork Chapter library when Gustavus Adolphus and his armies took this as war spoils in 1626. Many items from this lot will be lent to Polish institutions, just as they were during the 500th anniversary in the 1970s. The loans are handled in trust and high confidence by librarians on both sides, while parties outside the cultural heritage sector sometimes use exhibitions of this kind to voice claims for the permanent restitution of the same collections without regard to either the legal and historical aspects involved or to how this would affect future cooperation between custodians of historical collections in different countries. When a catalogue of the books taken from the Jesuit College of Braniewo in 1626, and now kept at Uppsala, was published jointly by Uppsala University Library and the National Library of Poland after a collaborative project, the director of the Polish National Library, Tomasz Makowski, stated his view on the matter in the preface:

> Can the cultural damage caused by the loss of such an intellectual centre be compensated today by the fact that the book collection escaped destruction and scattering, and has survived almost untouched in one place, like only few other historical items from similar time and representing similar value ever did on Polish soil? We will never be able to give a clear answer to this question. However, the fact that the library has survived in Sweden can now serve as evidence for the undeniable unity of European cultural and intellectual heritage.[14]

---

14  Tomasz Makowski, preface in Józef Trypućko, *The Catalogue of the Book Collection of the Jesuit College in Braniewo Held in the University Library in Uppsala = Katalog księgozbioru Kolegium Jezuitów w Braniewie zachowanego w Bibliotece Uniwersyteckiej w Uppsali*, eds. Michał Spandowski and Sławomir Szyller (3 vols., Uppsala/Warsaw: Uppsala universitetsbibliotek/Biblioteka Narodowa, 2007), 1, p. 11.

Since books looted in earlier centuries can today be found in library collections all over Europe, this now serves as a better incentive for international collaboration and exploration of a shared cultural heritage than as reasons for new and repeated conflicts. Several examples in the last decades have proven how fruitful such cooperative projects can be.

One such example was the reconstruction of the former Riga Jesuit college library (1583–1621), undertaken by the bibliographers of the National Library of Latvia in cooperation with the Uppsala University Library where the collection is now located. The Riga Jesuit college was a Catholic outpost in a Protestant environment and the collection incorporated in itself books from late medieval Catholic institutions and added new titles for the mission amongst Lutherans.[15] As described in several chapters of this volume, it was the first book collection to be ransacked by the Swedish forces during the wars of the seventeenth century, thus becoming a case of 'learning by doing' for the looters.[16] Taken as a war booty to Sweden in 1621, the Jesuit books from the largest city in the Baltic became part of Uppsala University Library founded the year before and commencing its activities the same year as Riga's conquest. The experience of bringing back a Catholic library as a war booty to the homeland was later perfected by the Swedish forces in Braniewo (Braunsberg), Frombork (Frauenburg), Würzburg, Mainz, Poznań, Olomouc, and Prague, just to mention the most important ones.[17] As the example of the Jesuit college in Riga shows, the looting of cultural artefacts cannot be seen only as acts of violence. In Riga the college and its book collection that represented pan-European learned culture like other Jesuit colleges in the north, were located in a hostile environment. The city had become Protestant already during the 1520s, and when Riga was conquered by Polish-Lithuanian forces in 1582, the Jesuit presence there was imposed on it, not chosen voluntarily. Most certainly the Riga Jesuit college library would have been destroyed by local protestants, who had revolted against the implementation of the Gregorian calendar by the Polish king Stephen Bathory (1533–1586) and the city council between 1584 and 1589,

---

15   Reinis Norkārkls, 'The Riga Jesuit College and its Book Collection', in *Catalogue of the Riga Jesuit College Book Collection (1583–1621): History and Reconstruction of the Collection = Rīgas Jezuītu kolēģijas grāmatu krājuma (1583–1621) katalogs: Krājuma vēsture un rekonstrukcija*, eds. Andris Levāns and Gustavs Strenga (Riga: Latvijas Nacionālā bibliotēka, 2021), pp. 90–111.

16   See contributions of Jonas Nordin, Peter Sjökvist and Laura Kreigere-Liepiņa in this volume.

17   Andrew Pettegree and Arthur der Weduwen, 'The Library as Totem: Building Ideology, Creating Targets', in *Catalogue of the Riga Jesuit College Book Collection (1583–1621)*, pp. 28–37, 35; see Nordin's contribution in this volume.

had it not been taken away by the Swedes.[18] In order to better understand the history of the collection and its fate, it has recently been reconstructed using a copy of the war booty list compiled by the chaplain of the Swedish court Johannes Bothvidi (1575–1635) and notes by the Swedish bibliographer Isak Collijn (1875–1949).[19] Without the relevant historical circumstances, which have given rise to later scholarly and bibliographical works, our knowledge of this collection would certainly have been much poorer if not altogether absent.

The collection taken from Riga to Uppsala also contained several books that were of great importance to Latvian culture. Uppsala University Library now holds a book with the oldest handwritten text in Latvian, the so-called Ghisbert's Lord's Prayer (c.1530), which was exhibited in Riga in 2017.[20] In 2021, the only full copy of the oldest surviving book printed in Latvian, the Catholic Catechism of Petrus Canisius (1521–1597), which used to be part of the college's books, was exhibited in the National Library of Latvia.[21] The exhibition gave rise to mixed reactions. While some visitors questioned why this national treasure should be returned to Uppsala and could not remain in Latvia, others argued that the catechism itself, a Jesuit product, symbolised colonial coercion. In the latter line of argument, the catechism embodied a culture and faith that had been imposed on Latvians by outsiders, namely German and Polish Jesuits who battled local Lutheran Baltic German pastors and noblemen.[22] Regardless of perspective, the reconstruction of the library allows posterity to grasp the value and importance of the former Jesuit collection not only for Latvian culture, but for the whole of Northern Europe.

---

18  Norkārkls, 'The Riga Jesuit College and its Book Collection', 92.
19  See contribution of Laura Kreigere-Liepiņa in this volume and *Catalogue of the Riga Jesuit College Book Collection (1583–1621)*.
20  Gustavs Strenga and Andris Levāns (eds.), *Luther: The Turn; Catalogue of the Exhibition, National Library of Latvia, Riga, 01.11.2017–04.02.2018* (Riga: Latvijas Nacionālā bibliotēka, 2017), p. 156; *Agenda sive benedictionale commune agendorum cuilibet pastori ecclesie necessarium* (Leipzig: Melchior Lotter, 1507), USTC 609610, Uppsala University Library, Riga 160; *Catalogue of the Riga Jesuit College Book Collection (1583–1621)*, no. 87.
21  Petrus Canisius, *Catechismvs Catholicorum* (Vilnius: Daniel z Lęczycy, 1585), USTC 6911452, Uppsala University Library, Utl. Rar. 174; the exhibition 'The Return: The Oldest Surviving Book in Latvian' at the National Library of Latvia (21.09.2021–29.01.2022); Renāte Berga, 'Sv. Pētera Kanīzija "Catechismus catholicorum" (Viļņa, 1585) – senākā līdz mūsdienām saglabājusies grāmata latviešu valodā', in Viesturs Zanders (ed.), *Grāmata Latvijai ārpus Latvijas: Kolektīvā monogrāfija* (Rīga: Latvijas Nacionālā bibliotēka, 2021), pp. 55–82; *Catalogue of the Riga Jesuit College Book Collection (1583–1621)*, no. 226.
22  See, Ilmārs Zvirgzds, 'Vecākā latviešu grāmata ir koloniālisma piemineklis' (The oldest Latvian book as monument of colonialism) www.satori.lv/article/vecaka-latviesu-gramata-ir-kolonialisma-piemineklis (last accessed 12 November 2022).

The phenomenon of book collections removed from their original locations and then reconstructed in modern times is recognized also in other parts of Europe. Probably the most well-known library taken as spoils of war in the seventeenth century is the Bibliotheca Palatina from Heidelberg. This Protestant library, containing around 5,000 printed books and 3,524 manuscripts, was taken by Maximilian of Bavaria (1573–1651) and his troops in 1622 and presented to the Pope. In the following centuries several attempts were made to restore the books to Heidelberg, and at the Congress of Vienna 847 German-language manuscripts were eventually handed over to the University of Heidelberg. The other books are still kept in the Vatican Library in Rome.[23] For the university's six hundredth anniversary in 1986, several items were lent from the Vatican for an exhibition in Heidelberg. In addition, since 2001 there ongoing work at the University Library of Heidelberg have aimed to reconstruct the Bibliotheca virtually.[24] We thus recognize yet another cooperation beneficial to several parties and of harm to no one.

Our goal with this book is in line with this idea. In the academic community and the cultural heritage sector, heated feelings have long since been replaced by mutual interests and cooperation across national borders to reconstruct and extract knowledge from the early collections. We believe that books and library collections are never static, but have long life cycles in which all aspects of the past belong to their historical narrative. We therefore study European libraries from three different aspects: their original creation in the late Middle Ages and after the Reformation; their later, often violent, relocation and first use in their new settings; and their reconstruction in modern times through cataloguing and re-assembling in physical and digital settings. Work of the latter kind has of course been substantially facilitated in later years by technological advances, although collaboration across borders started as early as the nineteenth century, and has been carried on continuously during the twentieth and twenty-first centuries. There are now many examples of successful transnational cooperation between librarians, bibliographers, and scholars of various backgrounds.[25] The violent past has created possibilities for fruitful

---

23  Karin Zimmermann and Maria Effinger, *Bibliotheca Palatina: The Story of a World-Famous Library* (2012), www.digi.ub.uni-heidelberg.de/en/bpd/bibliotheca_palatina/geschichte.html (last accessed 14 November 2022).

24  *Bibliotheca Palatina Digital*: www.digi.ub.uni-heidelberg.de/en/bpd/index.html (last accessed 14 November 2022).

25  See e.g. Beda Dudik, *Forschungen in Schweden für Mährens Geschichte* (Brünn: Carl Winiker, 1852); Ludwik Antoni Birkenmajer and Isak Collijn, *Nova Copernicana: Vorläufige Mitteilung über jüngst in Schwedischen Archiven und Bibliotheken aufgefundene, bisher unbekannte Autographen des Copernicus* (Cracow: Imprimerie de l'Université,

international collaboration and exchange in our time. This work, however, needs to be fertilised by continuous discussions about means, methods, theoretical framing, comparative examples, research possibilities, accessibility and many other aspects. It is our hope that the following chapters can contribute to this end.

---

1909); Eugeniusz Barwiński, Ludwik Antoni Birkenmajer and Jan Łoś, *Sprawozdanie z poszukiwań w Szwecyi: Dokonanych z ramienia Akademii Umiejętności* (Cracow: Nakłaem Akademii Umiejętności, 1914); Józef Trypucko, *Polonica vetera Upsaliensia: Catalogue des imprimés polonais ou concernant la Pologne des XV*$^e$*, XVI*$^e$*, XVII*$^e$ *et XVIII*$^e$ *siècles conservés à la Bibliothèque de l'Université royale d'Upsala* (Uppsala: Universitetsbiblioteket, 1958); Pawel Czartoryski, 'The Library of Copernicus', in Erna Hilfstein et al. (eds.), *Science and History: Studies in Honor of Edward Rosen* (Wrocław: Wydawnictwo Ossolineum, 1978); Józef Trypućko (ed.), *Braniewo: The Catalogue of the Book Collection of the Jesuit College in Braniewo held in the University Library in Uppsala* (3 vols., Warszawa: Biblioteka Narodowa, 2007); Thomas Tottie, 'Braniewokatalogen – ett mångårigt projekt' ('The Braniewo Catalogue – a Project of Many Years'), in Per Cullhed et al. (eds.), *I lag med böcker: Festskrift till Ulf Göranson* (Uppsala: Universitetsbiblioteket, 2012); Alicja Szulc and Renata Wilgosiewicz-Skutecka, 'O poznańskich rękopisach i starych drukach w zbiorach Biblioteki Uniwersyteckiej w Uppsali', *Biblioteka*, 18 (27), (2014), pp. 7–32, and in Swedish: idem, 'Redogörelse för efterforskningar i Sverige: Om handskrifter och äldre tryck från Poznań i Uppsala universitetsbiblioteks samlingar', *Biblis: Kvartalstidskrift för bokvänner*, 66 (2014), 52–65; Peter Sjökvist, 'Polish collections at Uppsala University Library: A History of Research', in Doroty Sidorowicz Mulak and Agnieszki Franczyk Cegły (eds.), *Książka dawna i jej właściciele: Tom drugi* (Wrocław: Wydawnictwo Ossolineum, 2017), pp. 237–244; and Peter Sjökvist, 'Books from Poznań at the Uppsala University Library', in Jack Puchalski et al. (eds.), *Z Badań nad Książką i Księgozbiorami Historycznymi: Polonika w z biorach obcych* (Warszawa: Wydawnictwa Uniwersytetu Warszawskiego, 2017), pp. 319–327. See also the current projects *The Swedish Booty of Books from Bohemia and Moravia 1646–1648: Bibliographic and Informational Portal*, www.knizni-korist.cz (last accessed 20 November 2022); and *Poznan Books at Uppsala University Library*, www.libris.kb.se, bibl:Uka db:POZN (last accessed 20 November 2022).

# PART 1

*Creating Libraries*

∴

CHAPTER 1

# Fifteenth-Century Manuscripts

*The Liturgical and Musical Testimonies from the Cistercian Nunnery in Riga*

*Laine Tabora*

Only a fraction of the liturgical books used in the former Cistercian nunnery of Saint Mary Magdalene in Riga has been preserved in the libraries in Uppsala and Vilnius, and no manuscript has survived from the nunnery in the city of Riga itself. Since most of the nunnery's books have vanished, the remaining sources are the only testimonies that narrate the spiritual and intellectual life of the nuns.[1]

After the closure of the nunnery in 1583, the nuns' books were added to the library of the local Jesuit college.[2] As they were no longer relevant to the new owners, some of these artefacts naturally went missing, whereas others were used as binding material for printed books, a common practice from the fifteenth to the seventeenth century.[3] Subsequently, in 1621, most of the Jesuit books along with the remains of the Cistercian nuns book collection was transferred to Sweden as war booty. According to existing research, in the collection of Uppsala University Library there are thirteen liturgical codices from the Cistercian nunnery of Riga.[4] These manuscripts are prayer books for the

---

1 This study presents some results of my PhD thesis at the Pontifical Institute of Sacred Music in Rome, under the direction of Prof. Dr. Franz Karl Prassl. I would like to express my gratitude to Jeremy Llewellyn for his revision of this chapter.

2 For more on the history of the Cistercian nunnery of Riga and its books, see Gustavs Strenga and Andris Levāns, 'Medieval Manuscripts in the Riga Jesuit College Book Collection: Manuscripts of the Riga Saint Mary Magdalene Cistercian Nunnery and Their Tradition', in *The Catalogue of the Riga Jesuit College Book Collection (1583–1621): History and Reconstruction of the Collection = Rīgas Jezuītu Koleģijas Grāmatu Krājuma (1583–1621) katalogs: Krājuma vēsture un rekonstrukcija*, eds. Andris Levāns and Gustavs Strenga (Riga: Latvijas Nacionālā bibliotēka, 2021), pp. 167–186. See also Otto Walde, *Storhetstidens litterära krigsbyten: En kulturhistorisk-bibliografisk studie* (2 vols., Uppsala: Almqvist & Wiksell, 1916–1920), I, pp. 49–51; Wolfgang Schmidt, 'Die Zisterzienser im Baltikum', *Finska kyrkohistoriska samfundets årsskrift*, 29/30 (1939), pp. 174–177.

3 See, for instance, Nicholas Pickwood, 'The Use of Fragments in Mediaeval Manuscripts in the Construction and Covering of Bindings on Printed Books', in Linda L. Brownrigg and Margaret M. Smith (eds.), *Interpreting and Collecting Fragments of Mediaeval Books: Proceedings of the Seminar in the History of the Book to 1500* (London: Red Gull Press, 2000), pp. 1–20.

4 Uppsala universitetsbibliotek (hereafter: UUB).

© LAINE TABORA, 2023 | DOI:10.1163/9789004441217_003

This is an open access chapter distributed under the terms of the CC BY-NC-ND 4.0 license.

personal use of the nuns and date to the fifteenth century. In terms of content, the larger part of the nuns' collection is composed of books of hours: C 438; C 454; C 467; C 474; C 486; C 487; C 488; C 491; C 503, designed for monastic use.[5] A smaller part of the collection consists of different types of breviaries: C 436 with a reduced office without nocturns; C 293 and C 434 contain the night offices; and C 477, a hymnary/collectary.[6] In addition to the manuscripts preserved in the Uppsala University Library, there is one psalter preserved in the Manuscript Department of the Library of the Lithuanian Academy of Sciences.[7] According to the inscription of ownership, it belonged to the Jesuit college in Riga and according to scholarship its origin is the Cistercian nunnery in Riga.[8] The present study is based mainly on an examination of five books of hours with musical notation, one psalter and two breviaries.[9]

Our overview of the liturgical and devotional practices of the Cistercian nuns of Riga is based on general liturgical and musicological analysis. These topics are studied for the first time here. One of the main focal points is the common liturgy of the Cistercian Order and its use in a nunnery in the far North. Another question concerns the concrete practice of the Riga Cistercian nuns: what the manuscripts at our disposal can tell us about the daily and festive liturgy of nuns. What was the function of the books of hours of the Riga Cistercians nuns, and what are their most characteristic features? Did the nuns celebrate the full liturgy of the hours like the monks, or did they only celebrate some parts of the office together, otherwise using further canonical hours within the context of private devotions.[10] In addition, the study investigates what the specifics are that characterise the liturgical calendar and the cult of

---

5   Lat. *liber horarum*, fr. *livre d'heures*.
6   For detailed medieval manuscripts catalogue descriptions, see Margarete Andersson-Schmitt et al., *Mittelalterliche Handschriften der Universitätsbibliothek Uppsala: Katalog über die C–Sammlung* (8 vols., Stockholm: Almqvist & Wiksell, 1988–1995); *The Catalogue of the Riga Jesuit College Book Collection (1583–1621)*.
7   Lietuvos mokslų akademijos Vrublevskių biblioteka (hereafter: LMAVB), *Psalter et cantica alia in usu Colleg. Rig. Soc. Iesu*, LMAVB RS F 22–96. I was able to securely identify this source as a manuscript of the nunnery; see also the following explanations.
8   The content of additional elements to the psalter shows a considerable overlap with other manuscripts from the nunnery of Riga, e.g., the most precise match is the list of Marian antiphons LMAVB RS F 22–96 fols. 149v–150v, presumably written with the same hand as the list on UUB C 477 fols. 123v–124rv. An analogous but partial list is present in UUB C 434 fol. 267v.
9   *Liber horarum* UUB C 438, C 467, C 486, C 487, C 488, *Psalterium Davidis* LMAVB RS F 22–96, *Breviarium* C 434 and C 436.
10  Cf. Thomas Csanády, *Breviarium monialium Seccoviensium: Über einige so genannte Seckauer Nonnenbreviere; Liturgiewissenschaftlicher Beitrag zur Frage der Lokalisierung einer Handschriftengruppe an der Universitätsbibliothek Graz*, (PhD thesis, Universität Graz, 2008).

saints in the nunnery and whether there is consistency with the other sources from the diocese? Finally, special attention is devoted to the musical material occurring in the manuscripts. In the bibliography concerning the books of hours, any reference to musical details is almost totally absent. How relevant is the musical notation present in monastic prayer books and can it reveal information about the nuns' communal and private prayer? During recent decades, research on female monastic practices, for example, in Northern Germany, has become increasingly more important.[11] In the case of Riga, however, there is no certainty about the motherhouse with which the nunnery was initially affiliated. Obviously, the nuns of Riga were related to the religious culture of Northern Germany from which presumably the first nuns were invited.[12]

At the end of the fifteenth century the Cistercian nunnery in Riga was of considerable size. A surviving charter from 1495 lists 53 Cistercian nuns, most of whom were of noble origin.[13] Because of the background of wealth of many nuns, the nunnery had the economic means to produce books or commission books and must have also had a considerable collection of both choral liturgical books and books for private prayer. Unfortunately, none of the nunnery's liturgical-musical manuscripts have survived.

The peculiar type of book of hours for monastic use, which forms a major portion of the surviving manuscripts used by the Riga nuns, represents two aspects of the nuns' ritual life: private piety and liturgy. On one hand, the content of weekday liturgies, which is common in these books of hours, very plausibly indicates that the nuns prayed in choir. It is also noteworthy that five books of hours (C 438, C 467, C 486, C 487, and C 488) contain musical entries, which is unusual for this type of book. The liturgical characteristics of the majority of the musical content of the manuscripts suggest their choral use. On the other hand, the books of hours were also designed for private use. The dimensions of the books have the features of a private prayer book: practicality and compactness. Given that the structure of this category of book is less uniform than other types of liturgical manuscripts, it can be concluded that there are no two identical books of hours.[14] In the case of the Riga Cistercians

---

11 Jeffrey F. Hamburger, Eva Schlotheuber, Susan Marti, and Margot E. Fassler, *Liturgical Life and Latin Learning at Paradies bei Soest, 1300–1425: Inscription and Illumination in the Choir Books of a North German Dominican Convent* (Münster: Aschendorff Verlag, 2016).

12 Schmidt, 'Die Zisterzienser im Baltikum', pp. 158–161.

13 *Liv-, Est- und Kurländisches Urkundenbuch: Nebst Regesten* (section 1, 12 vols; section 2, 3 vols., Riga: J. Deubner, 1853–1914), 2/1, (hereafter: LUB 2/1), no. 252.

14 Peter Ochsenbein, 'Stundenbücher', in Leo Scheffczyk and Remigius Bäumer (eds.), *Marienlexikon* (6 vols., St. Ottilien: EOS, 1988–1994), 6, pp. 320–322; Victor M. Leroquais, *Les Livres d'heures manuscrits de la Bibliothèque nationale* (Paris: Macon, Protat fréres imprimeurs, 1927), p. VII. See also Csanády, *Breviarium monialium Seccoviensium*.

every book of hours has a slightly different layout. Even though large parts of the layouts coincide, the disposition of content or additional texts varies to some degree, making these books individual and unique. Books underwent a continuous process of accumulation. After the main content by one or more scribes was finished, later owners or readers made their own additions, as is evidenced by the large number of different kinds of handwriting.[15] As a typical feature of a book intended for a female community, there is the presence of the Latin feminine ending in the prayer texts, as well as frequent textual errors and different entries in the vernacular, varying from short rubrics to entire prayers and devotional texts.[16] While the main characteristic of the private use of the book is the singular form, in books of hours these textual differences occasionally appear in the same prayer in different manuscripts. Another feature attesting to the personal use of a book is smaller sheets of paper, and drawn and printed images that occasionally appear among the pages.[17] All these observations indicate that part of the content of the book of hours constituted the private devotion of a nun and part was recited in choir.

## 1  The Nuns' *Consuetudo* of Prayer

Little is known about the ritual practices in the Cistercian nunnery of Riga. From the manuscripts at our disposal, however, it is possible to gain an insight

---

15  Although the books contain the hands of a well-trained copyist, there are numerous additions with less trained hands or hastily written pages, probably copied by the same nuns. E.g., in the book of hours UUB C 488 a great variety of hands appears including even an entry that seems to come from a scribe without writing practice, see UUB C 488, fol. 220r. Only one manuscript contains information from the scribe, it is the book of hours UUB C 438, where the inscription points out that the scribe was a man C 438, fol. 128v: 'Orate pro scriptore fratre vestro unum p[ater] n[oster]'. In addition, this manuscript in contrast to other books of hours, is written on paper, and its layout most differs from the other books of the same kind.

16  For instance, the widely known medieval prayer 'Here ihesu christe ik anbede dy', attributed to Pope Saint Gregory the Great, is present on front flyleaf recto of manuscript UUB C 486. The same prayer in Latin 'Domine ihesu christe adoro te' can be found also on fol. 1r of psalter LMAVB RS F 22–96. There is a wide collection of prayers in Middle Low German toward the end of the manuscript UUB C 474, fols. 190r–237r.

17  E.g., the handwritten and paper-printed prayers and fragments in Middle Low German in UUB C 486, fols. 161br–161fv. The smaller size paper sheets with liturgical texts at the end of breviary UUB C 436, fols. 156r–166v. Paper leaves with blessings in vernacular in UUB C 454 between fol. 87v and fol. 88r. Different illustrations appear on UUB C 477, fols. 1rv, 129v. Whereas, UUB C 491 contains two leaves (the front flyleaf verso and fol. 171v) with woodcut printed images.

into the daily and festive prayer life of nuns. An important aspect to consider is the fact that the nuns knew a large part of the Office by heart. Therefore, it was only natural that the manuscripts do not contain all the daily repetitions that were easily memorised.[18] Certainly, one manuscript alone cannot give a comprehensive view of the rhythm of the inner liturgical life of a monastic community; moreover, the presence of some elements intended for private use can also create a misleading impression regarding the celebration of the common liturgy. The night office with twelve lessons and the distribution and number of psalms in the liturgical hours revealed in the breviaries C 293, C 434, C 436 indicate the monastic cursus used in monastic families, especially those who follow the Rule of Saint Benedict, such as the Cistercians.[19] One of the indications is the number XII alongside the important feasts on the liturgical calendar of the Vilnius Cistercian psalter.[20] There is clear evidence verifying the observation of the Rule in the nunnery of Riga. A charter of 2 August 1255, which confirms the privileges of the Cistercian nunnery, indicates that Pope Alexander IV (pp. 1254–1261) promulgated the Rule of Saint Benedict and the Cistercians' statutes for the newly founded community.[21] Additional proof that the nuns followed Saint Benedict's precepts can also be found in the manuscripts. The book of hours C 486, which belonged to the last nun of the nunnery, Anna Noetken, contains a private confession of infractions of the monastic rule such as poor performance of the divine office and failure to observe the Rule of Saint Benedict.[22] In other books of hours, at the beginning

---

18   Chrysogonus Waddell, *The Primitive Cistercian Breviary (Staatsbibliothek zu Berlin, Preussischer Kulturbesitz, Ms. lat. oct. 402) with Variants from the 'Bernardine' Cistercian Breviary* (Fribourg: Academic Press, 2007), p. 29.

19   See Jörg Oberste, 'Constitution in progress: Der Zisterzienserorden und das System der "Carta Caritatis"', in Georg Mölich et al. (eds.), *Die Zisterzienser im Mittelalter* (Köln: Böhlau Verlag, 2017), pp. 31–43, here pp. 36–37; see also Albert Schmidt, 'Zusätze als Problem des monastischen Stundengebets im Mittelalter', *Beiträge zur Geschichte des Alten Mönchtums und des Benediktinertums*, 36 (1986), p. 67.

20   See Lila Collamore, 'Charting the Divine Office', in Margot E. Fassler and Rebecca A. Baltzer (eds.), *The Divine Office in the Latin Middle Ages: Methodology and Source Studies, Regional Developments, Hagiography; Written in Honor of Professor Ruth Steiner* (Oxford: Oxford University Press, 2000), pp. 3–11; see also Andrew Hughes, *Medieval Manuscripts for Mass and Office: A Guide to their Organization and Terminology* (Toronto: University of Toronto Press, 1982), pp. 50–80. The liturgical calendar is positioned at the beginning of the psalter. *Psalterium Davidis* LMAVB RS F 22–96, fols. 2r–7v.

21   LUB 3, no. 283.

22   UUB C 486, fol. 144r: 'Carissima domina dico deo et vobis culpam meam de omnibus defectibus meis De diuino officio male et indeuote persoluto ... De malis exemplis datis sororibus meis et feci contra regulam sancti benedicti ...' The later entry on fol. 1r reveals that the manuscript belonged to last nun Anna Noetken. See Nicolaus Busch, *Die*

of the *Confiteor*, one can find additional mention of Saint Benedict or in some cases Saint Bernard after the mention of God and the Virgin Mary.[23]

As noted earlier, at first glance one can observe in the surviving sources a very intense prayer life of the nuns, both in common and in private. Besides the regular Office, the centre of the Cistercian *Opus Dei*, the nuns' spiritual habits consisted of non-canonical daily observances such as memorials, additional offices, suffrages, preces and benedictions, Scripture readings, daily devotions, and penitential piety.[24] The custom of adding supplemental services to the canonical hours was a regular practice in the monasteries of the later medieval centuries and the books of hours are the main testimony about this custom in the Cistercian nunnery in Riga. Unlike Cistercian monks, female communities had much more liberty and independence in liturgical and spiritual activities.[25] A considerable quantity of votive observances indicates that they were given an importance similar to Office Hours.[26] Consequently, until the Reformation, besides the daily divine office, there was a rather complicated and dynamic system of votive services alongside the canonical office. These extensive ritual practices refer to a real need to support the founders, benefactors, family members, noble and clerical patrons and their dead with prayer; consequently, this reflects the principle that 'liturgy springs from life'.[27] Such an intense ritual life was only possible in monastic circumstances where prayer was the main obligation of a choir nun.

All the manuscripts from the nuns' collection show that their use depended on their content; for the daily prayer life they were used in combinations. The breviaries C 293, C 434 and C 436 contain the parts of canonical hours of the Proper for Sundays and feast days during the year: Christmas, Epiphany, Easter, Ascension, Pentecost, Trinity, Corpus Christi, and Sundays of Advent, after Epiphany, Lent Sundays, Sundays after Easter, Sundays after Pentecost,

---

*Geschichte der Rigaer Stadtbibliothek und deren Bücher* (Riga: Rigaer Stadtverwaltung, 1937), pp. 95–96; see also Leonid Arbusow Sr., *Livlands Geistlichkeit vom Ende des 12. bis ins 16. Jahrhundert* (Mitau: Steffenhagen und Sohn, 1913), pp. 152, 281.

23 For instance, UUB C 467, fol. 35v; C 488, fol. 40v; C 487, fol. 35v; C 438, fol. 70v: 'Confiteor deo et beate marie et sancto benedicto et omnibus sanctis....'; UUB C 486, fol. 37r: '... et sancto bernardo ...'.

24 For additional services, see Schmidt, 'Zusätze als Problem', pp. 9–17.

25 Elizabeth Freeman, 'Nuns', in Mette B. Bruun (ed.), *The Cambridge Companion to the Cistercian Order* (Cambridge: Cambridge University Press, 2013), pp. 100–124, here pp. 103–105.

26 See Leroquais, *Les Livres d'Heures*, pp. IX–XII; see also Hughes, *Medieval Manuscripts*, pp. 3–19; Schmidt, 'Zusätze als Problem', pp. 83–92.

27 Chrysogonus Waddell, 'The Early Cistercian Experience of Liturgy', *Cistercian Studies*, 12 (1971), pp. 77–116, here p. 88.

Sundays after Trinity.[28] Other sections are dedicated to the Sanctorale and Commune Sanctorum. In addition, breviaries contain smaller sections, such as the Hymnal and Collectary, and sections of lesser importance placed between the main sections, such as devotional offices of specific saints. The liturgical feasts marked in manuscripts are congruent between all three breviaries and correspond to the liturgical calendar of the Vilnius Cistercian psalter. In differing from other breviaries, the manuscript C 436, contains only diurnal offices (from Lauds to Vespers) of Sundays and feast days. This predisposition for daylight hours also occurs in the psalter section, which does not form part of other two breviaries. In addition, it also contains some itemised ferias of a privileged category: seasonal weekdays of Advent, especially, the fourth week of Advent, ferias during Octave of Epiphany, Lent and Eastertide. Overall, the ferial weekday office is a link between the breviary C 436 and the book of hours.

One type of book of hours, especially the kind designed for laity, is characterised by supplemental services without any presence of the rhythm of the liturgical year. The type designed for Riga's community contained an essential part of the nuns' monastic ferial office: both in Ordinary time and during prominent seasons of the Temporale. As one can observe from rubrics, the Office provided for *privatis diebus*, days during the weekdays when saints with a Proper office were not celebrated.[29] It includes the ferial format of the night office (Matins with two nocturns), Lauds, Vespers, and little hours from Monday to Saturday. Besides the ferial office, the books of hours, similar to the breviary C 436, contain different parts of weekday offices of Temporale Proper from Advent to Corpus Christi. These offices present Proper texts for more important ferias of the liturgical year, such as Rogation Days, Ash Wednesday, weekdays during the Lenten season, ferias of Holy Week, and weekdays of the octave of Easter, Ascension, Pentecost, and Corpus Christi.[30] Further offices include All Saints, and the Marian feasts (Purification, Visitation, Assumption and Nativity), the Dedication of the Church and Mary Magdalene. Manuscript rubrics do not provide clear indications as to when these offices were recited, but the ferial context of their content leads to the supposition that they are Proper texts of the weekdays during the octaves of these feasts.[31] The presence of Proper texts for feasts such as the Dedication of the Church and Mary

---

28  The number of Sundays differs between the manuscripts from twenty-four to twenty-six.
29  UUB C 486, fols. 40v, 131v; C 467, fols. 40r, 144r; C 488, fol. 45r; C 487, fols. 40r, 157v.
30  UUB C 486, fol. 157v the rubric 'in Rogacionibus'.
31  Not all Marian feasts (Visitation, Purification) in the manuscripts are marked with octaves, the historical sources show that the octave of Visitation was celebrated in the nunnery, see Hermann von Bruiningk, *Messe und kanonisches Stundengebet nach dem Brauche der Rigaschen Kirche im späteren Mittelalter* (Riga: Kymmel, 1904), pp. 557–558.

Magdalene, reported with two nocturns, attract major attention. It follows that these two feasts were relevant to the monastic community. Even though there is no proof about the relative octaves in the calendar, the Proper texts of these liturgical celebrations in the book of hours appear next to the other offices. They may have been celebrated, in practice, as primary feasts observed for the length of an octave. In light of another hypothesis, some ferias might have been assigned commemorative offices of a patron or other locally venerated saint, such as could have been the case of Mary Magdalene.[32]

The central and the most distinctive element of the book of hours is the Little Office of the Blessed Virgin Mary (*Officium Parvum Beatae Mariae Virginis*). Almost all books of hours belonging to the nuns of Riga begin with this office.[33] The Office of Virgin consists of one nocturn and three lessons celebrated in combination with the regular Office throughout the entire day, before the canonical hours, except Compline which was performed afterwards.[34] The manuscripts of the Cistercian nunnery do not include rubrics or special indications as to when this office was used, but traditionally in a major part of the liturgical year the Marian office was performed, during the weekdays, even though its uses can differ according to local customs. The Hours of the Virgin contain an indication of the possible festive context of this office through the presence of the hymn *Te Deum* in Matins.[35]

Besides the votive Marian service, these manuscripts contain the commemorative memorial Office of the Virgin for Saturday (*de beata Virgine in sabbato*), from which it originates. In fact, Saturday was highly privileged for the veneration of the Mother of God, this also being the case in the Church of Riga.[36] Besides the books of hours, this office can be found in breviaries C 436 and C 434, placed between the main sections.[37] Among other votive offices worth mentioning there exists a shorter Hours of the Cross (*Horae de Sancta Cruce*),

---

32  See Hughes, *Medieval Manuscripts*, p. 13.
33  *Officium Beate Virginis* UUB C 467, fol. 1r.
34  Schmidt, 'Zusätze als Problem', pp. 13, 87–88; see also Stefano Rosso, 'Il Sabato mariano in Occidente', in Ermanno M. Toniolo (ed.), *La Vergine Madre del VI secolo al secondo millennio* (Rome: Centro di cultura mariana "Mater Ecclesiae", 1988), pp. 165–189, here p. 180.
35  Normally in the regular Office the *Te Deum* was sung in Matins on Sundays (excluding Septuagesima and Lent) and for major feasts, as well as for weekdays of Christmas and Paschal seasons, this could indicate that the office was not scheduled for weekdays alone see, e.g., Collamore, 'Charting the Divine Office', pp. 4–6; Hughes, *Medieval Manuscripts*, pp. 53, 66.
36  Cf. Bruiningk, *Messe und kanonisches Stundengebet*, pp. 63, 169–170, 172.
37  The books of hours as well breviary UUB C 436 contain only the Vespers, while UUB C 434, fols. 240r–241v, and UUB C 293, fols. 95r–96v, contains Night Office with twelve Lessons positioned as follows between the main sections Temporale and Sanctorale (C 293),

usually assigned to Friday, and Office of the Dead, one of the oldest additional offices.[38]

One particularly important role of the female monastic community was its intercessory authority within the society of medieval Livonia. The memorial obligations observed by the nuns were rather important in maintaining social and familial networks. As an element of reciprocity, the material donations by benefactors were made in exchange for prayer obligations: spiritual offerings in the Mass, the divine office and other prayers.[39] The existing sources, including memorial records in the manuscripts, attest to the relationship between the Cistercian nunnery of Riga and other institutions, both religious and secular: confraternities, other orders and convents and individual supporters.[40] As indicated in the agreement between the Beer Carters' guild and the community, the nuns sang night vigils and masses for the deceased members of the confraternity.[41] One particularly noteworthy obituary appears on July 6 in the calendar of the Vilnius Cistercian psalter. The entry concerning the anniversary of the death of a man called Conrad: '*Anniuersarium domini conradi et so*[*ciorum*]'. Considering the fact that there is only one personal memorial record present in the calendar, this annual memorial must have been of particular importance for the book's owner or even for the entire Riga Cistercian nunnery.[42] Since memorial culture led to an increase in prayers for the departed, the Office of the Dead occupied a considerable amount of time

---

and the Common of Saints and Collectary (C 434). For more about the office, see Rosso, 'Il Sabato mariano in Occidente', pp. 165–189.

[38] Hughes, *Medieval Manuscripts*, pp. 13–14.

[39] See Gregory Leighton, 'Written and visual expressions of authority of female monastic institutions in Medieval Livonia: 13th to 15th centuries', *Studia Slavica et Balcanica Petropolitana*, 1. (2021), pp. 15–35; Mette B. Bruun and Emilia Jamroziak, 'Introduction', in *The Cambridge Companion to the Cistercian Order*, pp. 1–22, here pp. 10–14; Gisela Muschiol, 'Time and Space: Liturgy and Rite in Female Monasteries of the Middle Ages', in Jeffrey F. Hamburger and Susan Marti (eds.), *Crown and Veil: Female Monasticism from the Fifth to the Fifteenth Centuries* (New York: Columbia University Press, 2008), pp. 191–206, here pp. 192–195.

[40] E.g., the memorial present at the end of breviary UUB C 436 mentions Margrete Brynckke, probably the abbess of the Cistercian nunnery in Tallinn UUB C 436, fol. 167r: 'Item domen schref ÿnt ÿar (xlÿx) do vor starf selÿge margrete brÿnckke dess frÿdagess vor ÿubÿlate dat er got gnedÿch sÿ unde barmehertÿch'. See also Gustavs Strenga, 'Cistercian Networks of Memory: Commemoration as a Form of Institutional Bonding in Livonia and Beyond During the late Middle Ages', in Anu Mänd and Marek Tamm (eds.), *Making Livonia: Actors and Networks in the Medieval and Early Modern Baltic Sea Region* (Abingdon: Routledge, 2020), pp. 214–218.

[41] LUB 2/1, no. 252.

[42] LMAVB RS F 22–96, fol. 5r.

of the nuns' prayer life. This may have favoured the formation of an office characterised by local customs. The series of responsories in the Office of the Dead varies from source to source, which means identifying them can be useful in establishing the origin of a source. In the present case there is clear compatibility between the series of responsories in the books of hours associated with the Cistercian nuns of Riga. According to the research of Knud Ottosen, these series are attributable exclusively to these manuscripts of the Riga nunnery, which means that they constitute the local customs of this specific community, providing one more useful means of further clarifying the provenance of other manuscripts associated with the nunnery.[43]

## 2      The Liturgical Calendar and the Cult of Saints

Due to the scarcity of surviving liturgical sources from the diocese of Riga, the only two liturgical books that were available for a long time as the principal evidence about the cult of the saints were the fifteenth century Missal used in the cathedral of Riga and the diocesan Breviary (1513).[44] The liturgical calendar is an outstanding source and, fortuitously, one has been conserved in one of the fourteen liturgical manuscripts from the nuns' collection: the Vilnius Cistercian psalter.[45] Beside the calendar included in the *Missale Rigense*, the calendar of the psalter is the second one fully preserved from the diocese of Riga. This unique source is an important historically not only for the cult of the saints of the nunnery but also of the entire diocese.[46] Nevertheless, the presence of the liturgical feasts in the calendar still does not prove by itself their ritual celebration by the monastic community, but the necessary confirmation is contained by other liturgical components in the manuscripts. An overview

---

43    See Knud Ottosen, *The Responsories and Versicles of the Latin Office of the Dead* (Aarhus: Aarhus University Press, 1993), pp. 387–420. Published on the Cantus planus website: www.uni-regensburg.de/Fakultaeten/phil_Fak_I/Musikwissenschaft/cantus/ (last accessed 20 March 2021).

44    *Missale Rigense*, LU AB Ms. 1 and *Breviarium Rigensis* (Paris: Wilhelm Corver, 1513), LU AB R 2522, USTC 183289; both preserved in the Department of Manuscripts and Rare Books of the Academic Library of the University of Latvia. For information on *Missale Rigense*, see Guntars Prānis, *Missale Rigense Livonijas garīgajā kultūrā: Gregoriskie dziedājumi viduslaiku Rīgā* (Riga: Neputns, 2018), also Bruiningk, *Messe und kanonisches Stundengebet*.

45    For a more detailed study see Laine Tabora, 'Psalterium Davidis of the Cistercian Nunnery of Riga (LMAVB RS F 22–96) and its Liturgical Calendar', *Analecta Cisterciensia*, 71 (2021), pp. 119–169.

46    Anu Mänd, 'Saints' Cults in Medieval Livonia', in Alan V. Murray (ed.) *The Clash of Cultures on the Medieval Baltic Frontier* (London: Routledge, 2016), pp. 191–223, here p. 193.

and examination of written sources such as notices of the dedication of altars and chantries in the monastic church, presence of relics, and liturgical evidence in the manuscripts (proper texts, feast days' rubrics, litany of saints and suffrages) are needed for a comprehensive view. The present study will focus only on a few selected aspects of the cult of saints in the nunnery.

The Cistercian nunnery was located inside the city walls and considerable influence on the cult of saints is certainly derived from the diocese. For instance, the diocese's impact is particularly strong concerning some Marian feasts. One of these is the feast of the Presentation, celebrated on 21 November. The General Chapter of the Cistercian Order did not hasten to add the new feast to the Order's calendar. In fact, most of the Cistercian liturgical books give no notice of the feast until 1613.[47] Liturgical evidence in the manuscripts from the Cistercian nunnery of Riga dating back to the fifteenth century, however, reveals the nuns' practice of following the local custom of the diocese and incorporating this feast into their calendar.[48] Another Marian feast, which indicates local influence, is the feast of the Visitation. The general Cistercian calendar introduced it only in 1476, while in the diocese of Riga the feast is noted much earlier. The feast is assigned by a peculiar rhythmical office which apparently represents a proper tradition of Riga.[49] Consistency with the diocese appears even in such characteristic detail as the absence of prominent thirteenth-century saints such as Saints Anthony of Padua and Thomas Aquinas. Despite their cult and popularity throughout Europe soon after their canonization, there is no evidence of celebrations of these saints in any of the liturgical books from Riga. As some scholars have pointed out earlier, hesitancy in accepting new saints indicates a certain conservatism in the Church of Riga.[50] Overall, it should be emphasised that a comparison between the manuscripts of the nuns and diocesan sources reveals a certain conformity

---

47   Cf. Bernard Backeart, 'L'évolution du Calendrier cistercien', *Collectanea ordinis Cistercensium reformatorum*, 13 (1951), pp. 112–113.
48   The calendar of the psalter LMAVB RS F 22–96 contains a remarkable detail that attracts attention: on 21 November, next to *Columbani abbatis*, is reported *Presentatio*, the entrance is by the same hand, underlined without being highlighted in red. In addition, the breviaries, the hymnary UUB C 477 and the *Benedicamus* collection comprise this festivity.
49   As claimed by Antonie Schmid, the office is possibly a local creation of the diocese. See Antonie (Toni) E.M. Schmid, 'Stundengebet und Heiligenverehrung Magdalenenkloster zu Riga', in *Beiträge zur Kunde Ehst, Liv- und Kurlands*, 21 (Reval: Lindfors' Erbenpp, 1938), pp. 12–26, here pp. 15–22; see also Bruiningk, *Messe und kanonisches Stundengebet*, p. 346; Schmidt, 'Die Zisterzienser im Baltikum', p. 176.
50   Bruiningk, *Messe und kanonisches Stundengebet*, pp. 22–45; see also Mänd, 'Saints' Cults in Medieval Livonia', p. 222.

within the cult of saints, ordinarily known and venerated in northwestern and western Europe.[51]

In connection with the Proper celebrations of the Riga nuns' community, mention should be made of the feast of the patron saint and the Dedication of the Church. Cistercian houses were traditionally dedicated to Mary.[52] In fact, the first documents related to the Cistercian nunnery of Riga report the name of the Virgin Mary to whom the nunnery was devoted.[53] Nevertheless, according to historical sources, the patron saints of the monastic house appear in different guises over the centuries. Later written sources attribute other, presumably secondary, patronages, such as Saint Mary Magdalene, Saint Margaret, and the Eleven Thousand Virgins.[54] Among these holy women, highly celebrated in the Riga Church, the veneration of Saint Mary Magdalene is notably evident. In the fifteenth century, she appears as a patron saint of the nunnery. This dedication could be linked to the construction of the nunnery's church, over which Magdalene was chosen as patron.[55] Her particular veneration is clearly shown in the breviaries, the books of hours and even C 477 *Hymnarium et Collectarium*, which contain the antiphons of the Office of Mary Magdalene.[56] The set of manuscripts includes a large collection of hymns, including six hymns in honour of the patron saint, a noteworthy quantity.[57]

---

51   More on the saints venerated in the diocese of Riga, see Bruiningk, *Messe und kanonisches Stundengebet*, pp. 311–596. See also Tabora, 'Psalterium Davidis of the Cistercian Nunnery of Riga', pp. 133–136.

52   Emilia Jamroziak, *The Cistercian Order in Medieval Europe 1090–1500* (London: Routledge 2013), pp. 14, 174; see also Louis J. Lekai, *I cistercensi: Ideali e realtà* (Certosa di Pavia, 1989), p. 23.

53   Hermann von Bruiningk and Nicolaus Busch (eds.), *Livländische Güterurkunde aus den Jahren 1207 bis 1500* (2 vols., Riga: Jonck & Poliewsky, 1908–1923), 1, (hereafter LGU 1) no. 27; no. 36; LUB 3, no. 283a, LUB 1, no. 300, LUB 1, no. 336. Noticeably at the beginning the title has not yet been established and in the documents, in relation with nunnery, a reference to Saint James occurs as well. This reference could be associated with the convent's location near the church of Saint James, originally used by nuns until the construction of a monastic church.

54   The first time the name of Saint Mary Magdalene and Saint Margaret appears in the letter of indulgences issued on 15 January 1359, see Bruiningk, *Messe und kanonisches Stundengebet*, p. 581; other denominations: '*monasterium sancta Marie Magdalene Rigensis Cisterciensis ordinis*', LUB 8, no. 408; '*ad honorem Dei et sub vocabulo sancta Dei genetricis virginis Marie et sanctarum Undecim milium virginum*', LGU 1 no. 263. The denomination Eleven Thousand Virgins refers to Saint Ursula and her companions. See also Bruiningk, *Messe und kanonisches Stundengebet*, pp. 333, 474–476.

55   Bruiningk, *Messe und kanonisches Stundengebet*, pp. 324–325, 332–333, 475–476.

56   UUB C 477, fols. 126r–128r.

57   Schmid, 'Stundengebet und Heiligenverehrung', p. 23.

There is no evidence in historical sources about the exact date of the anniversary of the Dedication or even when the church was built, nor does the calendar provide the date of this highest ranking feast day.[58] From the location of Proper texts for the Dedication in the breviaries, one possible date is the month of November. According to Toni Schmid's study of manuscripts C 293, C 434, C 477, and C 486, the dedication date of the church was determined has having been between the 13th and 19th of November. This time span can be narrowed thanks to the rubrics present in the *Benedicamus* collection at the end of the manuscript C 438, as well the other manuscripts C 434, C 436, C 477, where the feast appears between Saint Brictius and Saint Anianus. On this basis, it may be assumed that the celebration occurred between 13th and 17th of November.[59]

The cult of saints in the Cistercian nunnery was also characterised by Cistercian liturgical practices which in the monasteries of the Order maintained uniformity. The calendar of the psalter demonstrates a typical designation of Cistercian Sanctorale feasts where the liturgical festivities are classified into feasts of twelve lessons and commemorations.[60] There is a perfect correspondence between Cistercian saints present in the calendar of the Vilnius Cistercian psalter and their commemorations inside the liturgical books of nuns.[61] The absence in the calendar and within the liturgical texts of an important saint of the Order such as Robert of Molesme (c.1027–1111), a standard in the Cistercian Order, should be noted, however. Furthermore, as far as

---

58 The monastic church is first indirectly mentioned in a mid-fourteenth century letter of indulgence. The document dated to 15 January 1359 assigned forty days of indulgence to the faithful who visit the monastic church on specific feasts of the year. See Bruiningk, *Messe und kanonisches Stundengebet*, p. 475. In addition, later indications of the altars of the monastic church can be found e.g., LUB 8, no. 408, 782; LUB 10, no. 150.

59 UUB C 438, fol. 125r; C 434, fols. 261v, 262r; C 436, fols. 125v, 126r; C 477, fols. 65r, 66r. See Schmidt, 'Die Zisterzienser im Baltikum', p. 177; see also Schmid, 'Stundengebet und Heiligenverehrung', p. 24.

60 In the calendar of the psalter LMAVB RS F 22–96 the commemoration is abbreviated with *con* (sic).

61 The calendar of the psalter includes liturgical days of Cistercian saints: *Mauri, Sotheris, Albini, Benedicti, Mamerti, Daciani et Rogaciani, Medardi, Cirici et Iulite, Translacio Benedicti, Eusebii, Mammetis, Bernardi, Genesii, Marcelli, Ewertii, Sequani, Andochi et Ruffi, Aniani, Columbani, Vitalis et Agricole* and *Chrysanthi et Darii*. Although Schmid already mentioned some of these saints in her study, the complete calendar, useful for comparison with the liturgical texts, was not available to her. See Toni Schmid, 'Ett breviarium från Magdalenenklostret i Riga', *Nordisk tidskrift för bok- och biblioteksväsen*, 18 (1931), pp. 271–273. Particular indication to Saint Benedict and Saint Bernard is observable in the collection of *Benedicamus* chants (UUB C 438 fols. 119v–130v) where both saints have a special chant in troped form assigned.

the Cistercian customs related to the calendar went, it should be emphasized that the nunnery maintained the Order's tradition of celebrating an annual commemoration of the deceased. Three out of four annual memorial days are present in the calendar: 11 January, the day of the commemoration of abbots, as well as deceased bishops of the order; 18 September, the commemoration of the first martyrs of the Order; and 20 November, the commemoration of relatives and parents. The calendar lacks only the commemoration of the deceased members of Order on 20 May, which was introduced in the Cistercian calendar in 1350.[62]

Another aspect characterising the cult of the saints in the Cistercian nunnery is the influence of its spiritual connectedness to other monastic communities. In the manuscripts, a Bridgettine influence can be observed. There is a substantial likelihood that it is mainly related to the relationships between the Cistercian nunnery of Riga and the Bridgettine convent in Pirita (Mariendal), founded in the early fifteenth century.[63] The liturgical influences are defined by the presence of saints such as Saint Joseph, celebrated on 15 January, and Saint Bridget of Sweden (1303–1373) on 6 October and 23 July. The 15 January date coincides entirely with that adopted by the Swedish dioceses.[64] However, the feast of Saint Joseph was one of the recently introduced feasts in the Church of Riga.[65] The fact that in Northern Germany the cult of Saint Joseph had a later start than in Tallinn (Reval) and Riga suggests the feast's Scandinavian origin. This was one of the specific features that led scholars to suppose Riga as being the provenance of manuscripts.[66] Saint Joseph's Day was especially

---

[62] In the calendar of LMAVB RS F 22–96 these memorial days are documented as: *Commemoratio episcoporum, Commemoratio primorum et martyrum* and *Commemoratio parentum*. Schmidt, 'Zusätze als Problem', p. 71. Cf. also Backeart, 'L'évolution du Calendrier cistercien', *Collectanea ordinis Cistercensium reformatorum*, 12 (1950), pp. 81–94, 307–316; 13 (1951), pp. 108–127.

[63] See Strenga, 'Cistercian networks of memory', pp. 214–218; see also Anu Mänd, 'The Cult and Visual Representation of Scandinavian Saints in Medieval Livonia', in Carsten S. Jensen et al. (eds.), *Saints and Sainthood around the Baltic Sea: Identity, Literacy, and Communication in the Middle Ages* (Kalamazoo: Medieval Institute Publications, 2018), pp. 101–143.

[64] See Hermann Grotefend, *Taschenbuch der Zeitrechnung des Deutschen Mittelalters und der Neuzeit*, 10th edition (Hannover: Hahnsche Buchhandlung, 1960). See an online version www.manuscripta-mediaevalia.de/gaeste/grotefend/grotefend.htm (last accessed 10 March 2021).

[65] There is no evidence that suggests that the cult of Saint Joseph may had been introduced into the Riga Church before the fifteenth century. See Bruiningk, *Messe und kanonisches Stundengebet*, pp. 452–456.

[66] Schmid, 'Stundengebet und Heiligenverehrung', p. 15; see also Bruiningk, *Messe und kanonisches Stundengebet*, pp. 452–453; Carl-Allan Moberg, *Die liturgischen Hymnen in*

commemorated in Riga and the printed breviary of Riga contains a slightly different Scandinavian rhythmical office for Saint Joseph. An analogous office can be found in breviary C 434, and a partial office in the other two breviaries C 293, C 436.[67] The second manifestation of Scandinavian influence is the presence of the liturgical feasts of Saint Bridget of Sweden in the nuns' manuscripts. Even the Litany of the Saints provides evidence of special devotion to the Swedish saint. In the litany present in C 487 (fols. 57v–60r) Saint Bridget is place as second among the female saints, directly after Saint Anna, while in the other books of hours she appears as third, after Saint Mary Magdalene. The calendar of the nunnery indicates her feast on 6 October, which is confirmed with the presence of antiphons from her office *Birgitte matris inclite* in C 436 and Bridgettine hymns in C 477 and C 434.[68] In addition, there is an indication that 23 July, the day of her death, was also commemorated by nuns.[69] The fact that Saint Bridget was venerated in a Cistercian context is a very intriguing and noteworthy feature because she was not a Cistercian saint. There must have been direct connections between the Cistercian monastic communities and the Swedish Bridgettine circles that produced these liturgical exchanges. In the case of Riga's nunnery, these presumably arose from the strong ecclesiastical relations with the Bridgettines of Pirita.[70]

It should be noted that two locally venerated saints are distinctive to the Riga community. Evidence for this consists of a cult of relics and the existence of a chantry in the monastic church. The calendar of the psalter reports several commemorations of the translation of relics (*translatio*). Not all these feast days can be confirmed as being celebrated liturgically, however. The liturgical texts offer only three of the six of these liturgical commemorations, namely, the feast of the translation of Saint Benedict, Saint Martin of Tours and the translation of Saint Gengulphus (*sancti Gangulphi martyris*), martyr of Burgundy. Particular devotion to this saint in the nunnery cannot go unnoticed. The calendar of the psalter contains as many as three liturgical days assigned to this

---

*Schweden* (2 vols., Kopenhagen: Einar Munksgaard, 1947), 1, p. 285; Grotefend, *Zeitrechnung des Deutschen Mittelalters*.

67  See also Schmid, 'Stundengebet und Heiligenverehrung', pp. 15–22.

68  The calendar of the psalter shows that in the nunnery of Saint Mary Magdalene the Saint was celebrated on 6 October, whereas in the Swedish dioceses the celebration was on 7 October.

69  Similar to *Breviarium Rigensis* (4, fols. 60r–61r) the indication of celebration on 23 July is found in the *Collectarium* part of UUB C 293, fol. 212v. For further information on *Officium Sancte Birgitte*, see Ann-Marie Nilsson, *Två hystorie för den heliga Birgitta* (Bromma: Reimers, 2003), see also Moberg, *Die liturgischen Hymnen*, pp. 301–302.

70  For memorial networks between Birgittines of Pirita and Cistercian nunnery of Riga, see Strenga, 'Cistercian networks of memory', pp. 212–231.

Burgundian knight. His liturgical day on 13 May, coincides with most of the calendars of German dioceses.[71] 4 May was the day on which the translation occurs, and 10 September is the day for the deposition of his relics. Noticeably, this is the only saint in the calendar to whom the deposition is given. The proper texts of manuscripts C 436, C 477, C 293, C 434 indicate only one prayer on the day of the translation. Furthermore, his name is reported in the litany of one of the books of hours; this certainly suggests that the saint was also venerated privately for special patronage.[72] It is not known if the cult of this saint in the nunnery was related to the relics available for veneration or if Saint Gengulphus was honoured as a patron saint for a more specific reason, such as his unique merits.[73] This is the only traceable mention thus far of the saint in the written sources of the diocese of Riga. Other evidence of special devotion to saints is given by the altars and chantries in the monastic church dedicated to specific saints. Six altars of the monastic church can be identified from the historical sources.[74] In particular it is worth noting Saint Procopius. The chantry in his honour in the monastic church was established on 8 July 1445.[75] The available sources show that the unique appearance of Saint Procopius in the diocese of Riga is associated exclusively with the Cistercian nunnery. Although the calendar of the psalter does not mention the Saint, the breviaries C 293, C 434, C 436, the hymnary/collectary C 477 and the collection of *Benedicamus* in C 438 contain an indication and Proper text of the Bohemian abbot. In Toni Schmid's opinion, the presence of Saint Procopius in liturgical texts was further proof that the manuscripts belonged to this specific nunnery.[76] It is pertinent to note that besides the manuscripts, there are only a few historical sources that report the notices of the liturgical feasts of the nunnery. One of these is the indulgence document issued by the papal curia in Avignon in 1359. That the feasts that appear in the liturgical manuscripts match those of the curial document is an important fact to note.[77]

---

71  See Grotefend, *Zeitrechnung des Deutschen Mittelalters*.
72  UUB C 503, fol. 39r.
73  Saint Gengulphus was particularly considered as the patron saint of deceived husbands and unhappy marriages. More on Saint Gengulphus see, e.g., Paul G. Dräger, *Das Leben Gangolfs* (Trier: Kliomedia, 2011).
74  See Bruiningk, *Messe und kanonisches Stundengebet*, p. 594.
75  LUB 10, no. 150, see Bruiningk, *Messe und kanonisches Stundengebet*, pp. 531–532. See also Schmid, 'Ett breviarium från Magdalenenklostret i Riga', p. 272.
76  Schimd, 'Stundengebet und Heiligenverehrung', p. 24. See also Bruiningk, *Messe und kanonisches Stundengebet*, pp. 472, 531.
77  There is no evidence of the feast of Saint Ivo (*Sancti Yvoni*) in the liturgical sources from nunnery. More on veneration of Saint in the diocese of Riga, see Bruiningk, *Messe und kanonisches Stundengebet*, pp. 65, 438, 582–583.

## 3  The Musical Material in the Cistercian Manuscripts

Since there are no known musical-liturgical manuscripts that fully present the nuns' musical practices in the nunnery of Saint Mary Magdalene, it is only possible to examine the pages with musical notation in seven of fourteen liturgical manuscripts for its liturgical context, practical purpose, and usage. These are five books of hours (C 438, C 467, C 486, C 487, C 488), a breviary C 436 and the Cistercian psalter now located in Vilnius. Unlike liturgical manuscripts, which in Cistercian circles have a high degree of uniformity, the book of hours is extraordinarily versatile and individually designed, including the nature of musical entries. The space dedicated to music in the manuscripts is not large, but nevertheless, due to its particularities, provides valuable information about the musical practice of the nuns' prayer life. The musical material varies from melodic incipits to complete compositions. Five books of hours contain the same notated Invitatory psalm *Venite*. In three of them (C 486, C 487, C 488) the *alleluia* antiphons are present. The manuscript C 486 includes two fully notated hymns for the feast of Purification of Virgin and two incipits of Paschal hymns, while the Vilnius Cistercian psalter contains two hymns with the same melody for the feast of the Ascension of the Lord. C 436 contains only one chant in notation form, but at the end of the manuscript C 438 can be found the selection of melodies of versicle *Benedicamus domino* and incipits of hymns and tropes of *Benedicamus* chants.

Musical material is not commonly encountered in a book of hours intended for private and devotional uses. Nevertheless, it could emerge in the books of monastic use. Incidentally, this feature confirms the characteristic appellation of nuns which appears in historical sources, namely, the singing virgins.[78] There is an obvious question: What were the criteria for choosing which chants in the prayer book should be notated? Because the musical material differs between the manuscripts, the primary reasons for its inclusion in the prayer books may also differ. Presumably, some musical entries may have been related to a peculiarity of a book, namely, that it was created not only for private devotion but also for ferial use within the liturgy.

The notation present in the manuscripts is an example of diastematic notation: the 'Gothic' script.[79] Gothic notation was characteristic for many Northern countries, but Sweden was an exception in using the square notation.[80] Correspondingly, evidence of Gothic notation in Sweden (Uppsala University

---

[78]  *singende vrouwen* (LUB 3, no. 1332) and *singende juncvruwen* (LUB 7, no. 372).
[79]  German: *Hufnagelschrift*.
[80]  See Moberg, *Die liturgischen Hymnen*, p. 82.

Library) is proof of the foreign origin of a manuscript. The notation present in each manuscript was copied by a particular scribe. The writing of the notator does not change inside each manuscript, apart from the C 487, where the *alleluia* antiphons are written with a different hand than the Invitatory psalm. However, the handwriting of the Invitatory psalms in C 487 and C 467 is identical. Likewise, the graphic forms of the notation do not differ between the sources and the notation's script is standardised. Greater differences can be observed in the accurate or more urgent and superficial form of records in, for example, C 438. While the copyist was unable to intervene and express his/her own individuality through the graphics of notation, this was possible by the use of accessory elements: catchwords, clefs, alteration signs and staff sign, *custos*. Four manuscripts that use the sign of *custos*, report variations in shape and size. Similar observations can be made for clefs.[81]

What can the musical compositions in the manuscripts reveal about the nuns' liturgy? The most common chant recorded in notation is the Invitatory *Venite exultemus* found in different places in five books of hours. Of all the books, C 488 shows most clearly its predetermined place in the liturgy, as attested to by rubrics and by its location in the text. The rubric *feria secunda ad matutinas* following the hymn *Sompno refectis artubus*, used for Matins on Mondays, confirms the ferial office context. Consequently, one can clearly see that nuns' ferial office was sung in choir.[82] The melody used for the Invitatory represents a simple tone which aligns with weekday circumstances.[83] The chant is noted in its entirety of six verses occupying four to eight folios, according to the manuscript in question. The manner of notation differs between manuscripts and in some manuscript the musical notation is divided by lines of the staff, showing the melody's relation to the text. This is notable indication, more so because the division of melody does not match between some of the Invitatories. Normally, the Invitatory chant was sung daily. Since it was easily memorised, there was no need for it to be written, at least not in its entirety. The way of structuring the melody with staff lines could indicate

---

81   The written features of these incidental and modest elements, as individual imprints of the copyist, are valuable information relating to the identification of the hand. The particularity in the shape and dimension of the *custos* can be locally characteristic and reveal the provenance of the manuscript. For more on the *custos*, see Gabriella Gilányi, 'Jelentéktelen kis apróság? A gregorián custos', *Magyar Zene*, 56 (4) (2018), pp. 385–397.
82   UUB C 488, fol. 143v.
83   With some variants the tone generally corresponds with the melodic version of VI tone, till now in use in Cistercians' liturgy. See *Antiphonarium Cisterciense pars prima* (Westmalle: Typis Ordinis, 1955).

some educational intent for a less experienced singer.[84] In effect, in the second strophe of C 467, the staff lines appear in red colour, while the Invitatory present in C 487 (copied by the same hand), does not represent any structuring of the melody. Beyond these five manuscripts, no other book of hours from the nuns' collections contains a notated *Venite*. Evidently, the notation was the personal choice of the book's owner.[85]

The most accurate script of musical notation is present in manuscript C 486.[86] This manuscript contains a 'musical section' that starts with *alleluia* antiphons on fol. 147r following the Invitatory and continues with two entire hymns for the feast of Purification: *Lux maris gaude celesti digna* and *Quod chorus vatum* (fols. 149v–152r). In addition to these hymns, in some later folios there appear two incipits of Paschal hymns: *Te lucis auctor personet* on fol. 156v and *Aurora lucis rutilat* on fol. 157r. In regard to these notated hymns, some peculiarities are worthy of commentary. At present, no complete, entirely notated and legible version of the hymn *Lux maris gaude* has been discovered.[87] Thus the entire notated melody for every stanza in C 486 is a valuable resource.[88] Even though its fortuitously notated form appears only in manuscript C 486, the same complete textual version can be found in two other manuscripts: C 477 fol. 84r and C 434 fol. 274v. No other book of hours contains this hymn. This may lead us to believe that in this case the choice of notation might have been a personal decision of the book's owner. C 434 specifies the hymn's liturgical use, giving the hymn's incipit for Lauds on the day of the Purification (fol. 126r). Alternatively, *Quod chorus vatum*, the second entirely notated hymn in the same manuscript, is provided for the Office of

---

84  This may be an indication that the verses of the *Venite* were assigned to young novices or even the convent's school children (*scholares, iuvencule*). For more on the children's roles in the liturgy, see Alison Noel Altstatt, *The Music and Liturgy of Kloster Preetz: Anna von Buchwald's Buch im Chor in its Fifteenth-Century Context* (PhD thesis, University of Oregon, 2011) Available at: www.works.bepress.com/alison-altstatt/12/ (last accessed 12 July 2021).

85  UUB C 467, fols. 170r–173v; UUB C 487, fols. 181r–184r.

86  This manuscript probably belonged to the last nun of Riga's convent, Anna Noetken.

87  *Analecta Hymnica Medii Aevi* 52 (hereafter: AH), no. 50; Ulysse Chevalier, *Repertorium hymnologicum: Catalogue des chants, hymnes, proses, séquences, tropes en usage dans l'église latine depuis les origines jusqu'a nos jours* (Louvain: Imprimerie Lefever, 1892), nr. 10846.

88  The hymn is found in two manuscripts. The first of these is the three-part breviary Wolfenbüttel HAB 169, 170 and 335 (D–W 169 fol. 15r) which presents the first four lines reported in notation. The second is breviary Wolfenbüttel HAB 1298, which contains melody of the V–VII line, unfortunately in ineligible notation. See Bruno Stäblein, *Hymnen: Die mittelalterlichen Hymnenmelodien des Abendlandes, Monumenta Monodica Medii Aevi* (MMMA) (12 vols., Kassel: Bärenreiter 1956–1999), 1, p. 589.

Matins.[89] There are no traces of the hymn *Lux maris gaude* in the printed diocesan Breviary; consequently, there is no evidence of the hymn's liturgical usage outside the Cistercian nunnery within the diocese.

Further information can be gleaned from the Vilnius Cistercian psalter, meant for private use, which transmits a hymn in notation. This hymn for the feast of the Ascension of the Lord is divided into two separate hymns: *Optatus votis* and *O grande cunctis gaudium*.[90] Two hymns are indicated as having the same melody and, incidentally, in the second hymn, both melody and text are copied in an inaccurate and imprecise way. For example, an error appears in the first stanza of the second hymn which, thanks to musical notation, is clearly evident. Instead of 'Quod partus nostre virginis' the copyist wrote 'Quod nostre partus virginis' (sic).[91] This feature in particular appears to be a common variant present in other manuscripts from the nuns' collection.[92] This textual version has no correspondence with the melodic line and is unsingable. Inasmuch as different manuscripts contain the same error, this observation provides significant information. Presumably, they were copied from a single source. The peculiar textual variant suggests that the musical notation did not ensure a particular version of the text which was, in some way, independent. From the context of the manuscript as a private prayer book, not intended for liturgical uses, the presence of notation likely serves as more of a decorative element than an indication for performance. Considering that hymns are compositions that retain the same melody for every stanza, there was no need to provide notation, much less to provide it for the entire piece. Such a decision reveals the personal attitude of the book's owner toward a particular chant, since it was the owner who made that choice.

Another noteworthy chant is the rhymed *Rector celi nos exaudi*, the unique chant accurately copied at the end of diurnal breviary C 436 fol. 155v, which illuminates another property of music in the prayer books. The chant could be identified by the context of the preceding rubric *Pro tempestate* which, in turn, locates the chant among the benedictions against inclement weather. The rhymed text, in its brevity and expressiveness, is a very clear and solemn prayer directly addressed to the Heavenly King. The origin of this invocative antiphon's text is unknown but is recognized as one of the most common and most beautiful prayers engraved on the bells of the medieval churches in different

---

89   The incipit of hymn can be found in UUB C 434, fol. 124r, as well in *Breviarium Rigensis* IV, fol. 16v.
90   LMAVB RS F 22–96, fols. 152v–153r. For melodical comparison see Stäblein MMMA 1, no. 60.
91   Cf., e.g., AH 51, no. 87, and Chevalier, *Repertorium hymnologicum*, no. 14177.
92   E.g., UUB C 477, fol. 93v; C 467, fol. 152r; C 488, fol. 123r; C 487, fol. 164v; C 434, fol. 280v.

parts of Europe. Such bells are also symbolically called 'peace bells'.[93] Despite the fact that this text was well-known in the medieval centuries and was musicalized, it occurs precisely in the context of impetratory orations for clement weather.[94] Even though intercessory orations for rain or clement weather are a common phenomenon in liturgical books such as those of rituals and the pontifical, chants added to benediction and prayer are rather exceptional in the breviary. In the present case, the musical addition to this prayer could be classified as part of personal devotion since it does not appear in other manuscripts of the nuns' collection, even without the music.

Finally, the last musical material to be examined is an extensive collection of 103 melodic indications of the versicle *Benedicamus Domino*. For most of these musical fragments transmitted on the last folios of C 438 (119v–130v), only the melodic and textual incipits are recorded. From 103 musical entries, nine melodies of the *Benedicamus* can be distinguished, from which only six are entirely notated. In addition, four troped versicles show that for the most prominent feasts of Church year and within this specific nunnery, the *Benedicamus* in troped form was used, increasing the richness and solemnity of the celebration. Indications of inaccurate and incomplete notation, as occur in other similar cases, suggest that this musical material served as a visual aid for the memory of the cantor who already knew the melodies by heart. The collection in question is organised in a *de tempore* system and the melodic incipits are indicated according to its liturgical usage. The rubrics consequently create a 'virtual' calendar of the most important festivities of the nunnery.[95] However, the *Benedicamus* collection presents incoherencies in the order of festivities, which interrupts the sequence according to the liturgical calendar. In addition, from comparison with the calendar of the Vilnius Cistercian psalter, the lack of some relevant feasts can be observed. Presumably, this was caused by later dismemberment and reassembling, which led to a codicological confusion concerning the order of the folios.[96] Since no other manuscript contains such a

---

93 Cf. Karl Walter, *Glockenkunde* (Regensburg: Friedrich Pustet, 1913), p. 203; see also Friedrich W. Schubart, *O rex gloriae, Christe, veni cum pace Amen: Ein uraltes Glockengebet; Ein Beitrag zur Glockeninschriftenkunde* (Baumann: Dessau 1896), pp. 3–4; Klaus Berger, *Leih mir deine Flügel, Engel: Die Apokalypse im Leben der Kirche* (Freiburg: Herder, 2018), p. 161.

94 A similar constellation of chants against inclement weather appears in *Rituale* Cod. Guelf. 1028 Helmst, fols. 117v–199v, see www.diglib.hab.de/mss/1028-helmst/start.htm?distype=thumbs-img&imgtyp=0&size= (last accessed 1 March 2021).

95 The feasts are indicated by rubrics, e.g., *Brigitte vidue, Augustini episcopi* etc. or *de virginibus, de confessoribus* etc. See also Moberg, *Die liturgischen Hymnen*, p. 57.

96 The relevant feasts between Saint Ambrose (4/4) and Saint Barnabas apostle (11/6) are missing.

collection, it can be assumed that manuscript C 438 belonged to someone who had the task of performing the intonation of the *Benedicamus* chant at the end of the liturgical celebration. This series of *Benedicamus* versicles refers to the most relevant feasts of the nunnery. Every feast was provided with a melody according to the classification of festivity. The primary reason for the use of different melodies was, presumably, to give a distinctive 'colour' or 'acoustic signal' for specific feasts or categories of feasts. This is one of the many examples of how music itself is a type of identification of different liturgical occasions.[97]

## 4   Conclusions

Since sources such as customaries, ordinaries, visitation records and even the choral liturgical manuscripts have not survived or have not yet been found, the small portion of the nuns' library at our disposal provides significant insights into the common and private ritual life of the Cistercian nuns of Riga. The manuscripts available for researchers in the libraries in Uppsala and Vilnius open a way of reconstructing, even in an incomplete and fragmentary manner, the prayer of the divine office, revealing the particulars of ritual practices based on common worship and private piety that have not yet been studied.

The sources confirm that breviaries like C 436 were used for the hours of feasts and prominent weekdays of the liturgical year; breviaries such as C 434 and C 293 were used for night offices of Sundays and feast days; while books of hours were used for the ordinary weekday office and ferias during the octaves of important feasts celebrated in the nunnery. Liturgical texts such as rhymed offices indicate relevant local liturgical practices of the female community in fifteenth-century Riga. Besides the canonical office, nuns experienced assorted votive services including the rich practice of Marian devotion and extensive memorial culture. This wide and intense prayer life was the result of numerous prayer obligations due to the commemorative bonds with the outside world.

The book of hours, the type of liturgical book that forms a major part of surviving codices, reveals an unusual content for a book of this kind. The most significant feature of the books of hours from the Riga nunnery is a combination between votive observances and weekdays office as well as different offices of the Temporale and the Sanctorale. This delineates the function of the book, which served not only for supplemental services but, particularly, for ordinary weekday liturgy throughout the entire liturgical year, including

---

97   Franz Karl Prassl, 'Pavlov's Dog and Liturgy: Listening and Recognition in Gregorian Chant', *De musica disserenda*, 9:1–2 (2013), pp. 253–269.

the festive octaves Proper of the local monastic community. An analysis of the content and comparison between the manuscripts suggests the community as a whole most likely recited supplemental services together, in addition to the canonical weekday office.

The cult of the saints of the Cistercian nunnery of Riga, as testified to by the nuns' breviaries and a unique source, the calendar of the Vilnius Cistercian psalter, reveals that, on the one hand, the monastic community had taken root in a concrete region which allowed it to be influenced by local religious practices and the regulations of the diocese. On the other hand, it demonstrates that the Cistercians' general practices of the veneration of saints remained unified with the larger family of the Order. Either way, the bonds with other religious communities and secular institutions, patrons and benefactors, had an important role in the development of the cult of saints in the nunnery. The manuscripts from the nunnery show a clear correspondence with the missal used in the cathedral of Riga and the printed diocesan breviary. Nevertheless, the several liturgical memorial days, until now unknown in the diocese of Riga, that appear in the columns of the calendar, are confirmed to have been celebrated liturgically in the nuns' breviaries.

Music in the books of hours has not yet received enough attention from scholars. Even though studies have been carried out on notated chants in late medieval prayer books and books for private use, conclusions related to music cannot be generalised. Thus, for example, well-known devotional books such as the fruit of the movement of piety *Devotio Moderna* (e.g., the Medingen prayer books), present a different reality: music for use within private devotional practice.[98] Likewise, the music present in the books of hours used by laypeople, which is a very rare occurrence, does not prove whether the notated music was intended for private performance or served only as a decorative element. These case studies, apparently, are not conversant with the reality of books of hours of the type used by the Cistercian nuns in Riga. Rather, the situation is similar to the fifteenth-century books of hours preserved in the Baden State Library from the Cistercian nunnery in Erfurt (Thuringia) which presents chants with the notation for the Office of the Dead.[99] These examples demonstrate the common liturgical prayer in the book of hours in a monastic context.

---

[98] Henrike Lähnemann, 'Bilingual Devotion in Northern Germany: Prayer Books from the Luneburg Convents', in Elisabeth Andersen et al. (eds.), *A Companion to Mysticism and Devotion in Northern Germany in the Late Middle Ages* (Leiden: Brill, 2014), pp. 317–341; Ulrike Hascher–Burger, 'Notation, Devotion und Emotion in spätmittelalterlichen Andachtsbüchern aus dem Kloster Medingen', *Musica Disciplina*, 55 (2010), pp. 33–73.

[99] Badische Landesbibliothek, Cod. St. Peter perg. 38 a; 66, 107.

The books of hours from Riga have a multifunctional character: they were used not only for individual prayer or votive services but also for weekday office performance. Musicological and liturgical analysis demonstrates that the nature of such musical elements as the Invitatory, alleluia antiphons, and versicles of the *Benedicamus*, is fully liturgical and very likely attests to their use precisely in the weekday liturgy. The intention of including musical examples in the book which, by its nature, is not a liturgical-musical book is a significant point of interest. Musical material, especially in books of hours and breviaries is not common at all and is thus of specific importance. There is no evidence that these chants were sung during the nuns' individual practices: on the contrary, their nature is liturgical rather than privately devotional. What was the reason for including chants in these books, or how and by whom were they performed? Explicating such performative scenarios remains one of the main questions for further research.

CHAPTER 2

# Gradual Formation and Dramatic Transformation

*Mendicant and Cistercian Book Collections in Late Medieval and Post-reformation Riga*

*Andris Levāns and Gustavs Strenga*

Most of the surviving medieval book collections in northern Europe were initially formed by religious communities. During the Reformation, they frequently became for the reformed institutions: universities, schools and municipal book collections, a kind of book depository and cornerstone for new libraries. After the secularisation of monasteries, friaries and convents the books once owned by these institutions or by individual monks, friars and nuns served pastors, professors, students and urban intellectuals. As the present study will demonstrate, during the late sixteenth century there were also instances when the books of old Catholic religious communities became the property of new ones, the colleges of the Jesuit Order. The use made of the books did not necessarily differ between followers of different beliefs. Some of these medieval books owned by Protestant or post-Tridentine Catholic institutions were meant to be forgotten and reused as raw material; they lay on the shelves unused, waiting for their parchment leaves to become binding material for works of Protestant or Counter-Reformation Catholic authors.

Medieval Riga, as other medieval Northern European cities of similar size, had numerous religious communities located within the city walls. In Riga, the friaries of the mendicants: Dominicans and Franciscans, and also a Cistercian nunnery were founded soon after the city was established in 1201. The Dominican convent of Saint John the Baptist was the oldest such institution, founded in 1234 when it received the old bishop's castle for use.[1] It remains unknown when exactly the Franciscan convent of Saint Catherine was founded, but it already existed around 1238.[2] The Cistercian nunnery of

---

1  Gertrud von Walther-Wittenheim, *Die Dominikaner in Livland im Mittelalter: Die Natio Livoniae* (Rome: Institutum historicum FF Praedicatorum, 1938), p. 7.
2  Leonhard Lemmens, *Die Franziskanerkustodie Livland und Preußen* (Düsseldorf: Schwann, 1912), p. 109; Jørgen Nybo Rasmussen, *Die Franziskaner in den nordischen Ländern im Mittelalter* (Kevelaer: Edition T. Coelde, 2002), p. 68; Anti Selart, 'Die Bettelmönche im Ostseeraum zur Zeit des Erzbischofs Albert Suerbeer von Riga (Mitte des 13. Jahrhunderts)', *Zeitschrift für Ostmitteleuropa-Forschung*, 56:4 (2007), pp. 475–499, here p. 485.

© ANDRIS LEVĀNS AND GUSTAVS STRENGA, 2023 | DOI:10.1163/9789004441217_004
This is an open access chapter distributed under the terms of the CC BY-NC-ND 4.0 license.

Saint Mary Magdalene was founded around 1256 through the efforts of the archbishop Albert Suerbeer (1253–1272/73) and it was located next to Saint James (St. Jakobskirche) church.[3] All three institutions, like friaries and nunneries elsewhere in medieval Europe, were physically located directly at the city walls, thus becoming part of the urban fortifications.[4]

Alongside the cathedral chapter, these communities were centres of literacy and book production. The book collections of the Riga Dominicans, Franciscans and Cistercian nuns have partially survived, despite the Lutheran Reformation that took place in Riga during the 1520s.[5] Because of confessional and political changes during the sixteenth and seventeenth century the surviving books of the Rigan Cistercian nuns and Franciscan and Dominican friars can be found in collections in Riga, Stockholm, Uppsala and Vilnius. The majority of Franciscan and Dominican books, mostly incunabula, remained in Riga and became part of the Riga city library (established after 1524) and are now held by the University of Latvia Academic Library.[6]

Most of the books from the Cistercian nunnery were inherited by the Jesuit college which was established after the Polish forces took control over Riga in 1582. These medieval manuscripts were kept in college library (1583–1621) and as part of that collection were taken as war booty to Uppsala, after the Swedish forces captured Riga in 1621.[7] Fourteen of them still survive as a part of the

---

3   *Liv-, Est- und Kurländisches Urkundenbuch: Nebst Regesten* (section 1, 12 vols; section 2, 3 vols., Riga: J. Deubner, 1853–1914), 1/1, (Reval: Kluge und Ströhm, 1853), (hereafter: LUB 1/1), no. 300; Wolfgang Schmidt, 'Die Zisterzienser im Baltikum und in Finnland', *Finska Kyrkohistoriska samfundets årsskrift*, 29/30 (1939/1940), pp. 1–286, here pp. 156–177; Gregory Leighton, 'Written and Visual Expressions of Authority of Female Monastic Institutions in Medieval Livonia: From 13th to 15th Century', *Studia Slavica et Balcanica Petropolitana*, 29 (2021), p. 15–35, here p. 24.
4   Johnny Grandjean Gøgsig Jakobsen, 'At Blackfriars Priory: Dominican Priories within Urban Geography in Medieval Scandinavia', in Edel Bhreathnach et al. (eds.), *Monastic Europe: Medieval Communities, Landscapes, and Settlement* (Turnhout: Brepols, 2019), pp. 331–356, here p. 340.
5   Leonid Arbusow, *Die Einführung der Reformation in Liv-, Est- und Kurland* (Leipzig: M. Heinsius, 1921); Martin Pabst, *Die Typologisierbarkeit von Städtereformation und die Stadt Riga als Beispiel*, (Frankfurt am Main: Peter Lang, 2015); Gustavs Strenga, 'Faith, Politics, Languages and Books. The Reformation in Riga (1521–1525)', in Andris Levāns and Gustavs Strenga (eds.), *Luther: The Turn; Catalogue of the exhibition, National Library of Latvia, Riga, 01.11.2017–04.02.2018* (Rīga: Latvijas Nacionālā bibliotēka, 2017), pp. 138–146.
6   Nicholaus Busch, *Die Geschichte der Rigaer Stadtbibliothek und Deren Bücher*, ed. Leonid Arbusow (2 vols., Riga: Rigaer Stadtverwaltung, 1937), 2, pp. 79–93; Rūta Jēkabsone (ed.), *Incunabula Bibliothecae Rigensis: katalogs* (Riga: Zinātne, 1993).
7   Reinis Norkārkls, 'The Riga Jesuit College and Its Book Collection', in *Catalogue of the Riga Jesuit College Book Collection (1583–1621): History and Reconstruction of the Collection = Rīgas jezuītu koleģijas grāmatu krājuma (1583–1621) katalogs. Krājuma vēsture un rekonstrukcija*, eds. Gustavs Strenga and Andris Levāns (Riga: Latvijas Nacionālā bibliotēka, 2021), pp. 90–111.

Uppsala University Library collection.[8] A psalter which formerly belonged to the Riga Saint Mary Magdalene nunnery is in the collection of the Wroblewski Library of the Lithuanian Academy of Sciences.[9]

Research on books once owned by the mendicant convents and female monastic communities is important for study of history of literacy and book culture. In recent decades there has been a considerable breakthrough in the research of literacy and book production in female monastic communities.[10] Surviving books from the mendicant and Cistercian collections shed light on book culture in late medieval Riga and reveal aspects of book production, ownership, and reading. Until the present, the historiography of medieval Riga mendicant and Cistercian book collections has not received the attention it deserves. Also, research has partially ignored Riga as a place of manuscript production and has not focused on the fate of the medieval books that belonged to the mendicant convents and the Cistercian nunnery after the Reformation.[11]

---

[8] Uppsala universitetsbibliotek (hereafter: UUB), C 293 *Breviarium*, 15th c., Riga; C 434 *Breviarium Cisterciense*, 15th c., Riga; C 436 *Breviarium*; C 438 *Liber horarum*, 15th c., Riga; C 454 *Liber horarum*, 15th c., Riga; C 467 *Liber horarum*, 15th c., Riga; C 474 *Liber horarum*, 15th c., Riga; C 477 *Collectarium et hymnarium Cisterciense*, 15th c., Riga; C 486 *Liber horarum*, 15th c., Riga; C 487 *Liber horarum*, 15th c., Riga; C 488 *Liber horarum*, 15th c., Riga; C 491 *Liber horarum*, 15th c., Riga; C 503 *Liber horarum*, 15th c., Riga; C 802 *De exterioris et interioris hominis compositione*, 15th c., Riga?; see the descriptions of the manuscripts in Margarete Andersson-Schmitt et al. (eds.), *Mittelalterliche Handschriften der Universitätsbibliothek Uppsala: Katalog über die C-Sammlung* (8 vols., Stockholm: Almqvist & Wiksell, 1988–1995) (hereafter: MHUBU); see also the manuscript catalogue of the Riga Jesuit college compiled by Laura Kreigere-Liepiņa and Renāte Berga in *Catalogue of the Riga Jesuit College's Book Collection (1583–1621)*, pp. 215–233; Schmidt, 'Die Zisterzienser im Baltikum und in Finnland', pp. 176–177.

[9] *Psalterium Davidis*, Lietuvos mokslų akademijos Vrublevskių biblioteka (hereafter: LMAVB, MAB) F 22 Bx 96; Laine Tabora, 'Psalterium Davidis of the Cistercian Nunnery of Riga (LMAVB RS F 22–96) and Its Liturgical Calendar', *Analecta Cisterciensia*, 71 (2021), pp. 119–169.

[10] Ingela Hedström, 'Vadstena Abbey and Female Literacy in Late Medieval Sweden', in Virginia Blanton et al. (eds.), *Nuns' Literacies in Medieval Europe: The Hull Dialogue* (Turnhout: Brepols, 2013), pp. 253–272; Jonas Carlquist, 'The Birgittine Sisters at Vadstena Abbey: Their Learning and Literacy, with Particular Reference to Table Reading', in *Nuns' Literacies in Medieval Europe*, pp. 239–251; Monica Hedlund, 'Nuns and Latin, with Special Reference to the Birgittines of Vadstena', in *Nuns' Literacies in Medieval Europe*, pp. 97–118.

[11] For the book history in medieval Riga, see Busch, *Die Geschichte der Rigaer Stadtbibliothek*, 2; for Latvian edition of the same book, see Nikolajs Bušs, *Rīgas pilsētas bibliotēkas un tās grāmatu vēsture* (2 vols., Rīga: Rīgas pilsētas valdes izdevums, 1937), 2; Toni Schmid, 'Stundengebet und Heiligenverehrung im Magdalenenkloster zu Riga', *Beiträge zur Kunde Estlands*, 21 (1937), pp. 12–26; Klaus Garber, *Schatzhäuser des Geistes: Alte Bibliotheken und Büchersammlungen im Baltikum* (Köln: Böhlau, 2007); Aija Taimiņa, '15. gs. metāla griezuma jeb "skrošu" gravīras un Rīgas patricieša Reinholda Soltrumpa grāmatu likteņi: Vēstījums ar atkāpēm par Aglonas bazilikas bibliotēkā jaunatrasto inkunābulu', *Mākslas*

This material allows us to see differences between the lifestyles of the male and female communities, gender aspect of reading and book production, and traits of female monastic spirituality that have been overlooked in the scholarship until now.

In order to reveal the complexity and regional importance of the book collections from late medieval Riga, the present study will focus on several research questions. What is known about the formation of these book collections? Where were the manuscripts used by the Cistercian nuns produced? Who were private donors of the books in these collections? What happened to the mendicant and Cistercian books during and after the Reformation? How did the city of Riga take over the mendicants' books and create its own book collection?

## 1  Places of Books. Formation of Mendicant and Cistercian Communities in Riga and Their Books

Throughout the Middle Ages the mendicant convents and Cistercian nunnery remained important institutions for the religious, social, and intellectual life of the city. Though these institutions in Riga were not marginal communities, almost no sources survive that would characterise individual friars and nuns. The books in this respect are especially valuable because they provide a brief glimpse into the intimate spiritual and intellectual lives of some of these individuals, the residents of late medieval Riga. Not only lifestyles and duties separated the mendicant friaries from the Cistercian nunnery. These communities hosted individuals of different backgrounds and this feature had an impact on the history of the institutions themselves and subsequently on the fate of their book collections.

Until the Protestant Reformation, the Dominican and Franciscan friars fulfilled two functions of great importance in north European urban societies. In Riga, as elsewhere, the mendicants served the townspeople as intercessors for the latter's deceased relatives, and, secondly, they performed public duties as scribes for both individuals and communal institutions: writing documents and writing letters for the illiterate. The mendicants were tightly integrated into the urban societies where they lived, giving them a public identity and communication opportunities in exchange for payments for their services. In this, they competed with the city council.

---

*Vēsture un Teorija*, 2 (2004), pp. 5–19; Guntars Prānis, *Missale Rigense Livonijas garīgajā kultūrā: Gregoriskie dziedājumi viduslaiku Rīgā* (Rīga: Neputns, 2018).

Most of the late medieval mendicants were of urban origin. The relationship between the local communities and mendicants in the Baltic Sea region changed during the late fifteenth century, when the reform of religious orders began. Both mendicant friaries in Riga were reformed. The Franciscan convent was reformed in 1463, and later, when other Franciscan friaries in Livonia were reformed, a new Livonia Custody was established.[12] It is not known exactly when the Dominican convent in Riga underwent reform; the first reform attempt took place in 1475–1476, led by the provincial of Saxony; and in the 1480s it was again listed among the convents of reformed *Congregatio Hollandiae*.[13] Though, in the beginning, in Northern European urban communities reform of the Dominican convents was popular, gradually the popularity of the Dominicans among townspeople diminished. In order to prevent disciplinary abuse, many friars who came from rich and influential families were transferred after the reform to convents elsewhere, and the convents were no longer staffed with 'local boys'.[14] The reactions of the urban communities to the Dominican reform in the long term were paradoxical. Though many of the Dominican convents in the Baltic Sea region were reformed with the support of the local city councils, and friars 'were living the most disciplined monastic life seen in the order for centuries,' during the Reformation the Dominican convents were those that were dissolved first. As Johnny Grandjean Gøgsig Jakobsen argues, the reform disrupted the existing social networks, making the Dominicans vulnerable to outside criticism, the local interests at stake having been reduced.[15] The reform pattern may have influenced the relationships between local communities and the Franciscans in a similar fashion. The events of the Protestant Reformation in Riga demonstrated that they were perceived by the local urban community as a foreign element, as agents of the old Catholic Church. The Franciscans and Dominicans had been the reformers' main opponents, engaging in a dispute with them in 1522 and taking

---

12  Rafał Kubicki, 'Mendicant Friaries in the Dominion of the Teutonic Order in Prussia and in Royal Prussia after 1466 until the Reformation', *Zapiski Historyczne*, 81 (2016), pp. 83–99, here p. 86.

13  Walther-Wittenheim, *Die Dominikaner in Livland im Mittelalter*, pp. 112–114; Petrus Franciscus Wolfs, 'Dominikanische Observanzbestrebungen: Die Congregatio Hollandiae (1464–1517)', in Kaspar Elm (ed.), *Reformbemühungen und Observanzbestrebungen* (Berlin: Duncker & Humblot, 1989), pp. 273–292.

14  Johnny Grandjean Gøgsig Jakobsen, 'The Dominicans and the Reformation in Northern Europe', in Per Seesko et al. (eds.), *The Dissolution of Monasteries: The Case of Denmark in a Regional Perspective* (Odense: University Press of Southern Denmark, 2019), pp. 75–103, here p. 79.

15  Jakobsen, 'The Dominicans and the Reformation in Northern Europe', p. 79.

part in diplomatic missions to counter the Reformation in Riga.[16] Three Rigan Franciscans in 1523 went with a secret mission to the Empire and to Rome to find support for opposition against the Lutherans.[17] On their return to the city, two of the friars, Antonius Bomhower and Burkhard Waldis (c.1490–1556), the latter later becoming a famous Lutheran author, were incarcerated.[18]

The Cistercian nunnery was in a very different position. Most of the Cistercian nuns were daughters of local noblemen. In 1495 the whole Cistercian community, the fifty-three nuns whose names were recorded, entered the Beer Carters guild. As this list demonstrates, most of the nuns belonged to Livonian noble families.[19] The nuns were not connected to the city's influential merchant families, yet the nuns' relatives (the local noblemen) were important patrons and guardians. There was an attempt to reform the nunnery of Saint Mary Magdalene during the late fifteenth century, and one of the city's overlords, the Master of the Teutonic Order's Livonian branch Wolter von Plettenberg (r. 1494–1535), supported this effort.[20] Most likely the reform of the nunnery had indeed taken place, though there is no confirmation of this in the historical record. The importance of the nobility's patronage revealed itself during the Protestant Reformation. If the mendicant convents were disbanded already in 1524, just two years after the beginning of the Reformation, the Cistercian nunnery survived the turbulence of the 1520s and continued to operate until the 1580s, though by that time it had only a few surviving nuns. The nobility's patronage did not allow the townspeople to expel the nuns from the city as they had done with the mendicants. This may explain why the nunnery (even with few nuns) and its books survived the Protestant Reformation.

The books that belonged to the Franciscan and Dominican convents before the fracture are the only hard evidence about the intellectual life of these religious communities. A number of features testify to the fact that the preserved incunabula and manuscripts did belong to the mendicants: provenance records and binding decoration, for example, ornamentation on leather

---

16  Arbusow, *Die Einführung der Reformation*, pp. 210–215; Pabst, *Die Typologisierbarkeit von Städtereformation*, pp. 219–220.

17  See, Arbusow, *Die Einführung der Reformation*, pp. 256–267.

18  Leonid Arbusow, 'Die Aktion der Rigaschen Franziskaner gegen das Vordringen des Luthertums und ihre Folgen', in *Sitzungsberichte der Gesellschaft für Geschichte und Alterthumskunde der Ostseeprovinzen Russlands aus dem Jahre 1913* (Riga: W. F. Häcker, 1914), pp. 21–70, here p. 53; Arbusow, *Die Einführung der Reformation*, p. 328.

19  LUB 2/1, no. 252; Gustavs Strenga, 'Cistercian Networks of Memory Commemoration as a Form of Institutional Bonding in Livonia and beyond during the Late Middle Ages', in Anu Mänd and Marek Tamm (eds.), *Making Livonia: Actors and Networks in the Medieval and Early Modern Baltic Sea Region* (London: Routledge, 2020), pp. 212–231.

20  LUB 2/1, no. 253.

covers, switch shape and chains (*catena*). Among the surviving medieval books in the former Riga city library collection, thirty-seven books were once owned by the Franciscans and fifteen books by the Dominicans, their identities having been established by Nicolaus Busch.[21] They represent, however, only a part of the books owned by the convents; nothing is known about the original size of these libraries in the early sixteenth century. The formation dynamics of these collections and the nature of subsequent changes can be observed only indirectly, based on the surviving books: most likely in the 1470s and 1490s the collections acquired a large number of incunabula. This can be explained both by the availability of printed texts because of Gutenberg's invention and the 'crisis' of manuscript culture, and also by the economic stability of the mendicants due to their active involvement in socio-political life of Livonia. In the second half of the fifteenth century, these factors also contributed to the systematic and purposeful consolidation of these book collections. This was also a time period during which the two convents were reformed. The preservation of fragments of these libraries is thought to have been influenced by both random choice and pragmatic selection by those who were in charge of the books after the Protestant Reformation. The mendicant convents in Riga not only acquired books, but also were the sources of books for other institutions. For example, a manuscript having a medical and theological content (Uppsala UB, C 180) was copied by a Dominican friar in Riga and then was taken to Prussia.[22] It shows that books belonging to the Riga mendicant convents could travel with their owner and be used or stored by other persons and institutions outside Livonia.

The books that once belonged to the Riga Franciscans are characterised by the following features: most of them, thirty-three in number are incunabula, printed between the years 1470/1475 and 1516, though items from the time between 1480 and 1490 are the most frequent. Four manuscripts created in the fourteenth and fifteenth centuries and once owned by the Franciscans have survived. Amongst these Franciscan books, there are three *Sammelbände*; in addition, some printed works have several separate volumes. The Franciscan convent also had received books from two private book owners. There is a book of Johannes Hammonis, alias Bonekamp, presumably a Franciscan friar in the Riga convent, who according to a property inscription owned a *Sammelband*

---

21   Busch, *Die Geschichte der Rigaer Stadtbibliothek*, 2, pp. 79–93.
22   *Nicolaus Stör. Guido de Monte Rocherii. Gerardus de Vliederhoven. Thomas a Kempis. Meidizinische Aufzeichnungen*, UUB C 180.

and donated it to the convent when he left the community in 1520.[23] The priest Reinhold Soltrump, of whom more later, during the late fifteenth century also donated his book collection to the Franciscans.

Although it has survived in an incomplete form, the library of the Dominican convent is represented by fifteen printed books, incunabula, one of which is a *Sammelband* with two texts bound together.[24] The chronological structure is similar: the years between 1475 and 1512, with the decades between 1480 and 1490 being represented by a larger number.

In the case of the Franciscans and Dominicans in Riga, it can be questioned whether the creation of these libraries and the use of their books reflect the local specificity together with the tradition of the convent. Likewise, we can query whether these collections followed the same pattern of formation as the libraries of the mendicant communities elsewhere in Northern Europe. The surviving printed books, most of which date from a time period between 1475 and 1512, only fragmentarily reflect the last stage of the book and literary culture of Riga's Dominican and Franciscan convents. Most of the manuscripts from these collections have almost completely perished, with just few books surviving.

The late medieval Northern European nuns were literate. For example, in Bridgettine Vadstena Abbey in the late fifteenth and early sixteenth century most of the nuns were literate at least in the vernacular.[25] In female monastic communities a considerable number of nuns were also able to read and write in Latin. As the surviving books from Riga show, bilinguality, as demonstrated by the presence of vernacular (Middle Low German) texts in the books in which most of the text is in Latin, was common. The importance of vernacular during the early sixteenth century increased.

There are fifteen manuscripts in the collection of the Uppsala University Library that have been attributed to the Cistercian nunnery in Riga. Thirteen of

---

23   Busch, *Die Geschichte der Rigaer Stadtbibliothek*, 2, p. 82, no. 14–17. The Sammelband consists of Franciscus de Platea, *Opus restitutionum usurarum et excommunicationum*, (Speyer: Peter Drach, 1489), USTC 748209, LUAB IK 164; Jacobus de Cessolis, *De ludo scachorum* ([Utrecht: Nicolaus Ketelaer und Gerardus de Leempt, 1474]), USTC 435228, Latvijas Universitātes Akadēmiskā bibliotēka [The University of Latvia Academic Library] (hereafter: LUAB) IK 56; Giovanni de Capua, *Directorium humanae vitae* (Strassburg: Johann Prüss, ca. 1489), USTC 746255, LUAB IK 113; to the volume a manuscript *Croedidimus jam dudum* is bound. On the last page of the manuscript the inscription is written: '*Joannes Hammonis in hoc se presentabat conventu anno virginei partus myllesimo quingentesimo vigesimo* [1520] / *Johannes Hammonis alias Bonekamp multum huic felicitatis optat conventui*'.
24   Busch, *Die Geschichte der Rigaer Stadtbibliothek*, 2, pp. 86–89.
25   Carlquist, 'The Birgittine Sisters at Vadstena Abbey', p. 247.

these manuscripts are the so-called books of hours and breviaries.[26] One of the manuscripts is a collection of works, in the Middle Low German, on monastic life by David de Augusta (c.1200–c.1271/72) that has been mistakenly attributed by Tage Ahldén to the Bridgettine monastery in Gdańsk (Danzig).[27] In addition to these manuscripts, in the Wroblewski Library of the Lithuanian Academy of Sciences there is a psalter that most likely belonged to the Riga Cistercians, and the only one of the nunnery's prayer books that has a calendar.[28] This, however, must have been only a part of books owned by the community of more than fifty nuns.

All of these manuscripts possess specific material and textual content-related features that indicate that they once belonged to the Riga Cistercian nunnery. The common features include the graphic and aesthetic mode of the script, the manner of binding and the rendering of the cover, the presence in the text of the Middle Low German language and the compliance of the content with the religious practices of the Cistercian nuns. According to Toni Schmid, numerous manuscripts have common liturgical traits that allow them to be attributed to the Saint Mary Magdalene nunnery.[29] Examination of the palaeographic and codicological features of these works allows for the characterization of the technical execution of these manuscripts as aesthetically simple; the manuscripts have no expensive miniatures or initials. It can be assumed that most of these manuscripts were created in Riga. This assumption is based on the specific features of the manuscript collection that serve as indicators of the presence of a local tradition in fifteenth-century Livonia and of the belonging of the texts to the Riga Cistercian nunnery, for which they were created and in which they were used.[30] It can also be assumed that for numerous manuscripts the Cistercian nuns were themselves the scribes, and the codicology of

---

26   UUB C 293; C 434; C 436; C 438.; C 454; C 467; C 474; C 477; C 486; C 487; C 488; C 491; C 503.
27   UUB C 802; Nikolajs Bušs, *Rīgas pilsētas bibliotēkas un tās grāmatu vēsture*, 2, p. 83; Tage Ahldén, *Nonnenspiegel und Mönchsvorschriften. Mittelniederdeutsche Lebensregeln der Danziger Birgittinerkonvente: Ein Beitrag zur Geschichte der mittelniederdeutschen Sprache und Kultur auf Grund der Handschrift C 802 Uppsala* (Göteborg: Elanders, 1952).
28   The manuscript is described in detail by Laine Tabora in this volume. *Psalterium Davidis cum canticis*, LMAVB, MAB F 22 Bx 96.
29   According to Schmid's liturgical analysis the manuscripts C 293, C 477, and C 434 belonged to a Livonian nunnery. See Schmid, 'Stundengebet und Heiligenverehrung im Magdalenenkloster zu Riga', p. 25.
30   Andris Levāns and Gustavs Strenga, 'Medieval Manuscripts in the Book Collection of the Riga Jesuit College: The Manuscripts of the Riga St. Mary Magdalene Cistercian Nunnery and Their Tradition', in *Catalogue of the Riga Jesuit College's Book Collection (1583–1621)*, pp. 166–187.

the manuscripts indicates the presence of a book-making 'workshop' in the nunnery or in close proximity of it.[31]

## 2      Individual and Collective: Acquisition, Usage and Ownership of the Mendicant and Cistercian Books in Late Medieval Riga

Numerous books once owned by the mendicants in Riga were donated by rich and influential individuals. One such provenance thread leads back to an exceptional clergyman in the late medieval period. Not many individual book owners in medieval Livonia are known. But the one in question was the archbishop of Riga, Friedrich von Pernstein (c.1304–1341), who according to three inventories (1324, 1325, one undated) owned a sizable book collection.[32] Friedrich von Pernstein was born of a noble Moravian family, the Medlow-Pernsteins, and his love of books might be explained by his capacious intellectual interests, possibly developed during his studies at the University of Bologna where in 1290 a certain *Fredericus de Boemia* had matriculated.[33] In the longest book inventory, compiled in 1325, seventy-one entries were been recorded and, in the case of archivalia, one entry had several items.[34] Likewise, surviving in the Vatican archives is an account of Friedrich's expenses from 1319, recording payments for book production: preparation of parchment, decoration with initials and writing.[35]

The early fourteenth century in Livonia was a turbulent time period. Between 1297 and 1330 a war was fought between the Teutonic Order, on one side, and the forces of the archbishop, other Livonian bishops and the city of Riga on the other.[36] Friedrich spent most of his time, more than thirty years of

---

31   See MHUBU 5, p. 154 to UUB C 454; Schmid, 'Stundengebet und Heiligenverehrung im Magdalenenkloster zu Riga', p. 26; Levāns and Strenga, 'Medieval Manuscripts in the Book Collection', p. 184.
32   Bernhart Jähnig, 'Friedrich von Pernstein (OFM) (um 1270–1341). 1304–1341 Erzbischof von Riga', in Erwin Gatz and Clemens Brodkorb (eds.), *Die Bischöfe des Heiligen Römischen Reiches 1198 bis 1448: Ein biographisches Lexikon* (Berlin: Duncker & Humblot, 2001), pp. 651–652; Kurt Forstreuter, 'Erzbischof Friedrich von Riga (1304–1341): Ein Beitrag zu seiner Charakteristik', *Zeitschrift für Ostforschung*, 19 (1970), pp. 652–665.
33   Forstreuter, 'Erzbischof Friedrich von Riga', p. 657.
34   Patrick Zutshi, 'Frederick, Archbishop of Riga (1304–1341), and His Books', in James H. Marrow et al. (eds.), *The Medieval Book: Glosses from Friends and Colleagues of Christopher De Hamel* (Houten: Hes and De Graaf, 2010), pp. 327–335, here p. 328.
35   Zutshi, 'Frederick, Archbishop of Riga', pp. 331–332.
36   Māra Caune, 'Rīgas pilsētas un Livonijas ordeņa karš 1297–1330. gadā', *Latvijas PSR Zinātņu Akadēmijas Vēstis*, 12 (1973), pp. 63–74; Manfred Hellmann, 'Der Deutsche Orden und die

his episcopate, not in conflict-torn Livonia, but in the papal court at Avignon, spending only a total of five years in Riga.[37] Accordingly, the inventories of 1324 and 1325 were compiled in Lyon and Paris, coinciding with one of his trips to Riga.[38] The books and documents served more that Friedrich's intellectual needs, because among the archivalia owned by Friedrich, there were numerous documents relating to the Riga archbishop's conflict with the Teutonic Order.[39]

Before becoming the archbishop of Riga, Friedrich had been a Franciscan friar active as a penitentiary at the papal curia and had started collecting books already at that time. In a 1332 response to Friedrich's petition, Pope John XXII (1316–1334) explains that Friedrich owned two kinds of books: those he had received as a Franciscan, and those he had acquired as the archbishop of Riga.[40] This meant that the earlier books had to be returned to the Franciscan order at some point, and Friedrich intended to do so, but the latter were at his disposal during his lifetime; in response, the Pope praised Friedrich's intention after his death to distribute books in the latter group to the Church of Riga and the Franciscan Order. Friedrich died in Avignon and the fate of his books remains unknown. As Patrick Zutshi writes, 'it has indeed proved extremely difficult to trace any books that were once in the possession of Archbishop Frederick'.[41] It is believed, however, that Friedrich donated his books to the Franciscan convent in Riga.[42] Yet after Friedrich's death, some of his books remained in Avignon and in the fourteenth century can be traced to the papal curia and the Franciscans there; one volume, *Ordinarium siue Pontificale fratris Frederici Archiepiscopi Rigensis ordinis fratrum Minorum et pertinent ad Ecclesiam Rigensem*, has survived at the Bibliotheca Apostolica Vaticana (Ms Borgh. 14).[43] It remains unknown how many of Friedrich's books were transported from Avignon to Riga after his death and how many of them were distributed to the cathedral chapter and the Franciscan convent.

---

Stadt Riga', in Udo Arnold (ed.), *Stadt und Orden: Das Verhältnis des Deutschen Ordens zu den Städten in Livland, Preußen und im Deutschen Reich* (Marburg: Elwert, 1993), pp. 1–33.

37   Forstreuter, 'Erzbischof Friedrich von Riga', p. 658; Manfred Hellmann, *Livland und das Reich: Das Problem ihrer gegenseitigen Beziehungen* (München: Verlag der Bayerischen Akademie der Wissenschaften, 1989), p. 18.

38   Forstreuter, 'Erzbischof Friedrich von Riga', p. 656, 658, 663.

39   Zutshi, 'Frederick, Archbishop of Riga', p. 328.

40   Forstreuter, 'Erzbischof Friedrich von Riga', p. 664; Zutshi, 'Frederick, Archbishop of Riga', p. 330.

41   Zutshi, 'Frederick, Archbishop of Riga', p. 330.

42   Bert Roest, *A History of Franciscan Education (c.1210–1517)* (Leiden: Brill, 2000), p. 228.

43   Zutshi, 'Frederick, Archbishop of Riga', p. 331.

Yet two thirteenth (or early fourteenth) century manuscripts with similar features, once owned by the Franciscans in Riga, have survived and it is plausible that they once were part of Friedrich's collection. One is a folio of David's Psalter (*Psalterium Davidis*), a costly thirteenth-century production, with illuminated miniatures, thought to have originated in western Europe.[44] The other book is a thirteenth-century folio manuscript of the Proverbs of Solomon (*Parabolae Salomonis*) that also has illuminated miniatures and most likely was produced in France.[45] Both of the manuscripts may have been copied in one workshop. The French connection and the high quality of the production are reasons to believe that these two folios come from Friedrich's book collection and were donated to the Franciscans in Riga or had been left in the convent during Friedrich's visit. Unfortunately, those are the only two surviving manuscripts from the former book collection of the Rigan Franciscans, and therefore it cannot be estimated how many of books likely to have been Friedrich's reached Riga and the Franciscan convent there.

Another notable book donor of the Franciscan convent in Riga lived in the age of book printing. A clergyman and notary, Reinhold Soltrump, resided in Riga during the 1460s and 1480s and owned a comparatively large book collection. He came from a family of influential merchants who had been part of the Riga political elite for several generations. His father, the burgomaster of Riga, Johann Soltrump, played a key role in city politics at the end of the fifteenth century.[46] Reinhold initially studied law at the University of Leipzig (1465) and then continued his studies at various Western European universities, probably in Strasbourg and Cologne, until he obtained a master's degree in 1474.[47] Around 1477, Reihnhold Soltrump returned to Riga.[48]

He was last mentioned in Riga sources around 1480, but he probably remained in Riga after that date.[49] Aija Taimiņa suggests that at least fifteen of Soltrump's books have survived; most of them are incunabula printed during the 1470s and 1480s, but the survivals also include some manuscripts copied by Soltrump himself.[50] Soltrump's book collection, which he had started

---

44  *Psalterium Davidis*, 13th c., Western Europe, LUAB Rk2676.
45  *Parabolae Salomonis*, 13th c., France, LUAB Ms. 4., Rk2669.
46  Heinrich J. Böthführ, *Die Rigische Rathslinie von 1226 bis 1876* (Riga: J. Deubner, 1877), pp. 105–106; Aija Taimiņa, 'Senākā zināmā Rīgai un Livonijai adresētā inkunābula (1487) un Broces noraksti', *Latvijas Zinātņu Akadēmijas Vēstis*, 66:4 (2012), pp. 106–119, here p. 110.
47  Taimiņa, '15. gs. metāla griezuma jeb "skrošu" gravīras', p. 9.
48  Leonid Arbusow sen. (ed.), *Livlands Geistlichkeit vom Ende des 12. bis ins 16. Jahrhundert* (Mitau: J. F. Steffenhagen und Sohn, 1913), p. 200.
49  Soltrump had numerous books printed in the 1480s.
50  Taimiņa, '15. gs. metāla griezuma jeb "skrošu" gravīras', pp. 9, 15–17.

gathering while studying in Western Europe, is unique in that it is the oldest known private book collection in Riga. During the fifteenth century, European intellectuals were beginning to build their own personal libraries; before that time only rulers and the highest clergy could afford to do so.[51] The wealth of the Soltrump merchant family probably played an important role in the creation of his collection, because otherwise a university-educated priest-notary with a ministry and a notarial position would hardly have been able to obtain enough funds to afford to buy so many books. Soltrump's collection included printed books and manuscripts, theological and legal literature, encyclopaedias, prose literature, and it is known that he also owned forty-nine metal engravings.[52] The books also include Soltrump's own notes, property records and painted initials. He made many additions to his printed books, especially in the form of red-painted initials, which look a little awkward; and he also rewrote several poems.[53] The work of Giampietro Ferraris (c.1364–c.1421), *Practica iudicialis*, testifies to the owner's relationship with his book: there are images of engravings pasted inside the covers, most likely chosen and painted by the owner Soltrump himself; and they are supplemented with religious poetry and the first letters of his name and surname.[54]

Reinhold Soltrump's choice of books reflected contemporary tastes. Among his books were the latest current editions of legal literature, and Soltrump did read these works, as evidenced by his notes on the pages.[55] He was a reader who felt it important to manifest his personality in his books with a recording and a picture. Thus, for example, in the aforementioned *Practica iudicialis* he also memorializes his father, Johann Soltrump, the burgomaster of Riga (1464–1477), with a recording, thus underscoring his family's collective memory.

As in the case of the archbishop Friedrich, it is unknown in what specific circumstances Reinhold Soltrump's books became part of the Franciscan book collection. Soltrump's last will has not survived, but the books were most likely bequeathed to the Franciscan convent after his death and became part of the

---

51   Andrew Pettegree and Arthur der Weduwen, *The Library: A Fragile History* (London: Profile Books, 2021), pp. 47–51.
52   Peter Schmidt, 'The Multiple Image: The Beginnings of Printmaking, between Old Theories and New Approaches', in Peter W. Parshall (ed.), *The Origins of European Printmaking: Fifteenth-Century Woodcuts and Their Public* (New Haven: Yale University Press, 2005), pp. 36–56, here p. 43.
53   Taimiņa, '15. gs. metāla griezuma jeb "skrošu" gravīras', pp. 9, 15–17.
54   Johannes Petrus de Ferraris, *Practica iudicialis*, Strassburg: Heinrich Eggestein, [1475], LUAB R IK 72.
55   Taimiņa, 'Senākā zināmā Rīgai un Livonijai adresētā inkunābula', p. 116.

city's book collection during the Protestant Reformation.[56] In such circumstances, the Franciscans, in return for the donated objects, had to offer Soltrump *memoria*, the remembrance of the dead, by celebrating Masses and liturgical prayers.[57] One book in the collection of the National Library of Latvia, originating from Nuremberg and not Riga, offers an example of book donation with a memorial intent. In a copy of *Biblia Germanica*, printed by Anton Koberger (c.1440/1445–1513), someone wrote on behalf of his wife Margareta (d. 1539) after the printer's death: 'This book was donated by the honourable Margareta Koberger. Whoever reads it, let him pray to God for her husband at the mass for the dead or [say the prayer] Hail, Mary for her [i.e. for Margareta].'[58] This obviously was a memorial donation.

Not many surviving books from the Riga mendicant convents have ownership inscriptions that would be evidence of the books' private usage by friars. The 1494 book *Copulata tractatuum Petri Hispani* that according to the inscription belonged to the Dominican convent (*Liber co[n]uentus Rygensis ordinis fratr[um] p[re]dicator[um]*) in the early sixteenth century was lent to individual friars.[59] The book contains numerous inscriptions of usage and the name of friar Cornelius Dulken (*Dulleken*) appears as one of the last users, after two other early sixteenth-century friars Johann de Arnheym and Simon Louwer.[60]

---

56    Busch, *Die Geschichte der Rigaer Stadtbibliothek*, 2, pp. 84–86.

57    Otto Gerhard Oexle, 'Die Gegenwart der Toten', in Herman Braet and Werner Verbeke (eds.), *Death in the Middle Ages* (Leuven: Leuven University Press, 1983), pp. 19–77; idem, 'Memoria als Kultur', in idem (ed.), *Memoria als Kultur* (Göttingen: Vandenhoeck & Ruprecht, 1995), pp. 9–78.

58    'D(i)z puch hat herein geschenckt die erber fraw Margretha Kobergerin wer darin list sol ire(m) haußwirt durch got ei(n) req(ui)em pete(n) od(er) ir ein Aue Maria.' *Biblia Germanica* (2 vols., Nürnberg: Anton Koberger, 1483), 2, USTC 740108, fol. 583v, National Library of Latvia, Riga, RH 40, II. This book had been bought by a private book collector and brought to the present day Latvia in the late nineteenth century.

59    Petrus Hispanus, *Copulata tractatuum Petri Hispani* [Nürnberg: Anton Koberger,] 1494. LU AB IK 159, fol. 1r.

60    Johann de Arnheym (most likely from Arnhem in the Netherlands) had been assigned to the convent in Riga in 1513, see Arbusow, *Livlands Geistlichkeit*, p. 10. Inscriptions in the book are the following: a) *Liber conventus Rygensis ad usum fratris Johannis Arnem* [crossed over and added:] *Cornelii Dulken* [by other hand]; b) [crossed over:] *Liber conventus Rigensis concessus fratri Simoni Louwer ad usum incertum*; c) *Frater Cornelius Dulken*; d) *Liber conventus Rigensis ad usum fratris* [crossed over:] *Johannis Arnem*; e) *Cornelii Dulken*; f) *Liber ordinis fratrum predicatorum conventus Rigensis ad usum fratris Simonis Louver ordinis eiusdem*; [On the other side of the cover page] a) *Liber fratris* [name erased] *ad usum incertum Rigensis conventus*; b) *Liber iste concessus est fratri Cornelio Dulken, Anno d. 1518 per manus fratris Wilhelmij Edelryc*; [on the last cover page:] *Liber conventus Rigensis ordinis fratrum predicatorum est concessus fratri Simoni Louwer ad usum incertum, ordinis ejusdem*. Petrus Hispanus, *Copulata tractatuum* ([Nürnberg: Anton Koberger],

Dulken had used this book shortly before the Protestant Reformation, in 1518. These numerous inscriptions demonstrate that the friars could reserve the convent's books for their individual usage by using the method of inscribing their name. Also, the name of friar Wilhelm Elderyc, a person possibly responsible for the convent's book collection, appears in the inscriptions. The book with his name, being the property of the convent, remained in Riga after the Reformation when it found its way into the book collection of the city.

Little is known about the production of manuscripts in late medieval Riga. Yet the manuscript of Uppsala University Library C 180 that contains numerous devotional and medical works, contains convincing evidence of local production.[61] According to two inscriptions in the book, it was copied in Riga's Dominican convent by friar Hinricus and priest Nicolaus Brasiator (*Braxator, Braxiatoris*, also *de Colmen*) in 1466/1467.[62] There is no information about the background of the friar Hinricus, but Brasiator's local origin and transregional career can be traced. Nicolaus Brasiator is identifiable as a Livonian (*de Liuonia*) student who matriculated at Rostock University in the winter semester of 1426/27 and later was a priest in Warmian (Ermland) diocese; around 1465 he was present in Riga and in Piltene (Pilten), the bishopric of Courland.[63] Most likely, Brasiator brought the book with him to Prussia, because at a certain point during the sixteenth century the book was in possession of a dean of Warmian diocese, Nicolaus, who in his testament donated it to the cathedral library of Frombork (Frauenburg).[64] Later, in 1626/1627, the book became war booty and was taken by Swedish forces from Frombork to Uppsala, to become part of the University Library collection.[65] This manuscript is a unique

---

1494), USTC 746482, LU AB IK 159; Bušs, *Rīgas pilsētas bibliotēkas un tās grāmatu vēsture*, 2, p. 76. See the concluding paragraphs of this chapter regarding fate of Cornelius Dulken.

61   UUB C 180.

62   'Per manus fratris hinrici etc de ordine predicatorum Anno domini M cccc lxvj [1466] sexta feria post Judica [28.03.] in conuentu rigensi de mane hora octaua Cui deus propicietur etc AmeN …: Scriptum per me nicolaum brasiatoris Anno d[omini] M cccc lxvij [1467] et finitum in die sancti vincencij martyris [22.01.].' C 180, fol. 129r and 254r; MHUBU 2, pp. 244–246; Bušs, *Rīgas pilsētas bibliotēkas un tās grāmatu vēsture*, 2, pp. 83–84.

63   Arbusow, *Livlands Geistlichkeit*, pp. 123, 358; Bušs, *Rīgas pilsētas bibliotēkas un tās grāmatu vēsture*, 2, p. 84. Matrikelportal Universität Rostock, www.purl.uni-rostock.de /matrikel/100038391, (last accessed 16 June 2022).

64   'Librum presentem dominis Nicolaus quandam huius ecclesie Varmiensis dyaconus necnon Vicarius pro testamento eidem ecclesie donauit etc.' C 180, fol. 1r.

65   About the Frombork's cathedral library, see Arno Mentzel-Reuters, *Arma spiritualia: Bibliotheken, Bücher und Bildung im Deutschen Orden* (Wiesbaden: Harrassowitz, 2003), pp. 160–161; about the inclusion of the Frauenburg's cathedral library's collection in the Uppsala University Library, see Peter Lebrecht Schmidt, *Traditio latinitatis: Studien zur*

example of Livonian book production, revealing cooperation between mendicant scribes and secular priests in copying manuscripts, most likely, for personal use.

There is another example of cooperation between local monastic communities. A late fifteenth-century book of hours contains a plea written by a scribe as part of the hymn in honour of Saint Mary, asking the nuns to 'pray for the scribe, your brother one Lord's Prayer' (*Orate pro scriptore fr[atr]e v[est]ro unu[m] p[ater] n[oster]*).[66] The manuscript, most likely, was of local, Livonian or even Rigan origins.[67] Yet it cannot be determined in which community: mendicant convent in Riga or Cistercian abbey in Padise (Padis), the manuscript was produced. The inscription testifies that the book of hours was created for use in a nunnery, namely, Saint Mary Magdalene's in Riga.

With the one exception of the book of hours once owned by Anna Noetken (discussed below), in the books of the Cistercian nuns traits of individual use and property inscriptions from the pre-Reformation period are hard to trace. It can be assumed that most of them, except those that have names of nuns recorded, were a property of the nunnery, and were not adapted for their personal needs by individual nuns.

## 3  Mendicant and Cistercian Books during and after the Reformation in Riga and Beyond

The Protestant-dominated historiography of the Reformation in Riga and the city's cultural history, in describing the founding of the Riga city library, have avoided confrontation with the fact that the city library's creation took place because of iconoclasm, looting, violence and expulsion of the mendicants from Riga. Narratives created by the Jesuits during the early seventeenth century have mythologised the history of the Cistercian nunnery and fate of its books after the Reformation in a similar fashion.

The Protestant Reformation swept away all Catholic institutions in Riga and their book collections, except for the Cistercian nunnery and the books of its nuns. Though their number gradually declined, these nuns continued their religious life in a Protestant city. The city government and the townspeople were not friendly towards them and continually contested the existence of

---

*Rezeption und Überlieferung der lateinischen Literatur*, ed. Joachim Fugmann (Stuttgart: Steiner, 2000), p. 20.
66   UUB C 438, fol. 128v.
67   MHUBU 5, p. 114.

the nunnery. Also, relatives of the nuns in the nobility sought to convince the few remaining nuns to give up their monastic lifestyle and nunnery's properties. The Jesuits, who arrived in Riga together with the Polish Lithuanian king Stephen Bathory (ruled 1575–1586) in 1582, played an important role in the further fate of the Cistercian books.[68] They were met by three elderly surviving nuns, who, according to the Jesuit narrative, were really old: Anna Tophel (also Toepell) was said to be a hundred and thirty years of age, and Anna Noetken (d. 1591) and Otilia Keiserling, who both were aged a hundred years.[69] Because they were given Saint James church and Cistercian nunnery as the spaces for their college, the Jesuits positioned themselves as the successors of the nuns who rightfully inherited all the nunnery's possessions and privileges.

The Jesuits wrote several texts about the 1583 founding of the Riga college, some of which contain emotional and detailed descriptions of the few remaining nuns opposing the Lutheran attempts to take over the nunnery and its properties.[70] These accounts also paid attention to the books and liturgical items owned by the Riga nuns. According to the accounts, the sisters' liturgical items were saved from the 'throats of the hungry heretics' and their hatred for many decades.[71] Nuns hid precious liturgical items and garments in buried chests: twelve Holy Communion goblets, several monstrances of pure silver, several golden wreaths adorned with jewels and pearls as well as several altar coverings made of Persian cloth and embroidered with gold and silver threads. They also hid the chasubles of priests and other similar objects.[72] Unlike the liturgical items and cloths, books were not hidden. According to the Jesuit narrative, during the mid-sixteenth century the remaining nuns had kept their

---

68   Norkārkls, 'The Riga Jesuit College and Its Book Collection', pp. 90–111.
69   Jacob Gretser, *Historische Erzehlung von dem Jungkfrawkloster S. Benedictordens zu Rigen, wie wunderbarlich dasselbig von der Zeit an, als sich die Lutherische Ketzerey erhebt, so lang erhalten, biß es den patribus der Societet Iesv, eyngeantwort vnd vbergeben worden*, (Ingolstatt: Elisabeth Angermaier, 1614), USTC 2094794, pp. 6–7, 25; Latin translation of the German text Jacob Gretser, 'Historia Monasterij Virginum Ordinis S. Benedicti, Rigæ, a tempore orientis hæresis Lutheranæ conseruati, vsque dum Patribus Societatis Iesv traderetur', in Henricus Ederus (ed.), *Religiosae Constantiae et Haereticae Fravdvlentiae Ac Violentiae, Dvo Ad Omnem Posteritatem Commemorabilia Exempla*, (Ingolstadt: Elisabeth Angermaier, 1615), USTC 2016851, pp. 1–15; Gretser, *Historische Erzehlung*, pp. 1–35; Erthmannus Tolgsdorff, 'Historia collegii Rigensis Societatis Jesu in Livonia [1582–1617]', in Jozefs Kleijntjenss (ed.), *Latvijas vēstures avoti jezuitu ordeņa archivos* (Riga: Apgāds Latvju Grāmata, 1941), 1, pp. 1–97, here pp. 14, 16.
70   See Levāns and Strenga, 'Medieval Manuscripts in the Book Collection of the Riga Jesuit College', pp. 166–187.
71   Gretser, *Historische Erzehlung*, p. 16.
72   Levāns and Strenga, 'Medieval Manuscripts in the Book Collection of the Riga Jesuit College', p. 173.

books of hours. They prayed in silence when the Lutheran preachers forbade them to sing and pray aloud, the preachers even covering their ears so as not to hear the nuns' 'sirenic songs'.[73] As the Jesuits wrote, the nuns managed 'for forty years' to safeguard the documents certifying the privileges granted to the nunnery in the hope that it would once again resume its activities. The Cistercian privileges and documents were kept in the archive of the Jesuit college and in 1585 they were copied into a manuscript that has survived.[74] The Jesuits reported that when Anna Noetken was approached by the Lutherans to give up the convent's properties, she had replied: 'they are not mine, but God's' (*non mea ista sunt, sed Dei*).[75] When the city council learned about the incident and became aware of its defeat and public humiliation, anger, envy and hatred flared at how the nuns had succeeded in keeping secret the existence of the nunnery's privileges so that nobody had been able to learn about them?[76] These events, taking place before the Jesuit arrival in Riga, were portrayed as a miracle.

Though all the books owned by the Cistercian nuns were produced in the late fifteenth century, the few property inscriptions in them originate from the post-Reformation era described by the Jesuits in their texts. Therefore these inscriptions show that medieval manuscripts were used by the Cistercian nuns decades after their creation and in very different circumstances. In one manuscript there can been found a memorial inscription beginning with the words 'this book was' (*Hic liber erat*), which permits with certainty for it to be considered as the property of the nun Anna Noetken.[77] Judging by the execution of the inscription in a cursive chancery hand and the mention of the place on the first page of the codex, the inscription was written in the Jesuit college, because Noetken died when the nunnery had already taken over by the Jesuits.[78] The manuscript itself shows vividly aspects of usage and adjustment of a late medieval manuscript for the purpose of individual religiosity. It is possible that Noetken was not the first user of the manuscript. The manuscript was of the late fifteenth century, so that she most likely had inherited

---

73  Tolgsdorff, *Historia collegii*, p. 8.
74  Gretser, *Historische Erzehlung*, pp. 5, 7. *Liber privilegiorum Collegii Societatis Jesu Rigensis*, Riga, *c*.1585, LUAB R, Ms. 61.
75  Tolgsdorff, *Historia collegii*, p. 9.
76  Gretser, *Historische Erzehlung*, p. 24.
77  'Hic liber erat Virginis Annae Netken vltimae monialis Monasterii S[anctae] M[ariae] magd[alenae] Rigae ordinis Cisterciensis quae in Christo obdormiuit 8 januarii hora pomeridiana p[rima] Anno 1591. Sepulta 10 Jan[uarii].' UUB C 486, fol. 1r.
78  Cf., e.g., UUB C 802, fol. 1r: 'Inscriptus Catal[ogo] Collegij Rigen[sis] Soc[ietatis] JESV A[nn]o 1589.' Also UUB C 503, fol. 1r: 'Inscriptus Catal[ogo] Collegij Rigen[sis] Soc[ietatis] Jesu a[nno] 1589.'

it from a nun of the previous generation. This book of hours features distinct typical traces of individual use and reading habits. A printed picture has been added to the book, depicting the Virgin Mary with the baby Jesus in a manger; prayers have been added, probably by the user herself; and printed texts of a religious nature have been added to the manuscript.[79] According to our palaeographical analysis, the written prayers in the text have been added to the main body during the late fifteenth or early sixteenth century. Thus, most likely, the prayers were written into and images added by an anonymous nun living before the Reformation or by Noetken herself during the very early years of her monastic life.

The names of two women: Margrete Bryncke and Katherina Varensbeke, are inscribed in two manuscripts that were most likely once owned by the Riga Cistercians.[80] They do not present sufficiently reliable evidence, however, to conclude that the two had been the users or owners of the books. Still, a bond between the two women and the Riga Cistercian nunnery can be established. In a breviary from the second half of the fifteenth century there is an inscription in Middle Low German that seems to be a memorial reminder of the deceased Margrete Bryncke: 'When the year [15]49 was written, then blessed Margrete Bryncke died on Friday before *yvbylate* [a day before the third Sunday after the Easter], may God be merciful and gracious to her'.[81] It is very likely that in this manner the still-living nuns perpetuated the remembrance of a recently deceased sister. Nothing else is known about Bryncke except the fact that she was the offspring of an influential family of vassals of the Teutonic Order in Courland.[82] One other book of hours, written in the sixteenth century, features name of Katherina Varensbeke in the same manner as in a breviary (C 436), where the name of a nun was inscribed at the very end of the book, a place that often served for notes of a memorial character.[83] In this case, too, the mentioned person had been a nun, whose liturgical memory was being perpetuated after her death with an inscription. It can be presumed that all these books may have been used as commemorative tools after the death of their users.

---

79  UUB C 486, fols. 1r, 161v, 161ar–161br.
80  UUB C 436, fol. 167r; UUB C 487, fol. 187v.
81  UUB C 436, fol. 167r: 'Jtem domen schref ynt yar xlyx do vor starf selyge margrete brynckke des frydages vor yvbylate dat er got gnedych sy vnde barmehertych.'
82  Strenga, 'Cistercian Networks', pp. 216, 226.
83  See Gabriela Signori, 'Leere Seiten: Zur Memorialkultur eines nicht regulierten Augustiner-Chorfrauen-Stifts im ausgehenden 15. Jahrhundert', in idem (ed.), *Lesen, Schreiben, Sticken und Erinnern: Beiträge zur Kultur- und Sozialgeschichte mittelalterlicher Frauenklöster* (Bielefeld: Verlag für Regionalgeschichte, 2000), pp. 149–184.

It is not known how many books were taken over by the Jesuits when they gained possession of the convent during the 1580s. The Cistercian nunnery during the late fifteenth century had around fifty nuns, and therefore the number of books the community needed for their daily religious life must have been significant.[84] The surviving books of the Riga Jesuit college that are now located in the Uppsala University Library show that many of them were bound in the parchment leaves from fifteenth-century manuscripts.[85] It is plausible that the parchment from the Cistercian manuscripts was reused as a binding material of new Jesuit books. If the binding material indeed came from the Cistercian manuscripts, the practice demonstrates the dynamism and practicality of the early modern book culture. The parchment manuscript books that were no longer in use were recycled as bindings of new printed material. The Cistercian books, most likely, were not part of the main book collection of the Riga Jesuit college library because most of them have no property inscriptions of the college. As Reinis Norkārkls has pointed out, the college had a repository in which spare copies and unused books were kept.[86] The relocation of the Jesuit books from Riga to Uppsala can also be seen as a re-evaluation of the Cistercian manuscripts conducted by their new owners, a step that probably saved them from being recycled into binding material.

The brutality and violence of the Protestant reformers in Riga, directed against the mendicant convents and the parish churches, laid the foundation for a new library. In early March 1524 just before Easter the mob of townspeople may have broken into the Franciscan convent and pillaged it. On 10 March there began iconoclastic attacks in the city's churches, recurring on two separate occasions of that year.[87] The city council reacted and took over the Franciscan books, keeping them as their property, but it remains unclear

---

84   Strenga, 'Cistercian Networks', p. 217.
85   Laura Kreigere Liepiņa refers to the research of Isak Collijn, see her, 'Bibliographical Reconstruction of the Book Collection of the Riga Jesuit College: The Layout of the Volume and the Organising Principles of Descriptions', in *Catalogue of the Riga Jesuit College's Book Collection (1583–1621)*, pp. 50–69.
86   Norkārkls, 'The Riga Jesuit College and Its Book Collection', p. 106.
87   On iconoclasm in Riga, see Sergiusz Michalski, 'Die protestantischen Bilderstürme: Versuch einer Übersicht', in Robert W. Scribner (ed.), *Bilder und Bildersturm im Spätmittelalter und in der frühen Neuzeit* (Wiesbaden: Harrassowitz, 1990), pp. 69–124, p. 93; idem, 'Bildersturm im Ostseeraum', in Peter Blickle et al. (eds.), *Macht und Ohnmacht der Bilder: Reformatorischer Bildersturm im Kontext der europäischen Geschichte*, (München: Oldenbourg, 2002), pp. 223–238, here pp. 231–232; idem, '"Hölzer wurden zu Menschen": Die reformatorischen Bilderstürme in den baltischen Landen zwischen 1524 und 1526', in Matthias Asche et al. (eds.), *Die baltischen Lande im Zeitalter der Reformation und Konfessionalisierung* (4 vols., Münster: Aschendorff, 2012), 4, pp. 147–163, here p. 147.

whether the city council came into possession of all books owned by the convents. The document that traditional research has considered as the foundation document of the Riga city library testifies that the city councillor, Paul Dreling (d. 1533/1536), passed on six books from the Franciscan convent to a Lutheran preacher, the former Catholic priest Nicolaus Ramm (d. 1532); these books, according to Dreling, were to be used for the common good (*vor dat gemene beste*).[88] Astonishingly, the document is dated 6 March 1524, which is indeed a very early date for the foundation of a Protestant book collection and creates doubts about the authenticity of the document date. The books lent were prints: a work of Cyprian, printed by Froben in Basel in 1521; a Latin Bibles from the late fifteenth and early sixteenth century; and Saint Augustin's sermons printed in Basel in 1494 and 1495.[89] Soon after, on 2 April, 1524, the Franciscans and most likely also the Dominicans were expelled and all the properties of the convents were taken over by the city.[90]

The narrative of the history of the city library produced in the nineteenth and twentieth century praised its 1524 foundation and created the impression that the collection was started during the violent phase of the Reformation. Yet this narrative does not properly reveal the attitude of the Riga city council towards the looted books. Nicolaus Busch argues that the city councillor, Paul Dreling, was responsible for the establishment of the *gemeine Kasten*; it was a newly created financial and charitable institution in which the resources of all the Catholic foundations and chantries had to be gathered. The books were thus part of these resources.[91] Many questions remain, however. Did the city council acquire the Franciscan books before the iconoclastic attacks began? Why did the city council support the confiscation of the books? Were they seen as liturgical instruments the confiscation of which would prevent the mendicants from practising their Catholic religiosity? Or were they seen as symbols of identity, so that taking the books would traumatize the mendicants as communities? Or were the books seen as having material value that through their sale could be turned into money? Various groupings in the city

---

88    The document was part of the Riga city library's collection, now is held by the Academic Library of University of Latvia, LUAB Rk 2675; Busch, *Die Geschichte der Rigaer Stadtbibliothek*, 2, p. 1; Pabst, *Die Typologisierbarkeit von Städtereformation*, p. 223; Garber, *Schatzhäuser des Geistes*, p. 55; Strenga, 'Faith, Politics, Languages and Books', pp. 138–146.

89    Klaus Garber, 'Die Bibliotheca Rigensis als Memorialstätte städtischer Kultur im alten Livland', in Michael Jaumann and Klaus Schenk (eds.), *Erinnerungsmetropole Riga: Deutschsprachige Literatur- und Kulturvielfalt im Vergleich* (Würzburg: Königshausen und Neumann, 2010), pp. 127–144, here pp. 129–130.

90    Arbusow, *Die Einführung der Reformation*, p. 300.

91    Busch, *Die Geschichte der Rigaer Stadtbibliothek*, 2, p. 2; Pabst, *Die Typologisierbarkeit von Städtereformation*, pp. 248–249.

in 1524 had practise in turning into money objects that were of no use after the Reformation. For example, the leadership of the Black Heads brotherhood, an elite group in Riga, sold their surviving altarpieces after the iconoclastic attacks.[92] Did the city councillors in 1524 know exactly what they wanted to do with the confiscated mendicant books? Were they following Luther's advice in his *An die Ratsherren aller Städte deutschen Landes* (1524) and really planned to establish a municipal library using the Dominican and Franciscan books?[93] Or was the library meant to create an intellectual base for new community of Lutheran preachers in the city? Most of these questions will remain without exact answers, though they have to be kept in mind when the events of 1524 and the supposed foundation of the city library are discussed.

There is one book that reveals a different fate of some of the Riga mendicant books during the Reformation. A surviving copy of *Gesta Romanorum*, printed in 1497 in Nuremberg, contains an ownership inscription of the aforementioned friar from the Dominican convent in Riga, Cornelius Dulken (*Frater Cornelius Dulleken hunc sibi vendicat librum*).[94] According to the inscription, he had come into the possession of the book and it was his personal property. As mentioned earlier, Dulken belonged to the Dominican convent in Riga in 1518; it is not known, however, whether just before the Reformation he was or was not transferred to other Livonian convents: in Tallinn (Reval) or Tartu (Dorpat). Such a possibility cannot be excluded, because after the Reformation a certain Cornelius Schurs (*Schursen*) de Dulken was a parish priest in Karja (Karris) on the island of Saaremaa (Ösel) and died there in 1550.[95] Saaremaa is closer to Tallinn and Tartu than to Riga. Dulken's ownership inscription must have been made when he was a friar in a convent before the Reformation and before his probable relocation to Saaremaa. After Dulken's death, the book was owned by a Livonian Catholic priest and bibliophile, Reinold Gemekow, who later led an active life in Prussia.[96] During the 1550s Gemekow was a priest of the bishopric Ösel-Wiek, the diocese in which Dulken may have been a priest

---

92   Dokumentesammlung des Herder-Instituts in Marburg Lahn 120, Schwarzhäupter Riga, no. 8, fol. 167. Arbusow, *Die Einführung der Reformation*, p. 294.
93   Martin Luther, *An die Radherrn aller stedte deutsches lands: Das sie Christliche schulen auffrichten vnd hallten sollen* (Wittemberg: [Cranach und Döring], 1524), USTC 637055.
94   *Gesta romanorum* (Nürnberg: Anton Koberger, 1497), USTC 740822, Kungliga biblioteket, Stockholm, (hereafter: KB), Inkunabel 462; Busch, *Die Geschichte der Rigaer Stadtbibliothek*, 2, p. 75.
95   Arbusow, *Livlands Geistlichkeit*, p. 190.
96   'Reinoldi Gemekow 1557', *Gesta romanorum*, KB, Inkunabel 462; Norkārkls, 'The Riga Jesuit College and Its Book Collection', p. 104; Hieronymus Rozrażewski and Stanislaus Kujot (eds.), *Visitationes Archidiaconatus Pomeraniae Hieronymo Rozrażewski Vladislaviensi et Pomeraniae Episcopo Factae* (3 vols., Toruń: S. Buszczyński, 1897), 1, pp. 17, 198, 270,

after leaving Riga. It seems that Gemekow collected the books of the deceased Catholic priests of that bishopric because he also owned incunabulas of other priests who had been active on Saaremaa.[97]

If the pre-Reformation Dominican from Riga and the post-Reformation priest from Karja are the same person, which is very likely, he must have taken along his personal copy of *Gesta Romanorum* after the closure of the convents in the Livonian cities. The fate of Dulken's *Gesta Romanorum* thus changes the perspective from which to view the fate of the Riga mendicant books during the Protestant Reformation. Apparently, the friars were allowed to leave the city with the books that belonged to them, but those of a convent were either pillaged by the townspeople or confiscated by the city council. This means that the city council may have taken over only those books that belonged to the convents, but not the personal books of individual friars. As this case shows, the friars may have taken their own books with them to the places where they continued their work. It is not known whether this volume returned to Riga when most of Reinold Gemekow's books became part of the Riga Jesuit college library during the late sixteenth century; the *Gesta Romanorum* holds a property inscription of the Jesuit college in Tartu.[98] The fate of this book once again was influenced by violence. When the Swedish forces during the Polish-Swedish war (1600–1629) overran Tartu, the book most likely was taken as a war booty to Sweden, where it became part of the royal library.

## 4    Conclusions

The surviving books of Riga's mendicant convents and the Cistercian nunnery help to characterise these religious communities. These book collections survived only partially, yet it can be presumed that the mendicants in Riga before the Reformation had the largest book collections in Livonia. The surviving printed material from the Franciscan and Dominican libraries originates mostly from the time period between 1475 and 1512. Considerable material resources had been spent to acquire the books necessary for the intellectual

---

275, 508–509; Arbusow, *Livlands Geistlichkeit*, pp. 63–64. See also the article of Laura Kreigere-Liepiņa in this volume.

[97]  In his collection Gemekow had a book once owned by the parish priest of Karmel (Kaarma), Henricus Lhaer. 'Domini Henrici a Lhaer paroci in Karmel possidet anno [15]58.' Johannes Andreas, *Sermones: Symbolum Nicaenum; Testimonia semper verus sit deus et verus homo* (Rome: Arnold Pannartz und Konrad Sweynheim, 1470.), USTC 993608, UUB 33:100, fol. 1r.

[98]  'Collegij Derpatensis Societatis Jesu 1598', *Gesta romanorum*, KB, Inkunabel 462.

life of the convents and the social, religious and judicial duties of the mendicants. As the example of Reinhold Soltrump's private book collection demonstrates, the mendicants, in this case the Franciscans, received large book donations that allowed them to develop their libraries. The case of the archbishop Friedrich and his books also points out that considerable book donations were made to convents in Riga already before the era of printing and the abundance of books that era brought.

The question of collective and individual book use in religious communities is essential. The example of the book owned by the Dominican convent (*Copulata tractatuum Petri Hispani*) demonstrates that the friars were able to claim books of the convent for their own personal use and did so by writing in their names. Yet the friars also had their own books. One of the readers of *Copulata tractatuum Petri Hispani*, friar Cornelius Dulken, owned a printed copy of *Gesta Romanorum* and, most likely, took it with himself when the Dominicans were banished from Riga in 1524. Similarly, one can follow private usage of books by the Cistercian nuns. When a nun died, her book (or books) became a collective property of the nunnery or probably were handed over to a younger nun. It is not known whether the manuscripts of Riga Cistercian nuns that were created in the late fifteenth century changed their owners or users. Yet several of the books were used by the sisters who remained in the nunnery after the Reformation even during the middle decades and the end of the sixteenth century. Then, the sisters were definitely not the first users of these manuscripts. The manuscript owned in the mid-sixteenth century by Anna Noetken must have been used and adapted by a nun that lived in the nunnery during the late fifteenth century. After the nuns died, their books were probably kept as memory aids that helped to commemorate the deceased users.

The books of the Riga Cistercian nuns have survived because the Jesuits, after the foundation of their college, took over the properties of the nunnery, including the books. As attested by the small number of the ownership inscriptions of the Jesuit College made in the manuscripts, they likely did not become part of the book repertoire used by the Jesuits. Many books, which were not used by them, were kept in a book depository rather than in the college library proper. In 1621, as the Swedish troops entered Riga, almost all the books that were at the disposal of the Jesuit college were brought to Sweden as war booty, likely without any consideration of whether they were part of the library proper or not. It is plausible that Jesuits themselves recycled the parchment manuscripts once owned by nuns for the book binding of newly acquired printed books. Yet, if the books had fallen into the hands of the Rigan Protestants, they would have perished. The other Protestants, the Swedes, who took them as war booty, must have seen some value in these old medieval manuscripts that possessed no aesthetic excellence.

In Riga the city's book collection was formed as a result of violence. Although in traditional historiography the origins of this collection is portrayed as the founding of the city library, the founding was rather a violent takeover of the books of the mendicants. The exact motivations of the city council are unknown and numerous questions remain. Nevertheless, this act of violence laid foundations for one of the first municipal libraries in Northern Europe.

CHAPTER 3

# The Printing of Missals and Breviaries as Ecclesiastical Authority in the Late-Medieval Baltic Region
*A Battle between Printers or between Bishops?*

Mattias Lundberg

A significant number of the books printed in or for the Baltic region before 1500 were liturgical volumes intended for use in a particular diocese. These were typically commissioned by a bishop or a consistorium to a local or itinerant printer. Such a print was an enterprise with few risks for a printer; if the diocese acquired and paid for the entire edition, the market and the quota of copies were guaranteed.[1] For a bishopric in Northern Europe the new innovation of print could be used to codify and enforce the particular *usus* of its Cathedral church, concerning feasts, texts and melodies that differed slightly from one diocese to another and which often stretched back for centuries. The *usus* of a Cathedral was expected to be imitated as closely as possible in the services of all parish churches throughout the diocese. The cost of a printed breviary, the rite for the Office to be learned by all priests in a diocese, have in some cases been estimated to have been around a fourth of the cost needed to produce a manuscript breviary.[2] Thus these books helped perpetuate the audible manifestation of which diocese a parish, city or collegiate church belonged to, with a greater degree of uniformity and at a lesser price than what had thitherto been possible.

The British Library *Incunabula Short Title Catalogue* and the *Gesamtkatalog der Wiegendrucke* at The Staatsbibliothek zu Berlin list thirteen missals, twelve breviaries and a number of psalters that could either through their

---

1  In a few cases, it seems that the copies were sold by the printer or bookshops, but then often with admonishments and exhortations from the bishop or consistorium to buy the book in question. Mary Kay Duggan, 'Reading Liturgical Books', in Kristian Jensen (ed.), *Incunabula and their Readers: Printing, Selling and Using Books in the Fifteenth Century* (London: British Library, 2013), pp. 71–82, here p. 74.
2  Jeremy Dittmar, 'Book Prices in Early Modern Europe: An Economic Perspective', in Shanti Graheli (ed.), *Buying and Selling: The Business of Books in Early Modern Europe* (Leiden: Brill, 2019), pp. 72–87, here p. 73.

---

© MATTIAS LUNDBERG, 2023 | DOI:10.1163/9789004441217_005
This is an open access chapter distributed under the terms of the CC BY-NC-ND 4.0 license.

titles, colophons, or elsewhere through discernable information in the printed material be linked to a diocese in the region surrounding the Baltic Sea before 1500.[3] These were published between 1478 and 1500 and span the region from Bremen in the West to Warmia in the East and Turku in the North. If one considers the geography and timeline of these around thirty printed items, certain patterns become apparent. It is surprising that this vast and unique material has not been subject to more intensive research. In 2011 Natalia Nowakowska could assert that:

> [t]o date, these episcopally commissioned incunabula have been the subject only of a handful of avowedly local studies, with the result that this class of early printed books has not yet been recognized, far less explored, as the European-wide ecclesiastical phenomenon that it is.[4]

The purpose of the present study is to examine closely the interplay between ecclesiastical authorities and individual printers in the Scandinavian region at the end of the fifteenth century.

## 1 The Print Genres of Missal and Breviary

Typically, a European diocese in the late fifteenth century would, if it could muster the funds, print a missal in folio (containing the sung and read texts for the mass of that diocese) and a breviary in quarto or octavo (containing the sung and read texts for the hours of the divine office for the diocese) together. These two books contained texts that were either read or chanted to memorized melodies and melodic accents. They therefore typically contain only a bare minimum of musical notation, but still enabled a priest to celebrate Mass and Office, possibly alongside a manuscript Gradual and Kyriale. This made Missals and Breviaries perfect printing products for dioceses and printers alike, something that doubtlessly accounts for the relatively large numbers of such editions. The more advanced books of Gradual (containing the chants for the Mass throughout the year, for a choir or specialized ordained singer) and the Antiphonale (containing antiphons and other melodies for the Office,

---

3  www.data.cerl.org/istc/ and www.gesamtkatalogderwiegendrucke.de/, respectively (last accessed 20 November 2022).
4  Natalia Nowakowska, 'From Strassburg to Trent: Bishops, Printing and Liturgical Reform in the Fifteenth Century', *Past and Present: A Journal of Historical Studies*, 213 (2011), pp. 3–39, here p. 4.

intended for the choir or a specialized ordained singer) required considerably more musical notation, and were rarely printed in Northern Europe before 1500. The *Graduale Sueticum* (the often-called *Graduale Arosiensis*) printed in 1493, most likely for the diocese of Västerås, stands out as an anomaly in this respect, in an otherwise predominantly manuscript-based book genre.[5] All the missals listed in Table 3.1 are in folio format. Breviaries are typically in smaller format, in quarto or octavo. As far as the mass is concerned, there were in addition to missals and graduals, also a separate sequentarium printed in Lübeck: the *Sequentiae: Prosae et sequentiae* (before 1491). The earliest printed Psalters are left out of the present study, since they served, in addition to strict liturgical use, also a separate market of private ownership, itself worthy of further study elsewhere.[6]

After 1500 the production of Missal and Breviary for a diocese often followed adjacently in time. This was for example the case when Trondheim (Nidaros) had both missal and breviary produced by different printers in 1519 (Ræff in Copenhagen, and Bienayse and Kerbriand in Paris, respectively). The liturgical printed works issued around the Baltic Sea before 1500, however, reveal a rather different pattern, with sudden bursts of printing activity relating to one type of book at the time within a specific region. Thus we will concentrate our study to the period up to 1500. The printing activity in the last quarter of the fifteenth century may in fact be interpreted as something of a competition or rivalry between dioceses, coupled with the maximizing efforts of the commercial trade of the printers contracted to produce the books. Before we enter into these investigations, the geographical delimitation at hand ought perhaps to be briefly addressed.

## 2     Two Geographical Centres

What, in actual fact, is to be included in the region of the Baltic Sea if geographical demarcation is to make cultural and ecclesiastical sense? The region is sometimes referred to as 'the hanseatic region' in relation to the late middle ages, but that would be misleading in our case, since such a definition would include also the North Sea region of Friesland and Holland (with no natural

---

5   Mary Kay Duggan, 'Early Music Printing and Ecclesiastical Patronage', in Andrea Lindmayr-Brandl, Elisabeth Giselbrecht and Grantley McDonald (eds.), *Early Music Printing in German-Speaking Lands* (London: Routledge, 2018), pp. 21–45, here p. 32.
6   Many psalters have been owned privately, as may be seen in *Kulturhistoriskt lexikon för nordisk medeltid* (Malmö: Allhems, 1956–1978): "Psalter" (vol. XIII, coll. 583–595).

nautical path except through the Danish strait of Helsingør) and cities as far south into Germany as Magdeburg and Erfurt. The latter cities belonged to the league, but had at this point few ecclesiastical connections with the Baltic. Moreover, many of the diocese cities were not joined with the league of the Hansa. For the purposes of our investigation we shall include printed matter for dioceses with borders directly adjacent to the Baltic Sea. That includes all of Denmark, the North-German coast from Bremen eastwards, the North-Polish coasts, Eastern Prussia, Warmia, present day Lithuania, Latvia and Estonia, the Finnish Gulf, and all of present-day Finland and Sweden.

Table 3.1 lists the printed works in question chronologically. One may observe that the Lübeck breviary of 1478 rather soon was followed by breviaries throughout the neighbouring region: Odense in 1482, Hamburg circa 1484, Bremen in 1486 and Schleswig 1489, after which point Hamburg and Bremen issued new breviaries, a 'second round' which seems hard to explain for liturgical or financial reasons. In the region surrounding the neck of Denmark five

TABLE 3.1  Missals and breviaries printed for dioceses of the Baltic Sea region before 1500

| Title | Printer | Year | Place | ISCTS | GW |
|---|---|---|---|---|---|
| *Breviarium Lubicense* | Brandis | 1478 | Lübeck | ib01164100 | 5374 |
| *Missale Sverinense* | Domus Horti Viridus | c.1480 | Rostock | im00725800 | M24768 |
| *Breviarium Othoniense* | Snell | 1482 | Odense | ib01173400 | 5418 |
| *Missale Othoniense* | Brandis | 1483 | Lübeck | im00679300 | M24591 |
| *Breviarium Hamburgense* | Gothan | c.1484 | Lübeck | ib01162300 | 5352 |
| *Missale Roschildense* | Schoeffer | c.1484 | Mainz | im00717700 | M24188 |
| *Missale Hamburgense* | Ghotan | c.1484 | Magdeburg | ib01162300 | M24407 |
| *Missale Upsalense* | Snell | 1484 | Stockholm | im00730000 | M24824 |
| *Breviarium Bremense* | Quentell | 1486 | Cologne | ib01150375 | 5291 |
| *Missale Slesvicense* | Arndes | 1486 | Schleswig | im00721800 | M24724 |
| *Missale Lubicense* | Brandis | 1486 | Lübeck | im00669500 | M24484 |
| *Missale Strengnense* | Ghotan | 1487 | Stockholm | im00722000 | M24732 |

TABLE 3.1  Missals and breviaries printed for dioceses of the Baltic Sea region before 1500 (cont.)

| Title | Printer | Year | Place | ISCTS | GW |
|---|---|---|---|---|---|
| Missale Aboense | Ghotan | 1488 | Unknown | im00644000 | M24188 |
| Breviarium Slesvicense | Arndes | 1489 | Lübeck | ib01180700 | 5375 |
| Breviarium Hamburgense | Grüninger | 1490 | Strassbourg | | 5353 |
| Missale Raceburgense | Koberger | 1492/93 | Nürnberg | im00686200 | M24647 |
| Breviarium Lubicense [novum] | Stuchs | 1490 | Nürnberg | ib01164300 | 5375 |
| Breviarium Hamburgense [novum] | Grüninger | After 1491 | Strassbourg | ib01162325 | |
| Breviarium Lincopense | Suchs | 1493 | Nürnberg | ib01164000 | 5373 |
| Missale Lubicense [novum] | Drach | c.1495 | Speyer | im00669600 | M24491 |
| Breviarium Sverinense | Bungart | 1495 | Köln | ib01183180 | 5471 |
| Breviarium Strengnense | Fabri | 1495 | Stockholm | ib01183000 | 5467 |
| Breviarium Upsalense | Fabri | 1496 | Stockholm | ib01187000 | 5499 |
| Breviarium Warmiense | Stuchs | Before 1497 | Nürnberg | ib01187390 | |
| Breviarium Othoniense [novum] | Brandis | 1497 | Lübeck | ib01173600 | 5419 |
| Missale Warmiense | Ruch, de Dumbach | 1497 | Strassbourg | im00731700 | M24838 |
| Breviarium Scarense | Stuchs | 1498 | Nürnberg | ib01179000 | 5458 |
| Missale Viburgense | Arndes | 1500 | Lübeck | im00730400 | M24831 |
| Missale Sverinense | Domus Horti Viridis | c.1500 | Rostock | im00725850 | M23994 |

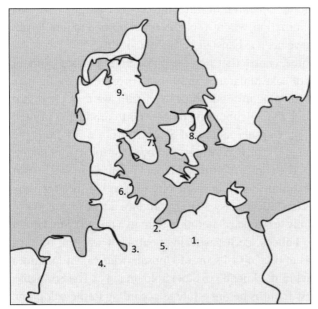

FIGURE 3.1　Dioceses with printed missals and breviaries 1478–1500: 1. Schwerin; 2. Lübeck; 3. Hamburg; 4. Bremen; 5. Ratzeburg; 6 Schleswig; 7. Odense; 8. Roskilde; 9. Viborg

breviaries were thus printed within two decades, all but one by printing workshops in the region (the 1486 Bremen breviary stands out, as it was printed in Cologne). Significantly, I will argue, not two of these ambitious printing enterprises employed the same printer.

If we turn to missals printed in the same region, affairs seem to have taken their start with the missal for Schwerin circa 1480. Odense followed in 1483, Roskilde circa 1484, and Schleswig and Lübeck both in 1486. This is within a period of only about five years, again mostly employing different printers (the exception is Lübeck, employing Brandis in their own city, which had previously been used also by the diocese of Odense). Taken together, seven different printers were active in Denmark during this period, none of which had a local background in Denmark.[7]

Interestingly, no breviary is known to have been printed in the Northern Baltic region of present-day Sweden and Finland until the area around the neck of Denmark had gone 'full circle' and started printing second editions.

---

7　Wolfgang Undorf, *From Gutenberg to Luther: Transnational Print Cultures in Scandinavia 1450–1525* (Leiden: Brill, 2014), p. 13.

The pattern, and the modus operandi of itinerant printers, almost resemble that of a biological dissemination, where a species is not pushed to new localities until all resources have been exhausted in the first locality.

The second geographical centre that may be noted from a closer study of Table 3.1 is the vicinities of Lake Mälaren in south-eastern Sweden (see fig. 3.2). In 1493 the diocese of Linköping printed a breviary. Again, we may see that it appears to have 'provoked' the neighbouring dioceses into producing printed breviaries: Strängnäs 1495, Uppsala 1496, and Skara (further away from the three Mälar dioceses) in 1498.[8] The two former employed the local printer family of Fabri in Stockholm. The choice of printer, place of publication and format makes sense, since Stockholm was a hanseatic city torn in half between the two dioceses, and it was a relatively easy affair to produce a text-based quarto book (there is considerably less musical notation than in a missal). Stockholm was also, in contrast to Lübeck, ecclesiastically 'neutral'. It was the bishops Kort Rogge of Strängnäs and Jacob Ulfsson of Uppsala who called Johannes Fabri (Latinization of 'Schmitt', 'Smedh') to Stockholm in 1495.[9] The Strängnäs breviary was issued a few months before – July 18 according to the colophon, whereas Ulfsson's breviary is dated September 30.

In the northern Baltic region it was also Ulfsson who first had a Missale printed for his diocese in 1484. Strängnäs followed in 1487 and Turku (Åbo, furthest away from lake Mälaren) in 1488. Again, this 'round' employed domestic or itinerary printers in the region (Snell and Ghotan in Stockholm). And just like in the neck of Denmark region, a 'second round' was later started, when Ulfsson had his second Uppsala missal printed by Jakob Wolff von Pforzheim in Basel, lavishly with much gold and colorization (see below).

We may note that both in the neck of Denmark region and in the Lake Mälaren region, the first diocese to produce a missal is also the first to start a new round of missals. The Schwerin missal of circa 1480 was supplanted by a new one only 20 years after (1500), an amazingly brief span in this period of time, given the efforts and costs of producing a printed missal made to order to a specific diocese. Just in the same way, the Uppsala missal of 1484 was followed by a new one in 1513.[10] As for breviaries, Lübeck led the way in 1478, and when the neighbouring dioceses had produced their equivalents, they had a

---

8   Nowakowska, 'From Strassburg to Trent', calls the surge in liturgical printing in Sweden 'a domino-style cluster', p. 11.
9   Isaac Collijn, *Svensk boktryckerihistoria under 14- och 1500-talen* (Stockholm: Gebers, 1947); Undorf, *From Gutenberg to Luther*, p. 48.
10  The brief span between the two Uppsala Missals have been the topic of an M.A. diss. by Kasper Ohlsson, *The Expensive Production of Missale Upsalense novum (1513) and the Short Life Span of Missale Upsalense vetus (1484)*, M.A. diss. (Department of Musicology, Uppsala University, 2020).

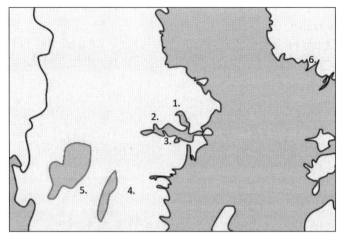

FIGURE. 3.2  Dioceses with printed missals and breviaries 1484–1500: 1. Uppsala; 2. Västerås; 3. Strängnäs; 4. Linköping; 5. Skara; 6. Turku

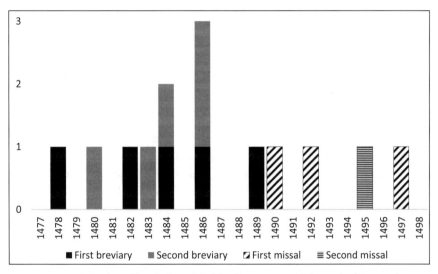

FIGURE 3.3  Missals and breviaries printed for dioceses around the neck of Denmark

new one issued in 1490, only twelve years after the printing of their earlier breviary. One ought of course not to be surprised that printers were eager to take on such new commissions soon after the previous liturgical print. But how to explain that the dioceses placed such new commissions based on an *usus* of text and melodies that had not been altered for more than a century?

The assumption that the two main geographical areas of competition in liturgical books are relevant seems to be corroborated further if we consider the present holdings of fragments and copies of the printed works. Surely, as any book historian knows, the secondary provenance can be convoluted or even deceptive, but the present holdings may at least give valuable hints of dispersion. The liturgical printed matter linked to Swedish parishes shows that a number of printed items from neighbouring dioceses have been owned by Swedish parish churches, but significantly not a single print from the neck of Denmark region.[11] This sense of locality and interchange between dioceses within one of the regions, but not between the two, invites us to try to understand the decisions and rationale behind the costly and labour-intensive production of these books.

## 3     Indications of Diocese Rivalry in Relation to Printed Books

In many of the diocese's printed works, the bishop is either mentioned as commissioner of the book, or at least in one way or another referred to in the colophons, typically also representing their crests (or, like in the Breviarium Scarense of 1498 and the Missale Lundense of 1514, physically portrayed in the form of stylized art).

We know from several felicitously surviving sources that Swedish bishops were acutely aware of the costs and labour required for producing a diocese liturgy in print. Uppsala archbishop Jacob Ulfsson produced two diocese missals during his episcopate, which may seem strange, especially since they reveal no substantial differences in contents as regards calendar, feasts or in the musical contents.[12] Since a new Missal was unlikely to have been needed due to lack of copies, nor was different in its scope or contents, it seems likely that the diocese in fact first and foremost wished to procure a more lavish book, something that seems to be supported by the surviving copies from what ended up as the final commission, with Wolff von Pforzheim in Basel 1513. The assumption of an 'arms race' of physical lavishness is supported by two other costly achievements of authority that Ulfsson undertook: the foundation of Uppsala University in 1477 (in competition with the proposed charter of Copenhagen), and the mural paintings of Albertus Pictor in many of the Uppsala diocese parish churches, where Ulfsson himself was in several cases painted into the murals alongside his crest. In Figure 3.5 (p. 399) we can see the gilding of one

---

11   Undorf, *From Gutenberg to Luther*, pp. 160–161.
12   The differences have been studied by Ohlsson, *The Expensive Production of Missale Upsalense*.

THE PRINTING OF MISSALS AND BREVIARIES 71

FIGURE 3.4    The final page of the *Missale Othoniense*, Brandis, 1483

of the copies of the second, Pforzheim-printed Uppsala missal. All the more surprising is the fact that this second edition had been in the making since at least 1508, only 24 years after the first Missale Upsalensis. This is known due to the surviving draft for a contract with Pater Hasse in Lübeck, which outlines an exact commission of 550 copies on paper and 150 on vellum (some folia, such as those containing the woodcut canon image were supposed to be on vellum also in the paper copies).[13] In this draft it is specified exactly which feasts should have which type of initial, and similar details.

The drafted contract with Hasse in Lübeck, later realized instead with Wolff von Pforzheim in Basel, mentions 700 copies, produced for a diocese that only had around 280 churches at the time. Was the more ambitious print meant to flood the market of diocese missals also for neighbouring dioceses around Lake Mälaren? At least we know that it *was* spread in the other dioceses, as Wolfgang Undorf has shown.[14] We also know that the diocese of Västerås had printed and procured their 1493 gradual at a high cost, as far as we know without calling it 'Arosiense' (title page or colophon has not survived).

What evidence is there, then, that bishops and consistoria deliberately compared their printing enterprises to those of others? Again, we may find evidence only after 1500, but we have little reason to assume that the situation

---

13    Letter is transcribed in Gustaf Edvard Klemming, *Sveriges bibliografi 1481–1600* (Uppsala: Akademiska boktryckeriet, 1889) p. 103.
14    Undorf, *From Gutenberg to Luther*, pp. 161–162.

would have been widely different earlier. Hans Brask, bishop of Linköping, knew, when he wrote to one of his canons on his way to Paris in 1524, how much Uppsala had paid for their 1513 missal, and wished to know also what Lund had paid for their 1514 missal.[15] Compared to the liturgically detailed draft contract between Uppsala diocese and Hasse in 1508, Brask seems even more concerned with the outer lavishness of the production of the breviary he now is planning:

> If it is possible for you to find out in Paris if we may have 800 breviaries printed for our church and for the blessed hours of the office, such as those printed in Lund with flourishes and figures framing all margins, and half of them more gilded and half of them gold. Ask about the books, when they may be bought and write back to us immediately. We presume you may procure this as good as you see fit yourself. And also ask about the cost of the missals that were printed in Paris for the Cathedral in Lund so that we may adapt our order according to how Uppsala had theirs printed in Basel.[16]

The two outlined commissions quoted here, none of which came to be realized in the form planned, seems to demonstrate what may be termed, for lack of a better term, 'diocesan rivalry'. The rivalry was one that could be heard in the singing from these books, but also (more importantly, it seems, to Ulfsson and Brask) a visually ascertainable episcopal authority in the gold, vellum and decorations mentioned. The aspirations for this outer extravagance may also explain why at this later stage, bishops turn to Paris and Basel, shunning the itinerant or Lübeck-based printers that had produced their 'first round' of breviaries and missals, as outlined in Table 3.1.

---

15   *Handlingar rörande Skandinaviens historia*, 13 (Stockholm: A. Wiborg, 1828) pp. 116–117. See also Undorf, *From Gutenberg to Luther*, pp. 273–274, and Ohlson, *The Expensive Production of Missale Upsalense*, p. 33.
16   Ibid: '… kan thet swa bare aat för eder at j till Pariiss tha vether ath vi aktom lata prenta vid viii c breffuer pro ecclesia nostra cum tali litera som Hore beate vore satte aat them i Lwnd cum floribus et figuris per omnes margines som the voro tenakulerede oc helffthena forgylt more eorum oc helffthena goltli, Förspören eder cum librariis om nesta köpet oc schriffuer oss til med förste bud. Vi förmoda vel ther gott kööp propter som i ther sielffue vel finnen. It. hörens oc före huad stycket gelder da missalibus the som trycktes parisiis pro ecclesia Lwndensi at vj motte laga vort kööp ther epter Vpsaliensis lothe tryckia sina in Basilea …'.

## 4   Commercial Aspects on Diocesan Liturgical Printed Works

Graheli and Pettegree have discussed what seems to have constituted a crisis in printing in the last quarter of the fifteenth century, pointing out that once the difficulties in selling out editions quickly became obvious, it was Europe's monarchs and bishops who kept the trade going.[17] The problem is summed up thus:

> The major problems all occurred in the area of sales: how to tell customers what was now available; how to get the books to them; how to judge the size of the market; how to arrange payment; which other artisan tradesmen needed to be involved in the process.[18]

None of these problems, bar perhaps the last one, did occur in an order such as that exemplified by the second Uppsala Missal or Linköping Breviary mentioned above. The number of copies were there agreed and supposed to be paid for beforehand, all to be delivered in bulk upon completion. The diocese must moreover themselves have provided the manuscript originals and closely overseen the editing process.[19] Thus it may be argued that the printing of liturgical books saved the situation for printers during the crisis that Graheli and Petegree have addressed. That a printer could still find himself in financial trouble and unable to print and deliver what has been pre-ordered is shown by the example of Michel Wenssler in Basel, who could commence printing a commissioned Breviarium only from loans from a third party.[20] After Wenssler had found himself increasingly indebted from 1487 onwards, he turned mostly to printing breviaries, missals, graduals and antiphonals for different dioceses.[21] Sarah Werner has pointed to the fact that the sequential production of large tomes in large quantities always put the printer in a vulnerable situation: until the final pages had been printed a workshop did not have

---

17   Shanti Graheli and Andrew Pettegree, 'How to Lose Money in the Business of Books: Commercial Strategies in the First Age of Print', in Shanti Graheli (ed.) *Buying and Selling: The Business of Books in Early Modern Europe* (Leiden: Brill, 2019), pp. 1–22, here p. 4.
18   Ibid.
19   This is mentioned, for example, in the colophon of the Nidaros breviary of 1519, where a diocese priest at the University in Paris was allocated the task.
20   Lucas Burkart, 'Early Book Printing and the Venture Capital in the Age of Dept: The Case of Michel Wenssler's Basel Printing Shop (1472–1491)', in Shanti Graheli (ed.), *Buying and Selling: The Business of Books in Early Modern Europe* (Leiden: Brill, 2019), pp. 23–54, here p. 49.
21   Burkart, 'Early Book Printing', p. 52.

one single book to sell. Since the earlier printed pages could consequently not be used to subsidize the latter, it was, as Werner puts it, 'all or nothing' with such commissions.[22]

As we can see in Table 3.1, a number of the printed works were produced on-site or in the vicinity of the diocese city. Some printers, like Ghotan, printed in no fewer than five cities in the Scando-Baltic region. The patronage that an itinerary printer temporarily enjoyed under a bishop or consistorium amounted to the opposite of competition on the free market. Surviving privilege documents such as those for Dold, Reicher and Mentzer to print the Breviary of Würzburg (Breviarium Herbipolense) in 1479 reveal a patronage situation similar to that of any tradesman brought to a medieval city:

> To them alone and to no one else have we given the opportunity to print accurately and in the best possible way these liturgical books … We have taken them and their families, their goods and chattels, under our dutiful and paternal protection and defence.[23]

Stephan Arndes was responsible for a number of the first liturgical printed books for the Baltic region and his career illustrates the close relationship between mobile proto-capitalist endeavour and ecclesiastical authority. Arndes moved from Italian lands to Schleswig in 1485, probably on request from Helrich von der Wisch, bishop of Schleswig.[24] There he printed the Schleswig missal in 1486. After moving to Lübeck, he printed the Breviary for Schleswig in 1489, but noticeably failing to secure the printing commissions for the diocese of Lübeck itself; this privilege went instead to Stuch in Nürnberg and Drach in Speyer, very far from the city. Instead Arndes printed the Missal for Viborg, further north into Danish land, and the Gradual for the diocese of Västerås, maintaining the city of Lübeck as his base. Arndes is in many respects an example of the opposite of an itinerary printer, as he held the largest printing workshop in Northern Europe, but received commissions from

---

22   Sarah Werner, *Studying Early Printed Books 1450–1800: A Practical Guide* (Hoboken: Wiley Blackwell, 2019), p. 24.
23   Quoted in Lionel Bently et al. (eds.), *Primary Sources on Copyright (1455–1900)* (Cambridge: Open Books, 2010), and discussed in context in Duggan, 'Reading Liturgical Books', pp. 22–23.
24   Duggan, 'Reading Liturgical Books', p. 31. See also Undorf, *From Gutenberg to Luther*, pp. 19 and 27–32.

afar, including from south-western Europe.[25] He also seems to have printed the Schleswig missal of 1486 without direct commission from the bishop.[26]

The crests of bishops had an important function in authorization and emblematic representation in book printing. When empty arms (without crests) are found in incunabula they could either merely represent a technical inability to produce the local crests with types, but could they also signal an openness to use in more than one diocese, or (within a diocese) for more than one consecutive bishop? Brandis produced printed liturgical books for the dioceses of both Lübeck and Odense. The final page of his 1483 Missale Othoniense comprises three coats of arms side by side (see Figure 3.4): one for the city of Lübeck (double eagle), one for the bishop (crosier outside empty split escutcheon) and one which may have been intended for Brandis' own crest. Karl Rønnow, bishop of Odense at the time, could have his crest entered by hand, but so could just as easily another bishop, such as his successor in Odense. Had he wished to, Brandis could surely have used woodcut crests as he did in other books (he was famous for his woodcut illustrations in his Josephus edition of 1475).

The diocese of Odense here stood alongside the city of Lübeck, itself a diocese city with Albert Krummendiek as bishop and for which Brandis produced both a Breviary and Missal. The colophon poetry in the Odense Missal includes the line: 'Me facit armari lubicana sed vrbsque parari / Ottoniense mode presulo sub karolo' ('I [the Missal] was made under the arms of Lübeck, but the city of Odense prepared me under bishop Karl'). Such intimations certainly need to be addressed in the analysis of mutual dependency of printers, city councils and bishops.[27] Previously it has been noted that printers often co-produced books by re-using contents that could be identical,[28] thereby maximizing production, but Brandis' dealings with Odense and Lübeck shows a balance of patronage within one single printed version, both in heraldry and in verse.

---

25   Alken Bruns and Dieter Lohmeier, *Die Lübecker Buchdrucker im 15. Und 16. Jahrhunderts: Buchdruck für den Ostseeraum* (Heide in Holstein: Boyens, 1994), p. 36.
26   Friedrich Bruns, 'Lebensnachrichten über Lübecker Drucker des 15. Jahrhunderts', *Nordisk tidskrift för bok- och biblioteksväsen*, 2 (1915), pp. 220–260, here pp. 252–253. Undorf, *From Gutenberg to Luther*, pp. 31–32.
27   See H.-O. Lange, 'Bidrag til Lübecks Bogtrykkerhistorie', *Bogvennen* (1893), for a discussion of Brandis, Rønnow and the city of Lübeck.
28   See Undorf, *From Gutenberg to Luther*, pp. 60–61 for such a case with Ghotan's books printed for Turku and Uppsala.

By the commissions from dioceses, printers moved to Baltic cities which would otherwise not have had a local printer, and the typical pattern was that a number of smaller and cheaper, commercially viable printed works were produced concurrently with the missals and breviaries.[29] This was not something which is likely to have concerned the bishops to any greater degree, but it is a fact that book history has focused more on these 'free speculation' market items rather than those commissions of liturgical books which in effect introduced printing in what is presently North-Western Germany, Denmark and Sweden.

## 5   Conclusions

It appears that the printing of breviaries and missals in the Scando-Baltic region before 1500 was a mutual game of patronage and investment by bishops and locally based or itinerary printers. This sets these printing commissions, with numbers of copies that often by far exceeded the number of churches and priests in the dioceses, in the light of different *usus*, local deviances in liturgical singing which had to be upheld against those of other dioceses, just at the very end of the crumbling Kalmar union, and the nascent Royal Kingdoms of Denmark and Sweden. While the printing press has often historiographically been depicted as a revolutionary force in Church history (in the hands of reformers in German-speaking lands), this study shows that the new technology could conversely be a powerful tool in upholding existing ecclesiastical and liturgical authority.[30]

The printers were most likely as disinterested and pragmatic in these ecclesiastical power struggles as were their fellow tradesmen who later helped pave the way for the reformation movements of Luther and other city reformers. They were predominantly tradesmen and businessmen. From the preserved drafted contracts and inquiries between the two parties, it seems that the bishops and dioceses were the perfect counterparts for the printers, namely wealthy and powerful authorities well-nigh interested in paying m o r e rather than less for a notable and locally discernibly liturgical print. The destruction rate of these books has been devastating in the light of the original size of editions.

---

29   Henrik Schück, *Den svenska förlagsbokhandelns historia* (2 vols., Stockholm: Norstedts, 1923), 1, pp. 29–35. Undorf, *From Gutenberg to Luther*, pp. 25–26.
30   See Nowakowska, 'From Strassburg to Trent', pp. 8, 10.

None of the aspiring bishops and consistoria around 1500 could of course fathom that in less than thirty years, the landscape of liturgical music printing was about to change forever. In fact, the rapid turnover of technology and new demands on the printed product just before the nascent North-European reformations is comparable to the rapidity of changes in music technology in the twentieth century.

CHAPTER 4

# A Game of Cities

*Driving Forces in Early Modern Scandinavian Book History*

Wolfgang Undorf

Every once in a while, attempts have been made to reduce a complex period in international book history by focussing on the history of a single country or on the rivalry of two cities.[1] But neither does the history of printing in the Netherlands replace the necessity of looking for other constitutive powers in a specific region and period of time, nor does that classical clash of ideological centres (Rome versus Wittenberg) alone write the history of Reformation and Confessionalisation in early modern Scandinavia. It is indisputable that Wittenberg rose to a position of uttermost importance for Protestant book printing in the middle of the sixteenth century from a very modest starting position.[2] Yet, for a long time, Wittenberg and its main 'brand' were of less importance at least with regard to the production of the printed books essential for the spread and consolidation of the Reformation in Sweden.[3] It is established practice to feature religion, geography or politics as the driving forces in history; nevertheless this is not sufficient in order to depict the correct image of the book market of that time. Scandinavian, especially Swedish and Danish, book markets which I will concentrate on in the present study, have never worked along clearly drawn lines dividing vernacular domestic and import markets from each other.

This is an understanding that expanded the longer I looked at certain actors and actions within early modern Scandinavian book history, as well as the statistics and bibliographical considerations pertaining to printing and distribution of books.[4] With regard to the book market and book trade, one has to

---

1  Kristina Lundblad, 'Föreställningar om förlag', *Biblis: Kvartalstidskrift för bokvänner*, 72 (2015/16), pp. 3–11. Anna-Maria Rimm, 'Elsa Fougt som internationell bokhandlare', *Biblis: Kvartalstidskrift för bokvänner*, 47 (2009), pp. 2–36.
2  Andrew Pettegree, *The Brand Luther: 1517, Printing, and the Making of the Reformation* (New York: Penguin Press, 2015).
3  Wolfgang Undorf, 'Reformation ohne Luther? Transnationale Druckkultur in Dänemark und Schweden in der Reformationszeit', *Bibliothek und Wissenschaft*, 49 (2016), pp. 263–280.
4  Otfried Czaika has contributed a number of articles and books to this field by focusing on lost and rediscovered Swedish religious books. See his article 'Ein weites und weitgehend

consider the important contributions by individual actors, places or powers that at times have been of major regional or even transnational importance as centres for book production or book trade. They join other driving forces and formative agents in history such as geography, climate or demography especially as stressed by the *Annales* school. The fact that there have been shifting centres, and at the same time shifting attention from the Scandinavian periphery as to what defines or what might create such a centre, allows us to ask questions about when and where new centres appeared and for what reasons.[5]

In early modern Scandinavia, religion was certainly one major driving force – but not the only one. The present study aims at investigating the interplay between mainly religion and other driving forces, such as geography, politics and people. To achieve this, it excludes typography or the technique of printing itself. There is no lack of studies highlighting some of the more well-known actors, and success stories but also obstacles that faced the emerging world of the printed book in the late fifteenth and early sixteenth century. On a general level, it is necessary to mention Andrew Pettegree's more structured view on centre and periphery in the period of the 'print revolution'. On a whole, Pettegree's description of the third, the outermost circle in the first century of print, is quite applicable to the situation in northern Europe, to be more precise, mostly Scandinavia and Northern Germany. Pettegree identifies a few actors or acting forces shaping the peripheral book markets, such as demography and local political elites.[6] Yet, he does not intend to explain the interplay of forces that shaped Scandinavian book history in greater detail. More fruitful in that respect is the approach of David Rundle in his sketch of the structure of humanist contacts, especially the main conclusion that 'the *studia humanitatis* were less about genius of place than mastery over space'.[7] Rundle's work on the development of the humanistic field and, at the same time, of the humanists achieving and teaching that same discipline in the fifteenth century, does fit

---

   unbekanntes Feld: Schwedische Gesangbücher und Lieddrucke des 16. Jahrhunderts', in Ottfried Czaika and Wolfgang Undorf (eds.), *Schwedische Buchgeschichte: Zeitalter der Reformation und Konfessionalisierung* (Göttingen: Vandenhoeck & Ruprecht, 2021), pp. 87–110.
5  Gina Dahl, *Books in Early Modern Norway* (Leiden & Boston: Brill, 2011). Wolfgang Undorf, 'Print and Book Culture in the Danish Town of Odense', in Benito Rial Costas (ed.), *Print Culture and Peripheries in Early Modern Europe: A Contribution to the History of Printing and the Book Trade in Small European and Spanish Cities* (Leiden: Brill, 2013), pp. 227–248.
6  Andrew Pettegree, 'Centre and Periphery in the European Book World', *Transactions of the Historical Society*, 18 (2008), pp. 101–128, here 106–107.
7  David Rundle 'Humanism across Europe: The Structure of Contacts', in David Rundle (ed.), *Humanism in Fifteenth-Century Europe* (Oxford: Society for the Study of Medieval Languages and Literature, 2012), p. 309.

almost equally well the book world of the sixteenth century. Because what the world of books and its history in Scandinavia reveal, is not the genius of that one place or of that one bookshop. It opens up a conceptual way of investigating which forcing agents executed at least some mastery over Scandinavian and Northern European space.

Given the undisputable importance of the international Latin book trade as one of the intrinsic characteristics of the development of the northern European book world, this world simply cannot be understood as having been self-sufficient.[8] A more recent study expands the number of driving forces shaping (at least regional) book history by reminding us of some of the borders that books had to tackle: the Protestant Reformation splitting the book market in two, political fragmentation increasing the number of border and customs controls in the way of imported books, and last but not least the division of Europe into territorial states.[9] The Scandinavian territorial states of the sixteenth century temporarily separated a domestic vernacular book market from a foreign, export-orientated Latin book trade.

One late effect of the Reformation and the formation of consolidated states in Europe, especially in central and northern Europe, is not only that today we have to discuss their impact on Scandinavian book culture. The disintegration of the (at least to a large extent) unified pre-Reformation Europe for a long time prevented book producers, traders and consumers during the sixteenth century from having access to the Latin and Catholic part of the world of books, no matter how much they might have fitted in with Pettegree's definition of the inner core in terms of book production.[10] This almost cataclysmic period of events makes it even more a necessity to contemplate frameworks, acting forces and individual actors that formed Scandinavian sixteenth-century book cultures. Does the transition from a Western Christianity, theologically orientated towards Rome, to the duality of Catholic and Lutheran and Reformed confessions mean that frameworks simply shrank without a change of character? They did so to a certain extent, yes. We can deduce certain parallels before and after 1525 (roughly speaking), but there were differences as well. Let us

---

8     Pettegree, 'Centre and Periphery', p. 107.
9     'Later, the Protestant Reformation, political fragmentation and the division of Europe into nation states challenged views depicting Europe as a unitary, organic entity.' Alessandro de Arcangelis, 'The Cosmopolitan Morphology of the National Discourse: Italy as a European Centre of Intellectual Modernity', in Tessa Hauswedell et al. (eds.), *Re-Mapping Centre and Periphery: Asymmetrical Encounters in European and Global Contexts* (London: UCL Press, 2019), pp. 135–154, here p. 135.
10    Pettegree, 'Centre and Periphery', p. 106.

begin our analysis by looking at the book trade starting in the middle of the fifteenth century.

## 1  Trade by Default

Until the Reformation, the places that had a major influence on Scandinavian print culture were the centres of international trade on the European continent that were looking for opportunities in the north. When it came to Mainz, the birthplace of printing, it is appropriate to start writing its book history with the start of book printing. Everywhere else, trade in books has preceded the printing of books, sometimes for decades.[11] This, of course, was all the more true the farther one travelled from central western Europe out into the peripheries of the continent. Books as merchandise travelled faster than printing presses.

Not long after the invention of printing and less than a generation before the first printers established offices in Scandinavia, the first printed books reached the shores of the Baltic Sea.[12] It was the most natural thing for a type of merchandise that fitted the needs of the Scandinavian readers but that also had to be traded in order to get a reward for the investment. This first period of the book trade in Scandinavia is characterized by reception rather than production. The earliest merchandise to a large extent consists of sought-after canonical literary works, their authors being far away from Scandinavia by time and space. While intellectual production in the modern sense of the word was not altogether unknown, intellectual reproduction still was the major business and encompassed the printing of (anonymously composed) liturgical books: the works of the church fathers and medieval theologians and standard school books, as well as pirated editions that met the market demand. The contents of late medieval and early modern Scandinavian book collections make it evident that much of the book trade did not necessarily involve identifiable authors at all.

This all-European book market was also dealing with relatively uniform merchandise, mainly liturgical books and scholastic literature. Being a commodity that fitted seamlessly the established transportation means and routes, books easily found their place among the merchandise with which the Hanse merchants dealt. Thus Lübeck became the natural centre for trade and printing, benefitting from its favourable geographical position on the southern

---

11  Hans Widmann, *Geschichte des Buchhandels* (Wiesbaden: Harrassowitz, 1975).
12  Wolfgang Undorf, *From Gutenberg to Luther: Transnational Print Cultures in Scandinavia 1450–1525* (Leiden: Brill, 2014), pp. 65ff.

coast of the Baltic Sea and as well as from its long-existing trade networks.[13] But the trade with books also benefitted from the generally homogenous liturgical and intellectual culture in pre-Reformation western Europe. That means that mastery of space was more decisive than any genius of place.

At a time when all liturgy was in Latin and, on the whole, 'Catholic' or Roman, variations in the liturgies used by churches, monastic orders and other larger religious bodies were negligible. Clerics and lay people all over Europe adapted foreign liturgical tools for use in their home dioceses: south German psalters were employed in the Swedish dioceses of Skara and Uppsala.[14] Nor was the use of Swedish liturgical books restricted to the dioceses they were originally printed for. The *Graduale Arosiense* for the diocese of Västerås, Sweden, and the *Manuale Upsalense* of 1487 for the archdiocese of Uppsala were demonstrably used simultaneously in the same parish, although they have been described by historians as partly incompatible.[15] The *Missale Dominicanum* produced by Wenssler in Basel in 1488 has a rather late Norwegian provenance, but its binding and other signs of provenance suggest strongly that at least this copy was imported to Norway before the Reformation.[16]

Foreign liturgical books were used, with minor or major adjustments, because they were needed but also thanks to the international character of the pre-Reformation Roman church. This specific aspect of the pre-Reformation period allowed Rome to determine the overall framework of the book trade, but Rome was never its centre.[17]

During these early years, the books, texts and ideas that were transferred from one place to the other determined the scale and nature of the Scandinavian market. There is overwhelming evidence of the capacity of this market: the speed with which printed books could cross Europe and the scale of the trade as reconstructed from contemporary sources.[18] Books produced in printing shops on the continent could easily take less than two years, and in some cases even less than one year, to travel to a destination in northern Europe, not only to Lübeck, Rostock or Hamburg from where they were shipped to Scandinavia, but also directly to Scandinavian markets and buyers as well. The 1483 Stockholm edition of the *Dialogus creaturarum moralisatus*

---

13   Alken Bruns and Dieter Lohmeier (eds.), *Die Lübecker Buchdrucker im 15. und 16. Jahrhundert: Buchdruck für den Ostseeraum* (Lübeck: Boyens, 1994).
14   Wolfgang Undorf, 'Ett okänt Psalterium – ett Hymnarium Scarense?', *Föreningen för Västgötalitteratur: Meddelande*, 2 (2003), pp. 6–7.
15   Undorf, *From Gutenberg to Luther*, p. 164.
16   Ibid., p. 156.
17   Ibid., pp. 66–70.
18   Ibid., pp. 70, 103.

was modelled directly on a Dutch print dated 1482.[19] In 1531 the later Finnish reformer Michael Agricola (c.1509–1557), then resident in the Finnish town of Turku/Åbo, acquired a copy of Martin Luther's *Ennarationes seu postillae* that had been printed in Strasbourg the year before.[20] It was the reliable trade web spun by the indefatigable travels of printer-publishers and their agents between Venice, Basel and Nürnberg to Frankfurt am Main, Leipzig and finally Lübeck or the Netherlands that made possible this speed.[21]

The scale of the trade was impressive, too, yet difficult to grasp on a broader base due to the lack of preserved books, provenances or archival evidence. Among others things, the qualities of a printed text, that is, its content and target audience, format and genre, significantly influenced its chances of survival. School books and pamphlets, broadsheets and letters of indulgence, prayer books and psalters disappeared speedily and almost entirely. The survival rates of printed books that can be deduced from our knowledge of edition sizes and archival information on the scope of the book trade indicate the domestic production as well as the import from continental printers of thousands of books each year throughout the period.[22]

These printer-publishers acted within the framework of the pre-Reformation church and the political landscape, but it is quite evident that it was never the religious or political centres or forces that alone determined the structure of the trade or the printing. So, within a relatively stable external framework, the internal power structures were slowly changing, due to, among other things, the actions of individuals involved in the trade, and also due to external actions. Towards the end of the pre-Reformation period, German printer-publishers were no longer able to maintain their exclusive role in the Scandinavian book trade, although the regional significance of printers in Lübeck and Rostock remained unchallenged on the whole. From the 1480s, other actors entered the Scandinavian scene, actors who were not dependent on Hanseatic trade or, specifically, the merchants of Lübeck. In the last decades of the fifteenth century, Dutch merchants were granted privileges by the Danish king in an attempt to outmanoeuvre the dominant Hanseatic League.[23] As we have

---

19   Isak Collijn, *Sveriges bibliografi intill år 1600* (3 vols., Uppsala: Svenska Litteratursällskapet, 1934–1938), 1, p. 25.
20   Otfried Czaika, 'Plinius världshistoria med Agricolas ägaranteckning', *Biblis: Kvartalstidskrift för bokvänner*, 51 (2010), pp. 30–39, here p. 37.
21   Undorf, *From Gutenberg to Luther*, pp. 83–85 with examples from the late fifteenth century.
22   Ibid., p. 120.
23   Hanno Brand, 'Baltic connections: Changing patterns in Seaborne Trade (c.1450–1800)', in Lennart Bes et al. (eds.), *Baltic Connections Archival Guide to the Maritime Relations of*

seen, this had an almost immediate impact on the book trade between the Netherlands and Scandinavia. Although in the long run Lübeck would lose its dominant position, in the early years Dutch books were still sent to Lübeck to be bound before they reached their Scandinavian destinations.

Lübeck and Rostock, members of the Hansa, had been crucial for Scandinavian, especially Swedish, trade for centuries. Lübeck in particular dominated the pre-Reformation book trade with Scandinavia, with Rostock catching up not before the 1520s. German book printers and sellers were drawn to Lübeck as the main port to trade with Sweden. For decades efficient and well-supplied book trading systems, with Lübeck, the centre of Hanseatic trade on the Baltic, at their heart, ensured that Scandinavia was supplied with a good range of high quality books, mainly from Germany and Italy.[24] The quality of this selection was superior to anything that could or, rather, might have been produced by printers active in Scandinavia. What is more, these editions were available at prices that Scandinavian printers could not afford to undercut.

The earliest Danish and Swedish printers all came from abroad, and their origins reflect the characteristics of the international trade network that connected Scandinavia to western Europe: most of the printers came from Lübeck and just the occasional odd one from the Netherlands or Hamburg. The technique of printing and its master craftsmen seemed to have followed in the footsteps of the trade, almost unintentionally, like a natural consequence.[25] But almost from the start, printing and customers could rely upon the structures and framework established by the trade: the first printers active on Scandinavian soil seem all to have been deliberately called upon by institutional and private customers.[26]

## 2       Printing on Demand

The earliest book trade did not generally involve the original intellectual production of printed editions of texts conceived by Scandinavian authors, nor the internal and external processing of explicit and informed orders by Scandinavian customers. This dynamic changed to a certain degree as soon as customers evolved into becoming more experienced book buyers, actively

---

   *the Countries around the Baltic Sea (including the Netherlands) 1450–1800* (3 vols., Leiden: Brill, 2007), 1, pp. 1–18.
24  Undorf, *From Gutenberg to Luther*, p. 83.
25  Ibid., p. 14.
26  Ibid., p. 13 on Danish commissions and p. 48 on Swedish commissions, all dated to the 1480s.

seeking to overcome geographical boundaries. In this way, Scandinavian customers established (usually short-lived) local and regional centres of printing within the realm of the Scandinavian kingdoms. But even individual actions could contribute to the establishment or, rather, elevation in a way, of foreign printing towns to towns of regional importance for Scandinavian book trade. That was the case with Paris and its importance for Denmark in the early sixteenth century or with Rostock and Sweden later in that same century. While Lübeck and Rostock, geographically speaking, were more of a natural choice, Paris was not. Paris was a major print town in its own right, but Danish individuals co-created Paris as a centre for printing for the Danish book market, which accidentally spilled over to the Swedish book market.[27]

Before the Reformation, for more than two decades from 1483–1504, four Lübeck-based printers produced Danish books abroad. The importance of Lübeck for the production of Swedish books abroad lasted even longer, from 1485 to 1523, with four printers employed in the production of different editions.[28] Already the production of the standard edition of the *Revelationes* of Saint Bridget of Sweden (1303–1373) had been outsourced to Lübeck, apparently due to the infrastructural challenges of this specific production, its volume and size.[29] Printers residing in towns outside Scandinavia every now and then received print jobs commissioned by religious institutions in all the Scandinavian countries. The earliest pro-Reformation works intended for the Scandinavian market were either ordered from and produced in Rostock, or imported by means that were largely informal, private and illegal.[30] But that was just another manifestation of the experience that private customers had developed with the continental book market and how they profited from it.

But the case of Paris in the beginning of the sixteenth century marked a new chapter in Scandinavian book history. For little more than a decade, between 1510 and 1520, Paris was the undisputed centre of printing Danish literature outside Denmark.[31] An indicator for the yet minor quantity on a European scale we are talking about here, is the fact that this was entirely the work of one man, Christiern Pedersen (c.1480–1554). A native of Roskilde, he was appointed dean at the cathedral in Lund in the year 1505.[32] Three years later, he left Denmark for Paris, where he continued his university studies and

---

27  Ibid., pp. 20, 87–95.
28  Ibid., pp. 18, 54.
29  Collijn, *Svensk bibliografi*, 1, pp. 117–128.
30  Undorf, *From Gutenberg to Luther*, pp. 85–86.
31  Ibid., pp. 18, 20–21.
32  Jens Anker Jørgensen, *Humanisten Christiern Pedersen: En præsentation* (Copenhagen: Reitzel, 2007).

also established a stable business relationship with Jean Badin (Josse Badius Ascensius), the major Parisian printer-publisher of the early sixteenth century. Several Danish books were printed in Paris during Pedersen's sojourn, most of them by Badin but also by several others: Jean Barbier, Thomas Kees and Guillaume Marchand, Wolfgang Hopyl, Jean Philippe, Jean Kerbriant and Jean Bieanayse as well as one unknown printer. While four printers in Lübeck produced nine titles over a little more than twenty years, these Parisian printing shops produced sixteen titles in less than half that time. Most of these titles were printed in the first half of the 1510s, commissioned directly by Christiern Pedersen.[33] Even after leaving Paris around 1514, he continued to sustain the trade connection, most prominently manifested in the Malmö list as well as his later contributions to the Danish national bibliography while he was in Antwerp around 1530.[34]

During his life span, Pedersen presents several examples of the importance that one single actor could have for book production for Scandinavia and the potential of certain cities becoming centres of Scandinavian printing. He was heavily involved in printing books in Danish in Leipzig 1517–1518 and Antwerp between 1529 and 1531.[35] Yet these later initiatives no longer had the long lasting effect as did his work in Paris.

I have previously described the Malmö list as a potent testimony of the power of the Danish book market and literary culture. The Malmö List is an inventory of books attributed to the then Danish town of Malmö, although the near-by city of Lund is mentioned as well, and to the aforementioned Christiern Pedersen. The inventory records 3,164 copies, a collection on a remarkable scale in any European context. It is not a private library and it cannot be ruled out that it might have been an institutional library either. Still, the List most probably represents the stock of a bookshop of regional importance. To a large extent, the Malmö List contains a large number of books that emanated in part directly from Pedersen's work as an editor and author in Paris. Other books document the trade with printer-publishers in Paris in which Pedersen appears to have been involved even after he returned to Denmark. Of the 204 titles registered, seven percent were probably printed in Paris, yet they represent 46% of all copies. That might have made quite an impact on the local and regional book markets. The large number of copies for single titles also

---

33  Lauritz Nielsen, *Dansk bibliografi: Med særligt hensyn til dansk bogtrykkerkunsts historie* (5 vols., Copenhagen: Gyldendalske Boghandel, 1919–1996).
34  On the Malmö list, see Undorf, *From Gutenberg to Luther*, pp. 87ff.
35  Jørgensen, *Humanisten Christiern Pedersen*, p. 14.

indicates deliberate decisions as to where specific titles should be produced.[36] In the context of and in competition with a European market based upon knowledge as well as personal connections, a local book market had by no means a natural advantage. That point is easily proven by the struggle for local printers to establish themselves at one place for a longer period of time.

The emergence of Paris even had repercussions for Sweden a few years into the 1520s. Documented evidence of the connections between Scandinavian customers and foreign printers is not common, but there are exceptions. A number of Swedish bishops were well aware of the products of foreign presses and of their qualities, and they did not hesitate to initiate long-distance contacts to obtain specific books. Georg Stuchs in Nuremberg was commissioned to print the two breviaries for Linköping in 1493 and Skara in 1498; Jacob Wolff von Pforzheim in Basel produced two printed liturgical books in 1513.[37] The correspondence of Hans Brask (1464–1538), the bishop of Linköping, in 1524 can stand as the final expression of the international connections involved in pre-Reformation printing. Brask was well informed about certain liturgical books printed for both Denmark and Sweden. This included Christiern Pedersen's edition of a Danish book of hours, *Vor Frue Tider*, printed in 1514 in Paris by Jean Badin; the *Missale Lundense*, also printed in Paris the same year; and the *Missale Upsalense* printed in Basel in 1513.[38] In a letter dated September 1524 and sent to Petrus Benedicti, then in Germany, Brask asked him to investigate how much the *Missale Lundense* had cost and how much it would cost to print 800 breviaries for the diocese of Linköping in the manner of the *Missale Upsalense*.[39]

The obvious decay of the united Scandinavian kingdoms and the introduction of the Reformation in the 1520s put an abrupt end to the promising trade connections established at least in part on the initiative of single customers. Even major investments made by religious institutions (most of the Scandinavian dioceses ordered liturgical books to be printed) or the occasional private customer could not provide the sort of long-term engagement and the market necessary for establishing a print centre and a firm basis for a sustainable print business, especially not in the emerging world of centralised

---

36   Undorf, *From Gutenberg to Luther*, p. 95.
37   Collijn, *Sveriges bibliografi*, 1, pp. 128–132, 169–175, 221–237.
38   Hedda Gunneng, *Biskop Hans Brasks registratur: Textutgåva* (Uppsala: Svenska fornskriftsällskapet, 2003), no. 256.
39   Undorf, *From Gutenberg to Luther*, p. 55.

territorial states. Yet they had had the potential of turning any specific place into an epicentre of printing in the pre-Reformation era.

This can be illustrated by the initiatives taken by Hans Urne (d. 1503), dean at Odense cathedral, which occurred in the most enigmatic period in Danish pre-Reformation book history. Between circa 1501–1503, Urne invested a total of 1583 Mark Lübisch, the equivalent of five times the value of the books exported from Lübeck to Scandinavia within a four year period 1492–1495, as recorded in the Pfundzollbücher. His collaboration with an otherwise unknown Lübeck-based printer, Simon Brandt (who possibly was the much better known Matthaeus Brandis), although not without its obstacles as revealed in the lawsuit from 1505 filed against the printer by the then deceased Hans Urne's brother Jørgen, nevertheless resulted in the production of at least nine editions and hundreds of copies. This was an enormous undertaking by a private customer, apparently the last of a series of collaborations between Hans Urne and the Brandis family over the years. Hans Urne must have been involved in the book trade on a significant scale, judging not only by the commission of the years 1501–1503, but also by the large number of copies of books bequeathed to his family in his will (dated 1503), which far exceed the numbers of single works that were to be found in any private book collections in Scandinavia at that time.[40] Yet, it didn't make Odense a Danish print centre of more than just short-lived local importance.

But the story is a wonderful example of what a single customer could achieve with the help of money, determination and experience within the book trade. We know nothing of Hans Urne's motives, they might have been purely economic altogether. Urne may have intended to do a good deed, in this case by commissioning the print of a diurnal and hundreds of school books: a large number of books were liturgical books printed for the church or school books printed for and bequeathed to poor pupils.[41] Although by helping society he may also have hoped to aid his soul's passage to heaven. In that case, religion might have proven to have influenced not only the general outline of the trade, but also directly a specific book trade enterprise. Anyway, what his engagement in the book business lacked was the stamina of external structures and movements. This becomes quite obvious as soon as the two major forces that determined the fate and nature of the sixteenth-century Scandinavian book trade entered the stage.

---

40   Ibid., pp. 36–47.
41   Ibid., p. 246.

## 3  Reformation, Confessionalization and National Politics

From around 1520, two new actors entered the scene: religion and (at least forms of proto-)nationalism.[42] The conflict between Protestantism and Catholicism skyrocketed Wittenberg into the position of the centre of Protestant printing. But soon, the book trade reconquered the more dynamic and complex state. One might say that monoculture never thrived in the world of books for long. The dynamic phase of this period stretches from a truly European pre-Reformation book market to the establishment of a new trans-national market after 1525, with the arrival of the Lutheran as well as the Low and Middle German book world in the second half of the sixteenth century. Lübeck was the place to go for printers from Cologne, Speyer, Nuremberg and Venice.[43] But the actions of individual customers could temporarily boost other places such as Paris or Odense as well to become international or regional print centres.

The discontinuation of a united Scandinavian kingdom as a result of the war between Denmark and Sweden at the beginning of the 1520s of course had repercussions in the Scandinavian book markets. Between 1523 and 1526, no books were printed in Denmark, while the number of acquisitions for the cathedral library in Västerås, Sweden, dropped to its lowest level in fifty years.[44] At the same time, though, Hans Brask, the last Catholic bishop of Linköping, Sweden, was able to establish a short-lived print shop that produced at least four books, making it the capital of political and religious turmoil. Brask also complained about the increasing illegal importation of Lutheran books in Sweden. He had come to realise that Lutheran books had been pouring into Sweden for some time, as he wrote in a letter dated March 1524.[45] In another letter from the same month, he reminded the brothers in the Birgittine monastery of Vadstena that it was forbidden to sell, buy, receive or read schismatic literature.[46] Yet, he had to admit that this had been going on for quite some years already.

---

42  Alexander Jacobson, 'Proto-Nationalism in Scandinavia: Swedish State Building in the Middle Ages', BA thesis (Seattle: University of Puget Sound, 2021), p. 7.

43  Heinrich Grimm, 'Die Buchführer des deutschen Kulturbereichs und ihre Niederlassungsorte in der Zeitspanne 1490 bis um 1550', *Archiv für Geschichte des Buchwesens*, 7 (1965–67), cols. 1153–1932.

44  Åke Åberg, *Västerås domkyrkas bibliotek år 1640 efter Petrus Olai Dalekarlus' katalog* (Västerås: Stifts- och Landsbiblioteket, 1973), p. 142; Wolfgang Undorf, 'Buchhandel und Buchsammeln in Schweden zur Zeit der Reformation und Konfessionalisierung', in Czaika and Undorf (eds.), *Schwedische Buchgeschichte*, pp. 13–54, here p. 15.

45  Undorf, *From Gutenberg to Luther*, p. 277.

46  Gunneng, *Biskop Hans Brask*, pp. 266–268 no. 197.

Here appears an aspect of the new major forces that in different ways were about to exert a heavy influence on the emerging new Scandinavian book culture. The Reformation divided western Christianity, and the break-up of the united Scandinavian kingdom resulted in the subsequent establishment of the new Scandinavian kingdoms of Denmark-Norway and Sweden (including Finland), respectively. These forces and the practical events they brought into play were the cause of the creation of a new phenomenon in printing and trading in Scandinavia: the emergence of illegal, schismatic and heretical texts as well as political propaganda, polemic works and written defences against them.

The years between 1522 and 1528 were a period of political and religious upheaval that started with the formal introduction of the Reformation in both countries against the background of a civil war between Gustav I Vasa (1523–1560) in Sweden and the Danish crown but also within the realm of the Danish kingdom itself.[47] The struggle for the establishment of new political orders resulted in a number of printed works in both countries. This is the first time that politics appears both as a driving and prohibitionary force on the Scandinavian book scene. In the middle of this period are the six editions in three different languages of the future king Gustav I Vasa and the Council's manifesto against the Danish King Christian II (1481–1559). As both the Low German and the High German versions were aimed at a German public, the first edition was printed in Lübeck, the other four were printed by the German printer Ludwig Dietz in either Lübeck or Rostock.[48] The same year, 1523, saw the proclamation of the Danish State Council in favor of the election of King Frederick (1471–1533), followed by the elected king's own letter addressing the German nation. Eight editions are known to have been published, three in Zwickau and five in Rostock.[49] In the 1590s, foreign presses were used again as publishing agents for the struggle between king Sigismund Vasa (1566–1632) and duke Carl (1550–1611).[50] Printing abroad provided the opportunity of easily reaching out to a continental public, and also the means to bypassing political and governmental suppression, usually in times of turmoil, but also

---

47 Martin Berntson, *Mässan och armborstet: Uppror och reformation* (Skellefteå: Artos, 2010). Ralph Tuchtenhagen (ed.), *Aspekte der Reformation im Ostseeraum* (Lüneburg: Nordost-Inst., 2004).
48 Collijn, *Sveriges bibliografi*, 1, pp. 286ff., 367.
49 Nielsen, *Dansk bibliografi*, 4, p. 165.
50 Collijn, *Sveriges bibliografi*, 3, *passim*.

at the end of the sixteenth century at the height of the confessional struggles in Sweden.[51]

Printing is a servant, not a master, and the Scandinavian monarchies made that point very clear when they regained their strength in the aftermath of the establishment of the new territorial kingdoms and of the Lutheran confession from the middle of the 1520s onwards. The outline of that 'new' world of books was defined by confessional borders (constituting the theological importance of Wittenberg for the rest of the sixteenth century), and also by the persistence of certain centres of printing that violated confessional boundaries, such as Frankfurt am Main and Basel for literature in Latin, as well as Lübeck and Rostock as the first addresses for printed works in German and the vernacular. The importance of Frankfurt am Main and Basel became evident and remained established as early as the 1530s and 1540s. That has been quite convincingly shown by Otfried Czaika in his reconstruction of the library of Sveno Jacobi (c.1480–1554), the bishop of Skara, Sweden, in the 1540s.[52]

The situations that politics, confessionalization and economy brought about in the new national book markets in Denmark and Sweden had quite strong similarities. In Denmark, the number of printing shops receded to a total of two for most of the sixteenth century, the corresponding number for Sweden being one.[53] Until the end of the century, the Scandinavian countries depended upon the major western and central European centres of printing for most of the literature consumed. Local, regional or even national book markets powered by one or two monopolised printing enterprises, satisfied the complementary basic literary needs of educational, liturgical, edifying literature as well as the information needs of the governments. Other literature was provided by an international book market.

But what was the immediate and long-term impact of the Reformation on Scandinavian book production? Thomas Kaufmann stresses in an article from 2015 the importance of printed texts in the vernacular languages not only for the Reformation as such, but also for the rise of a broad public sphere of reading and response.[54] The years between 1527 and 1542 and again between 1552

---

51 Kajsa Weber 'Buch und Konfessionskonflikt: Übersetzung, Kompilation und Paratext in Petrus Johannis Gothus' "Sköna och märkliga skriftens sentenser" (1597)', in Czaika and Undorf (eds.), *Schwedische Buchgeschichte*, pp. 111–130.
52 Otfried Czaika, *Sveno Jacobi: Boksamlaren, biskopen, teologen* (Stockholm: Kungliga biblioteket, 2013).
53 Undorf, 'Buchhandel und Buchsammeln', p. 15.
54 Thomas Kaufmann, 'Ohne Buchdruck keine Reformation?', in Stefan Oehmig (ed.), *Buchdruck und Buchkultur im Wittenberg der Reformationszeit* (Leipzig: Evangelische Verlagsanstalt, 2015), pp. 13–34.

and 1562 saw an impressive rise in the number of printed matter in the vernacular produced in Denmark. That corresponded in general with the development in Sweden.[55]

Beginning with the 1520s, literature in the vernacular became the predominant category in both Scandinavian countries, although there were differences. In Denmark we see predominantly religious and edifying contents, while Swedish production contained mostly religious and governmental publications. What both have in common is the fact that the introduction of the Reformation was more or less independent of a domestic production of pro-Reformation literature. If printing the works of Martin Luther was a clear sign of the Reformation of a country, then it is surprising to learn that the first complete Luther text in Swedish translation, *Undervisning om Herrans nattvard*, did not see the light of day until 1558.[56] After that, it took almost forty years before another four works by Luther were printed between 1587 and 1597. This is interesting, given the fact that Lutheran and pro-Lutheran writings were introduced to a Scandinavian public quite early and, if we believe the stout anti-Lutheran Hans Brask, a development that came too easily thanks to illegal imports.[57]

The situation in Denmark differed, though, from the Swedish with regard to its relation to the writings of Martin Luther. As early as 1526, the first translation into Danish of one of his texts appeared in print in Copenhagen, followed by another printed in Viborg 1528.[58] They were the first of a total of 44 of Luther's printed texts until the end of the sixteenth century (according to the Danish national bibliography).

The early Reformation is an act of transfer of ideas that includes the printed as well as the written and spoken word. With regard to the word of the Reformation and their main proponents, the success of the Reformation in Sweden did not depend on a domestic production of Lutheran and reformed literature. The Reformation was helped by a multitude of ways in reaching Scandinavia: letters, printed books, Scandinavian students in Wittenberg or the presence of continental reformers in Scandinavia. In the early Reformation-period, we can

---

55   Undorf, 'Buchhandel und Buchsammeln', pp. 16–17.
56   Collijn, *Sveriges bibliografi*, 2, pp. 239–241.
57   Brask had written to the Brigittine brothers in Vadstena in 1524, reminding them of the ban on selling, buying, receiving or reading Lutheran literature. He further admitted in a public letter to the citizens of Söderköping that Lutheran books had already been imported into the city by foreign merchants for some years; Undorf, *From Gutenberg to Luther*, pp. 275–278.
58   Nielsen, *Dansk bibliografi*, 1, no. 163.

almost speak in Sweden of a Reformation without Luther, that is, without his words, yet certainly not without his thoughts.

There was not just one print centre in the Scandinavian world; this sentence is just as true as another, namely, there was not just one centre of the Reformation. Import, selling and reading of reformed literature reveal a hidden power struggle over theological supremacy. Early modern Scandinavian book collections show signs of other reformers often occupying a quantitatively more important place than Martin Luther.[59] In effect, in the early modern period neither was Luther the main author of the Reformation nor was Wittenberg the main force in the Scandinavian book trade. In the libraries of Sveno Jacobi (c.1480–1554) and Hogenskild Bielke (1538–1605) in Sweden, and in the monastery at Øm and the library of Lutheran pastor Peder Sørensen (1542–1602) in Denmark, we generally find more books written by Philipp Melanchthon, Johann Bugenhagen (1485–1558), and Johannes Brenz (1499–1570) than by Martin Luther.[60] Brenz and other important reformers saw their works printed and distributed to northern Europe by publishers in Frankfurt am Main, Basel and Leipzig. This is a good illustration of the afore-mentioned thesis, that religion could set the framework for a book market that still developed largely according to its own inner dynamics, with readers creating collections that reflected this specific infrastructure.

## 4 Early Modern Book Imports

A monopolised domestic book market did not at all collide with book imports from abroad. The Scandinavian monarchies were aware of the limitations of domestic production and were often the first to perceive such limitations, the general lack of interest in printing books in one of the Scandinavian languages abroad, and the need for specialised literature that only an international market could satisfy. Communication with and knowledge of the capacities of foreign printer-publishers were an essential part of book importation. But sometimes even Scandinavian books reached readers outside their home countries, and

---

59   Undorf, 'Buchhandel und Buchsammeln', pp. 24–25; Undorf, 'Reformation ohne Luther?', pp. 273–276 and 280.

60   Czaika, *Sveno Jacobi*; Undorf, 'Buchhandel und Buchsammeln', pp. 25–46 (Hogenskild Bielke); Bo Gregersen and Carsten Selch Jensen (eds.), *Øm Kloster: Kapitler af et middelalderligt cistercienserabbedis historie* (Emborg: Syddansk Universitetsforlag, 2003); Hans Michelsen, *Peder Sørensen: En præst og hans bøger: en bog- og bibliotekshistorisk undersøgelse* (Roskilde: Roskilde Stiftsblad, 1995).

with this the information about the commercial opportunities that lay in the production of sought-after vernacular books.

The ecology of the world of the printed book is rich, with niches for specified groups of customers. Accordingly, print centres of importance for an ecclesiastic or academic audience were not necessarily equipped for the needs of a profane reader. The books collected by the Swedish politician Hogenskild Bielke over the span of fifty years provide a wealth of examples.[61] Here it is possible to highlight only a few aspects of the infrastructure of book-buying in Scandinavia. Of course, Swedish prayer books were sold in Finland, which at that time was an integrated part of the kingdom of Sweden. But it is a surprise to find Swedish psalters on the book market of the Danish capital Copenhagen in 1568, at a time when both countries were at war with each other.[62]

Captured during the Danish-Swedish war of 1567–1568, Hogenskild Bielke during his honorary captivity still was able to explore and exploit the book market of Copenhagen. The market was limited, yet international. Seventy to eighty percent of the 112 titles acquired by Bielke in 1568 came from German printer-publishers. Only eight percent were printed in Denmark. What should be underscored here is the relatively high number of Swedish books acquired by Bielke: nine percent. Neither geographical distance nor the ongoing war between Denmark and Sweden were obstacles to the importation of books to the Danish book market. One of the Swedish books acquired by Bielke was probably the *Catechismus* printed in 1567. Quite a few of the titles in Bielke's book list had been printed no later than 1567. That seems to apply particularly to the books from Stockholm and Leipzig. In the 1520s, the newly elected king of Sweden had complained that Christiern Pedersen's books were too widespread in Sweden for his taste.[63] So far we have no knowledge of any Danish complaint about Swedish religious books travelling the other way half a century later.

From the second half of the sixteenth century on, we can continue following Hogenskild Bielke, now in his exploration of the book market of Stockholm, the Swedish capital. The bulk of his library has been reconstructed in the University Library of Uppsala, including his book acquisitions from the beginning of the 1570s until the turn of the century.[64] We also have another book list dated 1578. If we combine all our information about the origins of the preserved books in

---

61   Wolfgang Undorf, *Hogenskild Bielke's Library: A Catalogue of the Famous 16th Century Swedish Private Collection* (Uppsala: Acta Universitatis Upsaliensis, 1995).
62   Undorf, 'Buchhandel und Buchsammeln', pp. 27, 30ff.
63   Undorf, *From Gutenberg to Luther*, p. 63.
64   Undorf, *Hogenskild Bielke's library*.

Hogenskild Bielke's book collection, we see the primacy of Frankfurt am Main, with almost double the numbers of titles as compared to Wittenberg and Basel (in second and third place, respectively). And almost all of these books were acquired in Scandinavia, mainly Stockholm. The analysis of the library of the former royal secretary, Henrik Matsson Huggut, leads to a similar result, except for an almost provoking lack of Swedish books: a majority of the identifiable editions was printed in Basel, Wittenberg and Frankfurt am Main.[65] Just as Bielke, after his return to Sweden in 1568 Huggut has been residing in central Sweden and Finland exclusively. So the books that he acquired after that date were books that had been imported to Sweden to be sold on the book markets of Stockholm and Turku/Åbo.

Religion influenced not only national and international politics, but also the general boundaries of the international book market of which Scandinavia was a part. That is why the book markets of Copenhagen and Stockholm were so firmly grounded in the central and northern European Lutheran or reformed sphere. But the practical configuration of the infrastructure that provided Scandinavia with books followed other criteria as well. What is striking when we look at the literature acquired by Bielke in the Frankfurt editions, is the variety of genres, from light fiction to history, from medicine and law to economics and religious literature. No other printing town in Europe could provide such a wealth of genres within a politically correct religious framework, and no politics or confession could do anything against it.

## 5 Printing Abroad in the Vernacular

The registration of books printed in Scandinavia or in Scandinavian languages in the context of contemporary inventories of private book collections is an absolute exception, mostly due to the lack of the books' status in the eyes of the owner or heirs. We therefore have to turn to institutional collections and recent findings in order to obtain information on where and when books in the vernacular were printed abroad. This enables us to identify long-term structures in the Scandinavian book market, especially a regional cluster of two cities, Lübeck and Rostock, that has been important for the Swedish book market at different times, though with two different approaches to that market.

It is easy to project a dichotomy on the early modern Swedish book market: on one hand, allegedly autonomous yet underdeveloped domestic book production answering to the needs of government and bureaucracy (royal

---

65   Undorf, 'Buchhandel und Buchsammeln', pp. 35–38, 59–60.

decrees, panegyrical printed ephemera) as well as religious and ecclesiastic authorities (liturgical books, psalmbooks and edifying literature); on the other hand, the importation of religious, academic and educational literature (mostly in Latin).[66]

Of academic interest here is the considerably larger late sixteenth-century market for religious and edifying literature that aroused the interest of foreign printer-publishers. Czaika has described a number of hitherto unknown Swedish editions of psalters, prayer books and separate editions of one or a few religious hymns.[67] The National Library in Stockholm has started to unearth and identify a number of fragments collected by its conservation workshop. This collection of mainly padding material from sixteenth- and seventeenth-century book bindings has already been shown to contain several fragments that appear to derive from previously unknown editions of Swedish religious and edifying literature.[68] In the light of these recent discoveries it becomes quite clear that the market for religious and edifying books was much larger and more specific, and domestic demand much higher than previously assumed. This created the business interest of the printer-publishers from Rostock and Lübeck, who were aware of an unsatisfied market with the potential to absorb larger numbers of books.

Among the books described by Czaika, we find both consecutive editions of previously published books as well as first editions that predate already known editions, sometimes by decades. So the demand for religious literature as well as the readiness to assume a commercial risk was quite high. Especially the Swedish psalter seems to have been a veritable blockbuster. One way or another, Lübeck and Rostock printers realised that their colleagues in Stockholm alone could not produce enough copies to satisfy the Swedish and Finnish markets.[69] Consequently, what they launched might be described as *Nachdrucke* or pirated printing, when viewed from an a-historical point of view. Actually, they were legitimate editions produced in substantial numbers of copies (at least 1,500–2,000 each) with an eye on making a profit. The list of thus far known editions of edifying literature printed in Lübeck and Rostock is impressive, as shown in Table 4.1 based on a rough reading of Swedish and Danish national bibliographies.

---

66  Ibid., pp. 53.
67  Czaika, 'Ein weites und weitgehend unbekanntes Feld'.
68  The signature is 288 Et 1 / 288 Bo 5. Among some 20-ish unidentified religious books there are for example 'Euangelia och Epistler' [Stockholm ca 1572?], 'Euangelia' [Lübeck ca 1607?], and a sixteenth century prayer book in Swedish.
69  The most recent discussion of circulation numbers of Swedish printed matter in Otfried Czaika, *Några wijsor om Antichristum (1536) samt handskrivna tillägg* (Skara: Skara stiftshistoriska sällskap, 2019), pp. 29–38.

TABLE 4.1  Religious books printed in Lübeck and Rostock for the Danish and Swedish markets

| Year | USTC | Genre | Place of print | Market | Title/Author |
|---|---|---|---|---|---|
| 1537 | 300262 | Postilla | Lübeck | Sweden | Postilla (Olaus Petri) |
| 1542 | 300258 | Psalter | Lübeck | Sweden | Hymnbook |
| 1552 | 302867 | Prayer book | Lübeck | Denmark | Prayer-book |
| 1556 | 302074 | Catechism | Lübeck | Denmark | Catechism (Martin Luther; transl. Peder Palladius) |
| 1556 | 302247 | Edification | Lübeck | Denmark | Jerusalem's misfortune (transl. Peder Tidemand) |
| 1556 | 302978 | New Testament | Lübeck | Denmark | Gospels and epistles |
| 1556 | 302247 | Passio | Lübeck | Denmark | Passio (Hans Tausen; transl. Peder Tidemand) |
| 1556 | 302360 | Psalter | Lübeck | Denmark | Hymnbook |
| 1557 | 302075 | Catechism | Lübeck | Denmark | Catechism (Martin Luther; transl. Peder Palladius) |
| 1558 | 302979 | New Testament | Lübeck | Denmark | Gospels and epistles |
| 1558 | 302175 | Prayer book | Lübeck | Denmark | Prayers (Bernardino Ochino; transl. Peder Palladius) |
| 1558 | 302383 | Psalter | Lübeck | Denmark | Psalm 51 (Hieronimo Savonarola; transl. Peder Palladius) |
| 1558 | 302361 | Psalter | Lübeck | Denmark | Hymnbook |
| 1561 | 302386 | Psalter | Lübeck | Denmark | Psalm 80 (Hieronimo Savonarola; transl. Peder Palladius) |
| 1564 | 300111 | Consolation | Rostock | Sweden | Book of Consolation (Laurentius Petri Gothus) |
| 1564 | 300112 | Prayer book | Rostock | Sweden | Prayer-book (Laurentius Petri Gothus) |
| 1565 | 302980 | New Testament | Lübeck | Denmark | Gospels and epistles |
| 1566 | 302076 | Catechism | Lübeck | Denmark | Catechism (Martin Luther; transl. Peder Palladius) |
| 1566 | 302362 | Psalter | Lübeck | Denmark | Hymnbook |
| 1567 | 302077 | Catechism | Lübeck | Denmark | Catechism (Martin Luther; transl. Peder Palladius) |
| 1568 | 302079 | Catechism | Lübeck | Denmark | Catechism (Martin Luther; transl. Peder Palladius) |

TABLE 4.1 Religious books printed in Lübeck and Rostock for the Danish and Swedish markets (*cont.*)

| Year | USTC | Genre | Place of print | Market | Title/Author |
|---|---|---|---|---|---|
| 1568 | 302248 | Edification | Lübeck | Denmark | Jerusalem's misfortune (transl. Peder Tidemand) |
| 1568 | 302981 | New Testament | Lübeck | Denmark | Gospels and epistles |
| 1568 | 302248 | Passio | Lübeck | Denmark | Passio (Hans Tausen; transl. Peder Tidemand) |
| 1568 | 302861 | Prayer book | Lübeck | Denmark | Prayer-book |
| 1568 | 302363 | Psalter | Lübeck | Denmark | Hymnbook |
| 1569 | 302872 | Prayer book | Lübeck | Denmark | Prayer-book |
| 1571 | 300087 | Psalter | Rostock | Sweden | Songs |
| 1572 | 302178 | Prayer book | Rostock | Denmark | Prayers (Bernardino Ochino; transl. Peder Palladius) |
| 1572 | 300440 | Prayer book | Rostock | Sweden | Prayers (Johannes Avenarius) |
| 1574 | 300462 | Psalter | Rostock | Sweden | Psalter (Petrus Michaelis) |
| 1575 | 302873 | Prayer book | Rostock | Denmark | Prayer-book |
| 1577 | 2215990 | Consolation | Rostock | Sweden | Restoration verse (Grosch, Johann; transl. Petrus Johanis Gothus) |
| 1577 | 300403 | Prayer book | Rostock | Sweden | Prayer-book (Petrus Johannis Gothus) |
| 1581 | 1700321 | Consolation | Rostock | Denmark | Book of Consolation (Jens Andersen) |
| 1584 | 300528 | Psalter | Rostock | Sweden | Hymns |
| 1584 | 300527 | Psalter | Rostock | Sweden | Songs |
| 1586 | 300519 | Catechism | Lübeck | Sweden | Catechism |
| 1586 | 302982 | New Testament | Lübeck | Denmark | Gospels and epistles |
| 1586 | 300520 | New Testament | Lübeck | Sweden | Gospels and epistles |
| 1586 | 300518 | Passio | Lübeck | Sweden | Passio |
| 1586 | 300522 | Psalter | Lübeck | Sweden | Hymnbook |
| 1586 | 300521 | Psalter | Lübeck | Sweden | Songs |
| 1587 | 302085 | Catechism | Lübeck | Denmark | Catechism (Martin Luther; transl. Peder Palladius) |
| 1587 | 303022 | Edification | Lübeck | Denmark | Jerusalem's misfortune (transl. Peder Tidemand) |

TABLE 4.1 Religious books printed in Lübeck and Rostock for the Danish and Swedish markets (*cont.*)

| Year | USTC | Genre | Place of print | Market | Title/Author |
|---|---|---|---|---|---|
| 1587 | 302849 | Passio | Lübeck | Denmark | Passio (Johannes Bugenhagen; transl. Peder Palladius) |
| 1587 | 302857 | Prayer book | Lübeck | Denmark | Prayer-book |
| 1587 | 302369 | Psalter | Lübeck | Denmark | Hymnbook |
| 1588 | 2213115 | Catechism | Lübeck | Sweden | Catechism |
| 1588 | 300467 | Passio | Lübeck | Sweden | Passio |
| 1589 | 300495 | New Testament | Lübeck | Sweden | Gospels and epistles |
| 1589 | 300496 | Psalter | Lübeck | Sweden | Hymnbook |
| 1590 | 300487 | Prayer book | Lübeck | Sweden | Prayer-book (Martinus Olai) |
| 1590 | 300488 | Prayer book | Rostock | Sweden | Prayer-book |
| 1592 | 300325 | Consolation | Rostock | Sweden | The Path to Deliverance (Petrus Johannis Gothus) |
| 1592 | 303358 | Edification | Lübeck | Denmark | Jerusalem's misfortune (transl. Peder Tidemand) |
| 1592 | 300326 | Edification | Rostock | Sweden | The Christian Knight (Johannes Spangenberg) |
| 1592 | 303352 | New Testament | Lübeck | Denmark | Gospels and epistles |
| 1592 | 303312 | Passio | Lübeck | Denmark | Passio (Johannes Bugenhagen; transl. Peder Palladius) |
| 1592 | 303291 | Prayer book | Lübeck | Denmark | Prayer-book |
| 1593 | 303334 | Catechism | Lübeck | Denmark | Catechism (Martin Luther; transl. Peder Palladius) |
| 1593 | 303357 | Edification | Lübeck | Denmark | Jerusalem's misfortune (transl. Peder Tidemand) |
| 1593 | 300279 | Edification | Rostock | Sweden | The Power of the Saints (Pseudo-Anselmus; transl. Petrus Johannis Gothus) |
| 1593 | 300305 | Edification | Rostock | Sweden | Sinner's Mirror (Hieronimus Savonarola; transl. Petrus Johannis Gothus) |
| 1593 | 303353 | New Testament | Lübeck | Denmark | Gospels and epistles |

TABLE 4.1 Religious books printed in Lübeck and Rostock for the Danish and Swedish markets (*cont.*)

| Year | USTC | Genre | Place of print | Market | Title/Author |
|---|---|---|---|---|---|
| 1593 | 303311 | Passio | Lübeck | Denmark | Passio (Johannes Bugenhagen; transl. Peder Palladius) |
| 1593 | 303305 | Prayer book | Lübeck | Denmark | Prayer-book |
| 1593 | 303339 | Psalter | Lübeck | Denmark | Hymnbook |
| 1593? | 1786204 | Prayer book | Lübeck | Denmark | Prayer-book |
| 1594 | 300296 | Catechism | Lübeck | Sweden | Catechism |
| 1594 | 1786205 | Edification | Lübeck | Sweden | Edification (Olaus Petri & Laurentius Petri) |
| 1594 | 300274 | New Testament | Lübeck | Sweden | Gospels and epistles |
| 1594 | 300295 | Passio | Lübeck | Sweden | Passio |
| 1594 | 303301 | Prayer book | Lübeck | Denmark | Prayers (Johannes Habermann; transl. Hans Christensen Sthen) |
| 1594 | 300290 | Prayer book | Lübeck | Sweden | Prayer-book |
| 1594 | 300291 | Psalter | Lübeck | Sweden | Hymnbook |
| 1594 | 300289 | Psalter | Lübeck | Sweden | Hymnbook |
| 1594? | 303304 | Catechism | Rostock | Denmark | Catechismus (Martin Luther; transl. Peder Palladius) |
| 1595 | 302457 | Postilla | Lübeck | Denmark | Postilla (Johannes Spangenberg; transl. Peder Tidemand) |
| 1595 | 303338 | Psalter | Lübeck | Denmark | Hymnbook |
| 1595? | 303354 | New Testament | Lübeck | Denmark | Gospels and epistles |
| 1596 | 302086 | Catechism | Rostock | Denmark | Catechism (Martin Luther; transl. Peder Palladius) |
| 1596 | 303023 | Edification | Rostock | Denmark | Jerusalem's misfortune (transl. Peder Tidemand) |
| 1596 | 302984 | New Testament | Rostock | Denmark | Gospels and epistles |
| 1596 | 302851 | Passio | Rostock | Denmark | Passio (Johannes Bugenhagen; transl. Peder Palladius) |
| 1596 | 302859 | Prayer book | Rostock | Denmark | Prayer-book |
| 1596 | 302372 | Psalter | Rostock | Denmark | Hymnbook |
| 1597 | 300398 | Consolation | Rostock | Sweden | Book of Consolation (Petrus Johannis Gothus) |

TABLE 4.1  Religious books printed in Lübeck and Rostock for the Danish and Swedish markets (*cont.*)

| Year | USTC | Genre | Place of print | Market | Title/Author |
|---|---|---|---|---|---|
| 1597 | 300388 | Luther | Rostock | Sweden | Sententier (Martin Luther; transl. Petrus Johannis Gothus) |
| 1598 | 300386 | Postilla | Rostock | Sweden | Book of Sermons (Petrus Johannis Gothus) |
| 1599 | 679534 | Edification | Rostock | Sweden | Kristlige riddaren (Caspar Huberinus; transl. Nicolaus Balck) |
| 1599 | 302917 | Psalter | Lübeck | Denmark | Psalmer |
| 1599 | 300353 | Psalter | Rostock | Sweden | The Book of Psalms |
| 1600 | 302088 | Catechism | Lübeck | Denmark | Catechism (Martin Luther; transl. Peder Palladius) |
| 1600 | 303336 | Edification | Lübeck | Denmark | Jerusalem's misfortune (transl. Rasmus Glad) |

The production in Lübeck and Rostock of books in the vernacular for the Swedish and the Danish markets show similarities, but also differences. The most surprising similarity is the fact that according to my count, the percentage of the foreign production of religious and edifying literature in the vernacular is in both cases 25% (see figures below). Both numbers cover a whole range of popular genres, concentrating on various forms of edifying literature, with prayer books and psalters in first and second place; apparently these were always in great demand.[70] Both cities produced large numbers of prayer-books and psalters. In third and fourth places for the Danish market one finds editions of catechisms and the New Testament for daily reading, the *Evangelier & epistler*. The Swedish market, by comparison, asked more for books of consolation and edification.

What is striking is the fact that printing in these genres was not especially frequent in either Denmark nor Sweden, speaking of the period from the 1520s to the 1560s, and definitely not in numbers of editions. But the numbers grew rapidly during the last three decades of the sixteenth century. In Denmark, the increase in the percentage of editions in certain genres before and after circa 1560 ranged from 138% (prayer books) up to 800% (Passio). If we examine

---

[70] On the case of the Swedish psalters, see Otfried Czaika, *Then Swenska Psalmeboken 1582* (Skara: Skara stiftshistoriska sällskap, 2016), p. 20.

the total output when divided between the periods from the 1520s to 1569 and from 1570 to 1600, the production during the last three decades exceeds that of the five preceding decades by 370%, on average.[71] The Lübeck and Rostock editions explicitly strengthened the market for some until then underrepresented genres, such as catechisms and the *Evangelier og epistler*.

With reservation for inaccuracies in computing the figures and our limited knowledge of the real output in the sixteenth century, the Swedish results with respect to domestic production are still quite staggering. Half of the genres analysed underwent a marked decline in the numbers of domestic editions, for instance the literature of consolation and edification, postillas and psalters. But when we consider the total number of printed works available during the sixteenth century and produced both in Sweden and abroad for the Swedish market, then we clearly see the importance of and the opportunity for the printers in Lübeck and Rostock. They did not produce only in genres that provided stable sales over the decade; they definitely helped to some extent to balance the supply demanded in genres that the Swedish printers had increasingly neglected since the 1570s, thus increasing especially the numbers of psalters available on the market during the period from the 1580s to the 1590s.

What then did Lübeck and Rostock produce in the main genres and what was their proportion of the total domestic production in Denmark and Sweden? In the Swedish case, there is extensive correspondence between the outcomes of the two producing segments, the domestic and foreign publishing. With the exception of the editions of the Catechism and prayer books, the proportions of productions are congruent with each other (see Table 4.1). The printers of Lübeck and Rostock together produced in concordance with the output of their colleagues in Stockholm. Remembering the limited numbers of editions that we have knowledge of, nonetheless, the proportions indicate that the German printers produced in accordance with the requirements of the market.

The situation in Denmark looks a bit different, though again it has to be remembered that the numbers of editions registered in the national bibliography is limited. The Lübeck and Rostock-based printers in this case still emphasised the production of editions in a complementary order. The most obvious case is the genre of consolation literature with only 1 title produced abroad against an impressive 39 within the realms of the Danish kingdom.

---

71  These figures are based on the number of printed works registered in the national bibliographies of Denmark and Sweden respectively.

TABLE 4.2   Religious books printed in Swedish or Danish in Sweden, Denmark and abroad in the sixteenth century

|  | Swedish books |  | Danish books |  |
| --- | --- | --- | --- | --- |
| Genre | Domestic | Foreign | Domestic | Foreign |
| Catechism | 16 | 3 | 13 | 10 |
| Consolation | 13 | 4 | 39 | 1 |
| Edification | 24 | 6 | 26 | 7 |
| New Testament | 10 | 3 | 8 | 9 |
| Passio | 10 | 3 | 8 | 6 |
| Postilla | 3 | 2 | 5 | 1 |
| Prayer Book | 12 | 6 | 19 | 12 |
| Psalter | 28 | 11 | 54 | 11 |
| Sum total: | 116 (7%) | 35 (23%) | 172 (75%) | 57 (25%) |

SOURCE: COLLIJN, *SVENSK BIBLIOGRAFI*. NIELSEN, *DANSK BIBLIOGRAFI*

## 6   Geography

The figures presented here seem to indicate not so much a significant rise in population at the end of the sixteenth century, but that Sweden and Denmark had entered a period of intensified confessionalization and increase of literacy, together with the growth of the market for edifying and religious literature, especially for prayer-books and psalters. Otfried Czaika has presented a well-founded theory that the number of psalters printed in Sweden alone might have reached totals from 20,000 to 80,000 at the least. This theory, among others, is based on an equally well-founded assumption that we might know about only half of all Swedish psalters printed in the sixteenth century.[72] We have reason to believe that the market for texts printed in the vernacular was stronger in both countries and, at the same time, that an international business was stronger than previously assumed. The number of copies of psalters alone printed in and for Sweden during the sixteenth century, therefore, might have been directed at a much wider market than just the feudal, ecclesiastical and urban elites. These figures also confirm another insight, namely, the existence of a north-eastern cluster of printing towns and its exceptional importance for

---

72   Czaika, 'Ein weites und weitgehend unbekanntes Feld', p. 103.

the book markets and the reading public in Denmark and Sweden. According to the Swedish national bibliography, Lübeck and Rostock were in fact the only continental towns producing books in the vernacular matching these genres for the Swedish market.[73] That was not quite the case with regard to the Danish market, which received a small numbers of relevant books from four other towns as well: Hamburg and Erfurt (one title each); Antwerp (eight titles from 1531, due to Christiern Pedersen's collaboration with the printer Willem Vorsterman); and Magdeburg (eighteen titles from the late 1530s to 1556). Yet, the quantitative contribution of these four printing towns to the Danish market is negligible in comparison to that of Lübeck and Rostock.

Finally, what does all this tell us about geography and its impact on the Scandinavian book trade and book culture in the sixteenth century? The four continental cities, besides Lübeck and Rostock, that contributed between one and a few editions each to the Danish of book market provide us with at least one interesting bit of information with regard to this question: that geographical vicinity was not decisive. Otherwise, the printers of Hamburg, directly on the border with Denmark, would have been in much wider demand.[74] Instead, we have to consider geography in connection with trade routes in general, and (quite literally) the speed at which books travelled in particular. From the start in the middle of the fifteenth century, books were able to travel long distances in a relatively short time. Within a single year, a Venetian print, dated 15 February 1493, reached Nuremberg, where it was bound together with a Koberger print, dated 1492, in a binding that had used printer's waste from the Schedel *Liber chronicarum* of 12 July 1493, finally reaching Rostock where it was acquired by a Danish student, Severinus Pauli. Another example is the Dutch 1482 edition of the *Dialogus creaturarum moralisatus* which provided the model for the edition printed in Stockholm the following year, 1483.[75]

As much as religion cannot be regarded other than a major force defining boundaries and framing conditions under which early modern book trade could take place and book cultures built up, the importance of religious centres at different times did not correspond with their relative importance in the book trade. Rome did not provide Scandinavia with books before the Reformation. And despite the transformation of Wittenberg from a sleepy provincial university town to a major player in the Protestant book world thanks to Martin Luther, its position in the middle of the world of the Reformation

---

73    Collijn, *Sveriges bibliografi*, 1, pp. xxvi–xxxi.
74    During the years 1489–1510, Johannes Borchardes was the only Hamburg-based printer of some significance before the Reformation; Undorf, *From Gutenberg to Luther*, p. 20.
75    Undorf, *From Gutenberg to Luther*, pp. 70, 201.

was not reflected in the same manner in sixteenth-century book collections. Geographically speaking, the distance between Copenhagen in 1568 and Frankfurt am Main was greater than the distance to Wittenberg. Still, the majority of the identified books acquired by the imprisoned Swedish officer Hogenskild Bielke in Copenhagen came from Frankfurt am Main and Stockholm despite the geographical distance and political obstacles. It is only after 1578 that Wittenberg rose to prominence and reached second place among the identified books in Bielke's book collection, possibly because of the transition from the period of establishment of the Reformation to the confessionalization of the Lutheran church.[76] The same trinity of printing places that dominated the Latin book collection of Hogenskild Bielke (Frankfurt am Main, Wittenberg and Basel) also did so among the places of origin in the library of Henrik Matsson around 1600.[77]

Within the primary boundaries of faith and nation, trade overcame geographical boundaries, and individuals found ways to at least temporarily draw new maps. It was hardly predictable that Odense would play a major role in Danish book printing immediately after 1500, except for the initiative and the money of Hans Urne.[78] And, as mentioned earlier, it was due to Christiern Pedersen's studies at the university in Paris and his major influence in the Danish church as dean of the cathedral in Lund, which was then seat of the Danish archbishop, that the printers of Paris gained that enormous importance in the 1510s. If we move our attention to the end of the sixteenth century, the national bibliographies of Denmark and Sweden suggest that certain individuals at different places actually gave rise to extensive publication activities. Usually this was a question of publications by Danes or Swedes living abroad, and not about the Scandinavian book market. Works in Latin written by Peder Palladius (1503–1560) and Niels Hemmingsen (1513–1600), Johannes Svenonius and Nicolaus Chesnecopherus (1574–1622) were printed abroad in larger numbers, but usually not for export back to their home countries.[79] Instead, what was exported to Scandinavia were mostly religious books in the vernacular for a mass market that has largely remained under the radar of book historians

---

76   Undorf, 'Buchhandel und Buchsammeln', pp. 29–34, 52.
77   Terhi Kiiskinen, *The Library of the Finnish Nobleman, Royal secretary and Trustee Henrik Matsson (ca. 1540–1617)* (Helsinki: Finnish Academy of Science and Letters, 2004).
78   Undorf, *From Gutenberg to Luther*, pp. 36–47.
79   Nielsen, *Dansk bibliografi*, 1–4; Palladius, nos. 1225–1226, 1256, 1258–1266, 1269, 1271, 1275–1286; Hemmingsen, nos. 743, 746, 748, 800–807, 811–812, 815–818, 820–833, 837, 840–847, 850, 852–854, 858, 861–865, 871–885, 906–909, 914–916. Collijn, *Sveriges bibliografi*, 1; Svenonius pp. 211, 231–232; Chesnecopherus, pp. 164, 196, 312–313.

due to the massive rate of destruction that affected prayer books, psalters, books of edification and consolation, and books in similar literary categories.

It is hoped that the present study helped to identify the main forces that shaped early modern Scandinavian book culture. Geography as well as religion seem to have provided a major overall framework for general trade and especially the book trade. Both established specific borders that admittedly limited the operational range within the book world and the prospects for individual customers for acquiring books to build collections. Of course, the most efficient border at that time was drawn by religion, especially when supported and upheld by the state, by censorship and force if necessary. Throughout the sixteenth century, this border was in fact a *conditio sine qua non* for trade and collection building, until the wars in the seventeenth century created, especially for Sweden, access to Catholic books on an unprecedented scale. Warfare and the political, economic and cultural ambitions of the Swedish government and its leading figures were then the new driving forces. They had such an enormous impact, at least on Swedish book culture, that for decades throughout the first half of the seventeenth century they dictated the terms on which Swedish libraries operated. Even though considered treasures and trophies at the moment of their 'acquisition' as well as in official declarations, within a short time war booty turned into a nuisance for the librarians and universities that had to deal with it.[80]

The wars of the seventeenth century provide an example of what at times was an overwhelming driving force shaping book history from the outside. Neither the number of books, the places of their printing or the contents of many of these books really corresponded with the needs of the receiving institutions in the long run. Nor did they fit well into the geographical boundaries of Swedish book, literary and academic culture at that time. Libraries and books were exploited, instrumentalized by politics. Most beneficial for Scandinavian book culture were the self-determined actions within the general boundaries set by certain major forces. These actions reveal reciprocal dynamics that cannot be fully explained by a Centre–Periphery paradigm based on geographic location or systemic position. What determined the range and characteristics of early modern Scandinavian book cultures was an intricate interplay of external and internal forces, revealing at times more or less predictable opportunities for printers, customers and readers.

---

80 Peter Sjökvist and Krister Östlund, 'Bokliga krigsbyten som kulturtransfer?', in Peter Sjökvist (ed.), *Kulturarvsperspektiv: Texter från en seminarieserie om specialsamlingar i Sverige* (Uppsala: Uppsala universitet, 2018), pp. 141–149, here p. 146.

CHAPTER 5

# English and Scottish Jesuits and Print Culture of the Sixteenth-Century Grand Duchy of Lithuania

*Hanna Mazheika*

On 6 May 1604, at Vilnius's (Wilno) Cathedral of Saint Stanislaus, the coffin with the remains of Prince Casimir Jagiellon (1458–1484) was moved from the crypt and placed at the altar. On 10 May 1604, an Apostolic letter issued by Pope Clement VIII was read, which allowed Casimir to be venerated as a saint in Poland and Lithuania.[1] Vilnius was to be the centre of his cult. The ceremony on 10 May 1604 was led by Bishop of Vilnius Benedykt Wojna (d. 1615) with the participation of the Chancellor of Lithuania, Lew Sapieha (1557–1633). During the celebration Sapieha accepted on behalf of King Sigismund III a Papal gift: a *labarum* with the effigy of Casimir. It was installed in the Cathedral where Casimir's relics were kept; in the same year, the foundation stone of Saint Casimir Church was laid in Vilnius. The procession then proceeded to the Academy of Vilnius where its students publicly read the commemorative poems they had composed to celebrate Prince Casimir's canonisation.[2] All of them were published by the Academy press under the title *Theatridium Poeticum Sanctissimo et Castissimo Poetae D[ivo] Casimiro* (A Little Poetic Theatre for the Most Venerable and Pious Blessed Poet Casimir).[3] Among the ninety-one poems four were composed by the Scottish students. Thomas Abercrombie wrote a poem entitled 'S. Casimirus miles Christianus'; the poem 'Anagramma ex nomine a S. Casimiri' was created by the Scot Joannes Nicolaus

---

1 Initiated by Sigismund III who sought to renew the cult of Saint Casimir, in 1602 Clement VIII issued the brief and approved the decision of the Sacred Congregation of Rites to proclaim the day of 4 March as Casimir's feast, but only within the Commonwealth. K. Paul Žygas, 'Dogma, Art and Politics: Roman aspects of St. Casimir's Chapel in Vilnius', *Journal of Baltic Studies*, 27 (1996), pp. 175–212, here p. 182.
2 Ibid., p. 183.
3 The edition of *Theatridium Poeticum* was bound with *Theatrum S. Casimiri: In quo ipsius prosapia, vita, miracula, et illustris pompa in solemni eiusdem apotheoseos instauratione, Vilnae Lithuaniae metropoli, v. Id. Maij, anno D[omi]ni M.DC.IV. instituta graphice proponuntur ...* ([Vilnae]: Typographicis Academiae Societatis Iesu, [1604]), USTC 250240; Jan Okoń, 'Pokłosie Skargowskie: "książki polskie" o św. Kazimierzu Jagiellończyku ... (na tropach druku i egzemplarza)', *Annales Universitatis Paedagogicae Cracoviensis / Studia ad Bibliothecarum Scientiam Pertinentia*, 11 (2013), pp. 44–60, here p. 58, n. 42.

---

© HANNA MAZHEIKA, 2023 | DOI:10.1163/9789004441217_007
This is an open access chapter distributed under the terms of the CC BY-NC-ND 4.0 license.

Dizos (his origin was not indicated in the publication); the third contributor of Scottish origin was Patrick Abercrombie with the poem 'Epitymbion;' and finally Joannes Petrevius (who was not designated as a Scot in the printed edition) published 'Grata perpetuitas – non Tutum patrocinium'.[4]

The process of the canonisation of Prince Casimir lasted for two decades and was concluded in 1621 when his name was included in the *Missale Romanum* and the *Breviarium Romanum*, which made him a saint of the whole Catholic Church rather than only within the boundaries of the Polish-Lithuanian Commonwealth. This meant that students of various ethnic origins from the Academy eagerly seized the opportunity to engage in the celebration of the memory of the Polish-Lithuanian prince who had been adopted as a patron of the Grand Duchy of Lithuania but who did not have full sainthood at that time and had never been an object of veneration among the Catholics of Western Europe. By looking at how much Scottish and English Jesuits were keen to support and advance the religious traditions of the host state, the present study seeks to reveal the extent to which they aligned themselves with the Catholic community of Lithuania and became accustomed to the local religious tendencies.

## 1   The Teaching Staff of English and Scottish Origin at the Academy of Vilnius

The Grand Duchy of Lithuania was subordinated to the Austrian Province of the Society of Jesus, but in 1574 the Superior General Everard Mercurian (1514–1580) created a separate Polish Province of the Jesuit Order covering the territories of Poland, Prussia, Lithuania and Muscovy, which existed in this form until the year of 1608 when the Lithuanian Province was separated from it. The Counter-Reformation in Poland-Lithuania took great advantage of educational exchange with other European countries. From its foundation as a Jesuit college in Vilnius in the late 1560s and upgraded to Academy in 1579, the institution attracted many foreign academics. It is worth noticing that Vilnius Academy offered Jesuit training of a level higher than other institutions of the region – those in Braniewo (Braunsberg) in Royal Prussia and Olomouc in

---

4   *Theatridium Poeticum*, fols. 31, 38, 50–51, 58, 65–66; Stanislaw Rostowski, *Lituanicarum Societas Jesu historiarum libri decem* (Paris: Victor Palmė, G. Lebrocquy, 1877), pp. 439–440. It should be pointed out that according to Poplatek Joannes Nicolaus Dizos was a Swede: Jan Poplatek, 'Wykaz alumnów seminarium papieskiego w Wilnie 1582–1773', *Ateneum Wileńskie*, 11 (1936), pp. 218–282, here p. 246.

Moravia – with a curriculum identical to that of the general school system of the Jesuit Order.[5] Unlike the college in Braniewo, the Vilnius College had the *studia superiora* which provided more mature courses at an advanced level. The structure of the Academy of Vilnius can be seen in the 1592 description made by a former student from England Samuel Lewkenor (*c*.1571–1615):

> Neere vnto the Church of S. Iohn Baptist, was lately erected a goodly and spacious Colledge, possessed by the Iesuites, in the base courtwherof are 6 schooles faire and large: the first for Grammer, the second for Poetrie, the third for Rhetorique, the fourth for Philosophie, the fift for Diuinitie, the sixt for cases of conscience, named of schoolemen Positiua Theologia. Therein also are many faire and spacious roomes, purposely prouided for publike disputations.[6]

Names of British academics and students have often been mentioned in the context of Anglo-Polish and Anglo-Lithuanian relations, but no picture has emerged of their role in the cultural development of the Grand Duchy. In the second half of the sixteenth century British recusants made much of education to re-establish Catholicism, and the Academy of Vilnius became an important academic centre on the Jesuit educational map, hosting a noticeable number of students of British origin. The ethnic composition of the first teaching staff varied markedly: there was a Croat, a Scot, an Irishman, a Belgian and two Czechs.[7] The presence of English and Scottish Jesuits among those working in Vilnius Academy was particularly noticeable in the last decades of the sixteenth century, even though the employment of the majority of them in the institution was usually short-lived or intermittent. John Hay (*c*.1546–1608), a Scot from Aberdeenshire, was the first British Jesuit to be attached to the staff. He came to Vilnius on 4 July 1570,[8] and taught rhetoric at the college from 1570 until February 1572, when he was sent on mission to Braniewo.[9] In

---

5 Oskar Garstein, *Rome and the Counter-Reformation in Scandinavia: Jesuit Educational Strategy, 1553–1622* (Leiden: Brill, 1992), p. 242.
6 Samuel Lewkenor, *A Discourse not Altogether Vnprofitable, nor Vnpleasant for Such as are Desirous to Know the Situation and Customes of Forraine Cities without Trauelling to See Them Containing a Discourse of All Those Citties wherein Doe Flourish at this Day Priuiledged Vniuersities: Written by Samuel Levvkenor Gentleman* (London: I[ohn] W[indet], 1600), USTC 514818, fol. 55r.
7 Jakub Niedźwiedź, *Kultura literacka Wilna (1323–1655): Retoryczna organizacja miasta* (Kraków: Universitas, 2012), p. 173.
8 László Lukács, *Catalogi personarum et officiorum provinciae Austriae S. I. T. I (1551–1600)* (Rome: Institutum Historicum Societatis Iesu, 1978), p. 327.
9 Lukács, *Catalogi personarum*.

the early 1570s, Hay undertook a public dispute concerning the sacrament of the Eucharist with two Lithuanian Protestants, theologian Andreas Volanus (1530–1610) and poet and translator Andrzej Trzecieski (c.1530–1584), defending the dogma of the real presence of Christ in the Eucharist.[10] The dispute was attended by a large number of the Protestant population of the town.[11] Hay was appointed lecturer in philosophy in 1573 and held this position until 1575.[12] He was an author of two collections of theses, published in Cracow in 1573 and 1574, which were to be used at disputations at Vilnius College during the inauguration of the academic years of 1573/1574 and 1574/1575.[13] William Lambert, an English coadjutor brother, joined the college in 1571 and continued to hold this position until 1573; he died in Lithuania, as indicated in the necrology of the Society of Jesus.[14] The English recusant Adam Brook (Brock), future rector of the Academy, arrived in Vilnius sometime between the years of 1574 and 1578, and there he pronounced his final vows as a Jesuit on 24 August 1578.[15] The English Jesuit James Bosgrave (c.1548–1623) arrived in Vilnius in 1576 and was professor of mathematics until 1580. The Scot Robert Abercrombie (1536–1613), a fellow-graduate of John Hay from Saint Andrews and a teacher of grammar and rhetoric, stayed in Vilnius between 1575 and 1580.[16] By 1580, all of them for different reasons left the Grand Duchy of Lithuania, when they came to the attention of John Rogers, an English agent in Poland, who asked Mikołaj Radziwiłł 'the Red' (1512–1584), the leader of the Protestants in Lithuania, for support in apprehending English recusants in the region.[17] Adam Brook however returned to Vilnius in the early seventeenth century to take up the post of

---

10   Ludwik Grzebień, *Encyklopedia wiedzy o jezuitach na ziemiach Polski i Litwy, 1564–1995*: www.jezuici.krakow.pl/cgi-bin/rjbo?b=enc&n=2126&q=0 (last accessed 17 July 2022); Rostowski, *Lituanicarum Societas Jesu*, p. 41.
11   Ibid., pp. 41–42.
12   Alasdair Roberts, 'Hay, John', *ODNB*: www.oxforddnb.com/view/article/12724?docPos=2 (last accessed 5 March 2017); Lukács, *Catalogi personarum*, pp. 321, 343.
13   Roman Darowski, 'John Hay, SJ, and the Origins of Philosophy in Lithuania', *The Innes Review*, 31 (1980), pp. 7–15, here pp. 10–11.
14   Lukács, *Catalogi personarum*, pp. 326, 344; Henry Foley, *Records of the English Province of the Society of Jesus: Historic Facts Illustrative of the Labours and Sufferings of its Members in the Sixteenth and Seventeenth Centuries*, 7:1: General Statistics of the Province; and Collectanea, Giving Biographical Notices of its Members and many Irish and Scotch Jesuits (London: Burns and Oates, 1882), p. 431.
15   Thomas M. McCoog, *'And Touching Our Society': Fashioning Jesuit Identity in Elizabethan England* (Toronto: Pontific Institute of Medieval Studies, 2013), p. 125, n. 13.
16   Martin Murphy, 'Robert Abercromby, S. J. (1536–1613) and the Baltic Counter-Reformation', *The Innes Review*, 50 (Spring 1999), pp. 58–75, here p. 63.
17   Hanna Mazheika, '"An Earnest Gospeller" and "a Dignified Martyr": Networks of Textual Exchange between the Grand Duchy of Lithuania and England, 1560s–1580s', in Richard

rector of the Academy in the period between 1602 and 1605.[18] He was especially favoured by the Bishop of Vilnius and honoured at the Academy.[19] In the late 1580s, John Howlett (c.1548–1589), instead of fulfilling his assigned mission in Transylvania, became professor of theology at the Academy in Vilnius, where he died on 14 September 1589.[20] In 1590, Laurence Arthur Faunt (1553/4–1591), an English Jesuit theologian, was appointed professor of theology; he too died in Vilnius a year later on 28 February 1591.[21] Another Englishman, Richard Singleton (c.1565–1602), was professor of dogmatic theology in Vilnius in 1600–1602, where he died during the plague on 13 April 1602.[22]

Every British member of the academic staff, except for William Lambert who was however highly valued by Cardinal Stanislaus Hosius (1504–1579) and to whom he served as a physician, had a university degree: Abercrombie and Hay had graduated from the University of Saint Andrews, Brook and Howlett were Oxford graduates.[23] Additionally, Abercrombie attended Louvain before entering the Jesuit novitiate. Richard Singleton studied at Rheims, Rennes and the English College in Rome.[24] Faunt graduated from Louvain and Munich, and went to the English College in Rome.[25]

Some of these Jesuits engaged in the life of the whole Jesuit province beyond the sphere of education. In 1579, Adam Brook was elected by the Polish Province as a delegate to attend the congregation of procurators held in Rome on 2 November 1579.[26] William Good, who was not associated with Vilnius Academy and never went to Lithuania, together with Brook, was sent to

---

Butterwick and Wioletta Pawlikowska (eds.), *Social and Cultural Relations in the Grand Duchy of Lithuania: Microhistories* (New York, Abington: Routledge, 2019), p. 169.

18 Grzebień, *Encyklopedia*: www.jezuici.krakow.pl/cgi-bin/rjbo?b=enc&n=7371&q=0 (last accessed 2 July 2022).

19 Foley, *Records of the English Province*, 7:1, p. 88.

20 Martin Murphy, 'Howlett [Howlet], John', *ODNB*: www.oxforddnb.com/view/article/14000?docPos=2 (last accessed 12 November 2022).

21 Martin Murphy, 'Faunt, Arthur', *ODNB*: www.oxforddnb.com/view/article/9210?docPos=1 (last accessed 12 November 2016).

22 Grzebień, *Encyklopedia*: www.jezuici.krakow.pl/cgi-bin/rjbo?b=enc&n=6137&q=0 (last accessed 14 March 2017).

23 Murphy, 'Robert Abercromby, s.j.', p. 61; James Lenaghan, '"The Sweetness of Polish Liberty": Sixteenth-Century British Jesuit Exiles to Poland-Lithuania', *Reformation*, 15:1 (2010), pp. 133–150, here p. 139.

24 Ibid., p. 140.

25 Marin Murphy, 'Faunt, Arthur', *ODNB*: www.oxforddnb.com/view/article/9210?docPos=1 (last accessed 12 November 2016).

26 McCoog, *'And Touching Our Society'*, p. 126.

represent the Province at the Fourth General Congregation on 7 February 1581 when the next Superior General was to be elected.[27]

In the last decades of the sixteenth and until the mid-seventeenth centuries, other English Jesuits worked at the Academy or resided in the capital of the Grand Duchy of Lithuania. According to the report by John Rogers on intelligence he had gathered in Königsberg in September 1580, '[the] Iesuit Confrers were most at Rome, more at Vilna and many in Brunsberge.'[28] Apart from about those belonging to the Academy, there is only partial information about the presence of English and Scottish Catholics in the city. Rogers does mention among those suspected of belonging to the Jesuit society and residing in England one Partridge, a goldsmith, whose son lived in Vilnius and was 'a favorer of Iesuiters.'[29] English Jesuit Thomas Malins (or Maglius) died in Vilnius in 1600.[30] Richard Gifford (c.1633–1697) and Christopher Robinson (c.1621–1685) joined the Jesuits in Vilnius on 5 September and 10 September 1647 respectively.[31] Robert Forster studied theology at the Academy of Vilnius before he was professed of the four vows on 24 August 1632.[32] In 1657, an English Jesuit, James Brent, died in Vilnius.[33] As for other towns of Lithuania it is known that Simon Jordan of Irish origin was rector of the Jesuit College in Polotsk (Połock) in 1651.

## 2  English and Scottish Students in the Grand Duchy of Lithuania

The success of the Academy was owed to its international character and the high European standards of training it offered, rather than by a very high number of students enrolled. The *peregrinatio academica* was a common phenomenon among European countries as well as within Poland-Lithuania: many

---

27  Rostowski, *Lituanicarum Societas Jesu*, pp. 89, 416.
28  John Rogers to Francis Walsingham, 10 October 1580, Elbing, Charles H. Talbot (ed.), *Elementa ad Fontium Editiones*, 4: Res Polonicæ Elisabetha I Angliæ regnante conscriptæ ex Archivis Publicis Londoniarum (Rome: Institutum Historicum Polonicum Romæ, 1962), p. 18.
29  Ibid., p 33.
30  Henry Foley, *Records of the English Province of the Society of Jesus: Historic Facts Illustrative of the Labours and Sufferings of Its Members in the Sixteenth and Seventeenth Centuries*, 7:2: Facts Illustrative of the Labours and Sufferings of its Members in the Sixteenth and Seventeenth Centuries (London: Burns and Oates, 1883), p. 962.
31  Grzebień, *Encyklopedia*: www.jezuici.krakow.pl/cgi-bin/rjbo?b=enc&n=1759&q=0, www.jezuici.krakow.pl/cgi-bin/rjbo?b=enc&n=5603&q=0 (last accessed 14 March 2017).
32  Foley, *Records of the English Province*, 7:1, pp. 275–276.
33  Ibid., p. 81.

students were transferred from Braniewo or other Jesuit colleges of Central Europe to Vilnius to gain a university education and to be able to follow the wider curriculum.[34] There are no surviving records on the representation of students in the Academy, but it is clear that some of the young men came from England and Scotland. According to research by Arūnas Grickevičius, during the period between 1585 and 1602 there were between 197 and 199 students in the Papal Seminary (a part of the Academy), ten of whom were from England and Scotland.[35] As the seventeenth century progressed, these numbers faded. This was observed because the educational structures for British recusants were finally set up on a firmer basis in the first decades of the century, with two Scots colleges established in Rome and Salamanca, in addition to the existing English colleges in Rome and Douai.

The register of the seminary at Vilnius Academy compiled by Jan Poplatek listed fourteen British expatriates matriculated in the last decades of the sixteenth and early seventeenth centuries. In contrast, the Jesuit College in Braniewo schooled more English and Scottish exiles: between 1579 and 1610, there were 25 students of British origin attending the school in this town of Royal Prussia.[36] Not all students of the Academy in Vilnius were Jesuits: there was a large number of Protestants undertaking studies.[37] There was only one British student registered in the 1580s: Andrew Lock, a Scot, matriculated at the college in Braniewo on 8 May 1582 and on 18 March 1584 he went to Vilnius to continue his *studia superiora* there.[38] In the 1590s, the number of Britons admitted to the Academy increased rapidly. Overall, in 1590 there were 35 students of different nations matriculated at the seminary.[39] Thomas Attomes

---

34   Garstein, *Rome and the Counter-Reformation*, p. 242.
35   The Vilnius Pontifical Seminary was set up as a part of the Academy of Vilnius in 1583. It offered education for young people who seemed to be destined for clerical or priestly vocation. Józef Bieliński, *Uniwersytet Wileński (1579–1831)* (3 vols., Kraków: W. L. Anczyca i Spółka, 1899–1900), 1, p. 83. Arūnas Grickevičius, 'The Seminary of Gregory XIII in Vilnius (1583–1655)', *Lithuanian Historical Studies*, 2 (1997), pp. 72–96, here pp. 79–80.
36   Among these students there were twenty-three Scots. See: Alphons Bellesheim, *History of the Catholic Church of Scotland* (3 vols., Edinburgh: William Blackwood and Sons, 1889), 3, pp. 455–456. James Lenaghan mentions two other students of British origin; they both entered the Jesuit Society in Braniewo but one of them died at a young age; the other one was the native of Poland-Lithuanian but his parents were of Scottish origin, and there is no information if he was a student at the Jesuit college: Lenaghan, 'The Sweetness of Polish Liberty', p. 141.
37   Tomasz Kempa, 'Religious Relations and the Issue of Religious Tolerance in Poland and Lithuania in the 16th and 17th Century', *Sarmatia Europea*, 1 (2010), pp. 31–66, here p. 44.
38   Jan Poplatek, 'Wykaz alumnów', p. 224.
39   Jan Poplatek, 'Zarys dziejów Seminarium Papieskiego w Wilnie 1585–1773', *Ateneum Wileńskie*, 7 (1930), pp. 170–228, here p. 177. Jakub Niedźwiedź, referring to the study of

(probably, Adams) from Shropshire in England studied at the Academy in 1590.[40] The Englishman Gwalter Honsonus entered the Academy in 1590 to start *studia inferiora* but had to leave Vilnius in 1592 for reasons of health.[41] Thomas Hathonus, an Englishman, spent a short period of time in Vilnius in 1592 before he was sent to the English College in Rome.[42]

Samuel Lewkenor, an Englishman mentioned above, enrolled at the Academy in 1592.[43] It was not his first university on the Continent: during his educational peregrination Lewkenor visited many universities around East-Central Europe, as he highly appreciated the education provided by Jesuits. In Poplatek's study he is described as a student of the seminary, but he hardly had any intention of becoming a Catholic priest nor of seeking to conduct missionary activities. He returned to England and later became a Member of the House of Commons.[44] Two Scots, William Douglas and James Lindsey, were admitted to Braniewo on 6 August 1596 and they both were sent to Vilnius on 29 November 1600 to continue their studies. Douglas died in the rank of Ensign during the siege of Smolensk of 1609–1611. Lindsey became a Jesuit in 1601 and soon after he returned to Scotland where he died in 1624.[45] Another two Scots, Thomas Abercrombie and David Leonard Kinnaird (Quinard), matriculated at the Jesuit school in Braniewo on 27 September 1599; on 28 December 1600, they embarked on a journey to Vilnius to continue their education at the Academy.[46] In 1601, Kinnaird became a Jesuit; he was imprisoned in 1626 for two years after Braniewo was seized by King of Sweden Gustavus Adolphus; after his release he was recruited as a chaplain in the Irish regiment of Colonel James Butler, and very likely participated in military campaigns, first in Royal

---

Ludwik Piechnik, *Dzieje Akademii Wileńskiej: Początki Akademii Wileńskiej, 1570–1599* (Rome: Institutum Historicum Societatis Jesu, 1983), provides the number of 600 scholars admitted to Vilnius Academy in the early 1590s. This estimation is notoriously slippery. According to the list of students provided by Poplatek, during the period between 1585 and 1601 there were 177 known scholars attending the institution. But it should be remembered that Poplatek's list contains only the names of those who attended the seminary at the Academy. Niedźwiedź, *Kultura literacka*, p. 175.

40 Poplatek, 'Wykaz alumnów', p. 232.
41 Ibid., p. 233.
42 Ibid.
43 Ibid., p. 238.
44 Alan Davidson and Simon Healy, 'Lewknor, Samuel (1571–?by1615), of Upton Cressett, Salop', in *The History of Parliament: The House of Commons 1604–1629*, ed. by Andrew Thrush and John P. Ferris (Cambridge: Cambridge University Press, 2010): www.history ofparliamentonline.org/volume/1604-1629/member/lewknor-samuel-1571-1615 (last accessed 18 July 2017).
45 Poplatek, 'Wykaz alumnów', p. 242.
46 Ibid.

Prussia and Germany against the Swedes and not long afterwards in Poland against the Muscovites during the Smolensk War of 1632–1634. He died in Nieśwież in 1648.[47] Butler, together with the Englishman Arthur Aston the Junior, was praised by the Protestant leader Krzysztof Radziwiłł (1585–1640) at the Sejm in March 1623 for their service under his command in the campaign of 1622, during which the town of Jelgava (Mitau) in the Duchy of Courland was captured.[48] Patrick Abercrombie from Scotland studied in Vilnius in 1604, after spending five years at school in Braniewo from 1596 till 1601 when he quit his studies, but soon he resumed his education.[49] The Scot Jan Petraeus (Joannes Petrevius) was among the scholars of the Academy in 1604.[50] William Abercrombie and Thomas Duff, both from Scotland, studied in Vilnius until 19 June 1610 when they were sent to Braniewo.[51] Edward Locke took his doctorate of philosophy at Vilnius Academy in 1650 and later became rector of the Irish College in Rome.[52]

3   **The Contribution of English and Scottish Jesuits to Printing Culture of the Grand Duchy of Lithuania**

Not only did Scots and Englishmen work or study at the Academy, but they made an impact on the development of printing culture of the Grand Duchy of Lithuania and contributed to the laudatory and commemorative poetry of the late sixteenth and early seventeenth centuries. Some publications issued by the printing press of the Academy of Vilnius provide additional information and cast some new light on the English and Scottish presence among the students. With the accession of Sigismund III Vasa to the Polish throne in 1587, the Jesuits of Poland-Lithuania produced a stream of complimentary propaganda about the new king. In 1589, the printing office of Mikołaj Krzysztof Radziwiłł 'the Orphan' (1549–1616), one of the most zealous Catholic defenders in the country, produced *Gratulationes Serenissimo Ac Potentissimo Principi Sigismundo III … In … Vilnam adventu factae Ab Academia Vilne[n]si*

---

47   Ibid.; Stephen Wright, 'Butler, James', *ODNB*: www.oxforddnb.com/view/article/4190?docPos=7 (last accessed 15 May 2017); Worthington, *British and Irish Experiences*, pp. 95–96; Rostowski, *Lituanicarum Societas Jesu*, p. 441.
48   Robert I. Frost, 'Scottish Soldiers, Poland-Lithuania and the Thirty Year's War', in Steve Murdoch (ed.), *Scotland and the Thirty Years' War: 1618–1648* (Leiden: Brill, 2001), p. 207.
49   Poplatek, 'Wykaz alumnów', p. 245.
50   Ibid., p. 246.
51   Ibid., p. 247.
52   Foley, *Records of the English Province*, 7:2, pp. 39–40.

*Societatis Iesu* [Congratulations to the Most Serene and Powerful Sovereign Sigismund III ... upon Arrival in Vilnius from Vilnius Academy of the Jesuit Order], a collection of eulogistic poems written by the students of Vilnius Academy in various languages.[53] It was issued on the occasion of the visit of the newly elected King and Great Duke Sigismund to the capital of the Grand Duchy. In the collection there was one overtly panegyric poem in English, called 'To the realme and people of poolande', celebrating the accession of Sigismund.[54] Based on the clumsiness of the verses and the fact that the names of some contributors provided at the end of the booklet were of Polish origin only, Wacław Borowy comes to the conclusion that the author was a Pole.[55] Given the noticeable presence of English-speaking Catholics in Vilnius in the late sixteenth century, however, it was not entirely unlikely that the poem was composed by a person of English origin, albeit one without poetic talent.

William Sotheron, an Englishman, contributed to at least three publications issued by the Academy. In 1594, he wrote two poetic tributes in Latin on the occasions of the deaths of his fellow scholars: Łazarz Kmita, the son of the Palatine of Smolensk Filon Kmita Czarnobylski (*c*.1530–1587), and Adauctus Kownacki.[56] In 1595, he was again among the contributors to express his grief about the deaths of Joannis Barscius, a fellow-student, and Jerzy Jurjewicz Chodkiewicz, the administrator of the Duchy of Samogitia.[57] All the commem-

---

53  *Gratulationes Serenissimo Ac Potentissimo Principi Sigismundo III ... In ... Vilnam adventu factae Ab Academia Vilne[n]si Societatis Iesu* (Wilno: Mikołaj Krzysztof Radziwiłł, 1589), USTC 250194; Wacław Borowy, 'Prześladowani katolicy angielscy i szkoccy w Polsce XVI wieku', *Przegląd Powszechny*, 219 (1938), pp. 110–124, here p. 117.

54  *Gratulationes Serenissimo*, sig. Fii^r.

55  Borowy, 'Prześladowani', p. 117. In contrast, the authorship of some poems in Finnish, Swedish and Latin was determined and ascribed to the students of Scandinavian origin matriculated at the Academy, see: Garstein, *Rome and the Counter-Reformation*, pp. 257–260; Isak Collijn, *Sveriges bibliografi intill år 1600* (3 vols., Uppsala: Svenska Litteratursällskapet, 1927–1938), 3, pp. 97–98.

56  *Parthenicae Sodalitatis in Academia Vilnensi Societatis Jesu: Threni in Exequiis Nobilissimi Clarissimiq. Adolescentis Lazari Philonis Kmitae Czarnobylski Palatinidae Smolenscen; eiusdemq; Academiae Alumni* (Wilno: Ex officina academica societatis Jesu, 1594), USTC 250351, sig. F2v–F3r; Karol Estreicher, *Bibliografia Staropolska*: www.estreicher.uj.edu.pl /staropolska/baza/wpis/?sort=nazwisko_imie&order=1&id=141330&offset=0&index=2 (last accessed 03 October 2015); *Oratio in exequiis nobilis et generosi adolescentis Adaucti Kownacki, studiosi academiae Vilnensis S. J. a Jacobo Evcholcio habita Vilnae in aede sacra D. Joannis ad stvdiosam ivventvtem III kal. aprilis MDXCIV* (Wilno: Ex officina academica Societ. Jesu, 1594), sig. B4r; Ramunė Dambrauskaitė, 'A Latin Funeral Oration from Vilnius (1594): Edited, with introduction and notes', *Humanistica Lovaniensia*, 44 (1995), pp. 250–269, here pp. 255–256, 269.

57  *Funebris Laudatio Et Threnodiae In Exequias ... Joannis Barscii A Studiosa Iuventute Conscriptae In Academia Vilnensi Societatis Iesu* (Vilnae, offic. Acad. S. J., 1595), USTC

orative stanzas produced by him were in Latin verse and were short. Sotheron's name cannot be found among the students in the seminary registry of the Academy but the publication clearly points both to his belonging to the institution and to the incompleteness of the known registry. Samuel Lewkenor published a poem on the death of Albrecht Radziwiłł, Duke of Ołyka and Nieśwież, in *Threnodiae, in obitum illustris[simi] Sac[ri] Rom[ani] Imp[erii] principis et domini, d. Alberti Radziwil[i] ducis in Ołyka et Nieswiz* [Laments, on the Death of the Most Illustrious Prince of the Holy Roman Empire and Master, Sir Albrecht Radziwiłł, Prince of Nieśwież and Ołyka] printed in Vilnius in 1593.[58]

There is nothing surprising in the fact that poetic works by English and Scottish students appeared in print as part of the volumes produced by the Academy. Composing poems was part of the curriculum of early modern institutions,[59] and similar examples could be found across Europe. Nevertheless, there are some cases when English or Scottish recusants published their literary works outside their training assignments. In 1605, Patrick Abercrombie, a student of Vilnius Academy, published a poem on the occasion of the wedding of a doctor of medicine James Arnott, a Scot, and Diana, a daughter of the resident of Vilnius Józef Sienkiewicz.[60] Likewise, three publications authored by the Scottish poet Andrew Leech (or Loch, or Andrzej Loeaechius, Loechius, Lechowicz, d. 1637), a former student of Vilnius Academy, were printed in Vilnius in 1599 and 1612.[61] In Lithuania, Leech very often chose to publish his

---

250357, sig. D<sup>v</sup>; *Parentalia in Obitvm Illvstris et Magnifici Domini D. Georgii Chodkievicii Generalis Capitanei Samogitiae. etc. etc. A Sodalibvs Congregationis Parthenicae, Academiae Viinensis, Societatis Jesv, mortem sodalis svi et moderatoris qvondam vigilantissimi, deflentibvs, conscripta* (Wilno: typographia Academiae Societatis Jesu, 1595), USTC 250366; Estreicher, *Bibliografia Staropolska*: www.estreicher.uj.edu.pl/staropolska/baza/wpis/?sort=nazwisko_imie&order=1&id=188832&offset=0&index=3 (last accessed 3 October 2015).

58   *Threnodiae in obitum illustrislsimij Sac[ri] Rom[ani] Imp[erii] principis et domini, d. Alberti Radziwil[i] ducis in Ołyka et Nieswiz, supremi M.D. Lit. marschalci, Caunen[sis] et Romburgen[sis] etc. capitanei ...* (Wilno: Ex officina Academica Societatis Iesu, 1593), USTC 250344, sig. G1r–v.

59   Michael Stolberg, 'The many uses of writing: A humanist physician in sixteenth-century Prague', in Andrew Mendelsohn, Annemarie Kinzelbach, and Ruth Schilling (eds.), *Civic Medicine: Physician, Polity, and Pen in Early Modern Europe* (London: Routledge, 2019), p. 71.

60   Patricius Abircrumbeus, *Epithalamium in nuptias nobilis et excellent. viri D. Jacobi Arnotti Scoti medicinae doct. peritissimi, nec non honestissimae et pudicissimae virginis Dianae Sienkiewiciae, Josephi Sienkiewicii viri clarissimae perillustris civitatis Vilnensis civis primarii filiae, Vilnae celebratas. A Patricio Abircrumbeo Scoto, ejusdem sponsi nepote grati animi testificationis erga scripta et oblata* (Vilnae: apud Joann. Karcanum, 1605), USTC 250246.

61   Andrzej Loeaechius studied at Vilnius Academy in 1584. For his biography and literary activities see, Agnieszka Borysowska, 'Andrzej Loeaechius i jego twórczość poetycka

poems in Protestant printing houses, and devoted part of his poetry to the members of the Radziwiłł family of both Calvinist and Catholic affiliations. Despite his links with the Calvinist branch of the Radziwiłłs, he was nevertheless one of the main suspects of the authorship of a pasquil entitled *Exetasis Epistolae Nomine Regis Magnae Britanniae, Ad Omnes Christianos Monarchos, Principes, & Ordines, scriptae* [The Ecstasy over the Letter written under the Name of the King of Great Britain, to all Christian Monarchs, Princes, and Orders], presumably printed in Braniewo.[62] This publication, written under the pseudonym of Bartholus Pacenius, whose real identity has not been uncovered, repudiated the Oath of Allegiance devised by King James VI of Scotland and I of England in 1606 to increase state control over his Catholic subjects. The pasquil infuriated the English king, who was jealous of his international reputation, and significantly fuelled his repugnance toward Catholics.[63]

---

(XVI/XVII w.)', *Slavia Occidentalis*, 54 (1997), pp. 17–28. Andrzej Loeaechius, *Epithalamium in nuptias Illustrissimi et Magnifici Domini D. Leonis Sapiechae, Cancellarii Magni Duc. Lit. Slonimscen. Markow. Pernavien. Miedzialien. etc. Capitanei: Et maiorum splendore Clariss: Virginis Elisabethae Radivillae, Illustrissimi Principia D. Christophori Radivilli Ducis Bierzarvm et Dubinki, Palatini Vilnensis, exercituum M. D. Lit. Generalis Solecensis, Urzendouiensis Capitanei nec non tenutarij Kokenhausensis, filiae Andreae Loaechii Scoti* (Vilnae: in officina Salomonis Sultzeri,1599), USTC 250400; idem, *Schediasmata duo quorum altero Illustriss. D. Reverend. in Christo Patris Nicolai Pac Samogitiae Episc. Encomium continetur, altero Perill. et Magn. D. Hieronymi Wołłowicz M. D. L. Supremi Thesaurarii Eudoxia exhibetur. Utrumque ex nominum eorundem Anagrammatismis ab Andrea Loaechio Scoto concinnatum* (Vilnae: apud Josephum Kartzan, 1612), USTC 250294; idem, *Schediasmata II Alterum Exequiis principis majorum splendore Illustriss: propriis Virtutibus Clarissim: D. Elizabeth Radziwiłłównae Celsissimae Memoriae Principis Christophori Radziwilli Ducis Birzarum et Dubinki, Palatini Vilnensis et Exercituum M. D. L. pref. Gener. filiae Illustr: Herois D. Leonis Sapiehae Mag. Duc. Lithuan. Mag. Cancell. Mohyloviensis &c. Capitanei Conjugis Desideratissimae. Alterum Memoriae Summi Viri Joannis Petri Sapiehae Capitanei Uswiatensis etc. Ducis copiarum quae pro Sigismundo III Poloniae et Sueciae Rege in Moscos seditionis socios arma gesserunt, posthumi honoris ergo ab Andrea Loeaechio Scoto facta dicata* (Vilnae: apud Petrum Blastum Anno 1612), USTC 250295.

62  Bartholus Pacenius, *Exetasis Epistolae Nomine Regis Magnae Britanniae, Ad Omnes Christianos Monarchos, Principes, & Ordines, scriptae: quae, Praefationis monitoriae loco, ipsius Apologiae pro iuramento fidelitatis, praefixa est* (Montibus: Adamus Gallus, 1609 and 1610), USTC 1506542, 1506678. For more information on this publication and surrounding events, see: Martin Murphy, 'James VI and I, the Scottish Jesuit, and the Polish Pasquils', in Teresa Bela, Clarinda E. Calma and Jolanta Rzegocka (eds.), *Publishing Subversive Texts in Elizabethan England and the Polish-Lithuanian Commonwealth* (Leiden: Brill, 2016), pp. 34–36.

63  Marc' Antonio Correr to the Doge and Senate, 9 June 1610, London, 'Venice: June 1610, 1–15', in Horatio F. Brown (ed.), *Calendar of State Papers Relating To English Affairs in the Archives of Venice*, 11: 1607–1610 (London: Longman, 1904), pp. 498–506 *British History Online*: www.british-history.ac.uk/cal-state-papers/venice/vol11/pp498-506 (last accessed

In April 1611, the English agent in Poland, Andrew Aidie, approached the Bishop of Warmia Simon Rudnicki (1552–1621), asking for help in discovering the author. The bishop alleged that he had read the book and felt it did not tarnish James's reputation: 'it was but controversies of religion.'[64] Another two Jesuits suspected of producing the pasquil were Robert Abercrombie, a teacher of grammar and rhetoric at the Academy of Vilnius in the 1570s, and a Jesuit from Wales, Griffith Floyd, who was professor of philosophy at Braniewo in 1604–1606.[65] When in August 1615 Floyd underwent a series of interrogations for his links with Braniewo, he claimed neither to have been in the town between 1609 and 1610 nor to have employed a printer, except for publishing philosophical theses and an oration of Saint Bernard.[66] Floyd presumed that the secret author was M.M. Maillan, 'a Gentleman of the Pope's Chamber', who had presented himself as an agent of the Duke of Lorraine.[67]

Although the number of Scots and Englishmen enrolled at the Academy or attached to the academic staff declined by the middle of the seventeenth century, the British connections in the Grand Duchy of Lithuania did not cease and the outcomes of exchange were unveiled already at the beginning of the seventeenth century. In 1601 or 1602, when Robert Abercrombie acted as Scottish Jesuit superior, in his letter to Father General Claudio Acquaviva (1543–1615) and Acquaviva's assistant for Northern and Eastern Europe George Duras, he pointed out that students in Poland, Lithuania and Prussia were allowed to attend Protestant sermons so as to improve their ability of challenging the beliefs and practices of their rivals in theological debates. He suggested introducing such a practice for some 'more spiritual sons' in Scotland.[68] In another example of cultural 'translation' during the mid-seventeenth century a part of the oeuvre written by Maciej Casimir Sarbiewski (1595–1640), a Jesuit priest of Vilnius Academy and a renowned Polish poet, was translated into English by

---

8 June 2017); Cyndia Susan Clegg, *Press Censorship in Jacobean England* (Cambridge: Cambridge University Press, 2001), p. 79.

64  Andrew Aidie to Robert Cecil, 15 April 1611, Danzig, Charles H. Talbot (ed.), *Elementa ad Fontium Editiones*, 6: Res Polonicæ Iacobo I Angliæ regnante conscriptæ ex Archivis Publicis Londoniarum (Rome: Institutum Historicum Polonicum Romæ, 1962), p. 102.

65  Patrick Gordon to James I, 29 October 1610, Danzig, ibid., p. 79; Grzebień, *Encyklopedia*: www.jezuici.krakow.pl/cgi-bin/rjbo?b=enc&q=FLOIDUS&f=1 (last accessed 27 June 2021).

66  Mary Anne Everett Green (ed.), *Calendar of State Papers Domestic, James I, 1611–1618* (London: Her Majesty's Stationery Office, 1858), pp. 303, 305.

67  Ibid.

68  Robert Abercromby to Claudio Acquaviva and George Duras, [s.d. ca. 1601/1602], [s.l.], Ginevra Crosignani, Thomas M. McCoog and Michael Questier (eds.), *Recusancy and Conformity in Early Modern England: Manuscript and Printed Sources in Translation* (Rome: Institutum Historicum Societatis Iesu, 2010), pp. xxix, 286, 287.

George Hils to express his royalist sentiments. It was printed in one of the most successful London printing offices, that of Humphrey Moseley, in 1646.[69] This bears evidence that textual exchange continued into the seventeenth century, despite the lack of any visible flow of English and Scottish Catholics to the Grand Duchy of Lithuania.

## 4   The Construction of the Martyrological Discourse in Poland-Lithuania and Its Connections to England

Polish-Lithuanian Jesuits paid particular attention to the use of the printing press, exploiting it fully to bolster the authority of the Catholic Church in the Commonwealth. They were quite successful in utilizing the power of the press to speed up the triumph of the Catholic Church in the Commonwealth under Sigismund III. The networks established by Polish-Lithuanian Catholics channelled a great amount of information, leading to the emergence of new literary genres and discourses.[70] Directing their gaze towards contemporary English martyrs to construct narratives of local Polish-Lithuanian martyrdom was a compelled measure, caused by a growing popularity of foreign Protestant martyrologies,[71] which not only began to circulate within the Polish-Lithuanian Commonwealth in the second half of the sixteenth century, but some of which were also translated into Polish.[72] In 1577, the Provincial of the Polish Province of the Jesuit Order Francisco Sunyer asked his fellow Jesuit Piotr Skarga (1536–1612), an ecclesiastic leader of the Counter-Reformation in Poland-Lithuania, to produce a volume of the lives of the saints based on

---

69   Maciej Kazimierz Sarbiewski, *The Odes of Casimire Translated by G.H.* (London: Humphrey Moseley, 1646); Krzysztof Fordoński, 'The Subversive Power of Father Matthias: The Poetry of Maciej Kazimierz Sarbiewski as Vehicle for Political Propaganda in England of the 17th Century', in Jacek Fabiszak et al. (eds.), *Crossroads in Literature and Culture* (Berlin: Springer, 2013), pp. 387–397, here pp. 391–392. There were some other translations of some of Sarbiewski's poems in the seventeenth century. See: George Gömöri, *The Polish Swan Triumphant: Essays on Polish and Comparative Literature from Kochanowski to Norwid* (Newcastle upon Tyne: Cambridge Scholars Publishing, 2013), p. 108.
70   For the detailed analysis of the adoption of foreign martyrologies to the religious situation in the Polish-Lithuanian Commonwealth, see, Mazheika, 'An Earnest Gospeller', pp. 169–182.
71   Mirosława Hanusiewicz-Lavallee, 'Recusant Prose in the Polish-Lithuanian Commonwealth at the Turn of the Sixteenth Century', in Bela, Calma and Rzegocka (eds.), *Publishing Subversive Texts*, pp. 18–19.
72   See, Mazheika, 'An Earnest Gospeller', pp. 170–174.

*De probatis sanctorum historiis* [Concerning the True Stories of the Saints] by the German Carthusian hagiographer Lorenz Sauer (Laurentius Surius).[73] The outcome of this endeavor became *Żywoty Swiętych starego y nowego zakonu* [Lives of the saints of the old and new covenant], issued in the Catholic printing press of Mikołaj Krzysztof Radziwiłł 'the Orphan' in Vilnius in 1579.[74] In the preface, Skarga explained that he considered daily readings of the lives of the saints, which had not existed in a written form in the Polish language before, as an essential tool for the affirmation of the authority of the saints and for the emulation of their lives. Under the influence of Cardinal Stanislaus Hosius, who had strong contacts with English recusants on the Continent, the author paid particular attention to the lives of the saints from the British Isles.[75] Hosius, whose theology was prominently featured in polemic literature in England, became an important opponent for English Protestant theologians. During the 1560s, he was attacked for his theology by Bishop of Salisbury John Jewel, the clergyman and author John Barthlet, the theologian William Fulke, as well as by the famous historian and martyrologist John Foxe in 1578.[76] Two of Hosius's writings, *Opus elegantissimum varias nostri temporis sectas & haereses ab origine recensens* and *De expresso Dei verbo libellus his temporibus*

---

73   Francis J. Thompson, 'The Popularity of Peter Skarga's Lives of the Saints among the East Slavs', in T. Soldatjenkova and E. Waegemans (eds.), *For East is East: Liber Amicorum Wojciech Skalmowski* (*Orientalia Lovaniensia Analecta*) (Leuven: Peeters, 2003), p. 122; Laurentius Surius, *De probatis sanctorum historiis, partim ex tomis aloysii lipomani, doctissimi episcopi, partim etiam ex egregiis manuscriptis codicibus, quarum permultae antehàc nunquàm in lucem prodiére, nunc recèns optima fide collectis per f. Laurentium surium carthusianum, tomus secundus, complectens sanctos mensium martii et aprilis*. (Köln: apud Johann Quentel (heirs of), 1571), USTC 631112.

74   Piotr Skarga, *Żywoty Swiętych starego y nowego zakonu z pisma świętego y z poważnych pisarzow y Doktorow koscielnych wybranych. Cz. 2* (Wilno: druk Mikołaja Krzysztofa Radziwiłła, 1579), USTC 250130.

75   Stanisław Windakiewicz, 'Skarga i Anglicy', *Sprawozdania z Czynności i Posiedzeń Polskiej Akademii Umiejętności*, 25:4 (1920), pp. 1–8. For more details on the ties between Hosius and English Catholics, see: Urszula Szumska, *Anglia a Polska w epoce humanizmu i reformacji (Związki kulturalne)* (Lwów: Skład Główny w Księgarni Krawczyńskiego, 1938), pp. 94–98; Clarinda E. Calma, 'Stanisław Hozjusz jako Patron I Protektor Elżbietańskich Rekuzantów', in Tomasz Garwoliński (ed.), *Iubilaeum Warmiae et Bibliothecae* (Olsztyn: Wydawnictwo Wyższego Seminarium Duchowego Metropolii Warmińskiej 'Hosianum', 2016), pp. 28–41.

76   Hanusiewicz-Lavallee, 'Recusant Prose', p. 16; idem, 'Brytania i Sarmacja – na krańcach Europy, Wśród krajów Północy', in Mirosława Hanusiewicz-Lavallee (ed.), *Kultura Pierwszej Rzeczypospolitej wobec narodów germańskich, słowiańskich i naddunajskich: Mapa spotkań, przestrzenie dialogu* (Warszawa: Wydawnictwo Uniwersytetu Warszawskiego, 2015), p. 135.

*accommodatissimus*,[77] were translated into English and printed in 1565 and 1567 respectively. The former work was published in English translation under the title of *A Most Excellent Treatise of the Begynnyng of Heresyes in Oure Tyme* by the English controversialist Richard Shacklock in the Spanish Netherlands and smuggled into England.[78] Shacklock added to the original dedication to Sigismund II Augustus a dedication to Queen Elizabeth. In 1566, the Church of England clergyman John Bartlett (Barthlet) published a reply to this translation under the title *The Pedegrewe of Heretiques wherein is Truely and Plainely Set out, the First Roote of Heretiques Begon in the Church*.[79] The other work by Hosius was translated by Thomas Stapleton, a Roman Catholic theologian, and printed in Louvain in 1567 under the title *Of the expresse word of God. A shorte, but a most excellent treatyse and very necessary for this tyme*.[80]

*Żywoty Swiętych* gained an importance in the religious culture of Poland-Lithuania, and new editions appeared several times in the late sixteenth and early seventeenth centuries, which Skarga expanded with additional information from English sources.[81] At least six editions were issued up to 1612, the year of Skarga's death.[82] Of particular interest is the final part of the

---

77 Stanisław Hozjusz, *Opus elegantissimum varias nostri temporis sectas et haereses ab origine recensens* (Paris: ex officina Jean Foucher, 1559), USTC 152717; idem, *De expresso Dei verbo libellus his temporibus accommodatissimus; item, Dialogus trimembris, isque elegantissimus, hac aetate pernecessarius, de communione sacrae Eucharistiae sub utraque specie, de sacerdotum conjugio* (Paris: apud Jean Foucher, 1560), USTC 152837.

78 Stanisław Hozjusz, *A Most Excellent Treatise of the Begynnyng of Heresyes in Oure Tyme, Compyled by the Reuerend Father in God Stanislaus Hosius Byshop of Wormes in Prussia: To the Moste Renomed Prynce Lorde Sigismund Myghtie Kyng of Poole, Greate Duke of Luten and Russia, Lorde and Heyre of All Prussia, Masouia, Samogitia &c. Translated out of Laten in to Englyshe by Richard Shacklock M. of Arte, and Student of the Ciuil Lawes, and Intituled by Hym: The Hatchet of Heresies* (Antwerp: AEg. Diest, 1565), USTC 407611; Peter Holmes, 'Shacklock, Richard', *ODNB*: www.oxforddnb.com/view/article/25188?docPos=2 (last accessed 7 March 2017).

79 John Barthlet, *The Pedegrewe of Heretiques wherein is Truely and Plainely Set out, the First Roote of Heretiques Begon in the Church, Since the Time and Passage of the Gospell, Together with an Example of the Ofspring of the Same. Perused and Alowed According to the Order Appoynted in the Queenes Maiesties Iniunctions* (London: Henry Denham, 1566), USTC 506448; Christopher Highley, *Catholics Writing the Nation in Early Modern Britain and Ireland* (Oxford: Oxford University Press, 2008), pp. 43–45.

80 Stanisław Hozjusz, *Of the expresse word of God: A shorte, but a most excellent treatyse and very necessary for this tyme* (Louvain: Jean Bogard, 1567), USTC 411358.

81 Hanusiewicz-Lavallee, 'Recusant Prose', p. 19.

82 There is no agreement on the number of the editions published before Skarga's death. Karol Estreicher provides the number of nine: Karol Estreicher, *Bibliografia Polska: XIX. stólecia*: www.estreicher.uj.edu.pl/skany/?dir=dane_xix_index|4 (last accessed 10 October 2015). According to Hieronim E. Wyczawski, the 1610 edition was the seventh one and

book, which is entitled 'A supplement about those lives of the holy martyrs who suffered for Christ, the truth and the Church during our ages' and contains the depiction of the persecution by Protestant authorities of English and French Catholics, and Jesuits abroad.[83] In the edition of 1585 of *Żywoty Swiętych*, as the connection that would allow the creation of a suitable background for introducing martyrological narratives in the Polish-Lithuanian Commonwealth, Skarga utilized the stories of the English Jesuit priest Edmund Campion (1540–1581), who was executed by the Elizabethan regime, and of James Bosgrave, former professor of mathematics at Vilnius Academy, who was imprisoned upon arrival in England together with Campion and other Jesuits, but was released following the interference of King of Poland, Stephen Báthory. By bringing to light the connection between Edmund Campion, who had never visited either Poland or Lithuania, and James Bosgrave, Skarga sought to adopt the figure of Campion as one of the local martyrs in order to create a martyrological narrative applicable to the situation in the Polish-Lithuanian Commonwealth where legislation, introduced by the Confederation of Warsaw of 1573, did not permit persecution of heterodoxy and therefore instances of violence against either Catholics or Protestants were not common.[84] Furthermore, Campion's writings, specifically his *Rationes Decem*, written in 1581, were widely exploited in Protestant-Catholic polemics in the Commonwealth. Not only was *Rationes Decem* printed in Latin in Vilnius in 1583,[85] but was also translated into Polish by Piotr Skarga himself as well as by Gaspar Wilkowski, a Catholic convert from Antitrinitarianism.[86] Both translations were issued by the same Catholic printing press in Vilnius in 1584. While Wilkowksi's translation of *Rationes Decem*

       the next edition did not appear before 1615, see: Hieronim E. Wyczawski, 'Piotr Skarga', in Hieronim E. Wyczawski (ed.), *Słownik polskich teologów katolickich*, (4 vols., Warszawa: Akademia Teologii Katolickiej, 1983), 4, p. 86. The same number is provided by Thompson, while she indicates that the editions of 1604 and 1612–1613 were listed by some scholars as nonexistent, see: Thompson, 'The Popularity', p. 141 n. 82. Janusz Tazbir considers the 1610 edition to have been the sixth one: Janusz Tazbir, *Piotr Skarga, Szermierz kontrreformacji* (Warszawa: Państwowe Wydawnictwo „Wiedza Powszechna", 1978), p. 101. For the editions of the *Acts and Monuments*, see: David Loewenstein, *Treacherous Faith: The Specter of Heresy in Early Modern English Literature and Culture* (Oxford: Oxford University Press, 2013), p. 105.

83    Piotr Skarga, *Żywoty Swiętych Cz. 2*, fol. 1122.

84    For the detailed examination of the function of the translations, see, Mazheika, 'An Earnest Gospeller', pp. 175–178.

85    Edmund Campion, *Rationes decem, quibus fretus certamen obtulit in causa fidei Edmundus Campianus e Societate Jesu* (Wilno: Mikołaj Krzysztof Radziwiłł, 1583), USTC 240322.

86    Idem, *Dziesiec wywodow dla ktorych Edmundus Kampianus z Londynu S. I. wszystkie heretyki co nauczensze w Angliey, na dysputatia okolo wiary wyzwal* (Wilno: druk. M. Ch. Radziwila, 1584), USTC 250159; idem, *Dziesiec mocnych dowodow, jz adwersarze*

aimed to refute the doctrine of the Antitrinitarians,[87] Skarga's translation had a different purpose. On the one hand, by detailing Campion's martyrdom he aimed to demonstrate atrocities committed by contemporary Protestant regimes against Catholics. On the other hand, by connecting Campion with the Polish-Lithuanian Commonwealth through the Catholic understanding of the Church as a Mystical Body of Christ in which Catholics of England and Poland-Lithuania were spiritually bound as one, he attempted to create the context in which the laity would come to realise the risk for any Catholic to be persecuted for their faith.

## 5  Conclusion

This present study has aimed to examine sixteenth-century Anglo-Lithuanian Catholic ties, revealing the influences of those contacts on the print culture of the Grand Duchy of Lithuania. As the Counter-Reformation solidly took root in both parts of the Polish-Lithuanian Commonwealth, offering safe havens to recusants from England and Scotland, profound British-Lithuanian Catholic ties were forged after the foundation of Vilnius Academy in 1579. All the publications produced with the involvement of British Jesuit students suggest that they were accustomed to life in Vilnius Academy as much as other foreign and local students and actively participated in the corporate life of the institution.[88] Many Englishmen and Scots were well aware that the wealthiest Lithuanian magnates, who professed Catholicism, were among the leading defenders of the Counter-Reformation. It would be fallacious to assert, however, that English and Scottish Catholics perceived the Grand Duchy of Lithuania as a purely Catholic state. In 1580, William Shepreve, a Catholic priest and scholar, who accompanied the English Catholic scholar Gregory Martin from Douai to Rome, sent a report to the rector of the English College in Rome. In it he wrote about Mikołaj Krzysztof Radziwiłł 'the Orphan', mistakenly calling him 'Prince or greate Duke of Lithuania,' and his stay in Bologna: 'This man what with the good diligence of the Jesuites [...] and other good instructions, hath so profited herein, that he resolved with him self to renounce all the errors, the

---

kosciola powszechnego, w porzadney o wierze dysputacyey upasc musza [Vilnius: typ. Mikołaj Krzysztof Radziwiłł, 1584], USTC 250154.

87   For a detailed analysis of the translation, see Clarinda E. Calma, 'Communicating Across Communities Explicitation in Gaspar Wilkowski's Polish Translation of Edmund Campion's Rationes Decem', *Journal of Jesuit Studies*, 1 (2014), pp. 589–606.

88   For the research on Scandinavian students in Vilnius Academy, see Garstein, *Rome and the Counter-Reformation*, pp. 233–265.

Schismatical and Diabolical and Paganical acts and opinions of that of his corrupted country.'[89] In contrast to William Shepreve, upon his return to England Samuel Lewkenor, a former student of the Academy of Vilnius, wrote and published in 1600 *A Discourse not Altogether Vnprofitable, nor Vnpleasant for Such as are Desirous to Know the Situation and Customes of Forraine Cities without Trauelling to See Them Containing a Discourse of All Those Citties wherein Doe Flourish at This Day Priuiledged Vniuersities*, in which he commented on the religious situation in Vilnius and on one of the Protestant members of the Radziwiłł family: 'Therein also is allowed one church for the Protestants, because the Woywod or Count Palatine thereof, the noblest of the Radziuilli professeth (if any) that religion.'[90]

Although in the second half of the sixteenth century Protestantism was one of the major confessional cultures of the Grand Duchy of Lithuania, having gained a significant foothold, the connections between English and Lithuanian Protestants were generally fortuitous. In contrast, the relationship between English recusants and Lithuanian Catholics was better structured, in comparison with occasional encounters between the Protestants of Lithuania and England, and the presence of English and Scottish Catholics within the Grand Duchy was much more noticeable than that of persons with a Protestant affiliation. Furthermore, Polish-Lithuanian Jesuits were more successful in exploiting the power of the press in advancing the triumph of the Catholic Church in the Polish-Lithuanian Commonwealth, engaging not only local writers but also authors of various ethnic origins. As a result, the networks established by Polish-Lithuanian Catholics with their counterparts abroad facilitated textual transmission between the countries, resulting in the construction of a martyrological narrative applicable to the situation in Poland-Lithuania.

---

89  George B. Parks (ed.), *Gregory Martin's Roma Sancta 1581* (Rome: Edizioni di Storia e Letteratura, 1969), p. 263.
90  Lewkenor, *A Discourse not Altogether Vnprofitable*, fol. 55v.

CHAPTER 6

# Pre-suppression Jesuit Libraries

*Patterns of Collection and Use in Northern, Central, and Eastern Europe*

*Kathleen M. Comerford*

Recent decades have shown the general public what librarians and historians of the book and of material culture have long known: collections of texts, whether by institutions, organizations, or individuals, are not static things. The development, for example, of Little Free Libraries around the world, and the replacement of many college and university libraries with Learning Commons, demonstrate that libraries are living entities, both responding to and creating trends, and adapting to significant challenges on multiple physical, economic, intellectual, and existential fronts.[1] They have historically been centres

---

1 Little Free Library (LFL), which calls itself 'the world's largest book-sharing movement,' is a US-based nonprofit serving more than ninety countries around the world, www.littlefree library.org/ (last accessed 17 March 2022). Each community, business, or individual which hosts a LFL provides a box, shelf, or basket for books, so that members of that community may borrow, lend, or donate books. That means that the collections are eclectic, but the LFL has designed programs to promote access to neighbourhoods which are underserved by traditional library systems and to support the reading and distribution of books which amplify diverse topics and authors. Detractors have argued that it can harm public library systems, disproportionately serves higher-income areas, and serves as a dumping ground for unwanted and out of date books (cf. Kriston Capps, 'Against Little Free Libraries,' *Bloomberg CityLab*, 3 May 2017, www.bloomberg.com/news/articles/2017-05-03/down-with-little-free -library-book-exchanges [last accessed 17 March 2022]). Nevertheless, LFL has garnered multiple awards, including a 2013 Innovations in Reading Prize from the (US) National Book Foundation – www.nationalbook.org/programs/the-innovations-in-reading-prize-archive/ (last accessed, 20 March 2022) – and the Library of Congress's Best Practices Award of 2015 for Creating a Community of Literacy – www.loc.gov/item/prn-15-210/library-of-congress- literacy-awards-publishes-2015-best-practices/2015-12-01/ (last accessed 20 March 2022). 'Learning Commons,' first embraced by academic libraries, is a term adopted by an increasing number of school and public libraries, to emphasize that they not only provide books and spaces to read them, but also furnish access to digital media, equipment for creating content, areas for remote and face to face education, and places to hold meetings, study groups, or other collaborative efforts. Cf. Steven Overly, 'The Download: Digital Commons, the Library of the Future?', *The Washington Post*, 21 July 2013, www.washingtonpost.com/business/capi talbusiness/the-download-digital-commons-the-library-of-the-future/2013/07/19/e62bfde0 -effe-11e2-a1f9-ea873b7e0424_story.html (last accessed 17 March 2022); Marlene Asselin and Ray Doiron (eds.), *Linking Literacy and Libraries in Global Communities* (London: Routledge,

---

© KATHLEEN M. COMERFORD, 2023 | DOI:10.1163/9789004441217_008
This is an open access chapter distributed under the terms of the CC BY-NC-ND 4.0 license.

of controversies regarding censorship, gatekeepers of specialized knowledge, hosts for cultural events, havens for those seeking a quiet spot, and so much more. As such, libraries are among the most versatile institutions in society. Yet few patrons pause to ask why specific books were chosen or rejected, or why certain texts have survived but others have not. This study addresses questions related to these collection and maintenance issues, by examining survivals of physical volumes with Jesuit library provenance, along with available pre-modern inventories from those institutions run by Jesuits. Studying these issues can provide insights into the intellectual life of the period stretching from the Reformations to the Enlightenment, including educational trends and priorities, as well as institutional constraints related to location and financing. My focus here is northern, central, and eastern Europe, with the hope of expanding comparative and contextual knowledge by including several areas not well represented in Anglophone studies of the sixteenth through eighteenth centuries.[2]

This study relies on data collected for my ongoing public and digital history initiative, the European Jesuit Libraries Provenance Project (EJLPP), formally launched in 2018 at www.jesuit-libraries.com. The EJLPP is a census of books known to have been in the possession of a European Jesuit college, professed house, probationary house, or museum prior to the papal suppression of the Society (which began in 1759 and was completed in 1773, excluding areas of Russia). At this writing, it consists of information about authors, printers, book titles, and institutions associated with over 5,300 titles, available

---

2016); and Dan Kennedy, 'In Session: York High School Abandons Traditional Library with Renovated "Learning Commons,"' *13newsnow.com*, 20 January 2020, www.13newsnow.com/article/news/education/york-high-school-learning-commons-library/291-cf3fb020-e28a-4e50-9148-bc8a119fd25f (last accessed 17 April 2022).

[2] Recent publications in the Open Access resource *Jesuit Historiography Online* www.dx.doi.org/10.1163/2468-7723-jho-all (last accessed 17 March 2022), help introduce Anglophone readers to the history of Jesuits in Bohemia, Croatia, Hungary, and Poland-Lithuania. These include Krzysztof Fordoński and Piotr Urbański, 'Jesuit Culture in Poland and Lithuania, 1564–1773', *Journal of Jesuit Studies*, 5:3 (2018), pp. 341–351; Andrea Mariani, 'The Contribution of the Society of Jesus to the Political Culture of Lithuanian Elites', *Open Political Science*, 2 (2019), pp. 153–173, here p. 154. Mariani's observations on the importance of Justus Lipsius, the myth of Venice, and contemporary Polish authors on the subject of politics in the Jesuit libraries of the Polish-Lithuanian Commonwealth, provide much food for thought and have aided my efforts to expand the Eastern European representation in the EJLPP. In addition, Paul Shore's '*Fragmentum Annuarium Collegii Societatis Iesu Claudiopolitani*: The Account of a Jesuit Mission in Transylvania, 1659–1662', *Reformation and Renaissance Review*, 8:1 (2006), pp. 83–106, seeks to address the unfortunately minor presence of Hungarian historiography in the Anglophone scholarly community focusing on the Society of Jesus prior to the opening up of Eastern Europe in 1989.

in a downloadable spreadsheet. The data can provide support and context to scholars of multiple disciplines, and allow for broader comparative studies than have generally been undertaken with respect to the study of Jesuit teaching, collecting, and book production and consumption. Thanks to the generous support of Georgia Southern University, a total of eleven undergraduate and graduate students and three Digital Commons specialists have assisted in various ways, including cataloguing photographs and creating data visualizations. In addition, the EJLPP includes contributions by individual researchers, and is partnered with the University of Uppsala Libraries and the CRAI Biblioteca. They have changed their name to CRAI Biblioteca de Fons Antic of the University of Barcelona.[3] We are currently working on agreements with other institutions and scholars. These enable us to expand the size and reach of the project, and to engage researchers working on similar undertakings in other parts of the world so that we can best achieve our shared goals of better understanding the Republic of Letters. In this article, I use data analysis to investigate aspects of Jesuit book collection and suggest some tentative conclusions about the intellectual history of the Society of Jesus based on the subjects, languages, and authors of those books and the locations where they were held.

## 1 Jesuit Libraries: A Brief Introduction

Libraries were one of multiple supports for the main institutional goals of the Society of Jesus: evangelization and education. The practice of Jesuit librarianship dates back to the foundation of the Society, beginning with passing references to acceptable texts for teaching and reading in the *Constitutions*, and continuing with local recommendations and regulations.[4] The latter included the 1551 *Rule* of the Roman College, which stipulated that the institution keep 'sufficient' books for the subjects taught there, and Jerome Nadal's (1507–80)

---

3 For further information, including photographs and biographies of the contributors, see www.jesuit-libraries.com/about-us (last accessed, 17 March 2022).
4 The *Constitutions* frequently mention books, and the virtues and dangers associated with reading. Part IV, Chapter 14, 'The Books to be Lectured on', has the most specific statements on books, but only identifies a handful of texts by name: the Old and New Testaments, the *Sentences* of Peter Lombard (1096–1160), and the works of Thomas Aquinas (1225–74) and Aristotle (384–22 BCE) are required, whereas Terence (c.195/85–c.159 BCE) is cautioned against. George E. Ganss, et al. (transl. and ed.), *The Constitutions of the Society of Jesus and Their Complementary Norms: A Complete English Translation of the Official Latin Texts* (St. Louis: Institute of Jesuit Sources, 1996), paragraphs 464–470, pp. 184–185.

1566 *Instructions Presented to the Provincial of the Rhine* which required that 'general books in each one of the faculties necessary for our student brothers are to be ... put in some place common to all' whereas 'the others,' presumably including those suspected of heretical content, would instead be housed in a locked room, for which the librarian would hold the key.[5] The 1567 *Regulae communes* for the Society were the first to include 'Rules for the Prefect of the Library,' requiring that he keep a copy of the Index, organize the books by subject and author, keep records of circulation, restrict use to those given permission by the Superior, and maintain the neatness of the space and the books.[6] In 1580, an update to this section empowered the librarian to request that his superior purchase 'necessary ... or ... very useful' books or dispose of the 'useless ones' in exchange 'for other better ones'.[7] Later *Regulae* of the sixteenth and seventeenth centuries contained 'Rules for the Novice Master,' to which were appended a list of roughly thirty titles, largely theological in subject, and vague suggestions for others to be considered (e.g., 'Thomas de Kempis, De Imitatione Christi, et alia eius Opuscula' [Thomas à Kempis, *Of the Imitation of Christ*, and others of his works]).[8]

The foundation of the Congregation of the Index in 1571 marked a shift in both librarianship and publishing. It institutionalized the practice of censorship, long a concern for the Catholic Church, and gave it permanent bureaucratic support. On the one hand, the Index of Prohibited Books, and a body with regular meetings revising that list, meant strong, formal restrictions, inhibiting intellectual inquiry. On the other, it meant convenience: this was a frequently updated catalogue of books which were never to be purchased or read at the Jesuit colleges, neatly organized into a document which must be

---

5 The *Rule* for the Roman College, in *Monumenta Ignatiana* series tertia, *Constitutiones et Regulae Societatis Iesu, Regulae Societatis Iesu (1540–1556)* (Rome: Monumenta historica Societatis Iesu, 1948), IV, Mon. 63, 'Regulae Collegii Romani (1550)', paragraph 11, pp. 270–71. Jerome Nadal, *Epistolae P. Hieronymi Nadal Societatis Jesu ab anno 1546 ad 1577* (Madrid: Lopez de Horno, 1905), 4, Monumenta Provincia Rhenanae, 54, pp. 330–331. Translation by Brendan Connolly, 'The Roots of Jesuit Librarianship: 1540–1599' (PhD dissertation, University of Chicago, 1955), p. 91. See also Brendan Connolly, 'Jesuit Library Beginnings', *The Library Quarterly*, 30:4 (1960), pp. 243–252.
6 *Regulae communes* (Rome: Collegio Societatis Iesu, 1567): 'Regulae Praefecti Bibliothecae'. USTC 832410. The book is not paginated.
7 Connolly, 'Roots of Jesuit Librarianship', p. 74; his translation of the 'Regulae Praefecti Bibliothecae'.
8 Cf. *Institutum Societatis Iesu. Regulae, Ratio Studiorum, Ordinationes, Instructiones, Industriae, Exercitia, Directorium* (3 vols., Florence: Typographia ss. Conceptione, 1893), 3, pp. 120–131, here pp. 121–122; *Regula Societatis Iesu* (Tarragona: Philip Mey, 1583), pp. 140–180, book list on pp. 143–145; *Regula Societatis Iesu* (Rome: Collegium Societatis Iesu, 1590), USTC 832498, pp. 97–117, book list on p. 99.

displayed for all to see. Abiding by it relieved librarians and prefects of certain difficult decisions. By the turn of the seventeenth century, Antonio Possevino, S.J. (1533-59) issued the two-volume *Bibliotheca selecta* (editions in 1593, 1603, and 1607). Possevino catalogued and occasionally discussed the contents of the books he considered necessary for a Catholic education, essentially outlining an ideal library.[9] This was not intended as a set of instructions, but instead served as a kind of 'library triumphant' or 'index of recommended books'. Such flexibility was important; one could never guarantee the availability of acceptable books, and to require a specific list would make at least the non-European missions nearly impossible. Essentially opposite sides of the same coin, the Index and the *Bibliotheca selecta* were fundamental to the development of Jesuit librarianship. Possevino's work can therefore provide modern scholars of Jesuit libraries with a set of guidelines which, when applied to inventories from individual pre-suppression libraries, can be used to determine whether or not Jesuits in the sixteenth and seventeenth centuries used identifiable collection practices, and whether, either by accident or design, the different college and residence libraries held books on similar subjects, collected texts in specific languages, favoured particular authors, et cetera.[10] Scholars who have attempted to recreate the libraries of institutions from the old Society have used both such inventories and surviving volumes for information. Examples include the very thorough work of historian Klára Jakó, who in a 1991 article attempted a reconstruction of the pre-1604 library in the Jesuit College in Cluj, and historian Andrea Mariani, whose more recent work focuses on the Polish-Lithuanian Commonwealth.[11]

---

9    See Luigi Balsamo, *Antonio Possevino s.i. bibliografo della Controriforma e diffusione della sua opera in area anglicana* (Florence: Olschki, 2006); Barbara Mahlmann-Bauer, 'Antonio Possevino's *Bibliotheca selecta*: Knowledge as a Weapon', in Manfred Hinz et al. (eds.), *I gesuiti e la Ratio studiorum* (Rome: Bulzoni, 2004), pp. 315-155; Alberto Biondo, 'La *Bibliotheca selecta* di Antonio Possevino: Un progetto di egemonia culturale', in Gian Paolo Brizzi (ed.), *La 'Ratio studiorum': Modelli culturali e pratiche educative dei Gesuiti in Italia tra Cinque e Seicento*, (Rome: Bulzoni Editore, 1981), pp. 43-75; Grant Boswell, 'Letter Writing among the Jesuits: Antonio Possevino's Advice in the *Bibliotheca Selecta* (1593)', *Huntington Library Quarterly*, 66 (2003), pp. 247-262; and Dirk Werle, *Copia librorum. Problemgeschichte imaginierter Bibliotheken 1580-1630* (Tübingen: M. Niemeyer, 2007).

10   See Kathleen M. Comerford, 'Jesuit Tuscan Libraries of the 1560s and 1570s: *Bibliotheca not-yet Selecta*', *Archivum Historicum Societatis Iesu*, 81, 162 (2013), pp. 515-531.

11   Klára Jakó, 'Az elsö kolozvári egyetemi konyvtar története és állományák rekonstruckcioja 1579-1604' (Reconstruction of the History and Collection of the First University Library of Kolozsvár [Cluj], 1579-1604), in *Erdélyi Könyvesházak I, Adattár XVI-XVII. századi szellemi mozgalmaink történetéhez* (Szeged: Scriptum, 1991). I am grateful to Éva Szeli of Arizona State University for her help in translating this title. Another example is Pierre Guérin, *Les Jésuites du Collège Wallon de Liège durant l'ancien régime* (Liège: Société des

Jesuit library beginnings were, therefore, not particularly proscriptive or prescriptive in the sixteenth century, but as librarianship developed, the collections began to fall into identifiable configurations. Among the reasons for this is the 1599 version of the *Ratio studiorum*, which made explicit provision for funding the library (which 'may under no circumstances be diverted to other uses') and directed the librarian to preserve the literary output of members of the Society and to follow the 'directions of the prefect of studies in regard to the circulation of books,' statements which indicate that the Society hesitated to impose narrow instructions.[12] The institutionalization of censorship within the Catholic Church, along with the development of a number of library treatises, including works by the Jesuit Jean Garnier (1612–81) and the Jesuit-educated humanist Justus Lipsius (1547–1606), introduced some more standardization.[13] Nevertheless, the book collections associated with the pre-suppression Society's colleges, houses, and offices show vast differences in the representation of authors, languages, and subjects. As a whole, European Jesuit libraries, from what we can discern in the twenty-first century, largely followed the topic patterns that can be identified in Possevino, as listed in the tables which follow, but with significant variations in emphasis according to place and time. This article explores some of those variations, focusing on the distinctions between collections in different geographical regions. Changes over time are more difficult to document, because librarians either did not take or did not preserve inventories on many occasions; however, I am including here some discussions on the developments in librarianship.[14]

---

bibliophiles liégeois, 1999), 1, an attempt to reconstruct the library of the Walloon Jesuit College in Liège, based on book lists from 1678, the mid-eighteenth century, and 1773, with a nineteenth-century catalogue of manuscripts, and a receipt for books (containing only the 'noms des acheteurs, les prix payés pour les different lots, mais non pas les titres de ces libres' ['names of the buyers, the prices paid for the different lots, but not the titles of the books']) sold in late February, 1779. See also Andrea Mariani, 'L'insegnamento delle scienze nelle scuole dei Gesuiti polacchi. Fra popolarizzazione e applicazione pratiche (1740–1773)', *History of Education & Children's Literature*, 7:1 (2012), pp. 319–339.

12  *The Jesuit* Ratio Studiorum *of 1599*, transl. Allan P. Farrell (Washington, DC: Conference of Major Superiors of Jesuits, 1970), 'Rules of the Provincial', paragraph 33, p. 11; 'Rules of the Rector', paragraphs 16–17, p. 17.

13  Jean Garnier, *Systema bibliothecae Collegii Parisiensis Societatis Jesu* (Paris: Sebastianus Mabre-Cramoisy, 1678); Justus Lipsius, *De bibliothecis syntagma* (Antwerp: Jan Moretus, 1602), USTC 1003389, see Thomas Hendrickson, *Ancient Libraries and Renaissance Humanism: The De bibliothecis of Justus Lipsius* (Leiden: Brill, 2017).

14  For a deeper exploration of Jesuit librarianship as it developed over the centuries, see my *Jesuit Libraries* (Leiden: Brill, 2023), doi: https://doi.org/10.1163/9789004517370 (last accessed 18 April 2023).

## 2 The EJLPP: Methodology and Overview

It is ironic to note that one of the best ways to study the libraries of the early Society of Jesus is to access the records of its dissolution. As governments across Europe and their global empires expelled Jesuits and outlawed the order, they saw to the recording of inventories of the Society's possessions. While these vary in detail, the documents created between 1759 and 1773 have provided a kind of library catalogue for many of the institutions which were shut down. Some institutions preserved earlier inventories, and as a result, researchers may discuss changes in holdings and collection patterns over time. What follows focuses on the records from the Professed House at Antwerp (inventory from 1660) and the colleges of Leuven (1635), Antwerp (1613), and Delft (1614), along with the Irish College at Rome (c.1630 and 1671), and the English College at Liège/Saint Omer (early seventeenth century) for a total of 1,246 titles.[15]

In addition to manuscript inventories, the EJLPP contains records for thousands of extant Jesuit-owned books. As of this writing, the vast majority of the titles (nearly 3,400) in the section of the EJLPP dedicated to surviving print copies come from Google Books, and another 281 from the Internet Archive, Hathitrust, and the Bavarian State Library combined. Approximately 23% of the entries were harvested from online library catalogues in the US, Austria,

---

15  Archive sources: Rijksarchief Antwerpen, Archief Nederduitse Jezuïetenprovincie (Flandro Belgica) [hereafter RAANJ(FB)] 3278: Bibliotheekcatalogus [Library catalogue] (s.d.); RAANJ(FB) 2045, Stukken betreffende een proces voor de Geheime Raad tussen Joachim Trognesius, boekdrukker in Antwerpen, aanlegger, en de provincie, verweerder, over het drukken van boeken voor de Sociëteit (1613) [Documents concerning a trial before the Secret Council between Joachim Trognesius, book printer in Antwerp, petitioner, and the province, defendant, about the printing of books for the Society (1613)]; RAANJ(FB) 2046: Catalogus van de boeken over architectuur, achtergelaten door P. Gulielmus Cornelii, overleden te Leuven in 1660 [Catalogue of the books on architecture left by P. Willem Cornelius, d. Leuven 1660], which contains books on many non-architectural subjects; and Rijksarchief Leuven, Jezuïeten College Leuven, 20. Catalogus van de schenkingen aan de bibliotheek, 1635 (Catalogue of donations to the library). Print sources: Delft Catalogue of 1614 (RAANJ[FB] 3002, fols. 2ᵛ–4ᵛ), transcribed by Paul Begheyn in 'The Oldest Jesuit Library Catalogue in the Dutch Republic: The Book Collection at Delft (1614)', in Pedro F. Campa and Peter M. Daly (eds.), *Emblematic Images and Religious Texts: Studies in Honor of G. Richard Dimmler, s.j.* (Philadelphia: Saint Joseph's University Press, 2010), pp. 71–88; Saint Omer catalogue, printed by Willem (Wim) Schrickx, in 'An Early Seventeenth Century Catalogue of Books from the English Jesuit Mission in Saint-Omer', *Archives et Bibliothèques de Belgique/Archief-en bibliotheekwezen in België*, 46 (1975), pp. 592–618; Irish College in Rome inventory, in Hugh Fenning, 'Some Irish Donors of Books to the Irish College in Rome, 1611–1678', in Dáire Keough and Albert McDonnell (eds.), *The Irish College, Rome, and Its World* (Dublin: Four Courts Press, 2008), pp. 45–63. I have transcribed all of these and made them available at www.jesuit-libraries.com/the-database (last accessed, 17 March 2022).

Belgium, Canada, France, Germany, Italy, Spain, Sweden, and the UK, without access to scans of the texts. I have proceeded with an eye to finding specific titles rather than by attempting to represent authors fully or to gather all the information from a given library catalogue. When I find reference in an article to a title which I think would be at home in a Jesuit institution in an article, and when I find a physical book with Jesuit provenance, I search for copies in libraries and in digital repositories.[16] Using extant copies of texts along with manuscript inventories can provide information on books which may have been lost over the centuries. This in turn gives the modern observer a better understanding of institutional priorities, because it does not depend on preservation of a specific text (or its provenance; during the suppression, some provenance marks were blotted out or excised). Please note that the quantitative and qualitative statements which follow should be understood as provisional. The EJLPP is a work in progress. Certain geographical areas of Europe are represented disproportionately. The new partnerships referenced above will be instrumental in balancing the scope, as we continue to integrate the data they make available to us.

Approximately 39% of the titles (2,093 entries) in the complete database of extant books with Jesuit provenance were held by 162 Jesuit institutions in regions which at the time were known as Bohemia, the Kingdom of Croatia, the Holy Roman Empire, the Kingdom of Hungary, the Low Countries, and the Polish-Lithuanian Commonwealth, heavily favouring Central Europe, and this article focuses on these establishments (see Figures 6.1a–b). The dominant institutions are the colleges in Munich (accounting for nearly 36% of the 2,093 titles), Prague (just over 18%), and Augsburg (slightly below 8%). No other single institution represents more than 2% of the total.[17] The books themselves

---

16  I have seen physical copies of 258 books (from Emory, Princeton, and Yale Universities, and the Folger Shakespeare Library), and have consulted photographs of title pages of another 107 at the CRAI Biblioteca de Fons Antic, University of Barcelona. Michael Davies-Powell of the University of Kent and the Middling Culture Project contributed six titles from the British Library. I began the EJLPP by identifying other surviving copies of the Yale and Princeton books, and continue this practice whenever I find a book with Jesuit provenance; I have since progressed to seeking out extant copies of books identified in the manuscript inventories. Since then, I have mined printed articles and books for authors and titles. As an example, I have used Mariani's 'Contribution of the Society of Jesus to the Political Culture of Lithuanian Elites'; cf. p. 159, nn. 45, 52, 53, 54, and 56. I have also come across several titles in bookseller and auction catalogues, but stopped searching those fairly early on, because of the likelihood that I would be unable to return to the source to find any further information I might want. I have retained those in the database; they account for less than 2.5% of the total.

17  I have been unable to identify with certainty the institutions for fifty-eight of the books, accounting for less than 3% of the total.

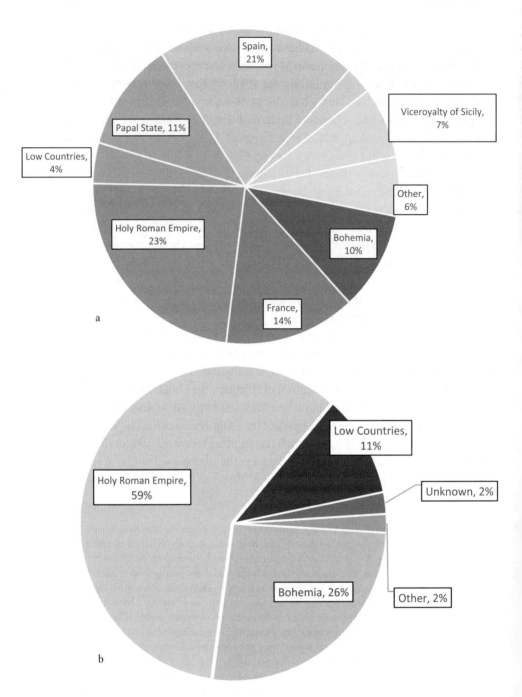

FIGURES 6.1   Geographical distribution of the Jesuit Libraries in the EJLPP and the identified subset. a) Distribution of Colleges/Houses in the EJLPP. b) Distribution of Colleges/Houses in the North, Central, and Eastern European Subset of the EJLPP

were printed in Catalan, Chinese, Dutch, English, French, German, Greek, Hebrew, Italian, Polish, Spanish, and Latin, heavily favouring Latin, and were written by authors from all over Europe, dating from ancient Greece and Rome to contemporary scholars, and include a single author from Peru: the Jesuit Diego Ruiz de Montoya (1562–1632). Authorship is dominated by the Italian peninsula, from which 32% of the total known writers hailed. The next largest geographical groupings are the Low Countries (12%), the Holy Roman Empire (14%), and Spain (15%). Only 2% of the authors in the Northern/Central/Eastern European subset were from Eastern Europe, the largest concentration of those from the Polish-Lithuanian Commonwealth, but also representing Bohemia, the Kingdom of Croatia, the Kingdom of Hungary, and the Principality of Moldavia. The inventories from the Low Countries include books in Arabic, Dutch, English, French, German, Greek, Hebrew, Italian, Spanish, and Latin, again heavily favouring Latin, with about 17% of the authors hailing from the Low Countries, 8% from England, Scotland, and Ireland combined, 7% from the Holy Roman Empire, and 7% from the Italian peninsula.

Although the official instructions on book collection for the Society were vague, the purposes of the Jesuit college and mission libraries were clear: the transmission and preservation of knowledge in subjects determined by the Society from its beginnings to be worthy of studies. The books which Jesuits kept generally reflect the advice in the *Constitutions* regarding the subjects which should be taught in the colleges: 'humane letters of different languages, logic, natural and moral philosophy, metaphysics, scholastic and positive theology, and Sacred Scripture'.[18] A more comprehensive listing of categories is the following, based in part on definitions devised by Joseph S. Freedman and Jill Kraye, in part on the categories identified in the *Bibliotheca selecta*, and in part on experience with multiple inventories. I have attempted to maintain some consistency in categorization of theological disciplines across the centuries, and at the same time have endeavoured not to adhere too strictly to a system of organization, as some works could clearly be used for multiple purposes.[19]

---

18   *Constitutions of the Society of Jesus*, Part IV, Chapter 5, paragraph 351, p. 188.
19   Cf. Joseph S. Freedman, 'Classifications of Philosophy, the Sciences, and the Arts in Sixteenth- and Seventeenth-Century Europe', *The Modern Schoolman*, 72 (1994), pp. 37–65, here 40–43, 47, and 49, explaining the differing understandings of philosophy in the sixteenth and seventeenth centuries, including consideration of the placement of ethics, family life, religious life, history, grammar, lexicography, and oratory; and Jill Kraye, 'Conceptions of Moral Philosophy', in Daniel Garber and Michael Ayers (eds.), *Cambridge History of Seventeenth-Century Philosophy* (2 vols., Cambridge, UK: Cambridge University Press, 1998), 2, pp. 1279–1316, here 1281, 1298. I have attempted to be as broad as possible in my definitions, because (for example) theological and philosophical disciplines changed across the centuries, and because some works could clearly be used for multiple purposes. See also Comerford, 'Jesuit Tuscan Libraries of the 1560s and 1570s'.

These labels are thus artificially applied, as many premodern library inventories were not arranged according to subject, and those that were organized that way both reflect varied definitions of the categories and show that the priority was listing books, not categorizing them. In several cases, for example, the first books inventoried were assigned to categories, but as the inventory progressed, adherence to these categories waned.[20]

TABLE 6.1  General subjects found in prescriptive materials and in Jesuit libraries in selected colleges in Europe prior to the suppression

| Subject (in alphabetical order) | Selected inventories from North and Central European colleges, 17th century #/% | | Extant books with provenance from North, Central, and Eastern European colleges #/% | | EJLPP as a whole #/% | |
|---|---|---|---|---|---|---|
| Ancient philosophy | 10 | 0.80% | 16 | 0.76% | 84 | 1.58% |
| Apologetics, controversies, and heresy | 200 | 16.05% | 145 | 6.92% | 283 | 5.33% |
| Ascetical theology | 10 | 0.80% | 11 | 0.52% | 29 | 0.55% |
| Astronomy, astrology, cosmography and cosmology | 9 | 0.72% | 41 | 1.96% | 153 | 2.88% |
| Bibliographies, dictionaries, libraries, and encyclopedias | 17 | 1.36% | 26 | 1.24% | 75 | 1.41% |
| canon and conciliar law | 10 | 0.80% | 40 | 1.91% | 144 | 2.71% |
| Empiricism, skepticism, and epistemology | 0 | 0% | 5 | 0.24% | 6 | 0.11% |
| Hagiography, martyrology, and spiritual biography | 29 | 2.32% | 120 | 5.93% | 319 | 6.01% |

---

20  For example, the exhaustive *Books in Cambridge Inventories* demonstrates that some private bookowners separated 'humanities' into different subjects (most often poetry and history), whereas others did not, and that both 'philosophy' and 'theology' were inclusive categories, which bookowning individuals did not divide into rational, theoretical, speculative, ascetical, or other subcategories. E.S. Leedham-Green, *Books in Cambridge Inventories: Book-lists from Vice-Chancellor's Court Probate Inventories in the Tudor and Stuart Periods. The Inventories* (2 vols., London: Cambridge University Press, 1986), 1.

TABLE 6.1 General subjects found in prescriptive materials (cont.)

| Subject (in alphabetical order) | Selected inventories from North and Central European colleges, 17th century #/% | | Extant books with provenance from North, Central, and Eastern European colleges #/% | | EJLPP as a whole #/% | |
|---|---|---|---|---|---|---|
| History (church) | 29 | 2.32% | 31 | 1.50% | 84 | 1.58% |
| History, travel, languages, and geography (non-mission territory of Europe) | 46 | 3.69% | 78 | 3.72% | 216 | 4.07% |
| History, travel, languages, and missions (Africa) | 1 | 0.08% | 5 | 0.24% | 18 | 0.34% |
| History, travel, language, and missions (Americas) | 3 | 0.24% | 28 | 1.34% | 81 | 1.53% |
| History, travel, languages, and missions (Asia) | 4 | 0.32% | 77 | 3.67% | 171 | 3.22% |
| History, travel, geography, missions, and navigation (global) | 11 | 0.88% | 44 | 2.10% | 100 | 1.88% |
| History, travel, languages, and missions (Europe) | 0 | 0% | 12 | 0.57% | 45 | 0.85% |
| Humanities | 282 | 22.62% | 274 | 13.24% | 815 | 15.47% |
| Jesuitica | 11 | 0.88% | 71 | 3.39% | 185 | 3.49% |
| Math (including architecture, geometry, and music) | 28 | 2.25% | 47 | 2.24% | 145 | 2.73% |
| Medicine, health, and anatomy | 19 | 1.52% | 28 | 1.34% | 154 | 2.90% |
| Moral theology | 40 | 3.21% | 116 | 5.53% | 257 | 4.84% |
| Natural history, botany and geology | 11 | 0.88% | 27 | 1.29% | 100 | 1.88% |
| Natural philosophy | 21 | 1.65% | 12 | 0.57% | 46 | 0.87% |
| Non-Christian religions and philosophy | 0 | 0% | 7 | 0.33% | 13 | 0.24% |
| Patristics | 52 | 4.17% | 12 | 0.57% | 60 | 1.13% |
| Practical and pastoral theology | 98 | 7.87% | 311 | 14.84% | 611 | 11.51% |
| Prayer and devotion | 58 | 4.65% | 211 | 10.07% | 400 | 7.55% |

TABLE 6.1  General subjects found in prescriptive materials (cont.)

| Subject (in alphabetical order) | Selected inventories from North and Central European colleges, 17th century #/% | | Extant books with provenance from North, Central, and Eastern European colleges #/% | | EJLPP as a whole #/% | |
|---|---|---|---|---|---|---|
| Scholastic philosophy, logic, and dialectic | 12 | 0.96% | 11 | 0.52% | 31 | 0.58% |
| Scholastic theology | 49 | 3.92% | 53 | 2.53% | 138 | 2.60% |
| Scripture and commentary | 108 | 8.66% | 149 | 7.11% | 347 | 6.54% |
| Systematic theology | 10 | 0.80% | 51 | 2.43% | 93 | 1.75% |
| Secular rhetoric | 42 | 3.37% | 32 | 1.54% | 73 | 1.39% |
| Theology (more than one kind, or unclear) | 8 | 0.64% | 0 | 0% | 22 | 0.41% |
| Unknown or unclear | 18 | 1.44% | 0 | 0% | 1 | 0.02% |

This chart allows for a comparison of inventories of colleges in the seventeenth century with a list constructed from surviving texts. Among the most obvious inferences one can draw from it relate to the disparities of representation. Those topics which were represented in large numbers in actual inventories (apologetics/controversies/heresy, humanities, and scripture and commentary account for more than 10% each) are consistent with the mission of the Jesuits, and for the most part were preserved in large numbers up to the present. A comparison with the EJLPP, however, shows that books on these subjects must have had a fairly low rate of survival. In the inventories from the Irish College at Rome, the English College of Liège/St. Omer, the colleges at Delft and Leuven, and the college and professed house at Antwerp, those subjects accounted for approximately 16% of the total collection; among those books still available in 2021, less than 7% were on those subjects. In the inventories, the humanities account for more than 22% of the books, while scriptures and commentaries represent over 10% of the titles; in each case, that is in the neighbourhood of twice the size of the percentage associated with the complete EJLPP. On the other hand, subdisciplines of theology which would be practical for priests (sacramental, pastoral, and liturgical theology as well as devotional texts) account for a total of about 12.5%, a full 50% *lower* than the EJLPP.

Looking closer, we can see that subjects associated with foreign missionary activity were fairly poorly represented in the collections of European libraries. Titles related to the history, travel, language, and missions of Africa, the Americas, and Asia together account for less than 2% of those mentioned in inventories from the Low Countries, Holy Roman Empire, British and Irish mission colleges, and Eastern Europe combined. In the EJLPP subset, those associated with the same regions total about 7%, as do those from the whole, suggesting that this kind of book had a high rate of survival. In some categories, the representation ratios are far closer: the highlighted lines in the chart show the subjects in which each category is within one-half of one percent of all the others. That is a limited group, represented by ascetical theology, bibliographies/dictionaries/encyclopaedias, empiricism/scepticism/epistemology, history/travel/missions (Africa), and non-Christian religions and philosophy. These total only about 2.6% overall. From the other direction, the large discrepancies between holdings in history/travel/languages/missions (Asia), patristics, prayer/devotion, practical and pastoral theology, and scripture and commentary, in which one grouping has significantly more or less than the other two, shows that focusing on surviving texts does not produce faithful reconstructions of suppressed libraries. While the subjects in each category are similar, the reconstructed collections do not very closely resemble the inventories.

## 3 Collection Patterns and Comparisons

Thus, although there was no standardized, comprehensive list of what titles or subject a Jesuit library ought to hold, and attempting to analyse developing librarianship from surviving texts is fraught with pitfalls, the library inventories and extant books do reveal certain collection patterns, either by design or by accident. To explore this issue deeper, and tease out more design and less accident, we turn to subjects in more detail, followed by language and then authorship.

The Society's emphasis on global evangelization, and the large numbers of Jesuits from all over Europe who served as missionaries, first raises the question of what those missionaries might have known about the territories that they evangelized. The *Ratio studiorum* required no training in the culture, history, or languages of Africa, the Americas, or Asia, or in similar subjects for European mission territory. Young men from colleges in Europe were sent to faraway places with little to no knowledge of those places, except the fantastic and heroic tales related in the annual letters describing triumphant conversions or terrifying battles for survival. Most of the libraries which appear in the EJLPP had large collections of texts focused on preaching or otherwise spreading the message of Christianity (i.e., both secular and sacred rhetoric, bibles or parts thereof, catechisms, and sacramental theology), to train students how to serve as priests. Foreign missionary activity, however, required a significant set of other skills, on subjects not well represented. Both the inventories and the surviving texts indicate that the students would have been woefully underprepared to confront the physical realities of travel and the demands of communication and survival outside Europe.[21] In the subset of available books in the EJLPP from North, Central and Eastern European institutions, slightly over 7% of texts are dedicated to the geography, history, and language of non-European territories, and just under 4% for European mission territories, percentages closely matched by the full database. The only non-European language in the subset was Chinese, vs. Arabic, Chinese, Guaraní, and Japanese in the complete group. On paper, the Society supported learning native languages. Letters from the 1580s and 1590s referred both to attempts to learn (for example) American tongues and to the need for stronger support from the leadership to do so. However, language acquisition remained a serious problem up to the suppression of the Society.[22]

In addition, while the average mission-bound Jesuit would have had access to many reports from the missions, including spectacular tales of martyrdom, heroic stories of successful conversions, and testimonies to the zeal of newly baptised Christians, he would have learned little practical information about the history, customs, geography, economy, or language of the region. Reports from the missions are decidedly general and formulaic, emphasizing the same points regardless of whether they describe Brazil or Japan. The dearth of books which could have trained missionaries better for their overseas work cannot be explained easily. The inventories of Antwerp, Delft, Leuven, Liège/Saint Omer, and the Irish College in Rome contain no mention of books on the subjects

---

21   On this, see Kathleen M. Comerford, 'Did the Jesuits Introduce "Global Studies"?' in David Whitford and Amy Leonard (eds.), *Embodiment, Identity, and Gender in the Early Modern Age* (New York: Routledge, 2021), pp. 197–209.

22   Cf. Andes Prieto, *Missionary Scientists: Jesuit Science in Spanish South America, 1570–1810* (Nashville: Vanderbilt University Press, 2011), pp. 109–10; Micah True, *Masters and Students: Jesuit Mission Ethnography in Seventeenth-Century France* (Montreal: McGill-Queen's University Press, 2015), pp. 58–60, 63; Liam Brockey, *Journey to the East: The Jesuit Mission to China, 1579–1724* (Harvard University Press, 2007), *passim*; Takao Abé, *The Jesuit Mission to New France: A New Interpretation in the Light of the Earlier Jesuit Experience in Japan* (Leiden: Brill, 2011), *passim*; and Qiong Zhang, *Making the New World Their Own: Chinese Encounters with Jesuit Science in the Age of Discovery* (Leiden: Brill, 2015), p. 299.

of the culture, geography, or history of European mission territories, and less than 2% of the total relates to all the non-European missions together. This is significantly smaller than the total in the full EJLPP and North/Central/Eastern European subset, which suggests that the survival of texts in these subjects is disproportionate to the interest institutions showed in collecting them.

The same geographical subset of the EJLPP shows other similarities with the subjects of the complete database. In the full set as well as in the section under consideration here, texts in what might be called 'reference' subjects (bibliography, dictionaries, encyclopaedias, and librarianship) account for about 1.4% of the total subjects; European history not related to missions (ancient history, art history, biography, chronology, and church history) for about 5.6%, and items specifically related to the work of the Jesuits (administrative issues, including *Rules* and mission letters) for about 3.5%. There are also striking differences. The North/Central/Eastern group of libraries had considerably smaller collections of texts on medicine, health, pharmacy, natural history, natural philosophy, astronomy, church law, and cosmology than the full set. On the other hand, they had a significantly larger percentage of books focused on moral theology, pastoral theology, prayer and devotion, and systematic theology. The reasons for these discrepancies are unclear; we have no evidence, for example, that colleges or houses in Poland-Lithuania were less interested in European history than those in Portugal, or that colleges in Spain were less concerned with moral theology than those in the Low Countries. Some volumes, in particular those related to devotion and martyrdom (including texts related to the missions, like the circular letters) were certainly studied in detail and by many people; they were meant to be read aloud to students at meals, and they were also read enthusiastically by those who wished to engage in the missions. As a result, such topics probably had a lower survival rate.

In earlier investigations, I remarked on a correlation of sorts which emerged from exploring the sixteenth-century inventories of the colleges in Florence and Siena, contextualized with brief remarks on the English mission college of Liège, which transferred to Saint Omer. There appeared to be a relative favouring of issues concerning the region in which the college was found: local authors, vernacular texts, and regional subjects for those vernacular tests.[23] Choosing nearby authors certainly made sense in terms of availability (both of books and

---

23  I made references to this correlation in several conference papers in 2014 (including at a conference celebrating the four hundredth anniversary of the foundation of the now-defunct Heythrop College of the University of London, which traced its ancestry to Liège/Saint Omer) and 2015, and at greater length in *Jesuit Foundations and Medici Power, 1532–1621* (Leiden: Brill, 2017), pp. 197–207.

authors) and cost of books (particularly in printing centres). In addition, the desire on the part of the Society to disperse its members (to send those who joined to regions in Europe remote from their families), suggests the necessity of providing the colleges with texts which would help foreigners understand their new locations.[24] Texts concerned with local issues and written in the local vernaculars could have been used to teach the members of the Society about the place where they were working. However, the vernacular texts in the Jesuit libraries I have studied rarely favoured local subjects, or community authors, with an important exception. The colleges which served missions, including the Irish College in Rome and the English college at Liège/Saint Omer, did favour books with regional connections, especially those printed locally. Trading large numbers of books from areas where Catholicism was inconsistently legal in early modern Europe could be dangerous, and as a result, the mission colleges relied on their own presses for their vernacular texts (and for many in Latin as well). This demonstrates that geography was important, but so, in a certain sense, was regional identity: for example, the libraries of the English colleges in the Low Countries had no books in Dutch and only eight in French, but seventy-four in English (out of a total of 124 titles).[25]

This should not be overemphasized. In the North/East/Central Europe subset of the EJLPP, with the exception of colleges serving hostile territory, the correlation between location and subject is very weak. One can find histories of Europe, but they are largely written in Latin; among the handful of texts on the subject in the vernacular languages of Europe are Italian-language histories of Italy, in Ingolstadt and Munich; several French-language histories of France, in Brussels, Mindeheim, Munich, Passau, Prague, and Tournai; German-language histories of the Holy Roman Empire, in Augsburg; and of Spain, in Italian, in Munich. A fair number of histories of the Low Countries

---

24　On the dispersion of Jesuits, see Gian Paolo Brizzi, 'Educare il Principe, formare le élites: i gesuiti e Ranuccio I Farnese', in Gian Paolo Brizzi et al. (eds.), *Università, Principe, Gesuiti: La politica farnesiana dell'istruzione a Parma e Piacenza (1545–1622)* (Rome: Bulzoni, 1980), pp. 133–211, here 157–168; Nigel Griffin, '"Virtue versus Letters": The Society of Jesus 1550–1580 and the Export of an Idea', in *European University Institute Working Paper*, 95 (Fiesole: EUI, 1984), pp. 22–26; A. Lynn Martin, 'Jesuits and Their Families: The Experience in Sixteenth Century France', *Sixteenth Century Journal*, 13 (1982), pp. 3–24, here 5–6, and *Jesuit Foundations and Medici Power*, pp. 183–188.

25　Maximilian von Habsburg has observed that 'the Jesuits became specialists in "cultural translation", forming a vital part of their conversion strategy', using the English mission as an example. Of the 'devotional works targeting English markets', 50% were written in Spanish, Italian, French and Latin; the remainder were in English. Maximilian von Habsburg, *Catholic and Protestant Translations of the Imitatio Christi, 1425–1650* (Farnham: Ashgate, 2011), p. 182.

can be found in colleges in that region, but those are in Latin. The colleges in Prague and Munich had comparatively significant collections of texts on European history: studies of Denmark, France, Lithuania, the Low Countries, the Holy Roman Empire, the Roman Empire, and Poland. In total, these represent less than 4% of the books identified in this subgroup of the EJLPP. Furthermore, only five books out of 2,093 consider the life and martyrdom of Stanisław Kostka, S.J. (1550–1568), the only Eastern European saint represented in the collection; eighteen more relate the tales of others martyred in the global missions, but these favour the English missions. The books related to the missions in the Holy Roman Empire and South-eastern Europe are concerned with combatting other religious traditions which could be found there (Protestantism and Islam), not with violence and sacrifice.

Colleges might have saved time and money by using not just local authors, but local Jesuits. Books about Jesuit martyrs, and those printed in the mission colleges, were more often than not written by members of the Society of Jesus. Did Jesuit librarianship develop to favour Jesuit authors in other subjects? Approximately 57% (3,006) of the titles in my complete database were written by members of religious orders; by comparison, about 65% of the titles in the North/Central/European subset were, and a considerably smaller number, just over 30%, can be found in the inventories. The remainder of the authors included ancient, medieval, and early modern writers associated with a variety of religious and secular professions. A total of 50 different religious orders, the majority of which were Jesuits, Dominicans, Franciscans of some kind, Benedictines of some kind, and Augustinians of some kind, are represented (see Figure 6.2). In both the full EJLPP and the North/Central/Eastern European subset, Jesuits dominated, more in the North/Central/Eastern colleges (over 82%) than in the whole, including Southern Europe (about 77%) and in the written inventories (nearly 67%). However, there is little apparent connection between the place of birth of the Jesuit author and the location of the library holding that author's books.

The complete EJLPP does demonstrate a marked increase in Jesuit authors in the college and residence libraries throughout the period between the foundation and the suppression. Joseph De Guibert observed that even a quarter century after Ignatius' death, the early lists of reading material for the colleges made little reference to the growing corpus of Jesuit-authored books.[26] That would change after the next quarter century. Approximately 20% of the

---

26  Joseph de Guibert, *The Jesuits: Their Spiritual Doctrine and Practice*, transl. William J. Young (St. Louis: Institute of Jesuit Sources, 1994), p. 217: in the 1581 list 'no spiritual writings published by Jesuits appear, except for the letters from the missions and the life of Ignatius'.

titles overall have provenance markings which include dates. Most of those are from institutions in Lyon (17%), Munich (36%), and Prague (8%), and they show a fifteen-fold increase between the sixteenth and seventeenth centuries in the number of texts authored by Jesuits, vs. a threefold increase for both Franciscans and Dominicans (which are the second- and third-largest represented religious orders). The practice of collecting new books written by members of religious orders declined in the eighteenth century, but Jesuits still dominated, and declined by less than other orders: they saw a 44% increase, vs. only a 14% increase among Dominican authors and a 25% increase among Franciscans. In other words, as Jesuit librarianship developed, a bias toward collecting Jesuit authors was clearly a part of it.[27] For the subset of books associated with institutions in North, Central, and Eastern Europe, of all the books authored by members of religious orders (65% of the titles), Jesuits accounted for over 88%, versus 3.8% for Dominicans and 2.6% for Franciscans.

The language issue, while related to the subject issue, is more complex. The sample college inventories, serving a population which spoke English, Dutch, French, and Italian, held a significant number of texts in those languages, accounting for close to 14% of the total books. Questions about the language of instruction in European institutions loom generally large in discussions of early Jesuit teaching. Allan Farrell noted that in the 1599 or final version of the *Ratio*, 'the amount of vernacular usage allowed both teacher and pupil was very considerable,' referencing several of the Rules for teachers of grammar, including a directive to have students translate dictation in other tongues to Latin, and permission to use the students' native languages in written composition.[28] Although the 'Common Rules for the Teachers of the Lower Classes' states that 'pupils should never be permitted to use their mother tongue in anything connected with class. ... Hence also the teacher must always speak Latin,' it also

---

27   This is clearly reflected in the pre-suppression libraries, yet Congregation 21 (1829), Decree 26 (17 and 18 in the manuscript version) hints at trouble: 'present circumstances do not so much require that Ours should be encouraged to write as that the compulsion which some experience to write and to publish their works should be reined in and held in check', John W. Padberg et al. (eds.), *For Matters of Greater Moment: The First Thirty Jesuit General Congregations. A Brief History and a Translation of the Decrees* (St. Louis, Mo: Institute of Jesuit Sources, 1994), p. 443. A reference to Congregation 11 (1651), Decree 18 (32 in the manuscript version), follows, reminding members of the 'severe and definite penalties' for publishing without permission, including 'privation of office, loss of active and passive voice, disqualifications from any honors and prelacies within the Society, even corporal punishment – all these to be decreed in proportion to the gravity of the transgression, as judged by the Superior', *For Matters of Greater Moment*, p. 325.

28   Allan Farrell, *The Jesuit Code of Liberal Education: Development and Scope of the* Ratio Studiorum (Milwaukee: The Bruce Publishing Company, 1938), p. 349.

TABLE 6.2  Representation of selected religious orders among authors in the inventories and the EJLPP

| Religious order | Representation at selected inventories from North and Central European colleges (percent of all religious orders/percent of all authors) | Representation in North, Central, and Eastern European subset of the EJLPP (percent of all religious orders/percent of all authors) | EJLPP as a whole (percent of all religious orders/percent of all authors) |
|---|---|---|---|
| Jesuits | 66.67/22.45 | 82.45/48.53 | 76.78/43.55 |
| Dominicans | 10.95/3.69 | 5.87/3.46 | 6.99/3.96 |
| Franciscans (all kinds) | 6.19/2.09 | 3.94/2.31 | 3.76/2.13 |
| Benedictines (all kinds) | 2.14/.72 | 1.05/0.61 | 2.10/1.19 |
| Augustinians (all kinds) | 4.29/1.44 | 1.16/0.66 | 1.76/1.00 |

permitted the teacher to interpret reading in vernacular languages, provided that he 'keep to the Latin word order as much as he can. In this way the ears of his pupils become accustomed to the Latin rhythm'.[29] The books which were to be read at table were also in Latin.

Seventy-two percent of the titles in the six inventories discussed here were in Latin, with another combined 6% in Arabic, Greek, and Hebrew. The remaining 22% were in Dutch, English, French, Italian, and Spanish, with more than 6% in English, nearly 6% in French, less than 2% each in Dutch and in Italian, and less than 1% in Spanish. The distribution of these languages is not particularly surprising: all of the books in Dutch and 98% of those in French are from libraries from the Low Countries, and 100% of those written in English were held in colleges serving the English or Irish missions. A total of about 13% of the titles are in the everyday languages of the people in the region housing the colleges or professed house (or, in the case of English, the language of the region to which the students were destined to serve).

With respect to the EJLPP, the most common language for the texts was Latin, accounting for over 79% of the North/Central/Eastern European group and 72% of the whole. The other texts were largely in European languages,

---

29  E.g., Rule 30, Farrell, *Jesuit* Ratio studiorum, pp. 64 and 67.

heavily favouring Western European tongues.[30] In the North/Central/Eastern European libraries, I have found only two books printed in Eastern European languages, both in Polish. In the complete data set, a total of four books were in the Eastern European languages: one each in Albanian and Croatian, and the other two in Polish. The Albanian-language text was held by the Professed House of Rome, and the one in Croatian belonged to a college in Paris. The inventories under consideration had no titles in Eastern European languages, and a tiny percentage, less than 0.25%, in German. Even noting that the vast majority of texts in these institutions were in Latin, this is a striking finding, at odds with southwestern European foundations. In particular, the dearth of texts in the languages spoken in Bohemia, Poland, Lithuania, Hungary, Croatia, et cetera, among surviving volumes is noteworthy. Five hundred thirty-nine books in my data set were held by institutions in Bohemia, the vast majority of those by the college in Prague. Not one of them is in a Slavic language, and only eight of them were authored by someone from Bohemia. Indeed, only 5% of the texts in the North/Central/Eastern Europe grouping were written by authors of the same nationality as the institution, and the vast majority of those are from the Holy Roman Empire. As for books in non-European languages, I have found one each in Persian and Japanese, two each in Arabic and Chinese, and twenty-four in Hebrew. Among these, the one Chinese-language book, and ten of the Hebrew books, were kept in Northern, Central, or Eastern European libraries.

Geography is important to the language issue in other ways as well. The presence of many authors who would have called themselves 'Romans' in the classical period muddies identification of place within the Italian peninsula as a whole, but also throughout the Europe and the non-European Mediterranean. In states like the Low Countries and Spain, multiple languages were spoken. Many small, independent states of the Italian peninsula shared a common vernacular; in the viceroyalties of Naples and Sicily, Spanish as well as the local dialects of Italian were spoken. These facts considerably complicate the task of determining whether or not local collection preferences can be discerned. Over 13% of the texts in the full database were written by authors of the same nationality as the institution, with a significant bias toward far western and southern Europe. Approximately 18% of the books associated with French libraries were in the French language, and approximately 32% of those from Spanish libraries were in Spanish. By contrast, about 9.6% of the books in

---

30  In order of representation, these were Italian, French, German, Spanish, English, and Dutch. Rarely, one can find texts in Asian, African, or American languages; on this, see Comerford, 'Did the Jesuits Introduce "Global Studies"?'

libraries in the Holy Roman Empire were in German. In the inventories, nearly 63% of the books in the English and Irish missions were written in English, as compared to less than 2% of the books in Dutch-speaking Low Countries institutions which were in Dutch. In the available inventories from the Low Countries and the English and Irish mission colleges, more than 16% of the titles were certainly written by authors from those regions; the vast majority of those (over 96%, accounting for almost 15.9% of the whole) were from the Low Countries. That relationship between author and place is expressed more weakly in the surviving books in the EJLPP: 13% of the texts were written by authors from the same geographical area as the institution, with Spain accounting for more than 30% of those, followed by France (24%), the Holy Roman Empire (20%), the Low Countries (nearly 5%), and Bohemia (less than 2%). In the North/Central/Eastern Europe subset, 11% of the texts were written by authors from the regions where the colleges were housed. Most of those (79%) were in the Holy Roman Empire, with the Low Countries trailing considerably (16%).

## 4 Conclusions

This examination of the rich heritage of Jesuit librarianship uses two complimentary approaches: identification of titles from manuscript or published inventories, and seeking out physical or electronic copies of actual texts with verifiable Jesuit provenance. I have attempted to understand libraries in the colleges in North, Central, and Eastern Europe by investigating the appearance of given subjects, the presence of members of religious orders among the authors of texts, and the use of vernacular languages. As I continue to add to the database, I expect to see my observations shift and become more nuanced, but several tentative conclusions are suggested by the data. First, vernacular texts were widely available in Jesuit college and residence libraries. While Latin dominated, sixteenth, seventeenth and eighteenth-century Jesuits and their students had access to books in most of the European languages, but southern and western European languages were far easier to find, even in Eastern Europe. Second, the availability of texts in the English language, and focused on English martyrdom, at the continental Irish and English colleges shows a strong commitment to those missions which is not mirrored by texts focusing on the missions in Eastern Europe, Asia, Africa, or the Americas. Among the many issues related to this point, only vanishingly small percentages of books were available in languages from outside Europe. Third, while we associate Jesuit education with good training in the humanities, logic, preaching, and missionary activities, based on the advice in the *Constitutions* regarding the subjects which should be taught in the colleges, texts on these subjects were far eclipsed in their libraries by scholastic theology, moral theology, and scripture commentary. Fourth, some of our assumptions are quite close to the mark: Jesuit institutions favoured Jesuit-authored texts, and they collected large numbers of books related to casuistry and controversial theology. Further exploration of the vast intellectual and material heritage of the Society of Jesus, in particular with reference to the European missions and Eastern Europe, will surely lead scholars onto firmer ground in understanding the importance of early modern information management.

# PART 2

## *Relocating Libraries*

∴

CHAPTER 7

# Building a Nation through Books

*From Military to Cultural Armament in Seventeenth-Century Sweden*

*Jonas Nordin*

The Swedish empire in the seventeenth century was a precocious and overstretched creation. In less than a generation, Sweden went from being an unnoticed peripheral state on the outskirts of Europe to dictating the terms of continental politics. Long-term reputation and real influence, however, could not depend on weapons alone. In an international order based on authority cultural renown was also vital to gain admiration and respect from other states, and Sweden had a long way to go to meet this requirement. The Protestant Reformation had created a spiritual divide between Sweden and large parts of Europe, having disassembled much of the cultural and educational infrastructure, including libraries. The present study explores the ideological background to the large-scale confiscations of libraries and looting of books in the Swedish wars of the seventeenth century. How were the objectives of these acquisitions formulated and by whom? In what environments did the pillaged books find new homes? To what extent were the purposes of the lootings fulfilled and the books put to use in their new surroundings?

Historian Andrew Pettegree has argued that books had lost their role as status objects already in the sixteenth century. If a private individual, such as a middle-rank official of the Paris *Parlament*, Antoine du Prat, by 1550 could have accumulated a personal library of 4,000 volumes, 'then Europe's crowned heads had to look to other forms of conspicuous consumption to awe foreign visitors and their subjects.'[1] What was the situation then, when we turn to countries like Sweden, where not even the largest public library could boast of having 4,000 volumes? Here, the collecting of books was not about conspicuous consumption but rather a matter of meeting practical needs. By the end of the sixteenth century, there was only one printer in the Swedish realm and he rarely produced more than two or three books per year. Private book

---

[1] Andrew Pettegree, 'The Renaissance Library and the Challenge of Print', in Alice Crawford (ed.), *The Meaning of the Library: A Cultural History* (Princeton: Princeton University Press, 2015), pp. 72–90, here pp. 75–76. The argument is expanded in Andrew Pettegree and Arthur der Weduwen, *The Library: A Fragile History* (London: Profile Books, 2021), ch. 4.

collections were insignificant and no public libraries existed. There was no substantial knowledge production in Sweden and, from the Reformation on, even much of cultural importation had come to a halt.

To be sure, Swedish scholars had rarely contributed in any substantial manner to European learning in the medieval centuries. Saint Bridget (c.1303–1373) stands out as one of very few Swedes of some international renown. The monastery that she founded in Vadstena became a hub for manuscript production and around 1500 held what was probably the largest library in Scandinavia, with somewhere between 900 and 1,300 books. The core of the library was a vast collection of sermons and the monastery had a unique standing as a centre for religious instruction, but mainly it served the immediate needs of the brothers and sisters. Certainly, through tomes containing Aristotle and the Church Fathers, Avicenna and Raimundus Lullus, as well as books on metaphysics, astronomy and mathematics, the mainstay of European education was represented in Sweden, but it was a thin stream and it only ran in one direction.[2]

The late medieval centuries brought strong expansion of learning with many newly established universities and not least thanks to the art of printing, but the intellectual drive that Europe experienced came to a halt in Sweden. Scandinavia's first university was founded in Uppsala in 1477, but its activities were discontinued in the 1520s. Swedish customers had already had books printed in Northern Germany some years before the first book was printed in Sweden in 1483 by the Lübeck craftsman Johann Snell. He and another itinerant printer, Bartholomeus Ghotan, successively installed their print shops in Stockholm in the 1480s. In spite of a promising start in that decade, however, Swedish print production all but crumbled in the early 1500s and saw only slow progress in the following years. Some production of books intended for domestic use continued to be outsourced to print centres outside Sweden, especially Lübeck and Rostock. These printings are included in the graph below (Figure 7.1). Until 1580, foreign-printed items represent twenty-five percent of the corpus in the Swedish national bibliography edited by Isak Collijn, and their proportion rises to just under fifty percent in the last two decades of the sixteenth century.[3] When considering these figures, we need to bear two

---

2  Ville Walta, *Libraries, Manuscripts and Book Culture in Vadstena Abbey* (Helsinki: Helsinki University, 2014). For a new estimate of the size of the library, see Jonas Nordin, 'Hur stort var klosterbiblioteket i Vadstena?', *Biblis: Kvartalstidskrift för bokvänner*, 94 (2021), pp. 34–44.
3  Isak Collijn, *Sveriges bibliografi intill år 1600* (3 vols., Uppsala: Svenska litteratursällskapet, 1934–1938). Cf. Henrik Schück, *Den svenska förlagsbokhandelns historia* (2 vols., Stockholm: Norstedts, 1923), 1, pp. 95–102; Wolfgang Undorf, 'Buchhandel und Buchsammeln in Schweden

things in mind. First, much, if not most, of the material printed abroad that has been included in Collijn's bibliography was not intended for the Swedish market; some examples of this are the many Dutch, German or English translations of Saint Bridget's writings. The most successful Swedish book of the era was undoubtedly Olaus Magnus' *Historia de gentibus septentrionalibus* (see below). All thirteen editions of this book before 1599 were printed abroad, but only the first was aimed at a Swedish audience, and then only partially. Second, the fact that a part of Swedish book production was located abroad rather underlines my argument that Sweden was on the cultural fringe of Europe and unable to meet even a comparatively modest demand for books. With these observations having been made, I will concentrate on domestic printing. The poor output is especially visible during the reign of King Gustav I Vasa (1523–1560), and by the end of the century a mere 429 titles, or thereabouts, are certain to have been printed in Sweden.[4] Of the 429 known domestic titles, the privileged Royal Printer in Stockholm, who in effect was the sole printer in the realm after 1526, had produced 382, or almost ninety percent.[5]

Using international research, church historian Otfried Czaika has argued that the real print output in Sweden might have been twice as large as the surviving print items suggest.[6] This is an arbitrary although by no means unreasonable assumption, but it is based on international comparisons and, if the model is correct, it does not change the relative proportions of the Swedish and foreign print output. If we only include identified domestic titles, the number of printed works did not rise above five per year on average, and with all the foreign works included, the figure would still not exceed 5.5. Even if we double these figures the number would remain unimpressive, especially in the first half of the century.

---

zur Zeit der Reformation und Konfessionalisierung', in Otfried Czaika and Wolfgang Undorf (eds.), *Schwedische Buchgeschichte: Zeitalter der Reformation und Konfessionalisierung* (Göttingen: Vandenhoeck & Ruprecht, 2021), pp. 13–54, esp. pp. 14–23.

4 For single volumes detected since Collijn's bibliography, cf., e.g., Otfried Czaika, *Then Swenska Psalmeboken 1582: Utgåva med inledande kommentar* (Skara: Skara stiftshistoriska sällskap, 2016), pp. 22–24. The print output in sixteenth-century Sweden is discussed by, e.g., Wolfgang Undorf, Remi Kick, and Otfried Czaika, in Czaika and Undorf (eds.), *Swedische Buchgeschichte*.

5 The Uppsala Chapter printed a circular letter in 1535, and Jürgen Richolff was commissioned to print the Swedish Bible in 1540–41; he produced four other print works during the same period.

6 Otfried Czaika, *Några wijsor om Antichristum [1536] samt handskrivna tillägg: Utgåva med inledande kommentarer* (Skara: Skara stiftshistoriska sällskap, 2019), pp. 17–38.

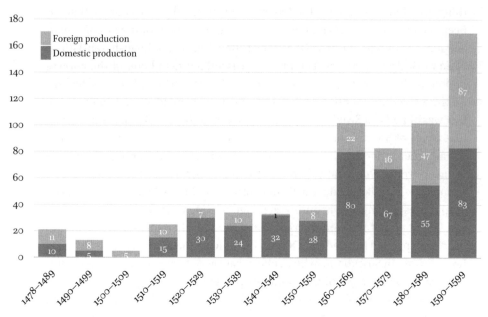

FIGURE 7.1    Swedish domestic and foreign print production 1478–1599: number of titles
SOURCE: ISAK COLLIJN, SVERIGES BIBLIOGRAFI INTILL ÅR 1600, 1–3 (UPPSALA: SVENSKA LITTERATURSÄLLSKAPET, 1934–1938). NOTE: ALTHOUGH SOME ADDITIONAL PRINTED WORKS FROM THE PERIOD HAVE BEEN IDENTIFIED SINCE COLLIJN'S BIBLIOGRAPHY, IT DOES NOT AFFECT THE OVERALL PICTURE. THE NUMBERS IN THE BARS ONLY REFER TO PRINTED MATTER REGISTERED IN COLLIJN.

The main, not to say only, accomplishments of domestic printing in the century were the Swedish translation of the New Testament in 1527, of the whole Bible in 1541, and of the New Testament into Finnish in 1548. In fact, the two most important works of Swedish book production of the period and the only two examples of Swedish renaissance humanism were printed in Rome by two exiled Catholic archbishops, the brothers Johannes and Olaus Magnus. Their magna opera, *De omnibvs Gothorvm Sveonvmqve regibvs* (1554) and *Historia de gentibus septentrionalibus* (1555), were fine representations of the very few vestiges of Nordic erudition. As expatriates, the Magnus brothers longed for their native country, and as deposed representatives of the proper Catholic faith, they felt the urge to remind the world that there existed an exposed part of Christianity in the far North. Both works were highly successful and had a disproportionate influence on the image of Sweden and the Swedes internationally. Two Rome editions of *De omnibus* were followed by another three in Basel, Cologne, and Wittenberg, and a Swedish translation was printed in Stockholm in 1620. *Historia* was an even greater success, with no less than twenty-one editions and translations into French, Italian, Dutch, German, and English.[7] The influence of these two books far exceeded anything that may have been produced by the Royal Printers in Sweden, and, ironically, left a long-lasting negative mark on the image of Sweden abroad.[8] The urge for information about the rising European great power was such that as late as 1669 Johannes van Ravesteyn in Amsterdam could print a 12:o edition of *Historia*, long after the passing of its best-before date. Through its inability to utilize the printing press, the Swedish Crown had left much of the prerogative of interpretation to its enemies.

## 1  A Nation Poor on Books

King Erik XIV (ruled 1560–1568) and his brother and successor Johan III (ruled 1569–1592) were not unaffected by renaissance humanism and they both eagerly read the works of the Magnus brothers, but their cultural activities had little effect outside court circles. One of the largest private book collections in the realm belonged to Councillor Hogenskild Bielke (1538–1605) and comprised around four hundred printed and manuscript books, of which about 290 are known to us. It was primarily a reference library of contemporary books in the fields of theology and law.[9] The only comparable private book collection in the realm is supposed to have been that of Per Brahe the Elder (1520–1590). In his instruction for the upbringing of aristocratic boys to be perfect courtiers, he stressed the value of reading, which nevertheless came second to horsemanship and the use of arms. Brahe's advice was sturdy and practical:

---

7  Elena Balzamo, *Un archevêque venu du froid: Essais sur Olaus Magnus (1490–1557)* (Paris: L'Harmattan, 2019); Erling Sandmo, 'Historien om en Historia: Olaus Magnus i et bokhistorisk perspektiv', in Aasta M. Bjørkøy etc (eds.) *Litterære verdensborgere: Transnasjonale perspektiver på norsk bokhistoria 1519–1850* (Oslo: Nasjonalbiblioteket, 2019), pp. 56–80.
8  Cf. Otfried Czaika, 'Det svenska riksrådets censur av David Chytraeus' krönikor på 1590-talet', in Otfried Czaika, Jonas Nordin and Pelle Snickars (eds.), *Information som problem: Medieanalytiska texter från medeltid till framtid* (Stockholm: Kungliga biblioteket, 2014), pp. 78–95.
9  Otto Walde, 'En svensk boksamlare från Vasatiden: Hogenskild Bielke och hans bibliotek', in *Uppsala universitetsbiblioteks minnesskrift 1621–1921: Med bidrag av bibliotekets forna och nuvarande tjänstemän* (Uppsala: Uppsala universitetsbibliotek, 1921), pp. 193–267; Wolfgang Undorf (ed.), *Hogenskild Bielke's library: A catalogue of the famous 16th century Swedish private collection* (Uppsala: Uppsala universitetsbibliotek, 1995); Arne Losman, 'Adelskap och boklig bildning', in Jakob Christensson (ed.), *Signums svenska kulturhistoria: Renässansen* (Lund: Signum, 2005), pp. 151–179, here pp. 151–155.

He [the noble student] must also have some experience in the seven liberal bookish arts, although they may not be fully perfected since other chivalric exercises may stand in the way; however, there are some parts a courtier cannot dispense of, and, understandably, no one can be eloquent without *artes discendi* [learning skills, viz. *artes liberales*]. ... If we are to begin with the reading of useful books, it is above all important to know that the world is full of books on many things that human reason has conceived, authored and comprehended, but not all of them are of the same value, as is stated in *Ecclesiastes*, twelfth and last chapter. Therefore, one must choose the very best and most judicious *autores* that one can read.[10]

According to Brahe, the important subjects were liberal arts, Latin, theology, political science, warfare, law, rhetoric, history, and ethics. Beside two modern writers, Philip Melanchton and Jean Bodin, he mentioned Erasmus and Petrarch, while the rest consisted of around a dozen classical authors, from Aristotle to Justinian. 'More useful authors could certainly be enumerated, but these are sufficient for a courtier (*aulicum*), who, for the sake of other chivalric exercises, cannot spend time on reading many books.'[11] As stated in the referred passage in *Ecclesiastes* (12:12): 'of making many books *there is* no end; and much study *is* a weariness of the flesh.'

Indeed, the future King Charles IX (ruled 1604–1611) revived Uppsala University as a decidedly Protestant school in 1593, but operations did not begin to prosper until the reign of Gustavus Adolphus (ruled 1611–1632). The latter introduced a new and determined cultural policy that also affected libraries.

10   'Så måste han ock hafwa någon Förfarenheet uthi the Siu frije Booklige Konster; Kan thet icke blifwe så fullkomligit för andre öffningar skull, såsom thet kunda förhindra, så är thet lijkwäl något ibland hwart Styckie, såsom een *Aulicus* ingalunda kan wara föruthan, som man kan förstå ther uthaff, at ingen kan blifwa något Wälltalande, *Artes discendi* föruthan. ... Och effter nu till thet första, här effter förmält warder om nyttige Bökers Läßning. Så skall man thet weeta, at Werlden är full aff Böker, om allehanda Ting, som Menniskligit Förnufft hafwer kunnat uptänckia, författa och begrijpa, och äro icke alle gode, effter såsom *Ecclesiastes* skrifwer uthi thet 12. och senaste Cap: Så måste man uthwälia sig the aldrebäste och förståndigeste *Authores* som man hafwa kan, at läsa uthi', *Gamble Grefwe Peer Brahes, Fordom Sweriges Rijkes Drotzetz, Oeconomia, eller Huußholdz-Book, För ungt Adels-folck. Skrifwin Anno 1581* (Visingsborg: Johann Kankel, 1677), pp. 11–12. Cf. the modern critical edition: John Granlund and Gösta Holm (ed.) *Oeconomia eller Hushållsbok för ungt adelsfolk* (Stockholm: Nordiska museet, 1971), pp. 15–20, with commentary pp. 229–232.

11   'Mera nyttige *Authores* kunde wäl upräcknas, men thesse äre nogh för een *Aulico*, som för andre Ridderlige öffningar icke kan gifwa sig Tijd at läsa månge Bööker igenom', *Gamble Grefwe Peer Brahes, Fordom Sweriges Rijkes Drotzetz, Oeconomia*, p. 16.

In 1611, he appointed the first royal librarian, two years later Uppsala University received its first printer, and a university library was founded in 1620. Thus, both the king's capital city and the rehabilitated university had new libraries created for the benefit of the realm, but neither of them had any collections to boast of. The foundation for the library in Uppsala consisted of books from the discontinued Franciscan convent at Gråmunkeholmen in Stockholm. It had been the home of a productive scriptorium in the medieval period, and both Johann Snell and Bartholomeus Ghotan seem to have installed their temporary print shops within its premises in the 1480s. In the second half of the sixteenth century, the abandoned properties were used as storehouse for the book collections that at the time of the Reformation had been confiscated from churches, monasteries, private individuals (including Hogenskild Bielke), as well as from the Catholic King Sigismund (ruled 1592–1599), among others. This motley collection, possibly exceeding 4,000 volumes, and consisting largely of scholastic writing and Catholic liturgy, became the core of the university library.[12] In addition, the books of the early Vasas were brought from Stockholm to Uppsala, but their numbers were probably quite unimposing. According to a list from 1568, Erik XIV owned 217 printed and handwritten books, and according to another list from 1571, Johan had 56 volumes in his possession.[13] Admittedly, none of these lists shows the full extent of their respective collections, but one biographer's conclusion, that King Erik 'gathered a library that equalled or even surpassed those of contemporary Northern European princes', does not convince.[14] The Danish King Christian III (ruled 1536–1559) mustered some 2,000 books during his lifetime, and his subject

---

12   Otto Walde, 'Konung Sigismunds bibliotek och Gustaf Adolfs donation 1620–21: Ett bidrag till Upsala universitetsbiblioteks äldsta historia', *Nordisk tidskrift för bok- och biblioteksväsen*, 2 (1915), pp. 317–332.

13   'Concept till Inventarium öfver konung Erik XIV:s böcker; upprättadt den 27 september 1568', in *Handlingar rörande Skandinaviens historia*, 27 (Stockholm 1845) pp. 380–390; 'Konung Johan III:s boksamling år 1571: Ett hittills otryckt bokförteckningskoncept av Rasmus Ludvigsson', *Lychnos: Lärdomshistoriska samfundets årsbok* (1937), pp. 212–220. See also Claes Annerstedt, *Upsala universitetsbiblioteks historia intill år 1702* (Stockholm: Norstedts, 1894) pp. 6 ff., and Harald Wieselgren, *Drottning Kristinas bibliotek och bibliotekarier före hennes bosättning i Rom jemte en öfverblick öfver de kungl. biblioteken i Sverige före hennes regeringstid* (Stockholm: Norstedts, 1901), pp. 3–13; on Erik's library: Astrid Nilsson, *Royal Marginalia: King Eric XIV of Sweden as a Reader* (Lund: Centre for Language and Literature, 2021), pp. 39–41.

14   'han hade samlat ett bibliotek som tålde jämförelse med eller överträffade samtida nordeuropeiska furstars': Ingvar Andersson, *Erik XIV*, fourth ed. (Stockholm: Wahlström & Widstrand, 1979), p. 162.

Henrik Rantzau (1526–1598), governor of Schleswig and Holstein, had a library of more than 6,300 volumes, to name but two examples.[15]

Beside the donation of books, Gustavus Adolphus assigned 200 silver *daler* per year, a sum that was raised to 300 *daler* in 1621, for the university library's maintenance.[16] This sum, about 3.6 percent of the university's annual budget, had to cover not only the procurement of books, but also the upkeep of the library building.[17] The grant remained at the same level until the middle of the century, and during the years 1641–1649, it was only enough to buy fifteen books per year.[18] Admittedly, acquisition rose to nearly sixty-five books annually during the next five years, but had this been the only way of obtaining books, it would have taken a very long time to create a library collection of any significance. The war with Poland in the 1620s, however, initiated a new and determined way of procuring books wholesale.

## 2   Organized Looting of Books

When he was a child, Gustavus Adolphus was taught that the same hand maneuvered the pen and the sword. In 1604, the crown prince's teacher, Johan Skytte, published 'A Short Treatise: On the Crafts and Virtues That a Young Prince Should Strive to Attain':

---

15  Harald Ilsøe (ed.), *På Papir, Pergament og Palmeblade ... Skatte i Det Kongelige Bibliotek* (Copenhagen: Det Kongelige Bibliotek, 1993), p. 13; S. Birket Smith, *Om Kjøbenhavns Universitetsbibliothek før 1728, især dets Håndskriftsamlinger* (Copenhagen: Reitzels, 1982 [1882]) p. 20; M. Posselt, 'Die Bibliothek Heinrich Rantzau's', *Zeitschrift der Gesellschaft für Schleswig-Holstein-Lauenburgische Geschichte*, 11 (1881), pp. 69–124, pp. 82–83; Nan Dahlkild and Steen Bille Larsen (eds.), *Dansk Bibliotekshistorie: Biblioteker for de få. Biblioteker for de få; tiden før 1920* (2 vols., Århus: Aarhus Universitetforlag, 2021), I, p. 84.

16  Gustavus Adolphus' resolution on the University and the order of the school system, 13 April 1620; idem, ordinance on the number of professors, salaries, and several other matters at Uppsala University, 7 July, 1621; Claes Annerstedt, *Upsala universitets historia*, Bihang 1: Handlingar 1477–1654 (Uppsala: Schultz, 1877), pp. 155, 175.

17  A financial plan from September 1620 set the annual budget of the entire university to 8,210 silver *daler*; Annerstedt, *Upsala universitets historia*, Bihang 1, pp. 158–160. In 1652, when Mazarin's former librarian Gabriel Naudé was hired to cater Queen Christina's books in Stockholm, he received an annual salary of 3,000 silver *daler*; Wieselgren, *Drottning Kristinas bibliotek*, p. 38; Christian Callmer, *Königin Christina, ihre Bibliothekare und ihre Handschriften: Beiträge zur europäischen Bibliotheksgeschichte* (Stockholm: Kungliga biblioteket, 1977), pp. 73.

18  Annerstedt, *Upsala universitetsbiblioteks historia*, p. 76.

According to the most learned and wise Masters' faithful advice and opinions, a young Lord and Prince should train himself thoroughly in the following exercises: firstly, in a true and proper religion and worship; secondly, in the wonderful and fine adornments that the study of books abundantly informs, delivers and bestows on us all; and lastly, in all those chivalric bodily exercises, which are a foundation and preparation to all things martial, and which makes a good soldier and an illustrious warrior prince.[19]

Gustavus Adolphus took the lesson to heart, and war, religion, and bookish exercises merged from his very first campaign onwards and became a matter of national pride. Typical is the king's motivation for establishing a domestic paper production:

Since God the Almighty has gifted us Swedes with soul and reason and skills, in equal measure with other nations, and here in the kingdom nothing is lacking that paper can be made of, we are determined to set up a paper mill in Uppsala.[20]

He also drew attention to the fact that

many much-needed books are in demand, both in the schools and academies here in the kingdom, which is a big reason why studies and bookish ingenuity cannot reach the perfection that it rightfully should and we would like to see.[21]

---

19  'Effter the Höglärde och klokaste Mästares trogne Råd och Betänckiande, skal en vng Herre och Furste vti thesse effterföliande Stycker, sigh flijteligen öfwa och bruka: Först vthi en rätt och sannskyllig Religion och Gudztiänst: Sedan vthi the Härlige och sköne Prydningar, som the Boklige Konster rijkeligen oss allom medhdela, skäncke och förähre: Och til thet sidste vthi alle Ridderlige Kropsens öfningar, hwilke äre ett Fundament och Præparatif til alle Krijgzsaker, och göra en godh Soldat och berömmelig Krijgz-Furste.' Johan Skytte, *Een kort Vnderwijsning: Vthi hwad Konster och Dygder en Furstelig Person skal sigh öfwa och bruka then ther täncker med tijden lyckosamligen regera Land och Rijke* (Stockholm: [Anund Olufsson], 1604), USTC 253116, p. 11.

20  Gustavus Adolphus' letter 8 January 1612, quoted from Schück, *Den svenska förlagsbokhandelns historia*, 1, p. 120.

21  'många högnödige böker, både Vthi skolerna och Academierna här Vthi wårt Rijke desidereres, och sådant wara een stoor orsaak, hwarföre studier och Boklige kånster icke kunne komma till den profection, som det sigh med retta borde och wij giärna såge', privilege for the book printer Johan Matthiæ, 21 February 1628, quoted from Henrik Schück, *Bidrag till svensk bokhistoria* (Stockholm: Föreningen för bokhandtverk, 1900), p. 29.

This attitude prevailed during the whole, so called, age of imperial greatness and the looting of books continued through the Thirty Years' War, the wars of Charles X Gustav, and the wars of Charles XII in the early 1700s. A pattern can be discerned, however, in the different directions taken by the looted books at different times. Most of the books seized by Gustavus Adolphus became public property, principally through the university library in Uppsala; under Queen Christina (ruled 1644–1654), the flow of books was redirected to the royal library in Stockholm (and eventually to Rome and the Vatican Library); whereas from the 1660s onwards, most books ended up in private collections. There are, of course, exceptions to this general pattern during each period.[22]

It is impossible to say how large a share of the books in Swedish libraries in the seventeenth century was made up of war booty. The field marshal and royal councillor, Count Jakob De la Gardie (1583–1652), erected the most sumptuous palace, known as *Makalös* (Sans pareil), in Stockholm in the early seventeenth century. He left a select library of some 229 titles, arranged by the four 'faculties' of theology, law, medicine, and philosophy, including history and fortification. Although he made his living from warfare and spent most of this time in the field, there are no signs of booty among his books. They seem to have been carefully handpicked to suit the owner's needs and interests; for instance, among his books there were only works on Lutheran theology, a feature rarely encountered in the looted libraries.[23] Jakob De la Gardie's consumption might have been conspicuous in some ways, but this did not extend to his books. It was a different situation with his son, Chancellor Magnus Gabriel De la Gardie (1622–1686), who amassed the largest private library in the realm with perhaps as many as 8,000 books, cared for by several librarians.[24] In the 1680s, when it was sequestered by the Crown, the library had an estimated value of 14,866 Swedish *daler*, a sum which would buy 1,650 barrels of rye or 6,500 barrels of beer when a copy of Johannes Schefferus' newly published *De antiqvis verisqve regni Sveciæ insignibus, liber singularis* (Stockholm: Nicoalus Wankijff, 1678), 325 pages with 47 copper engravings, cost 2 *daler*, 16 *öre*.[25] A large portion of

---

22  The fundamental account of Sweden's looting of books is found in Otto Walde, *Storhetstidens litterära krigsbyten: En kulturhistorisk-bibliografisk studie* (2 vols., Uppsala: Almqvist & Wiksell, 1916, 1920); Swedish looting of manuscripts in the Thirty Years' War is especially considered in Callmer, *Königin Christina, ihre Bibliothekare und ihre Handschriften*, pp. 94–147.

23  The handwritten catalogue is published in Göran Axel-Nilsson, *Makalös: Fältherren greve Jakob De la Gardies hus i Stockholm* (Stockholm: Kommittén för Stockholmsforskning, 1984), pp. 237–242.

24  Losman, 'Adelskap och boklig bildning', pp. 176–179.

25  Nils G. Wollin, 'Karl XII:s torg', *Samfundet Sankt Eriks årsbok* (1925), p. 76. All price comparisons taken from Lars O. Lagerqvist, *Vad kostade det? Priser och löner från medeltid till våra dagar* (Lund: Historiska media, 2013), p. 121.

this library consisted of war booty, but we cannot tell to what extent. De la Gardie let his underlings scout private libraries during the Swedish campaigns in Denmark in 1658–1659. Among the more important collections he claimed for himself were those of Jørgen Reedtz, Gunde Rosenkrantz, and Anders Sørensen Vedel. Reedtz's library contained some 550 items; of the others, we have no reliable figures, but it is assumed that they were substantially larger.[26] In the late 1650s De la Gardie already had a substantial basis for his book collection in the great library of the Danish historiographer Stephanus Johannis Stephanius (1599–1650), which he had bought and paid for already in 1652. About a thousand of Stephanius' books can be identified in Uppsala University Library, in the National Library of Sweden, as well as in private collections, but these are only a fraction of the original number.[27] To complicate matters even more, Stephanius' library contained books from the former Jesuit colleges in Erfurt and Heiligenstadt, which were ransacked by the Swedes in the 1630s.[28] How these books found their way to Denmark has not been established, but their presence there make it even more difficult to single out proper booty in De la Gardie's library. At any rate, De la Gardie was a cultured and well-read person, but he also used architecture, art, and books as a means of displaying his influence and fortunes on a thitherto-unprecedented scale.[29]

Another great collector, Count Per Brahe the Younger (1602–1680), was procurator of the realm (*riksdrots*, nominally the highest office under the Crown) and Sweden's largest landowner. He saw himself as a sort of viceroy and behaved almost like an independent prince in his own county around Lake Vättern in southern Sweden. Brahe was the actual founder of the university in Turku (Åbo) in Finland, and in 1666 he established a private printing works at the island of Visingsö in Lake Vättern, employing the printer Johann Kankel from Gdańsk (Danzig). Between 1667 and 1685, Kankel produced a total of 53 printed items of various thicknesses and sizes, ranging from single sheets to tomes of more than 500 pages.[30]

Brahe was one of the most impressive representatives of a new generation of Swedish aristocrats, possessing cultural interests and an urge to establish

---

26   Walde, *Storhetstidens litterära krigsbyten*, 2, pp. 234–235, 242, 270–271, 319–322, 315–357, 367–370, 372–373, 377, 382–383.
27   De la Gardie paid 1,700 *riksdaler* for the printed books and an additional 200 *riksdaler* for the manuscripts. The library was transported to Stockholm in ten large chests. Otto Walde, 'Stephanii bibliotek och dess historia', *Nordisk tidskrift för bok- och biblioteksväsen*, 4 (1917), pp. 261–301, here pp. 298–301; idem, *Storhetstidens litterära krigsbyten*, 2, pp. 244–247.
28   Walde, 'Stephanii bibliotek och dess historia', pp. 265–266.
29   Walde, *Storhetstidens litterära krigsbyten*, 2, pp. 233–381.
30   Sven Almqvist, *Johann Kankel: Per Brahes boktryckare på Visingsö* (Stockholm: Almqvist & Wiksell, 1965), with bibliography of Kankel's works, pp. 131–147.

themselves on the same level as their counterparts on the continent. He had travelled through Denmark, Germany, England, the Netherlands, and Italy, and had spent a total of six years at the universities of Giessen and Strasbourg, where he supplemented his German and Latin with studies in French, Hebrew, and some theology. Following his father's intervention, he turned his focus to more noble exercises, and learned to ride, dance, fence, and play the lute. Throughout his travels, Brahe bought books and gathered a library of some 1,500 volumes in all areas of knowledge, ranging from pharmacology to fortification but with special emphasis on theology, history, law and *philosophia naturalis*. About a hundred of his books were war booty, which he had acquired in 1653 when he married Beata De la Gardie, widow of the Field Marshal Lennart Torstenson (1603–1651), commander of the Swedish troops in Germany during the Thirty Years' War and a notorious looter. Brahe had served as colonel for four and a half years under Gustavus Adolphus but did not pursue a military career. Through indirect conduits, he nevertheless got his share of the war booty that circulated in Sweden. The amplitude of his library also illustrates the remarkable expansion of book culture since Hogenskild Bielke's days, two generations earlier.[31]

One of the best-documented book collections of the era was located in Skokloster Castle. This residence has been described as a giant *Kunstschrank* or museum with its interior decorations, art, handicraft, scientific instruments, maps, and books.[32] At the death of its creator, Carl Gustaf Wrangel (1613–1676), the Skokloster library consisted of about 2,400 volumes, which were divided into four inheritance lots.[33] One of them is still stored at the castle (supplemented with several books from the other lots). Modern estimates suggest that

---

31  Walde, *Storhetstidens litterära krigsbyten*, 2, p. 438; Jonas Nordin, 'Per Brahe d.y:s Tänkebok', *Personhistorisk tidskrift*, 88 (1992), pp. 75–95, here 82–87; Losman, 'Adelskap och boklig bildning', pp. 166–170. For Brahe's estate holdings and building activities, see Fredric Bedoire, *Guldålder: Slott och politik i 1600-talets Sverige* (Stockholm: Bonniers, 2001), pp. 37–46.

32  Arne Losman, *Carl Gustaf Wrangel och Europa: Studier i kulturförbindelser kring en 1600-talsmagnat* (Stockholm: Almqvist & Wiksell, 1980), p. 234.

33  For an overview of the library collections at Skokloster, see Arne Losman, 'Tre rekonstruerade 1600-talsbibliotek på Skokloster', *Livrustkammaren: Journal of the Royal Armoury*, 11:8 (1969), pp. 227–240; idem, 'Skoklosters slotts bibliotek i ett östersjöperspektiv' in Kerstin Abukhanfusa (ed.) *Mare nostrum: Om westfaliska freden och Östersjön som svenskt maktcentrum* (Stockholm: Riksarkivet, 1999), pp. 228–240; Arne Losman and Elisabeth Westin Berg, 'Skokloster', in Bernhard Fabian et al. (eds.), *Handbuch deutscher historischer Buchbestände in Europa*, 7:1 (Hildesheim: Olms, 1998), pp. 217–221, also available at www.fabian.sub.uni-goettingen.de/fabian (last accessed 6 December 2022); Janis Kreslins, 'Skokloster Castle Library', in David H. Stam (ed.), *International Dictionary of Library Histories* (2 vols., Chicago: Fitzroy Dearborn, 2001), 2, pp. 695–698.

only about 10 percent of the book stock was war booty, but this estimate is certainly too low. Emma Hagström Molin has pointed out that scholars have underestimated the amount of booty because of the lack of sources, whereas Wrangel's orders through contacts in Hamburg, Amsterdam, The Hague, Frankfurt am Main, and London, have been minutely recorded.[34]

A contemporary catalogue divided Wrangel's books into ten subject areas, and, within the subject of theology, more than 75 percent of the preserved volumes consist of war booty. This is indeed not characteristic of the whole collection, and if we had the opportunity to examine its full extent, the total size of the booty would probably end up more towards the lower part of the wide range. Since almost three quarters of Wrangel's original library has been scattered, however, this can never be more than a guess.[35] How representative the Skokloster library was of aristocratic book collections in general is even harder to surmise. The best we can say is that the influx of looted books in Sweden was significant, but its share of the realm's total book stock at any given time may never be known, especially in the case of private collections. What the robbed books in turn may have meant for the edification, reputation or entertainment of the new owners is of course even more difficult to determine. The Italian philosopher and diplomat Lorenzo Magalotti, who met Carl Gustaf Wrangel on several occasions in the 1670s, portrayed him thus: 'He delights in many things, likes books and letters, although, to tell the truth, he is not very well educated. He is never idle: he either reads or works at his lathe or models houses and fortresses'. Historian Arne Losman has described Wrangel as 'increasingly educated but never learned'.[36] On a different note, Chancellor Axel Oxenstierna's brother Gabriel was certainly not alone when he lamented about his son: 'he has absolutely no inclination for his books, but only to war, and whatever he studies it is of no use.'[37]

---

34    Emma Hagström Molin, *Krigsbytets biografi: Byten i Riksarkivet, Uppsala universitetsbibliotek och Skokloster slott under 1600-talet* (Göteborg: Makadam, 2015), pp. 176, 196. Cf. Losman, *Carl Gustaf Wrangel och Europa*, pp. 182–192.

35    Walde, *Storhetstidens litterära krigsbyten*, 2, pp. 249–263; Elisabeth Westin Berg, 'Krigsbytesböcker i biblioteken på Skokloster', in Sofia Nestor and Carl Zarmén (eds.), *Krigsbyten i svenska samlingar* (Stockholm: Livrustkammaren, 2007), pp. 109–111; Hagström Molin, *Krigsbytets biografi*, pp. 196–198.

36    'Si diletta di molte cose: ama i libri ed i letterai, benché, per dirne il vero, non sia troppe delicato; non sta mai ozioso, o legge o lavora al tornio, o modella case e fortezze': Lorenzo Magalotti, *Relazioni di viaggio in Inghilterra, Francia e Svezia*, ed. Walter Moretti (Bari: Laterza, 1968), p. 319. 'alltmer bildad men aldrig lärd': Losman, *Carl Gustaf Wrangel och Europa*, p. 234.

37    'han slett ingen lust haffuer till sin book, uthan till kriget, och alt hvadh han studerar ähr uthan nytta': Gabriel Gustafsson Oxenstierna to Axel Oxenstierna, 13 January 1633, in

As far as public libraries are concerned, the data are somewhat better, although we can only estimate the size of the collections even in them. As indicated above, Uppsala university library at its founding in 1620 may have received a nucleus of somewhere between four and five thousand volumes. Thirty years later, the library is estimated to have had somewhere in the region of 8,600 volumes or more, with the lion's share of the increase consisting of war booty. Looted books may thus have accounted for about 40 percent or more of the library's collections. Of the around 1,165 manuscripts, well over half would have come from foreign pillaging.[38] For the royal library in Stockholm, the proportion was probably even higher until the middle of the seventeenth century. The books of the previous kings had been sent to Uppsala and what arrived instead, before Queen Christina began to buy large foreign collections, was to a large extent war booty.[39] For example, of the 953 manuscripts listed in the royal library's oldest catalogue from 1651, only four are known with certainty to have been there already in the sixteenth century.[40]

The looted books sent home by Gustavus Adolphus to Uppsala (and to a lesser extent to Stockholm) were taken mainly from Riga, Braniewo (Braunsberg), Frombork (Frauenburg), Würzburg, and Mainz. In all cases, these were libraries that belonged to the religious institutions and persons that were the Swedish king's adversaries: Jesuit colleges, chapters, monastic and mendicant libraries, prince bishops, and other Catholic dignitaries. This was important from both a legal and a moral point of view. On the one hand, goods were being seized in accordance with the laws of war; on the other, enemies of the evangelical faith were deprived of spiritual sustenance, which instead was now put into service of the unadulterated religion.[41] According to the Bishop of Strängnäs, Laurentius Paulinus, it pleased God if Swedish weapons succeeded in conquering 'the renowned colleges and magnificent libraries of our enemies, which they abuse for the suppression of the true faith, but which

*Rikskansleren Axel Oxenstiernas skrifter och brefvexling* (15 + 12 vols., Stockholm: Norstedts, 1890), 2:3, p. 284.

38 Annerstedt, *Upsala universitetsbiblioteks historia*, pp. 14–15. Otto Walde thought that Annerstedt's estimation was too low both in the number of books and the proportion of booty; idem, 'Konung Sigismunds bibliotek', pp. 317–318.

39 Eva Nilsson Nylander, *The Mild Boredom of Order: A Study in the History of the Manuscript Collection of Queen Christina of Sweden* (Lund: Lund University, 2011), pp. 45–63.

40 Cf. Christian Callmer (ed.), *Katalog över handskrifterna i Kungl. biblioteket i Stockholm skriven omkr. 1650 under ledning av Isaac Vossius* (Stockholm: Kungliga biblioteket, 1971).

41 See, e.g., Walde, *Storhetstidens litterära krigsbyten*, 1, pp. 15–19; Hagström Molin, *Krigsbytets biografi*, pp. 47–56; Ulf Göranson, 'Kulturarvskrigsbyten och den rättsliga utvecklingen från Grotius', in Peter Sjökvist (ed.), *Bevara för framtiden: Texter från en seminarieserie om specialsamlingar* (Uppsala: Uppsala universitetsbibliotek, 2016) pp. 73–82.

in our hands could be brought again to their proper use, which is to honour God, strengthen the defence of our Christian faith, and continue all commendable and useful studies.'[42]

To identify and retrieve and, when necessary, select particular items from the captured book collections required some expertise. If a selection had to be made, manuscripts and celebrated authors were preferred, but, if possible, the entire library should be sent home to be sorted and assessed in peace and quiet. Archives that could provide information about the enemy's actions, facilitate the administration of conquered areas, and provide historical edification were sought after. While Gustavus Adolphus was alive, the king himself took active part in the selection, assisted by field preachers. Later, the selection process was transferred to the secretaries of the field chancellery, trained in languages and political science.[43] In early 1643, Axel Oxenstierna issued the following order to the Commander-in-Chief Lennart Torstenson:

> Likewise, if the Lord Field Marshal conquers any Papist cities, where any grand and costly libraries are being kept, as happened last summer with Neus, [and] Olomouc, he should command the secretary, or else some certain, trustworthy, experienced, and knowledgeable man, who knows how to use the opportunity to collect and preserve the said libraries, and to ship them here at a safe moment, in order to improve the libraries of the Realm's academies and gymnasiums.[44]

Oxenstierna's instructions contain several interesting pieces of information. The purpose of the cultural policy was paramount: the books would be used to fill empty school libraries. The army must use the skills at hand to carry out

---

42   'wåre Fijenders nampnkunnige collegia och sköne Bibliotheker, hwilke the missbruke till then sanne Religionens vndertryckellse, men här kunne föras till genuinum usum igen, som är Gudhi till ähra och wår christelige Religions kraftigare förswarelse sampt alle berömmeliga studiers nyttige fortsettning'; Paulinus to Axel Oxenstierna, 1 Aug. 1634, quoted from Walde, *Storhetstidens litterära krigsbyten*, 1, p. 25.
43   Walde, *Storhetstidens litterära krigsbyten*, 1, pp. 19–25. For the importance of archives, cf. Inger Dübeck, *Fra gammel dansk til ny svensk ret: Den retlige forsvenskning i de tabte territorier 1645–1683* (Copenhagen: Rigsarkivet, 1987).
44   'I lijka måtto ther her Fälldtmarskallken får någre papistiske orter in, ther sköne och kostelige bibliotheker ähre till finna, som uthi förledne Sommar skedde medh Neus, Olmitz [Olomouc], at han wille befalla Secreteren, eller elliest någon wiss, godh, förfahren och förtrogen man, som weet till taga den legenheeten i acht, at sambla och conservera samma bibliotek, och låta widh säker legenheet sända dem hijt öfwer, at ther medh förbättra bibliotheken uthi Rijkzens academier och gymnasier.' Memorial for Gabriel Oxenstierna, 21 Jan. 1643, quoted from Walde, *Storhetstidens litterära krigsbyten*, 1, p. 345.

the mission and the books should be handled with care. Furthermore, it was explicitly declared that only the libraries of the *enemy* could be looted in this way. Depriving the 'papist' and the Jesuit of his intellectual tools was not only a just punishment; it was also a protective measure for the evangelical side and an opportunity to allow the books to be used in the service of the true faith. To what extent Catholic liturgical manuals and other 'papist' books could really fulfil their intended function in Lutheran Sweden and, above all, in its educational institutions is a question that to some extent divides scholars. The dominant view, however, is that the benefits were severely limited by the somewhat haphazard methods of acquisition. The university library in Uppsala had two floors with separate entrances. The upper floor contained the proper working library where useful and representative books were kept. The lower floor was more of a storage room for less valuable or damaged books. Some of the duplicates or books otherwise deemed useless were sold or traded for other books, whereas several parchment manuscripts had to sacrifice their pages to the university bookbinders and the city's organ builders. More than four hundred manuscripts were destroyed this way before 1691. In view of the large influx of unusable literature, the Consistory's ordinance of 1646, that the scarce acquisition grants should only be used to purchase pure doctrinal gospel books, is understandable.[45]

## 3    Might or Right?

Was the seizure of war booty justified or legal at the time? The seventeenth century was an era of continuous warfare, but it also witnessed the birth of international law. The right of the strong that had previously prevailed was increasingly being replaced by principles based on natural law, according to which there were certain fundamental rights and obligations that must be taken into account even in war and diplomacy. In this context, reference is often made to the Dutch lawyer Hugo Grotius and his *De jure belli ac pacis* ('On the Laws of War and Peace'). If a war was legitimate, it was also lawful for the victor to take booty under certain conditions, according to Grotius. This concerned, for example, munitions but also the public property, including cultural

---

45    Peter Sjökvist, 'On the Order of the Books in the first Uppsala University Library Building', *Journal of Jesuit Studies*, 6 (2019), pp. 315–326, also in Swedish as 'Om böckernas ordning i Uppsala universitetsbiblioteks första byggnad', *Biblis: Kvartalstidskrift för bokvänner*, 85 (2019), pp. 65–71; idem, 'Litterära krigsbytens öden i Sverige', *Biblis: Kvartalstidskrift för bokvänner*, 89 (2020), pp. 21–26.

objects, of the defeated enemy. Such transfers of ownership were afterwards regulated in peace agreements and were thus approved by both parties.[46]

Grotius published his influential treatise in 1625, while the large-scale Swedish book robberies had begun already in Riga in 1621.[47] Then again, these matters had occupied lawyers already in the medieval centuries (e.g. Thomas Aquinas) and Grotius had pondered the subject in previous works.[48] Moreover, the Italian jurists Pierino Belli in his *De re militari et de bello* (1563) and Alberico Gentili in his *De jure belli commentatio prima* (1588; extended and revised as *De jure belli libri tres*, 1598) had already laid the groundwork for the law of nations (*ius gentium*), including for the laws of war. Gentili drew heavily on Greco-Roman natural law and Jean Bodin's theories on sovereignty, and there is reason to believe that his work inspired the articles of war issued by Gustavus Adolphus in 1621, to which all soldiers in his armies were bound by oath. These articles emphasized the military chain of command and the soldiers' duty of obedience; articles 90–101, especially, contained regulations on looting and the treatment of civilians.[49]

---

46   Fritz Redlich, *De praeda militari: Looting and Booty 1500–1815* (Wiesbaden: Franz Steiner, 1956), on Swedish practices, see esp. pp. 10–11, 25, 31–32, 35, 44, 47, 54–56, 61; Philippe Contamine, 'The Growth of State Control: Practices of War, 1300–1800. Ransom and Booty', in idem (ed.), *War and competition between states* (Oxford: Clarendon, 2000), pp. 163–193.

47   About the Riga spoils, see *Catalogue of the Riga Jesuit College Book Collection (1583–1621): History and Reconstruction of the Collection = Rīgas Jezuītu Kolēģijas Grāmatu Krājuma (1583–1621) Katalogs. Krājuma Vēsture un Rekonstrukcija*, eds. Andris Levāns and Gustavs Strenga (Riga: Latvijas Nacionālā bibliotēka, 2021).

48   Callmer, *Königin Christina, ihre Bibliothekare und ihre Handsschriften*, pp. 94–98; Bo H. Lindberg, 'Spoils and trophies', in Fred Sandstedt et al. (eds.), *In Hoc Signo Vinces: A Presentation of the Swedish State Trophy Collection* (Stockholm: The National Swedish Museums of Military History, 2006), pp. 37–49; Hannes Hartung, '"Praeda bellica in bellum iustum?" The Legal Development of War-Booty from the 16th Century to Date: A Chance of Bettering Museum Practice?', esp. pp. 25–30, and Claudia Reichl-Ham, '"Keiner soll auf Beuth gehen ohne Wissen und Willen seines Hauptmannes": The War-Booty Laws of the Holy Roman and Habsburg Empires in Theory and Practice from the 16th to the 19th centuries', both in Sofia Nestor (ed.), *War-Booty: A Common European Cultural Heritage* (Stockholm: Royal Armoury, 2009); Hans Blom (ed.), *Property, Piracy and Punishment: Hugo Grotius on War and Booty in De Iure Praedae* (Leiden: Brill, 2009); Ryan Greenwood, 'War and Sovereignty in Medieval Roman Law', *Law and History Review*, 32 (2014), pp. 31–63, e.g., pp. 50–51; Andrew Blom, 'Grotius and Aristotle: The Justice of Taking Too Little', *History of Political Thought*, 36 (2015), esp. pp. 101–107; Ove Bring, 'Kulturella krigsbyten och folkrättslig utveckling', *Svensk juristtidning*, 102 (2017), pp. 274–288, here pp. 274–279.

49   *Krijgs articlar som fordom then stormechtigste furste och herre, herr Gustaff Adolph then andre och store, Sweriges, Göthes och Wändes konung, storfurste til Finland, hertig vthi*

Gustavus Adolphus issued the articles of war on 15 July 1621, shortly before the siege of Riga. In line with their spirit, the repossessions made after the fall of the city included only the so-called cadukes. This term, *caducus*, originated in Roman Law and referred to property without a legal heir or, in a figurative sense, orphaned property in general.[50] After the conquest of Riga in September 1621, the officials of the Polish king and the city's Jesuits were expelled. The property they left behind was considered forfeited to the Swedish Crown, while the rest of the city's population was left in peace, at least to the extent that the royal judiciary could exercise control. Procedure of this kind governed the book plundering undertaken by the Swedish Crown; a prerequisite for the booty to serve its intended use was that it be captured in a reasonably good order. During the Thirty Years' War, the Swedish government, headed by Axel Oxenstierna, came to lean on Grotius' authority. It was, of course, helpful that Grotius was engaged in Swedish diplomatic service during the last ten years of his life.[51] What licentious soldiery and unruly officers did, however, was not easy to control in all situations. A Lutheran pastor near Dresden fled into the woods when Swedish troops ravaged his hometown during the Thirty Years' War. When he returned, he discovered that the Swedish army chaplain had taken thirty-two of his private and most valuable books from the church vestry.[52] This was clearly no orderly confiscation, neither was it an action against an enemy of the evangelical faith.

In some instances, the Swedes saw their spoils as the restoration of Swedish property. The sixteenth-century library on Gråmunkeholmen in Stockholm 'was looted by the Jesuits, who during the time of King Johan III ravaged our church and our Helicon [i.e., our literature]', wrote Uppsala university library's chronicler Olof Celsius in 1745.

> In Uppsala library you will find books, which in the margin of the title page have the following note: 'Inscribed in the catalogue of the Jesuit order's in Sweden library', where they [the Jesuits] have crossed out the words 'in Sweden', but so poorly that they can be easily read, and written

---

*Estland och Carelen, herre vthöfwer Ingermanland, etc. loffwärdigst i åminnelse, hafwer låtit göra och författa, A. M. DC. XXI* (Stockholm: Peter van Selow, 16[42]), USTC 252255.

50  On the concept of cadukes in this context, see Walde, *Storhetstidens litterära krigsbyten*, 1, p. 46; Hagström Molin, *Krigsbytets biografi*, pp. 59–60.
51  Cf. Henk J.M. Nellen, 'Hugo Grotius's Political and Scholarly Activities in the Light of his Correspondence', in *Property, Piracy and Punishment*, pp. 16–30, e.g., pp. 19–20, 27.
52  Pettegree and Weduwen, *The Library*, p. 137.

'Braunsberg' instead, after they left the country and secretly went to Braunsberg with this loot.[53]

Interestingly, Celsius did not see this Jesuit institutional library as the property of the Catholic order, but as national Swedish property. Provenance marks show that some of these books had already travelled between Jesuit colleges in northern Europe and Stockholm as many as three times in the sixteenth century.[54] Another book with an itinerant history was an edition of Thomas Aquinas's *De veritate catholicæ fidei contra errores infidelium*, printed by Henricus Arimininensis in Strasbourg in 1479, and bound by the bookbinder Niels in Vadstena not long thereafter. It must have been confiscated during the Reformation and ended up in the Crown's book warehouse on Gråmunkeholmen, where a short-lived counter Reformational seminar was formed in 1576 under a Jesuit headmaster, Laurentius Nicolai Norvegus. In 1580, Laurentius and his colleagues were expelled together with fifteen apostates, the departing persons taking many of the books with them. The present volume is marked 'Ex Biblioth. Cath. Ecclæ Olom.' for Olomouc, where it was captured by the Swedes in 1642, brought back to Stockholm and finally placed in Uppsala University Library.[55]

The largest and most infamous Swedish plunder took place in the so-called Lesser Town in Prague in the summer of 1648, just a few months before the Westphalian peace agreement was signed. Through this last advance, not only did the Codex Gigas ('Devil's Bible') and the Codex Argenteus ('Silver Bible') fall into Swedish hands, the total spoils, according to contemporary estimates, amounted to an astonishing 7 million *riksdaler*'s worth. By comparison, France's subsidies to Sweden in 1638–1648 amounted to 5.4 million *riksdaler*, which was just above the monetary settlement the Swedish Crown was granted

---

53 'Inveniuntur libri, in Bibliotheca Upsaliensi, hoc signo notati ad marginem titularis folii: *Inscriptus catalogo Bibl. Soc. Jesu in Suetia*, ubi expunctis vocibus *in Suetia*, ita tamen ut facile legi possint, vocabulum *Braunsberg* reposuerunt postquam, relicto Regno, Brunsbergam se clam, cum hac præda, contulissent.' Olof O. Celsius, *Bibliothecæ Upsaliensis historia* (Uppsala: Regiæ academiæ Ups. impensis, 1745) pp. 16–17. Swedish translation by Sten Hedberg, *Uppsala universitetsbiblioteks historia* (Uppsala: Almqvist & Wiksell, 1971). Cf. Isak Collijn, 'Bibliotheca "Collegii Societatis Jesu in Suetia": Några bidrag till kännedomen om jesuiternas boksamling på Gråmunkeholmen', *Nordisk tidskrift för bok- och biblioteksväsen*, 1 (1914), who enumerates 54 works in 34 volumes, now in Uppsala, that belonged to the Jesuit school.
54 Collijn, 'Bibliotheca "Collegii Societatis Jesu in Suetia"', pp. 157–158.
55 Isak Collijn, 'Råd och anvisningar till en svensk bokbindare under medeltiden', *Samlaren*, 24 (1903), p. 144–145.

in the peace treaty for the disbandment of its troops.[56] The Osnabrück Treaty included special stipulations regarding booty. Goods and possessions that were still in their original place were to be restored, but everything that had already been removed would be kept by the new owners (article XVI:15). All previous conflicts, claims and suffered injustices were to be disregarded after the ratification of the treaty.

## 4      The Spoils of Charles X Gustav

Peace did not last long and in the summer of 1655, Sweden broke the truce with Poland that had been concluded in Stuhmsdorf in 1635. The reasons were many and cynical, but the formal points included religious schisms and unresolved claims in relation to the Polish Vasa branch. Archival documents of Swedish provenance were thus on the lists of desired booty when administrative centres were conquered.[57] As before, there was also an interest in larger book collections. Books were brought to Uppsala especially from Jesuit colleges and monasteries in Vilnius and Poznań; they were also extorted from the royal library in Warsaw.[58] According to the peace treaty, all archives and official documents as well as the royal library from Krakow were to be returned unless they had already been shipped to Sweden.[59] This last provision was overlooked by Otto Walde, which has led to much misunderstanding in later research. Regardless of moral viewpoints, it was in full accordance with the peace settlement that the books already brought to Stockholm remained there. Many of these books were later destroyed when fire demolished the royal castle in 1697.

Some of the Swedish schools and universities sought to reserve future book acquisitions for their own libraries. Soon after Charles X Gustav had declared his second war on Denmark, he received the following petition from Johannes Terserus, bishop in Turku in Finland:

---

56   Walde, *Storhetstidens litterära krigsbyten*, 1, pp. 308–333; *Från Femern och Jankow till westfaliska freden* (Stockholm: Generalstabens litografiska anstalts förlag, 1948), pp. 369–399.
57   On the devastation in Poland, including libraries and archives, caused by Swedish troops during the wars of Charles X Gustav, see Mirosław Nagielski et al., *Förödelse utfört av svenskarna i Polen under åren 1655–1660* (Warszawa: Solar, 2011); also published in Polish as *Zniszczenia szwedzkie na terenie Korony w okresie potopu: 1655–1660* (Warszawa: Wydawnictwo DiG, 2015). The authors remark that the destruction of archives makes it difficult for historians to reconstruct the extent of the devastation even today.
58   Walde, *Storhetstidens litterära krigsbyten*, 1, pp. 1–176.
59   Treaty of Oliwa, 23 April 1660, § 9. See also Peter Sjökvist, 'Freden i Oliwa och restitutionen av bokliga krigsbyten', *Biblis: Kvartalstidskrift för bokvänner*, 68 (2014/15), pp. 20–23.

if it so pleases the good Lord to continue to bless His Royal Majesty's victorious arms and to place Copenhagen in the hands of His Royal Majesty, [it is hoped that] His Royal Majesty should remember the Academy in Turku with [a donation of] some print items as well as libraries.[60]

As a rule, however, during the wars of Charles X Gustav it seems that booty ended up in private hands to a greater extent than before. 'Following the example of the ancient Romans, the illustrious men of Sweden also installed libraries on their estates, where they could rest their weary minds', wrote Olof Celsius with reference to this period.[61] Among the most distinguished of these collections he listed those belonging to Schering Rosenhane, Per Brahe the Younger, Magnus Gabriel De la Gardie, and the diplomat and councillor Clas Rålamb. All of them contained varying amounts of war booty. A significant part of Rosenhane's collections is today kept at the National Library of Sweden, while De la Gardie's and Rålamb's books came to rest in Uppsala after the Crown's 'reduction' (re-acquisition) of noble estates in the late seventeenth century. Per Brahe's books were for the most part scattered or consumed by fire, but remains can still be found at Skokloster, which is also home to portions of Carl Gustaf Wrangel's spoils from Poland and Denmark, mentioned earlier. As secretary of the chancellery, Emund Figrelius Gripenhielm (1622–1675) was inspector for the royal library and was thus able to secure duplicates from its collections. This way, he formed an impressive library of 6,000 volumes, including many books looted from Poland and Denmark. Gripenhielm's book collection was purchased by Charles XI and donated in 1684 to the library of the newly established university in Lund, where it still remains. The fortifications officer Erik Dahlbergh, who carefully sketched the Polish cities before they were just as carefully burned down by the Swedes, liked to pilfer individual volumes in the subject areas that interested him: topographical works, architecture, engineering, martial arts, classical writers, among other subjects.[62] It should be added

---

60  'där den högste Gud än ytterligare välsignar H. K. M:ts segersälla vapen och gifver Köpenhamn uti H. M:ts händer, H. K. M:t ville då ihågkomma akademien i Åbo med något tryck såväl som bibliotek', quoted from Walde, *Storhetstidens litterära krigsbyten*, 1, p. 29.

61  'Erexerunt etjam illustrers in Svecia viri, more Romanorum veterum bibliothecas in Tusculanis suis: ubi animos curis defatigatos relaxarent'; Celsius, *Bibliothecæ Upsaliensis historia*, pp. 37–38. On looted books in private collections in Imperial Rome, see Christian Jacob, 'Fragments of a History of Ancient Libraries', in Jason König et al. (eds.), *Ancient Libraries* (Cambridge: Cambridge University Press, 2013), pp. 57–82, p. 73.

62  An extensive inventory list of Dahlbergh's books, paintings and engravings in October 1654 is printed in Ernst Ericsson and Erik Vennberg, *Erik Dahlbergh: Hans levnad och verksamhet* (Uppsala: Almqvist & Wiksell, 1925), pp. 159–167.

that much booty ended up in other countries via foreign officers in Swedish service.

Rich profits were amassed also during the wars with Denmark, not infrequently from private libraries. Charles X Gustav's first Danish campaign lasted only six months, from August 1657 to February 1658, and its rapid course limited the possibilities for pillaging. The second Danish war, which began in August 1658, however, meant that Swedish troops were stationed on Danish soil for a year and a half, creating a good opportunity for both sanctioned and improvised looting. As before, the Swedes tried to uphold the principle of only confiscating 'orphaned' goods. This included collections that had been abandoned after the flight of the owners, and collections that had been evacuated from their original location in order to be hidden. Particularly rich loot was taken in conquered fortresses that served as depots for refugees. The Danish wars brought home magnificent trophies of historical and artistic value to the Crown, such as Queen Margaret's robe, Frederik II's canopy and a large number of bronze sculptures from Frederiksborg Castle.[63] The existence of book pillaging we know primarily by reference to objects that ended up in private collections and that arrived in public institutions only indirectly. Most of the Crown's confiscations, on the other hand, were probably destroyed when the royal castle in Stockholm burned down, which makes its actual extent difficult to estimate.

## 5   Charles XII's War in Poland

It is not always possible to determine with certainty whether the books with Polish provenance that can be found in Sweden today were originally taken during the campaigns of Charles X Gustav in the 1660s or during those of Charles XII (ruled 1697–1718) in the early eighteenth century. It seems, however, that book plundering was less common during the later war. This may have several explanations: the Swedish public collections were already saturated after almost a century of replenishment; the tastes of the Swedish officers had become more refined, and they were no longer content with books in bulk unless their more specific interests could be met in the Polish libraries;

---

63   Görel Cavalli-Björkman, 'Krigsrov från München, Prag och Fredriksborg i Nationalmuseum', in Sofia Nestor and Carl Zarmén (eds.), *Krigsbyten i svenska samlingar* (Stockholm: Livrustkammaren, 2007), pp. 79–91; Barbro Bursell, 'War-Booty in Swedish Collections', in Ann Grönhammar (ed.), *Krigsbyte – War-Booty* (Stockholm: Royal Armoury, 2007), pp. 35–48.

increasingly mobile warfare did not allow for accumulation and shipping of a large volume of booty. Among those who are known to have brought books back with them from the campaign is Olof Hermelin, professor of law in Tartu (Dorpat), chancellor and royal historiographer. Charles XII had his headquarters in Heilsberg 1703–1704 and during this stationary period there was plenty of time for a connoisseur to choose books in peace and quiet. Hermelin sent home two coffers to Stockholm with books taken from the bishop's library. Among his spoils were several older manuscripts, of which at least a few over a dozen were donated by his son Carl Hermelin to the library of the Turku Academy, where they were destroyed in the great city fire of 1827.[64]

Charles XII's Polish campaign offered the last opportunities for the soldiers of the Swedish great power to plunder libraries of any significance. One or two Russian books have evidently found their way to Sweden, but mostly the Russian campaign passed through areas that did not present any real opportunities for literary spoils. The last large collection of books that was shipped to Stockholm and enriched the royal library was not the result of pillaging, but of a rescue operation. The Swedish university in Tartu near the Russian border had already been disturbed by warfare in the reign of Charles X Gustav, and in 1699 the university was moved to greater safety to the coastal town of Pärnu (Pernau). Due to the war, the university library's books never came to rest in the new environment but lay packed in coffers until 1709 when they were rushed to Stockholm together with the entire academic consistory. This can stand as a thought-provoking epilogue to the whole Swedish book-robbery era, meaning that not even the books that the Swedish authorities themselves had collected necessarily met all the needs in the home country. 'The Pärnu Library was certainly rich in older books,' wrote the royal librarian Magnus Celsius in 1751, 'which in any case have their value; but with these also came a number of textbooks and others of insignificant value, which are unlikely to find their place in the magnificent hall where the royal library will be set up shortly.'[65] For almost a century, Swedish librarians had had to deal with this tension between

---

64   Walde, *Storhetstidens litterära krigsbyten*, 2, pp. 184–189; Sven Olsson, *Olof Hermelin: En karolinsk kulturpersonlighet och statsman* (Lund: Gleerupska universitetsbokhandeln, 1953), p. 569.
65   'Dives quidem erat Pernaviensis supellex librorum antiquiorum, ... quibus utique suum pretium est; at comitabatur hos multitudo Scholasticorum, aliorumque vilioris pretii librorum, qui quum etiam ab aquis damnum acceperint huc transportandi, in splendido atrio, quo brevi collocanda erit Bibliotheca Regia, locum vix obtinebunt.' Magnus O. Celsius, *Bibliothecae Regiae Stockholmensis historia brevis et succincta* (Stockholm: Lars Salvius, 1751), pp. 187–188; Pettegree and Weduwen, *The Library*, p. 156.

useful and useless books. However, at the same time Sweden ceased to be a great power, it could no longer be considered culturally backward.

## 6     Successful Cultural Rearmament

As we have seen, the early sixteenth century was a period of rapid cultural transformation in Sweden with the reopening of Uppsala University, the establishment of public libraries, and several reforms promoting studies both domestically and abroad. The university in Uppsala was followed by new universities in Tartu 1632, Turku 1640, Lund 1668, as well as the university in Greifswald (founded 1456), which came under Swedish dominion with the Peace of Westphalia. There had not been any regular book traders in Sweden in the sixteenth century. The royal printer vended his own products, and the occasional German peddler travelled the country, but from the 1530s onward, book import was generally restricted. The first stationary bookseller cum publisher settled in Stockholm in the 1590s. To promote the university, Gustavus Adolphus issued a privilege for a book trader in Uppsala in 1616. Although there were many changes and interruptions within the trade, at least Stockholm and, for most of the time, Uppsala had permanent purveyors of books from then on.[66]

There was also a rapid growth in the number of printing establishments. From 1613 there were two print shops in Stockholm, and from 1630 there were three. The numbers fluctuated from three to five during the rest of the century, but from the 1690s there were never fewer than six. Uppsala had a printer from 1613, and for long periods, there were two. Other cities with printing presses were Västerås (from 1621), Strängnäs (1622–), Linköping (1635–), Turku (1642–, two from 1668), Gothenburg (1650–), Lund (1664–), and Viborg (1689–). Other cities had printers for shorter periods: Kalmar (1626–1635), Norrköping (1682–1683), Nyköping (1645–1650), and Malmö (1659 through the 1690s with interruptions). Count Per Brahe had a private printing press at his residence on Visingsö (1667–1685).[67] In the conquered provinces, Sweden either acquired

---

66    Isidor Adolf Bonnier and August Hånell, *Anteckningar om svenska bokhandlare intill år 1935*, 2: Stockholm och Uppsala (Stockholm: Bonniers, 1935); Magnus Bernhard Swederus, *Boklådorna i Uppsala 1616–1907: Ett bidrag till den svenska bokhandelns historia* (Uppsala: Lundequistska bokhandeln, 1907).

67    Gustaf Edvard Klemming and Johan Gabriel Nordin, *Svensk boktryckeri-historia 1483–1883 med inledande allmän öfversigt* (Stockholm: Norstedts, 1883), pp. 156–222. See also Per S. Ridderstad, 'Tryckpressens makt och makten över tryckpressen: Om tryckerietableringar i det svenska riket 1600–1650', in Sten Åke Nilsson and Margareta Ramsay

or established new print shops. Riga had had a printer on permanent basis since 1588 and received a second one in 1675, equipped with royal privilege. The Swedish governor general installed a printer in Tartu in 1630, and the gymnasium in Tallinn (Reval) employed its own in 1634.[68] The residential city Szczecin (Stettin) in Pomerania had a printer from 1533, as did the university in Greifswald from 1582. The Swedish Crown established yet another in Stralsund in 1628. In 1651, shortly after the Swedish takeover, a printer was called to Stade, the Swedish residential city in Bremen, whereas Wismar, the seat of the Swedish appeals court in the German provinces, got its first printer in 1663.[69]

The output in the amount of printed matter consequently saw a continuous growth. The yearly average of titles printed within the realm, which was eight or nine in the 1590s, more than tripled in the following decade and the numbers increased at a steady pace throughout the century (apart from a short stagnation during the reigns of Queen Christina and, perhaps less surprising, Charles X Gustav). There was an average of a hundred titles printed per year in the 1600s, as compared to less than five each year in the 1500s. According to Eltjo Buringh and Jan Luiten Van Zanden, the total output of printed matter on a European scale increased by 131 percent in 1601–1700, as compared to 1451–1600. The equivalent rise in Sweden, according to the same source, was more than 6,400 percent, from 89,000 to 5.8 million copies! These numbers call for some caution. Buring and Van Zanden admit that the margins of error for their estimates 'are no doubt relatively large, especially for the earlier period,' but even if we were to substantially increase the earlier output and decrease the later, the growth would still be extraordinary.[70]

---

(eds.), *1600-talets ansikte* (Nyhamnsläge: Gyllenstiernska Krapperupsstiftelsen, 1997), pp. 345–356.

68  Arend Buchholtz, *Geschichte der Buchdruckerkunst in Riga 1588–1888* (Riga: Müller, 1890), pp. 17–18; Martin Klöker, *Literarisches Leben in Reval in der ersten Hälfte des 17. Jahrhunderts (1600–1657): Institutionen der Gelehrsamkeit und Genese städtischer Gelegenheitsdichtung* (Berlin: De Gruyter, 2005), ch. 5.

69  Gottlieb Mohnike, *Die Geschichte der Buchdruckerkunst in Pommern* (Stettin: Bülow, 1840), pp. 49–65, 72–84; Josef Benzing, *Die Buchdrucker des 16. und 17. Jahrhunderts im deutschen Sprachgebiet*, second ed. (Wiesbaden: Otto Harrassowitz, 1982), pp. 165–167, 428, 431–435, 495.

70  Eltjo Buringh and Jan Luiten Van Zanden, 'Charting the "Rise of the West": Manuscripts and Printed Books in Europe, a Long-Term Perspective from the Sixth through Eighteenth Centuries', *The Journal of Economic History*, 69 (2009), pp. 409–445, pp. 416–417. If Buringh and Van Zanden's quantities are combined with the numbers in my figures 7.1 and 7.2, the average print run before 1600 would be just above 200, and in the seventeenth century about 490, which does not seem unreasonable.

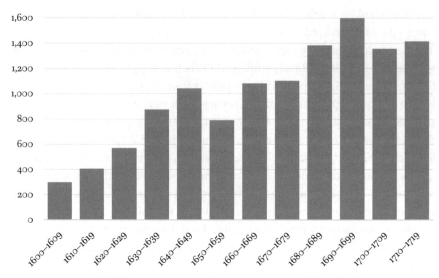

FIGURE 7.2  Swedish domestic print production 1600–1719: number of titles
SOURCE: THE SWEDISH NATIONAL UNION CATALOGUE LIBRIS, DATABASE: SVETRYCK. NOTE: PERIOD PRINTED MATTER WITHOUT KNOWN YEAR OF PRODUCTION HAS BEEN OMITTED FROM THE CHART.

Ironically, or perhaps consequently, the growth of printed matter is also reflected in the number of censorship laws. In the sixteenth century, when the realm had only one printer who worked on royal assignment, there was no need for legal restrictions; his work was properly supervised by the corrector, appointed by the king. In 1630, the printer Eric Schroderus received royal privilege to print books without interference from the Crown. He was a trusted individual who had the support of the authorities and could thus be his own corrector.[71] The first real censorship law was issued only in 1661.[72] It required all printers to submit two copies of every book to the Chancellery of the Realm before dissemination. A ban on a book could mean a substantial economic loss to the printer, and therefore within a year it was ruled that, instead, the authors' manuscripts should be submitted for consideration and approval *before* printing. Religious books were examined by the episcopal consistories and academic books by their university equivalents. But in 1684, all other

---

71  Klemming and Nordin, *Svensk boktryckeri-historia 1483–1883*, p. 164; Schück, *Den svenska förlagsbokhandelns historia*, 1, pp. 66–69.
72  Procedures for the Chancellery of the Realm, 22 September 1661, printed in *Samling af instructioner rörande den civila förvaltningen i Sverige och Finland*, 1, ed. Carl Gustaf Styffe (Stockholm: Hörberg, 1856), pp. 327–365, cf. esp. §§ 8 and 14.

BUILDING A NATION THROUGH BOOKS 177

printing was left to a newly created *censor librorum*, who was to oversee the print shops within the realm as well as the importation of books. It became customary that the *censor librorum* doubled as custodian of the royal library.

There can be no doubt that the Swedish Crown pursued a very conscious cultural policy and actively strove to emulate the more advanced European nations. In light of the Crown's objectives, the result must be described as nothing less than a success. In the eighteenth century, Sweden lost its great-power status and was still located very much on the European periphery, but it was no longer considered a backward and underdeveloped country. The favourable portrayal that the Swedes received in 1723 in the *Neu-eröffnetes Amphj-Theatrum*, a compilation of ethnographic accounts, would most certainly not have been bestowed on them a century earlier.

> The Swedes have fine features, large bodies, strong limbs, are courageous, resistant and sincere, polite and mannerly in conversations. Nature has destined them to become soldiers, and for a century, the nation has gained a tremendous reputation in warfare. In those studies, they are quite successful, as well as in other useful arts and sciences. The only thing they have been accused of, this far, is their good fortune, which has made them unbearable to other nations.[73]

It is perhaps telling that Sweden lost its great-power status in the North to Russia, another nation that aspired to gain recognition in the eyes of her neighbours. Like Swedish rulers a century earlier, the Russian sovereign, Czar Peter I (ruled 1682–1725), took all the inspiration he could from the most advanced European nations and sought to replant their practices in his homeland. Many solutions, including bureaucratic names and titles, were copied from his Swedish foe. Swedish was even one of the three modern languages (besides French and German) that was taught at the ambitious Glück Gymnasium that operated in Moscow between 1703 and 1715. From being only a receiver, Sweden

---

73   'Die Schweden sind fein vom Gesichte, groß von Statur, starcken Gliedmassen, am Gemüthe tapffer, beständig und aufrichtig, in Conversation höfflich und artig. Die Natur hat sie gleichsam zu Soldaten gebohren, und die Nation hat sich von einem Seculo her im Kriege ungemein renomirt gemacht. Jn denen Studien bringen sie es zum Theile ziemlich hoch, wie auch in andern guten Künsten und Wissenschafften. Das eintzige, was man bißher an ihnen ausgesetzet hat, ist, daß sie bey ihrem Glücke hochmüthig, und daher frembden Nationen undertäglich worden.' *Neu-eröffnetes AMPHJ-THEATRUM, Worinnen Nach dem uns bekanten gantzen Welt-Kreits, Alle NATIONEN Nach ihrem Habit, in saubern Figuren repräsentiret* ... (Erfurt: Johann Michael Funcken, 1723), 'Europa', no. 41.

had transformed into a provider and bestowed the model for Russia's military reforms and new state bureaucracy.[74]

A generation later, in 1756, the Professor of Physics at the university in Turku, Carl Fredrik Mennander, amazed at the progress of Swedish learning compared to the previous century. Then all but the simplest books had been imported from abroad, and a learned man's library consisted of little more than the Bible, Aristotle, Plutarch, and Ptolemy.

> Today our printing presses are operated by Swedish hands. They do not toil exclusively with translations alone, but also with the works of our native scholars, who now find previously absent publishers as well as rewards; and not only spread learning and wisdom at home, and make us into an enlightened people, but also give us the same reputation among foreign peoples. The works of our scholars are so desirable to the foreigners, that many, the wisest of them, out of impatience to acquire their contents, do not have time to wait for them being translated to their own languages, even though they are effectuated with adequate haste, but begin to learn Swedish.[75]

Mennander also acknowledged the importance of spoils of war in the building of large public libraries under Gustavus Adolphus and Queen Christina, 'although that, which had arrived under the beat of drums, soon mostly went away under the sound of pipes'. But those methods of procurement were now no longer necessary, he concluded.[76]

---

74   Erik Anners, *Den karolinska militärstraffrätten och Peter den stores krigsartiklar* (Uppsala: Almqvist & Wiksell, 1961); Claes Peterson, *Peter the Great's Administrative and Judicial Reforms: Swedish Antecedents and the Process of Reception* (Stockholm: Stockholm University, 1979); Lindsay Hughes, *Russia in the Age of Peter the Great* (New Haven: Yale University Press, 1998) pp. 102, 107, 110, 117, 119–120, 127–128, 138, 143, 181, 218–219, 305, 328–329, 347, 371. Cf. also Ylva Haidenthaller, *The Medal in Early Modern Sweden: Significances and Practices* (Lund: Mediehistoriskt arkiv, 2021), pp. 192–193.

75   'Våra Prässar röras nu af Svenska händer. De svettas icke under blåtta öfversättningar, utan ock under våra Inhemska Lärdas arbeten, som nu finna så länge saknade Förlags-män och belöning; samt icke allenast utsprida Lärdom och Vitterhet hemma, och göra oss til et uplyst folk, utan ock sätta oss i samma anseende hos främmande Folkslag. Våra Lärdas arbeten äro för Utlänningarna så begärlige, at åtskillige, de vittraste ibland dem, af otålighet at inhämta deras innehåll, icke hunnit afbida öfversättningarna deraf på sina språk, hvilka ske nog skyndsamt, utan begynt lära sig det Svenska.' Carl Fredrik Mennander, *Tal om bok-handelen i Sverige, hållit för Kongl. Vetenskaps Academien vid præsidii afläggande, den 8 maji 1756* (Stockholm: Lars Salvius, 1756), pp. 14–15.

76   Mennander, *Tal om bok-handelen*, p. 10.

CHAPTER 8

# War Booty of Books from Olomouc
## Catholic Libraries in Lutheran Sweden

*Lenka Veselá*

About 25,000 books were taken to Sweden from the Czech lands at the end of the Thirty Years' War. The first books to be seized in 1645 were from Mikulov and Olomouc, where the Swedes confiscated the largest aristocratic library in Moravia (the Dietrichstein Library) as well as church and monastic libraries. Three years later, the Swedes acquired extensive collections from Prague (especially from Prague Castle) where the most extensive booty was the biggest library in the Czech lands, the Rosenberg Library, and the Habsburg collections.[1]

Compared to the attractive monarchical and aristocratic collections taken from Prague Castle (1648) and Mikulov Castle (1645), the ecclesiastical libraries from Olomouc have appeared less appealing to researchers, and thus have gone unexamined for many decades. Furthermore, research into the looted books from Olomouc is complicated mainly because no original catalogue has been preserved; the remains of the book collections from there are dispersed across dozens of institutions in Sweden and other European countries.

Olomouc was the third-largest city in the medieval Czech lands and an important religious and administrative centre in Moravia.[2] During the Thirty Years' War, Olomouc became a crucial strategic target for the Swedish army in its battles with the Habsburg imperial troops. The city was taken by an armed force under the command of General Lennart Torstenson (1603–1561) in 1642, and consequently Olomouc served the Swedes as a stable military base for the following eight years. It was not until 1650 that the last troops left the city due to unpaid contributions to Sweden, two years after signing the Treaty of Westphalia.[3]

---

1 This study is a result of the research funded by the Czech Science Foundation as the project GA ČR 22-06083S 'The Swedish War Booty of Books from the Czech Lands'.
2 Jindřich Schulz (ed.), *Dějiny Olomouce* (2 vols., Olomouc: Statutární město Olomouc – Univerzita Palackého v Olomouci, 2009).
3 A summary of the Swedish occupation of Olomouc: Miroslav Koudela, *The Swedes in Olomouc 1642–1650* (Olomouc: DANAL, 1995); Miroslav Koudela, 'Za třicetileté války', in *Dějiny Olomouce*, I, pp. 333–336.

© LENKA VESELÁ, 2023 | DOI:10.1163/9789004441217_010
This is an open access chapter distributed under the terms of the CC BY-NC-ND 4.0 license.

Olomouc was a traditional seat of significant ecclesiastical institutions: among the most ancient was a bishopric with a Chapter and a Premonstratensian convent, both founded in the twelfth century. Minorites and Dominicans settled in Olomouc in the thirteenth century and the circle of religious orders in Olomouc was expanded again by the Carthusian monastery and Augustinian and Franciscan convents in the fifteenth century. After the Hussite Wars, Olomouc remained a Catholic town with a bishop's seat but the development of these institutions was negatively influenced by the religious turbulence of the fifteenth and sixteenth centuries, the Hussite Wars, and, in particular the Lutheran Reformation, which was especially influential within the German population of Olomouc. Most convents and monasteries, however, stabilized their status and position after the re-catholicisation of the seventeenth century. The Catholics strengthened their position both locally and provincially thanks to the arrival of two new religious orders in Olomouc: the Jesuit college (1566) and the Capuchin convent (1614). In the middle of the seventeenth century, under the Swedish occupation, there were, besides the Chapter, ten monasteries and convents, of which two were nunneries.[4] These institutions constituted an essential component in the city's organization, which needed to be taken into account by the Swedish garrison.

During the occupation, the Swedish troops confiscated a substantial part of the institutional libraries in Olomouc. Although they did not take the opportunity to seize all of the available book collections, their bounty of books from Olomouc ranks as the largest where Catholic libraries are concerned. Even today, we do not know what books were in the libraries taken from Olomouc and how many, nor can we be sure which have been preserved until the present.[5] What has negatively affected the interpretation of these events is a single dramatic, austere, and incomplete description of the Olomouc confiscations, reliance on which has been evident in the scholarly literature to date.[6]

---

4 They were houses, convents and monasteries of the following orders: Jesuits (from 1566), Franciscans (1453), Minorites (from 1214), Augustinians (from 1425), Premonstratensians (1078), Carthusians (1437), Capuchins (1614) and Dominicans (1239).

5 The only comprehensive information regarding the Olomouc book booty can be found in the studies by Otto Walde and Beda Dudík, which were published more than one hundred years ago. Beda Dudík, *Forschungen in Schweden für Mährens Geschichte* (Brünn: Winiker, 1852); Beda Dudík, *Iter Romanum: Im Auftrage des Hohen maehrischen Landesausschusses in den Jahren 1852 und 1853* (2 vols., Wien: In Commission bei F. Manz & Comp., 1855); Otto Walde, *Storhetstidens litterära krigsbyten: En kulturhistorisk-bibliografisk studie* (2 vols., Uppsala: Almqvist & Wiksell, 1916–1920).

6 The primary source for describing the book confiscations was the chronicle written by a Minorite friar Jakub Pavel Zaczkovic. It was made available by the editor Beda Dudík as

The looted books from Olomouc are now being explored in my research project, which, among other objectives, aims to map all preserved specimens of books plundered from the Czech lands between 1646 and 1648.[7] Although my investigation is at its outset, it is already apparent that the case of Olomouc is in some respects different from the taking of spoils of war from other cities. For instance, despite the general recommendations and explicit governmental orders to confiscate the libraries in Olomouc, the Swedish commanding officers did not appear to have shown much interest in them.

The present study aims to reconstruct the course of the confiscation of books in Olomouc, and thereby to reveal the circumstances that influenced this process. Was the case of Olomouc different and more specific than confiscation in other cities? The second major focus of the study is the second life of the books from Olomouc in their new cultural environment, after their removal to Sweden. I would like to underscore in the present study that the interruption of the natural development of the Olomouc libraries is not to be perceived only negatively, and that the insights into surviving books from the city may offer positive research perspectives.

## 1  The Course of Book Confiscations in Olomouc

The capitulation treaty, signed in 1642 by the city representatives and the Swedish garrison, guaranteed inviolability of the assets owned by the ecclesiastical institutions and the Chapter in Olomouc. From the very beginning, however, the treaty came into conflict with the practical needs of the Swedish troops. Shortly after seizing the city, the Swedes tore down all buildings outside the city walls for strategic military reasons. Among them were two convents, the Premonstratensian and the Capuchin.

Against all odds, this violent act does not seem to have affected the relationship between the convents, monasteries and the Swedes in a negative way. In the first phase of the Swedish occupation, there were no significant clashes between the Swedish garrison and the locals. Although the Swedish commanders perceived the ecclesiastical institutions as places of potential resistance, at the same time they respected their sovereignty and even, as did the locals,

---

*Chronik des Minoriten-Quardians über die Schwedenherrschaft in Olmütz 1642–1650* (Wien: Gerold & Comp., 1881).

7   The research results are presented in the database of preserved books on a web portal with map visualizations and other informative sources: *The Swedish Booty of Books from Bohemia and Moravia 1646–1648*, available on www.knizni-korist.cz/en (last accessed 20 July 2022).

used them for hiding personal valuables. Swedish officers and commanders would visit the Jesuit college and even attend sermons. The Franciscan convent had even closer relations with the Swedish garrison. The convent superior, Michal Jahn, became the confidante of the Swedish commander, Georg Paykull (1605–1657), and an unofficial mediator between the city elite and the military garrison.[8]

The atmosphere in the city started to deteriorate, however, due to the increasingly tense military-economic situation. After the first escalation in the autumn of 1643, Jesuits were expelled from the city and the Augustinian convent was plundered, while other religious institutions were saddled with high contributions. Another critical point was the Emperor's attempt at conquering Olomouc in 1644, supported by the above-mentioned superior of the Franciscan Friary, Michal Jahn. In the act of vengeance, the Franciscan convent was ransacked, and the situation of the religious orders in Olomouc became unsustainable. As a consequence, most of the inhabitants living in the ecclesiastical institutions gradually abandoned the city.

It was precisely at this moment when, according to the Olomouc Chronicle of the time, the systematic plundering of the books in the monastic libraries occurred. The author of the chronicle, Minorite friar Jakub Pavel Zaczkovic, says that what initially triggered the devastation was the accidental discovery of the Jesuit library, which the Jesuits had concealed before leaving the city, and which was unintentionally revealed by the last administrator of the Jesuit college, Jiří Pelinka.[9] Though Zaczkovic's Chronicle of occupied Olomouc is a valuable resource, it raises several issues. First, since it was written after a substantial time interval, the chronology of events is unreliable. Second, the Minorite friar was influenced by biased assertions and interpreted events unfavorably with respect to the Swedish occupants and local 'enemies', the Jesuits, who were seen as adversaries by the Minorites.

It cannot be completely ruled out that individual books had already been taken from the convents and monasteries during the attacks of 1643 and 1644. My assumption, nevertheless, is that book confiscation in the libraries was neither systematic nor organized until 1645. From the very beginning, the Swedish garrison led by Commander Georg Paykull showed no interest in the thousands of books located in the convents, monasteries, ecclesiastical institutions, or

---

8  Martin Elbel, *Město a klášter: Františkánský konvent v raně novověké Olomouci* (Praha: Nakladatelství Lidové noviny, 2017), pp. 22–25.
9  *Chronik des Minoriten-Quardians*, pp. 575–576.

homes of Olomouc townspeople, thus ignoring the 1642 order of the Swedish Chancellor Axel Oxenstierna to requisition the libraries.[10]

The Swedish commanders' lack of interest is apparent from, for instance, how the convents located outside the city walls were demolished. There was a deserted library in the Premonstratensian convent, dating to the twelfth century, which the canons had vacated before the city was occupied.[11] Some of its books were destroyed during the demolition of the convent, while the rest were successfully moved to the Minorite convent. As documented in Jesuit accounting records, the Swedes sold several missals from the Premonstratensian convent to the Jesuits.[12] Neither did the Swedes attempt to appropriate the library of the Capuchin convent, which was torn down in 1642. The Capuchins moved their books to the inner city of Olomouc without any trouble.

The fact that the books were still in Olomouc in the hands of their original owners in 1644 is shown in one of the books preserved at the University Library in Leiden.[13] An eyewitness wrote down in Czech an account of the unsuccessful attempt by the Emperor's army to conquer Olomouc in 1644. He remarked that 'many people died on both sides' in the course of a few hours (Figure 8.1). Unfortunately, we do not know either the writer's name or which library the book came from.

I am assuming that the Olomouc libraries were not confiscated before the end of 1645 and that the initiative did not come from the local Swedish commander but was the result of intervention from higher military and political authorities. In the autumn of 1645, the war commissioner, Johannes Bussow, was sent to Olomouc to make an inventory of the confiscated books and prepare them for transportation to Sweden. However, in my view, the main reason

---

10   Walde, *Storhetstidens litterära krigsbyten*, 1, p. 229; Generally speaking, the confiscation praxis was introduced by the military order issued by Gustavus Adolphus in 1621, see more in Emma Hagström Molin, 'Spoils of Knowledge. Looted Books in Uppsala University Library during the Seventeenth Century', in Gerhild Scholz Wiliams et al. (eds.), *Rethinking Europe: War and Peace in the Early Modern German Lands* (Leiden: Brill, 2019), pp. 256–257.

11   Their library contained at least 699 books; this number indicating the order of the books in the original catalogue of the monastery was preserved on the front page of the incunable stored in the Royal Danish Library in Copenhagen, Inc. Haun 196, see the database *The Swedish Booty of Books from Bohemia and Moravia 1646–1648*.

12   *Chronik des Minoriten-Quardians*, p. 575; Zdeněk Orlita, 'Olomoucká univerzitní knihovna od svého založení do zrušení jezuitského řádu (1566–1773)', in Zdeněk Orlita (ed.), *Chrám věd a múz: Dějiny Vědecké knihovny v Olomouci* (Olomouc: Vědecká knihovna v Olomouci, 2016), p. 17.

13   Helfrich Emmel, *Sylva Quadrilinguis* (Praha: Daniel Adam z Veleslavína, 1598) USTC 567757, Universiteitsbibliotheek Leiden (721 C 15).

for his expeditious mission was not the ecclesiastical Olomouc libraries, abandoned in the languishing or completely deserted convents for two years. The main incentive was, it seems, the unexpected acquisition of the large aristocratic library, which was taken over by the Swedes in Mikulov Castle in the autumn of 1645. This library belonged to the Austrian-Moravian family of Dietrichstein and contained more than eight thousand books, making it the second-largest private library in the Czech lands.[14] Since the Swedish garrison could not stay in Mikulov permanently, it was thought necessary to move the library to Olomouc post-haste. Olomouc, 130 kilometers away, was chosen because it had been a long-term, stable Swedish base.

Unlike the looted books from Mikulov and Prague, the book collections in Olomouc were not confiscated en masse, perhaps except for the Jesuit library, which was, as far as we know, taken in its entirety.[15] As for other libraries in the convents, perhaps even the Chapter library, the Swedish commissioner selected only some of the books.[16] That confiscations were only partial seems to be confirmed by the fact that single books from the original fund of the Olomouc convents have been preserved across the Czech lands. These are mainly incunables from the Franciscan and Augustinian convents, and they have been preserved in significant quantities, especially in the Olomouc Research Library (Vědecká knihovna v Olomouci).[17] Another piece of evidence is the insignificant number of books (so far only two registered books) preserved from the libraries of male Olomouc Dominicans and Minorites in Sweden and elsewhere. None of the preserved books from the Dominican and Augustinian nunneries have surfaced yet, but perhaps their libraries were so small that they were not subjected to the Swedish requisition.

It remains unclear in what manner and how many books were confiscated from the Chapter library, the second largest after the Jesuit library and the oldest in Olomouc. The library of the Olomouc Chapter had been in continuous

---

14  Miroslav Trantírek, *Dějiny mikulovské zámecké knihovny* (Mikulov: Okresní vlastivědné muzeum, 1963); Burkhard Seuffert, 'Bibliothek und Archiv auf Schloss Nikolsburg in Mähren vor 1645', *Zentralblatt für Bibliothekswesen*, 42 (1925), pp. 253–259.

15  Nearly 200 books were allegedly saved from the Swedes; according to Jana Mačáková, they were hidden in the basements of the townsmen and in the Carthusian monastery: Jiří Žáček, *Jezuitský konvikt: Sídlo uměleckého centra Univerzity Palackého v Olomouci. Dějiny – stavební a umělecké dějiny – obnova a využití* (Olomouc: Univerzita Palackého, 2002), pp. 23–24.

16  *Chronik des Minoriten-Quardians*, p. 576.

17  Francyszek Bajger, *Česká františkánská knižní kultura: Knihovny minoritů, františkánů a kapucínů v průběhu staletí*, Dissertation (Ostrava: Ostravská univerzita, 2007), pp. 412–423; Jiří Glonek, 'Pozdně gotické vazby z moravských františkánských klášterů (Brno, Olomouc, Uherské Hradiště, Znojmo)', *Bibliotheca Antiqua* (2017), pp. 32–76.

existence since the twelfth century, its flowering having taken place in the fourteenth and fifteenth centuries when it possessed 250 manuscripts. A part of the earlier collection still forms part of the Chapter library, preserved today in Olomouc.[18] Since the Chapter administrators had managed to move the Chapter archive to Vienna before the occupation, a theory emerged that together with the archive, a part of the Chapter library might also have been moved. Both were supposed to be returned from Austria to Olomouc after the Swedes finally left the town in 1650.[19] My preliminary assessment, which needs to be confirmed by further research, is that, together with the archive, the administrators of the Chapter moved out only some of the precious medieval manuscripts which were traditionally an organic component of the Chapter archive, and that the rest of the library remained in Olomouc. On the one hand, the move would have involved thousands of books, whose transportation would have been overly complicated; and, on the other, the Chapter library collection had not been well looked after already for several decades before the occupation. In 1645, a partial book requisition presumably took place in the Chapter library and some other convents and monasteries. The main difference between Chapter library and monastic libraries lies in the quantity of the seized books; The Swedes probably gained only dozens or hundreds of books in convents and monasteries that had small collections, whereas the confiscation from the Chapter numbered more than 1,200 (see Table 8.1 below). Furthermore, the Chapter library is unique because it allows us to establish the approximate ratio of confiscated books to those left untouched.[20] Based on the preserved manuscripts and incunables, it seems that approximately two thirds of the book collection was moved to Sweden while the rest remained in Olomouc.

Moreover, some libraries were left entirely untouched by Swedish confiscations. For instance, the extensive library of the Carthusian monastery in Olomouc contained hundreds, maybe thousands, of books in the seventeenth century. Surprisingly, no one has explained how the medieval fund of the Carthusian library, preserved until today almost intact, survived in the

---

18  Miroslav Flodr, *Skriptorium olomoucké: K počátkům písařské tvorby v českých zemích* (Praha: SPN, 1960); Markéta Poskočilová, *Geneze historie a skladba souboru prvotisků z fondu kapitulní knihovny v Olomouci*, Masters thesis (2 vols., Olomouc: Filozofická fakulta Univerzity Palackého v Olomouci, 2017).
19  Štěpán Kohout, *Kde voní pergamen: Čtrnáctero návštěv rukopisné knihovny olomoucké kapituly* (Olomouc: Univerzita Palackého v Olomouci, 2009), p. 11.
20  However, only the manuscripts and some incunables can be compared with certainty. Find more about the transported part of the Chapter library in the database of the preserved books: *The Swedish Booty of Books from Bohemia and Moravia 1646–1648*.

Olomouc Research Library.[21] This collection contains at least 250 preserved manuscripts. The fate of the Carthusian monastery during the Swedish occupation is still somewhat unclear and is not even mentioned in the Minorite chronicle from that time. It is possible that the Carthusians concealed the library or removed it temporarily. The Carthusians were the only order that remained in Olomouc throughout the entire occupation of the city and, as far as we know, avoided any serious conflict with the Swedish garrison. This might have given the Carthusian monastery greater protection than others.

The respect that the Swedes showed for the property of the monasteries in which monks remained is supported by evidence from other cities. There was a Capuchin convent with an exciting library near the emptied Mikulov Castle (where the Swedes had seized the Dietrichstein library in 1645), which, to the best of our knowledge, did not suffer any harm under the Swedish occupation. Similarly, the Swedes did not make claims to the private libraries of the Olomouc townsmen, even though some of these comprised hundreds of books and often surpassed in size the collections of smaller local monasteries.[22] The only exception was the library owned by Ferdinand Julius Zirckendorfer, a city council member whose books appear in several Swedish libraries. Zirckendorfer's library was officially confiscated, along with his other assets, as a punishment for conspiring with the enemy.[23]

Comprehensive confiscations, it seems, thus occurred, only in the religious institutions that were abandoned or that had tense relations with the Swedes during the occupation (Jesuits, Franciscans, and Augustinians). Confiscations in other communities were conducted as formalities, and it cannot be ruled out that some convents were completely spared (Carthusians). There were several reasons for this course of events. Despite the uneasy situation in the city, the Swedish garrison strove to maintain, to some extent, the legal status of the monasteries and ecclesiastical institutions as well as the inhabitants, treatment that was stipulated by the capitulation treaty in 1642. Furthermore, the Swedes may have considered irrelevant those book collections that remained significant in the Czech or Catholic context.

---

21 Find more about the medieval fund of the library in Tomáš Černušák, 'Knihovna dolanských kartuziánů jako historický pramen', *Problematika historických a vzácných knižních fondů Čech, Moravy a Slezska*, (1997), pp. 30–34; Jiří Glonek, 'Knihvazačská dílna olomouckých kartuziánů', *Bibliotheca Antiqua* (2013), pp. 40–61.

22 Jaroslav Miller, 'Zchudlé město bohatých měšťanů?', in Martin Elbel, Ondřej Jakubec (eds.), *Olomoucké baroko: Proměny ambicí jednoho města* (2 vols., Olomouc: Muzeum umění Olomouc, 2010), 1, p. 73.

23 Walde, *Storhetstidens litterära krigsbyten*, 1, p. 241. Preserved specimens can be found in the database *The Swedish Booty of Books from Bohemia and Moravia 1646–1648*.

For all that, the book bounty from Olomouc was vast. The Swedish military commissioner Bussow made a thorough inventory of the books and prepared them for transport to Sweden. As a reward for his contribution to the Moravian book bounty, he was ennobled by Queen Christina (1626–1689). After his departure, the sealed barrels with books had to remain in Olomouc for one more year before their transport by General Wittenberg's troops. The books were transported in two stages. The first to be shipped came from the Dietrichstein library and the Capuchin library (November 1646), and was followed by the Jesuit library and other book collections, including the Chapter's library which departed two months later. The books arrived in Głubczyce (Leobschütz) during the winter of 1646–1647 and subsequently traveled to Głogów (Glogau). Then they were shipped on the river Odra on fourteen small vessels to Szczecin (Stettin), arriving in Stockholm in May 1647.[24]

## 2   The Scope of the Book Booty from Olomouc

Although some of the book collections escaped confiscation, the booty from Olomouc ranks in its scope as the greatest acquired by the Swedes, at least as far as ecclesiastical libraries are concerned. By comparison, in 1621 the Swedes confiscated approximately a thousand books in a Jesuit college in Riga, and five years later, roughly 2,200 books in the Jesuit college of Braniewo (Braunsberg). There is no precise estimate of how many books were looted from Poznań in 1655 which, besides the Jesuit library, comprised collections from some monasteries, but it was probably somewhere between two and six thousand.[25]

Similarly, the scope of the Olomouc book booty was unknown, even as an approximation, until recently. Unlike in Prague or Mikulov, none of the catalogues from Olomouc have been preserved (that is, the one compiled by Johann Bussow before the transportation, in addition to some older catalogues of the monasteries that sources mention as having existed).[26] Despite facing this obstacle at the start of my research, I have sought to estimate the scope

---

24   Dudík, *Forschungen in Schweden*, p. 40, 50.
25   Peter Sjökvist, 'Books from Poznań at the Uppsala University Library', *The Central European Journal of Social Sciences and Humanities* (CEJSH), (2017), pp. 319–328; Peter Sjökvist, 'Polish Collections at Uppsala University Library. A History of Research', in Dorota Sidorowicz-Mulak and Agnieszka Franczyk-Cegły (eds.), *Książka dawna i jej właściciele* (2 vols., Wrocław: Wydawnictwo Ossolineum, 2017), 2, pp. 237–244.
26   Walde, *Storhetstidens litterära krigsbyten*, 1, p. 245. Handwritten *ex libris* in the books indicate that there were older catalogues for the Jesuit and Premonstratensian library.

of the book booty in Olomouc, focusing both on the overall picture and on several of the libraries.

In the past, research into the looted books from the Czech lands used a rough estimate from the size of preserved book collections from several libraries whose original content is known. For instance, researchers looked into Rosenberg's library, which was the largest and oldest aristocratic library in the Czech lands. It contained nearly ten thousand volumes and was taken from Prague Castle in 1648. Another library, for which research exists, was owned by an Austrian knightly family in the service of the Habsburgs, the Becks from Leopoldsdorf; it later became part of the Dietrichsteins' library in Mikulov.[27] The preserved manuscripts can be compared to the catalogue made at the royal library in Stockholm in 1650.[28] The research I have conducted in all these areas of the book booty from the Czech lands and Moravia points to the same conclusion: compared to the former quantity, only 20 per cent of the books have been preserved.[29]

Two main factors can explain this low proportion of preserved books. First, in contrast to the book booties from Lithuania and Poland, those from the Czech lands were primarily designated for the royal library in Stockholm, which experienced a destructive fire in 1697. The fire destroyed three quarters of the royal collections, including an untraceable number of books from the Czech lands. Second, during the first years after they arrived in Sweden, some of the books found their way to other locations, which is also of some significance. Queen Christina gave larger and smaller book collections to individuals and Swedish ecclesiastical and educational institutions. After her abdication in 1654, she took hundreds of books from the Czech booty to Rome; however, only manuscripts have been preserved in her private library.[30]

Furthermore, minor losses occurred while the books were transported to Sweden or shortly before. Yet these losses were far less significant than those of the war booty from Prague, which took place two years later. In Prague, dozens, perhaps even hundreds of books were appropriated by several Swedish

---

27 Lenka Veselá, *Knihy na dvoře Rožmberků* (Praha: Knihovna Akademie věd ČR – Scriptorium, 2005); Lenka Veselá, *Ritter und Intellektueller: Hieronymus Beck von Leopoldsdorf (1525–1596) und seine Bibliothek* (Frankfurt am Main: Peter Lang, 2017).
28 Lenka Veselá, 'Rukopisy a švédská knižní kořist z českých zemí', *Studie o rukopisech*, 50/1 (2020), pp. 25–45.
29 Veselá, *Knihy na dvoře Rožmberků*, p. 261; Veselá, *Ritter und Intellektueller*, p. 267.
30 Eva Nilsson Nylander, *The Mild Boredom of Order: A Study in the History of the Manuscript Collection of Queen Christina of Sweden* (Lund: Lund University, 2011).

commanders for their private collections.[31] Among these persons was a military counselor in the service of Sweden, Alexander Erskine (1598–1656), whose 'inappropriate' interest in books had also been observed in Olomouc. He was admonished for stealing from the Olomouc book bounty by Queen Christina herself.[32]

Today, almost 1,800 preserved books have been successfully traced from the Olomouc booty, now dispersed in nearly twenty libraries across Europe. Assuming that, as in other cases, approximately 20 per cent of the Olomouc books were preserved, their total number at the moment of transportation could have amounted to between eight and nine thousand volumes.

The most extensive library was the collection of the Olomouc Jesuit college, probably the only one that was confiscated in its entirety, approximately six thousand volumes (Table 8.1). The reason for this uncompromising approach, which differed from that of other Olomouc ecclesiastical institutions, could be that in the eyes of the Swedish elites, the Jesuits were perceived as 'enemies'. Nearly 1,300 books have been preserved from the Jesuit library; they indicate that the Jesuits would acquire books from traditional sources and gifts from supporters of high rank, especially Olomouc bishops and members of the Order. The preserved remains of the original Jesuit library reveal a wide range of private and hitherto completely unknown collections: among the most interesting, the books of a Catholic cleric, Jan Sarkander (1576–1620), deserve special attention. This controversial pastor was tortured to death in Olomouc during the Bohemian Revolt in 1620, and in 1995 he was beatified. His books entered the library as a legacy of his brother, Mikuláš Sarkander. The Jesuits in Olomouc employed acquisition strategies that reached not only the libraries of competing Olomouc institutions (Dominicans, Franciscans, and the Cathedral Chapter) but also several older ecclesiastical-educational institutions (the Cathedral school and the bishop seminary). Founded after 1566, the Jesuit library contained large quantities of older literature and a surprising number of incunables (of which 320 are preserved). The Jesuits also engaged with the Swedish soldiers to buy old manuscripts from the demolished Premonstratensian convent in 1642.

---

31  Robert Rebitsch, Jenny Öhman and Jan Kilián, *1648. Kriegführung und Friedensverhandlungen: Prag und das Ende des Dreißigjährigen Krieges* (Innsbruck: Innsbruck University Press, 2018), pp. 295–320; Emil Schieche, 'Umfang und Schicksal der von den Schweden 1645 in Nikolsburg und 1648 in Prag erbeuteten Archivalien', *Bohemia*, 8 (1967), pp. 111–133.

32  Pavla Slavíčková, 'Nové materiály švédské provenience k dějinám města Olomouce', *Acta Universitatis Palackianae Olomucensis: Facultas philosophica. Historica*, (2007), pp. 129–137, p. 133.

Such a progressive approach as this was used by the newer orders to create their libraries, in contrast with the stagnating libraries of traditional medieval monasteries and convents. The approach can also be seen with the Capuchins, who settled in Olomouc as late as 1614. Although they lost their entire library during the Bohemian Revolt, they built a new book collection of considerable scope during the following thirty years, amounting to hundreds of volumes (Table 8.1).

The books preserved from Olomouc also reflect more significant sociocultural changes in the book culture of the local ecclesiastical institutions, as, for instance, in the ways that personal sponsorship strategies changed. It was mainly Olomouc bishops who would donate books to monasteries and convents, while at the beginning of the seventeenth century, this activity was assigned to the congregation of the chapter deans. There was also a change in the spectrum of the recipients. Traditionally, the members of the Cathedral Chapter would bequeath their private libraries to the Chapter library; in the seventeenth century, however, we observe a clear trend of book donations to different Olomouc ecclesiastical institutions.

## 3  Catholic Libraries in Lutheran Sweden

As has already been noted by Peter Sjökvist, looted books served primarily as cultural capital in their new environment.[33] The same applies to the vast majority of books brought from Olomouc, which became, for another three centuries, a passive historical fund for several Swedish institutions, in much the same way as any collection of old books in other libraries. The short period after they arrived in Stockholm (1648–1654), a time of both intellectual and political turbulence, deserves attention. Here we can look more closely at the books that Queen Christina gave away to single individuals and institutions, before leaving Sweden, and the role of the Olomouc collections in these donations.

Books from Olomouc found their way into private hands less frequently than those from the aristocratic libraries of Prague and Mikulov. This is unsurprising, as most of the Olomouc books consisted of Catholic theological literature; those that did fall into private hands tended to deviate from this thematic

---

33  Peter Sjökvist and Krister Östlund, 'War Booty at Uppsala University Library', paper presented at *IFLA WLIC 2017 – Wrocław, Poland – Libraries. Solidarity. Society*, available on www.library.ifla.org/id/eprint/1687 (last accessed 20 July 2022). See also Emma Hagström Molin, *Krigsbytets biografi: Byten i Riksarkivet, Uppsala universitetsbibliotek och Skoklosters slott under 1600-talet* (Göteborg: Makadam, 2015).

content and reflected the interests of the new owners. For example, Magnus Gabriel De la Gardie (1622–1686) obtained as a gift from Queen Christina a collection of Olomouc incunables with legal texts.[34] Queen Christina chose several manuscripts from the Olomouc Chapter and Jesuit college for her private library, which she transported to Rome after her abdication in 1654. These were precious parchment manuscripts with classical texts, created in Florence in the fifteenth century.[35] Furthermore, in compensation for unpaid wages (and perhaps less legally), several books from the royal library were selected by the Queen's librarian, Isaac Vossius, and some others ended up in the private collection of his successor, Edmund Gripenhielm, inspector of the royal library in Stockholm.[36] Their humanist interests coincided with the chosen books from Olomouc that dealt with modern science: books on geography, mathematics, astrology, and current editions of classical and patristic works or bilingual editions of biblical texts. Most of them originated in the Olomouc Jesuit library.[37]

Even more interesting is the range of books distributed to the bookshelves of Swedish institutions and the intention behind their destination. Queen Christina gave approximately five hundred looted books to the Västerås gymnasium (upper secondary school) and between 2,000 and 2,500 books to the Strängnäs Chapter.[38] In both cases, approximately 70 per cent of the books came from the Olomouc book booty.

Researchers disagree on how to interpret these book donations. Some authors claim that Queen Christina wanted to create an intellectual base for the schools of higher education that had been founded not long before in both cities. Others argue that it was an elegant way for the Queen to dispense with books that she found uninteresting or were duplicated in the royal collection.[39] My analysis of both collections revealed that both the endowments consisted

---

34   These books can be found in the University Library in Uppsala, see the database *The Swedish Booty of Books from Bohemia and Moravia 1646–1648*.
35   The selection of the books was done hastily by the librarian Isaac Vossius; however, this was probably the Queen's intention. Veselá, 'Rukopisy a švédská knižní kořist z českých zemí', pp. 41–42.
36   Christian Callmer, *Königin Christina, ihre Bibliothekare und ihre Handschriften: Beiträge zur europäischen Bibliotheksgeschichte* (Stockholm: Kungliga biblioteket, 1977), pp. 41–42.
37   See the database *The Swedish Booty of Books from Bohemia and Moravia 1646–1648*.
38   Eugeniusz Gawryś, *Slavica Arosiensia* (3 vols., Stockholm: Almqvist & Wiksell, 1961), 3, p. 11 and card catalogue Praedae Bellicae Arosiensis at Stadsbiblioteket Västerås; Ragnhild Lundgren, *Strängnäs domkyrkobibliotek: Systematisk katalog över tryckta böcker = The Cathedral Library in Strängnäs: Systematic Catalogue of Printed Books* (2 vols., Skellefteå: Artos Academic, [2017]).
39   Walde, *Storhetstidens litterära krigsbyten*, 1, p. 26; František Horák, 'Dodatková a souhrnná zpráva o průzkumu humanistických bohemik za léta 1966–1968', *Listy filologické*, 92 (1962), p. 360.

mainly of theological texts by Catholic authors and included only a few books (such as textbooks, dictionaries, language manuals, or ancient literature) that would be of use for teaching at school. Thus, the donated books could not be said to have fulfilled 'educational' functions in any of the cases.[40]

Comparing the structures of the donated theological literature in greater detail, it seems that the selection for the Chapter library in Strängnäs was made with greater care, especially in the range of authors representing different religious learnings. What I would argue is that the religious and, at the same time, multi-confessional nature of the books donated to the Strängnäs Chapter was not random. It was Queen Christina's symbolic act of support for the Strängnäs Bishop, Johannes Matthiae Gothus (1592–1670), and his controversial (for the Lutheran institution) ecumenical attitudes.

Bishop Matthiae was an extraordinary figure in orthodox Lutheran Sweden. He was strongly influenced by Ramism, which, within the Lutheran Church, sought to (though rather unsuccessfully) advance Christian humanism, with elements of ecumenism. Bishop Matthiae had a close relationship with the Queen not only because of his tolerance towards different religious attitudes: in his youth, he had also worked as her tutor.[41] Thus, the Queen's book gift to the Strängnäs Chapter was well-considered, reflecting the crucial role of their like-minded philosophical-religious attitudes. This symbolic subtext is reinforced by the fact that the Bishop immediately started to open the donated book collection to the public. Not only did he perform a symbolic act by giving everyone access to the catalogue, as he mentioned in 1663, but moreover, by storing the volumes in the Strängnäs Cathedral, he made them, in practice, available at a publicly accessible place. Books by Catholic and Calvinist authors, who were, in Lutheran Sweden, strictly forbidden, thus entered the public domain.[42]

There was yet another influential factor: the scope of the Strängnäs gift differed fundamentally from other similar gifts aimed at Swedish educational institutions. The academy in Turku/Åbo and the university library in Uppsala, for example, received volumes from the Czech book booty numbering only in the tens. The gift for the school in Västerås was somewhat less extensive, however, compared to the Strängnäs gift. The underlying intention was not explicit,

---

40   Lenka Veselá, 'Užitečné, či nepotřebné? Knihy z Čech a Moravy jako dar královny Kristiny švédským vzdělávacím institucím v polovině 17. století', in Lucie Pavelková et al. (eds.) *Knihovny a jejich majitelé: Odraz zájmu a touhy po poznání* (Brno: Moravská zemská knihovna v Brně, 2018), pp. 63–73.
41   Callmer, *Königin Christina*, pp. 15–16, 28.
42   Lundgren, *Strängnäs domkyrkobibliotek*, p. 21.

nor did it have the potential for educating local students. It seems that in this case, the Queen merely granted the request that the gymnasium had repeatedly made to obtain looted books ever since its founding. In this case, the aim was to fill empty shelves with books regardless of their content, that is, it was a typical display of the distribution of cultural capital.

All said, even the 'positive phase' in Strängnäs did not last long in the history of the Chapter library. Following the abdication of Queen Christina in 1654 and her subsequent conversion to Catholicism, Johannes Matthiae's position in the leading establishment became unsustainable. He was accused of religious syncretism and, a few years later, forced to resign from his office. Already in the seventeenth century, the Strängnäs library became a closed book collection whose origin was still perceived as disparate and unnatural.[43]

## 4   Conclusions

The case of the Swedish book booty from Olomouc is extraordinary in several respects in the context of confiscations during the Thirty Years' War. First, the reconstruction of the confiscations revealed that this process did not follow any simplified scheme, as may seem to be the case from narrative sources of that time or from the historiography that followed. The Swedish military command in Olomouc, led by Georg Paykull, did not show interest in the Olomouc collections, despite the official and unequivocal position (Gustavus Adolphus's articles from 1621 and General Torstenson's order in 1642). The Swedish command did not use the opportunity to seize monastery and convent libraries, either during their demolition (Premonstratensian and Capuchin convents) or random plundering in 1643 and 1644. What influenced the course of the book confiscations, besides the absence of motivation and interest on the part of the Swedish command, was an atypical situation of long-term occupation of the city, the necessity to co-exist on a long-lasting basis, and to respect, at least informally, the legal status of ecclesiastic institutions as well as their inhabitants.

The confiscations from Olomouc libraries did not start until 1645 when the Swedish high command sent the military commissioner Johann Bussow. Under his authority, there was a massive seizure of the local ecclesiastic libraries. It

---

43   Emma Hagström Molin, 'The Materiality of War Booty Books: The Case of Strängnäs Cathedral Library', in Anna Källén (ed.), *Making Cultural History: New Perspectives on Western Heritage* (Lund: Nordic Academic Press, 2013), pp. 131–139.

was by no means comprehensive, however. The only library that was confiscated in its entirety was that of the Olomouc Jesuits, whereas other book collections were seized only partially. It seems that some book collections, for instance, that of the Olomouc Carthusians, were spared entirely. Still, between eight and nine thousand books were confiscated, giving Olomouc the leading position in the Swedish spoils of war from ecclesiastic institutions.

After they arrived in Sweden, the books looted from the Czech lands faced diverse fates compared to the book bounties from Jesuit libraries in Poland or the Baltic lands that were destined for the newly founded university library in Uppsala. The books from the Czech lands were assigned to the royal library in Stockholm, though some were donated to institutions or individuals by Queen Christina. The historical events that followed, mainly the fire at the Royal Palace in Stockholm in 1697, meant that only approximately 1,800 looted books from Olomouc were preserved; these are, furthermore, now scattered across more than twenty Swedish and other European institutions.

Although only a small part of the former libraries has survived, the preserved books represent a unique source that reflects the actual state of ecclesiastical Olomouc libraries in the middle of the seventeenth century, irrespective of later acquisitions. They constitute a unique micro-research laboratory that allows us to explore the course of confiscations in Olomouc, their approximate scope compared to other countries, and the fate of the books in Sweden. Research into the transported Olomouc libraries poses a challenge not only in the tracing of personal and institutional libraries, but also in the investigating of their potential to impact broader socio-cultural issues, such as the book transfer amongst diverse ecclesiastical institutions in certain locations.

Without a doubt, the role of the looted books from Olomouc fundamentally changed in their new environment. Most of them assumed the role of passive cultural capital in the following centuries. A closer look into the frantic period in the first years after the Czech books arrived in Stockholm (1648–1654) reveals, nevertheless, several extraordinary, though short-term historical episodes. In this respect, the most significant is Queen Christina's gift to the Strängnäs Chapter, which was one of the most important spiritual centres in Sweden. With this significant gift, which mainly originated in Olomouc, the Queen wanted to support the ecumenical stance of Strängnäs Bishop Johannes Matthiae. The new library in Strängnäs, freely accessible to the public for several years, aptly illustrates the atmosphere of religious tensions at the time, where an essential factor was the symbolism of artifacts, including books.

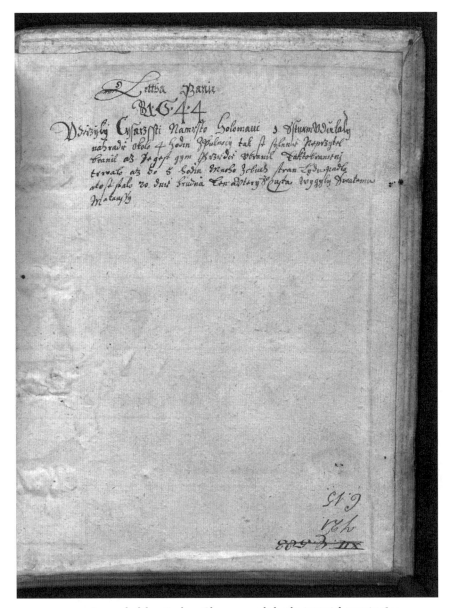

FIGURE 8.1     A record of the attack on Olomouc made by the imperial army in 1644. Helfrich Emmel, *Sylva Quadrilinguis* (Prague: Daniel Adam z Veleslavína, 1598), Universiteitsbibliotheek Leiden (721 C 15)

TABLE 8.1   Libraries confiscated in Olomouc in 1645

|  | Number of preserved books (state of research in 2022) | Estimated number of transported books |
|---|---|---|
| Jesuit college | 1,267 | c.6,300 |
| Chapter library | 241 | c.1,200 |
| Premonstratensian convent | 90[a] | more than 699 |
| Capuchin convent | 89 | c.450 |
| Franciscan convent | 58 | c.280 |
| Augustinian convent | 33 | c.170 |
| Dominican convent | 13 | c.80 |
| Bishop's seminary | 6 | x |
| Convent of Friars Minor Conventual | 3 | x |
| Carthusian monastery | 1 | x |
| Summary | 1,788 | c.9,000 |

a   Probably books stored in the Minorite convent in 1642 (see the text above).

CHAPTER 9

# Useful Literary Spoils of War from Riga at Uppsala University Library

*Peter Sjökvist*

The Swedish King Gustavus Adolphus (ruled 1611–1632) in the war against Poland entered Riga with his troops on 16 September 1621, when the city had finally fallen after a long siege.[1] Although the king was in general quite lenient towards its citizens, there were some obvious exceptions. The properties of the Polish king and of the Jesuit Order, which had started its activities in the city in 1583, were accordingly confiscated, and all movables belonging to the Jesuit College were taken and inventoried on the king's order.[2] The members of the Jesuit Order were forced to leave. It is not known exactly when the College's library was loaded onto ships bound for Stockholm, but in November of the following year it was presented at the castle by the clergyman Johannes Bothvidi (1575–1635), who initially was commissioned to take care of the library, to the vice-chancellor of Uppsala University, Laurentius Olai Wallius (1588–1638). He was the head of the learned institution that was now to receive the library as a donation from the Crown. Gustavus II Adolphus had the ambition to make the university in Uppsala a scholarly institution of international stature, and by donating literary spoils of war to its library one problem was seemingly taken care of: the books that were needed arrived in great numbers. The collection from Riga would soon be followed by several others, looted from libraries on the continent during the seventeenth century.[3] Taking books from the

---

1 As always in the case of literary spoils of war taken by the Swedes, the fundamental study is Otto Walde's magisterial doctoral thesis *Storhetstidens litterära krigsbyten: En kulturhistorisk-bibliografisk Studie* (2 vols., Uppsala: Almqvist & Wiksell, 1916–1920). The case of Riga is discussed in the first volume on pp. 42–52. For a more detailed account of the war when Riga surrendered, see *Sveriges krig 1611–1632*, 2: Polska kriget (Stockholm: Generalstaben, 1936).
2 On the history of the Jesuit College in Riga, see Reinis Norkārls, 'The Riga Jesuit College and its Book Collection', in *Catalogue of the Riga Jesuit College Book Collection (1583–1621): History and Reconstruction of the Collection* [CRJCBC] = *Rīgas Jezuītu kolēģijas grāmatu krājuma (1583–1621) katalogs: Krājuma vēsture un rekonstrukcija*, Gustavs Strenga and Andris Levāns (Riga: Latvijas Nacionālā bibliotēka, 2021), pp. 90–111.
3 The collections looted from Braniewo and Poznań have been or are the subjects of recent projects at Uppsala University Library, in collaboration with librarians from Poland. A catalogue of the Braniewo collection was published in 2007; see Józef Trypućko, *The Catalogue of*

© PETER SJÖKVIST, 2023 | DOI:10.1163/9789004441217_011
This is an open access chapter distributed under the terms of the CC BY-NC-ND 4.0 license.

institutions of confessional enemies in order to meet the demands for literature at home, however, was not an ideal solution when education at Uppsala aimed primarily at training clergymen and officials loyal to the state.[4] It is a truism that not all books from a Jesuit College could be considered useful at a Lutheran university in an age of confessionalization and conflict. Nevertheless, it is essential to investigate what kind of books and literature was or could be useful, and to suggest the reasons why. With the help of some catalogues, both early modern and very new ones, that cover the Riga collection and Uppsala University Library in the first half of the seventeenth century and today, the present study will seek to contribute to that discussion.[5] To start with, we have to survey the material we have to work with, and how library contents were arranged at the time.

## 1    Catalogues and Registers

The Johannes Bothvidi mentioned earlier was the alleged, though doubted, author of an inventory that listed the contents of the library from Riga together with some other taken items. This inventory is still extant at Uppsala University Library, and it consists of 893 titles, 61 unbound items, and a number of household utensils.[6] Gustavus Adolphus reminded of the necessity of

---

the Book Collection of the Jesuit College in Braniewo Held in the University Library in Uppsala = Katalog księgozbioru Kolegium Jezuitów w Braniewie zachowanego w Bibliotece Uniwersyteckiej w Uppsali, eds. Michał Spandowski and Sławomir Szyller (3 vols., Uppsala/Warsaw: Uppsala universitetsbibliotek/Biblioteka Narodowa, 2007). Modern catalogues of the Poznań spoils are being created presently. As regards the Polish collections in Uppsala, see also Peter Sjökvist, 'Polish Collections at Uppsala University Library: A -History of Research', in Dorota Sidorowicz-Mulak and Agnieszka Franczyk Cegła (eds.), Książka dawna i jej właściciele (2 vols., Wrocław: Wydawnictwo Ossolineum, 2017), 2, pp. 237–244. For information on the Poznań project, see Peter Sjökvist, 'Books from Poznań at the Uppsala University Library,' in Jack Puchalski et al. (eds.), Z badań nad książką i księgozbiorami historycznymi: Polonika w zbiorach obcych (Warsaw: Bractwo Kawalerów Gutenberg, 2017), pp. 319–327.

4   Cf., e.g., Erland Sellberg, Kyrkan och den tidigmoderna staten: En konflikt om Aristoteles, utbildning och makt (Stockholm: Carlssons, 2010), pp. 370–371. An example from the time is the statement in Laurentius Olai Wallius' program Decretum super vexationes humanitatis fere omnis expertes, dated 11 August 1633 at Uppsala: subolem ... literis et virtute erudiendam committunt, ut post parentis sui obitum Dei cultor existat, et patriae servitor.

5   Cf. especially Renāte Berga, 'Rara et Cara. Collection of Rare Books and Books of Cultural and Historical Significance in the Riga Jesuit College', in Catalogue of the Riga Jesuit College Book Collection (1583–1621), pp. 134–149.

6   Uppsala University Library (UUB) U 271, digitized version: www.urn.kb.se/resolve?urn=urn:nbn:se:alvin:portal:record-248017 (last accessed 20 July 2022). Cf. Claes Annerstedt, Upsala universitetsbiblioteks historia intill år 1702 (Uppsala: Wahlström & Widstrand, 1894), p. 9, and

making such a register in November 1626, and Johannes Bureus (1568–1652) wrote to Laurentius Olai Wallius, the vice-chancellor, about the matter at the same time when he, Bureus, was going through the books that had been looted in Prussia in the same year. The Riga inventory is likely to have been created after that date.[7] The list, however, does follow an original at Stockholm Castle, as is stated in some notes at the end of the extant inventory, but this original has not been identified in our time. We could presume that the original had come about already in Riga, since, as we saw, the Swedes had been ordered by the king to register all goods taken there.[8]

As Isak Collijn later noticed when starting a project to reconstruct the Riga collection at the beginning of the twentieth century, the Bothvidi inventory is not complete. At Uppsala University Library there are today books with a Riga provenance that are missing in the list. In addition, the bibliographical details in the inventory are not always correct, and the information given there very rudimentary. The arrangement of the books in the inventory is simple: they are classified only according to format and to whether they were bound or not.[9] On the other hand, there are also books on the Bothvidi list that are not at Uppsala University Library today, because some were discarded and others sold at auctions of duplicates over the centuries.[10]

In spite of its obvious deficiencies, the Bothvidi list will have an important role in the rest of the present study as a complement to and a very early forerunner of the new catalogue of books from the Jesuit College of Riga that was released at the beginning of 2021 by Laura Kreigere-Liepiņa and Renāte Berga at

---

Antoaneta Granberg, 'Carolina Redivivas samling från jesuitkollegiets bibliotek i Riga och Isak Collijns arkiv', in Per Ambrosiani, Per-Arne Bodin, and Nadejda Zorikhina Nilsson (eds.), *Må Novgorod fröjda sig: Hyllningsskrift till Elisabeth Löfstrand* (Stockholm: Institutionen för slaviska och baltiska språk, finska, nederländska och tyska, Stockholms universitet, 2016), p. 80.

7   Walde, *Storhetstidens litterära krigsbyten*, 1, p. 49. Cf. Johannes Bureus, 'Anteckningar av Johannes Thomae Agrivillensis Bureus', *Samlaren*, 4 (1883), p. 102, and Emma Hagström Molin, *Krigsbytets biografi: Byten i riksarkivet, Uppsala universitetsbibliotek och Skokloster slott under 1600-talet* (Göteborg: Makadam, 2015), p. 123.

8   Cf. Granberg, 'Carolina Redivivas samling från jesuitkollegiets bibliotek i Riga och Isak Collijns arkiv', p. 80.

9   Isak Collijn, *Jesuitkollegiets i Riga bibliotek: Bidrag till dess historia*, unpublished essay, UUB 475 D:2, digitized version: www.urn.kb.se/resolve?urn=urn:nbn:se:alvin:portal:record-400144 (last accessed 20 July 2022).

10  See further Peter Sjökvist, 'Litterära krigsbytens öden i Sverige', *Biblis: Kvartalstidskrift för bokvänner*, 89 (2020), pp. 20–26. Polish version: 'Losy księgozbiorów zagrabionych w czasazh wojen szwedzkich w XVII w', in Dorota Sidorowicz-Mulak and Agnieszka Franczyk-Cegła (eds.), *Kolekcje prywatne w zbiorach książki dawnej* (2 vols., Wrocław: Wydawnictwo Ossolineum, 2020), 1, pp. 252–264.

the National Library of Latvia.[11] The work of Kreigere-Liepiņa and Berga, which was able to use Collijn's above mentioned archive material extant at Uppsala as a starting point, means that there is for the first time ever a published register covering the books from the Jesuit College of Riga.[12] In connection to this event, the books from Riga have been gathered at Uppsala University Library, in an attempt to reconstruct the collection physically in one place, and they are now located in the Library's magnificent Book Hall. Titles of books from Riga that we know have been at Uppsala from the start until now, and that can be found both in the oldest and newest inventories, will help us to see how this collection was received in its new environment during the first decades in Uppsala, when we identify them in the first library catalogues from 1638–1641.[13]

The intention here is thus to try to see which books from the Jesuit College of Riga were considered useful at the Lutheran university of Uppsala at the beginning of the seventeenth century by examining how they were located on the shelves once the contents had been studied and evaluated.[14] In order to do so, we must first briefly describe how the library collection was arranged at the time, since the extant catalogues are in reality shelf lists and are arranged according to subject and format.

## 2    The Seventeenth-Century Library

Although, of course, there had been books at Uppsala University since its beginnings in 1477 and an inventory of the book collections had been ordered at the ecclesiastical Uppsala Assembly in 1593, the university library was not formally founded until two royal decrees of 1620 and 1621. With the first decree came donations of collections from the Crown's depot Gråmunkeholmen in Stockholm, containing the confiscated libraries of noblemen and of old

---

11   *Catalogue of the Riga Jesuit College Book Collection (1583–1621)*. In the rest of this chapter, records in this catalogue will be referred to only as CRJCBC and with record numbers.

12   See further, Laura Kreigere-Liepiņa, 'Bibliographic Reconstruction of the Book Collection of the Riga Jesuit College', in *Catalogue of the Riga Jesuit College Book Collection (1583–1621)*, pp. 50–68.

13   For valuable case studies on the importance of book lists for a purpose like this, see the conference volume Malcolm Walsby and Natasha Constantinidou (eds.), *Documenting the Early Modern Book World: Inventories and Catalogues in Manuscript and Print* (Leiden: Brill, 2013).

14   This article is thus a parallel to a previous study of mine. See, Peter Sjökvist, 'The Reception of Books from Braniewo in the 17th-century Uppsala University Library', *Biblioteka*, 24 (33) (2020), pp. 101–116.

monasteries, among other things.[15] At the beginning of the 1620s, nonetheless, there was still no single building destined for the purpose. When the books from Riga came to Uppsala in 1622, they were first placed in the southern chancel of the cathedral. In 1626, however, a small edifice in two floors next to the cathedral and the new main university building Gustavianum became available to house the library collections, and the books from the cathedral, the Riga collection and the Crown depot collection, among others, were soon carried in on the upper floor. In the following year, the literary spoils of war from Braniewo (Braunsberg) and Frombork (Frauenburg) arrived at Uppsala and were stored on the lower floor.[16]

In spite of the order by Gustavus Adolphus that the collections should be registered and a catalogue made, it took more than a decade until such an undertaking was finished. The result was a handwritten catalogue in two volumes, one covering the *bibliotheca superior* and another the *bibliotheca inferior*, which mirrored how the books were arranged in the library. The catalogue was in fact a collection of shelf-lists of books according to subject and format.[17] I have myself discussed the order of the books in this first university library in other articles, and I will not repeat all the details and arguments here.[18] May it suffice to mention that the library was built in two floors with split levels and contained three rooms on each floor. Obviously, the building was of very poor quality. There were constantly recurring complaints at the university council about the poor conditions the books had to endure, especially on the lower floor, where they were allegedly even at risk of destruction. But while the lower floor suffered heavily from moisture, the roof was leaking repeatedly on the upper floor. What we see, however, is that the books in the upper library were arranged according to the four faculties and the professorial chairs, while

---

15   See further Otto Walde, 'Konung Sigismunds bibliotek och Gustaf Adolfs donation 1620–1621: Ett bidrag till Uppsala universitetsbiblioteks äldsta historia', *Nordisk tidskrift för bok- och biblioteksväsen*, 2 (1915), pp. 317–322; and Åke Davidsson, 'Gustav II Adolfs bokgåvor till akademien i Uppsala', in *Gustav II Adolf och Uppsala universitet* (Uppsala: Uppsala universitet, 1982), pp. 93–110.

16   Annerstedt, *Upsala universitetsbiblioteks historia*, pp. 8–12. The cathedral had generally housed the books of the university before the formal foundation of the university library.

17   Uppsala University Library (UUB), Bibl. arkiv K2 and K3. Both are available in digitized versions online: urn.kb.se/resolve?urn=urn:nbn:se:alvin:portal:record-270360 (K2), and urn.kb.se/resolve?urn=urn:nbn:se:alvin:portal:record-270365 (K3), (both last accessed 7 December 2022).

18   See Peter Sjökvist 'On the Order of the Books in the First Uppsala University Library Building', *Journal of Jesuit Studies*, 6 (2019), pp. 315–326; idem, 'Literary Spoils of War in Uppsala in Practice', *Biblioteka*, 25 (34) (2021), pp. 127–140; and idem, 'The Reception of Books from Braniewo', pp. 101–116.

the lower was more of a storage room for literature that was not really useful for the regular teaching at the university, where the Jesuit classification of theology from Braniewo had in fact been retained for many titles by Catholic authors. When the books were taken from their original locations, they were placed in chests according to subject, supposedly according to how they had been arranged in Braniewo. In Uppsala, as it seems, they were at first simply arranged on the shelves in the same order.

Step by step, books that were considered relevant at the university were selected and moved to other sections of the library. And, as already mentioned, large portions of the books written by Catholic authors and with a confessional Catholic content were by default assumed to be less useful at this very Lutheran university. In dissertations and propaganda of the time the Pope was here compared with Antichrist and the Jesuits described as his deceitful, cunning and blood-thirsty followers.[19] In addition, several books in the library at the end of the 1630s were duplicates, since the libraries of the learned Catholic institutions from which they were taken frequently held copies of the same or similar editions.[20] In such cases, in Uppsala one copy was placed on the upper and one on the lower floor. Nor were the books perceived as Calvinist judged to be very useful, and many, though not all, were stored on the lower floor, under the heading *libri Calvinianorum*.[21] According to the catalogues of the time, there was thus a separation of the library into one floor for the actual and current university library, containing the most useful books arranged according to the four faculties, and one where duplicate copies and less useful books were stored.[22] This is our starting-point.

19   See Sjökvist, 'Literary Spoils of War in Uppsala in Practice'. Cf. Hans Helander, *Neo-Latin Literature in Sweden in the Period 1620–1720: Stylistics, Vocabulary and Characteristic Ideas* (Uppsala: Acta universitatis Upsaliensis, 2004), pp. 321–336.
20   In 1626 looted books arrived from Catholic institutions at Frombork and Braniewo. In 1636, looted books arrived from Catholic institutions at Würzburg and Mainz.
21   UUB, Bibl. arkiv K 2, pp. 119–122.
22   This division can also be verified in explicit contemporary sources, such as a poem by the Uppsala professor of music and poetry Jonas Columbus (1586–1663) on the Swedish victory at Braniewo (*Victoria Brunsbergensis*): 'Hic ubi nubiferas alte est educta sub auras/ ingentis precii libros quae continet aedes,/ et duplex ample librorum conficitur grex./ Dividuus paries omnes qui ponitur inter/ foetibus a sanis scabiosa peculia nobis/ plurima quae data sunt abs te Brunsberga repellit'. Jonas Columbus, manuscript at Linköping Diocese Library, W 28. Apograph at UUB, R 383. There is also a short note stating the same thing in prose in a history of Uppsala by Johan Eenberg (d. 1709), a former employee of the library, from the beginning of the eighteenth century: 'Det förste academiske bibliothek är ... inrättadt åhr 1620, uti det huset, som står uti nord-wäst på domkyrkiogården (därest nu är Consistorium Academicum), hwarest uti öfre wåningen de förnämste, och i under

## 3    Aims

With the help of the Bothvidi inventory and Kreigere-Liepiņa and Berga's new catalogue of books from the Jesuit College, in the following discussion we will seek to locate specific titles from Riga in the first (1638–1641) catalogues of the Uppsala University Library, proceeding section by section. To begin with, we need to address the questions of usefulness and classification in the new environment of these books. What kind of titles from Riga were useful enough to be placed on the *upper* floor and in the actual library that was arranged according to the four faculties? Which kind ended up in the storage of mostly Catholic literature on the *lower* floor? A second aspect of relevance comes from a comparison of the handling of the Riga books with that of the books from Braniewo and Frombork, which I have discussed in a previous article.[23] The latter books were initially stocked on the lower floor. Some categories of them also stayed there, with several books in fact still in the very same order as they had been listed by Johannes Bureus when he inventoried the spoils from those places at Stockholm Castle. Others were found more useful and moved to the upper floor. With most of the books from Riga the opposite can therefore be expected to have taken place. Books relevant for the teaching at the university are likely to have stayed and were relocated to the upper floor, while less useful books were moved down. We can assume that the Riga books were not kept together to the same degree as the books from Braniewo, since they were not carried into the storage part but into the rooms comprising the active university library. In addition, this assumption receives support from the fact that the arrival of the books from Riga at Uppsala was even questioned by librarians themselves some decades later.[24] The following discussion may be dry, but it does reveal interesting aspects concerning the judgement and valuation of learning and literature at a small but significant university in the outskirts of Europe during a turbulent period. It should also be stressed that we can track only a limited number of books here, since the entire collection originally contained more than 900 titles.

---

        wåningen de sämbre böcker blefwe då planterade, och stode til åhr 1691'. Johan Eenberg, *Kort berättelse af de märkwärdigste saker som för de främmande äre at besee och förnimma uti Upsala stad* ... (Uppsala: Werner, 1703–1704), p. 56.

23    Sjökvist, 'The Reception of Books from Braniewo'.

24    The librarian Harald Vallerius in a list of extant registers in 1678 mentioned the inventory of the Riga books, and added: 'but we do not know for sure whether these came here or not' (*Men man icke wist wet om de äre hitkomne eller icke*). UUB Bibl. arkiv K6, p. 597.

## 4 Bibles and Languages

To begin with, the location of some books from Riga in the classification scheme of the first catalogues is obvious. Martin Luther's Bible, printed in Magdeburg in 1536, for instance, and part of the spoils, could be found on the upper floor, in the first room among the other Bibles.[25] The same was the case with the German Bible printed in Lübeck in 1494 and containing comments by Nicolas de Lyre;[26] a Bible in Dutch printed in Harlingen in 1585;[27] and the German edition of the Bible created by Johann Dietenberger and printed in 1582.[28] Not all Bibles, however useful they normally were, were located in that section. A Dutch Bible printed in Delft in 1581, for instance, could be found on the upper floor under *Theologi*.[29] The New Testament in Polish, printed in Kraków in 1594, ended up on the lower floor, under the heading *Libri Polonici*.[30] Books in the Polish language were not only inaccessible to most people at Uppsala for linguistic reasons, but could at the time also be suspected of containing theologically doubtful material. Other books in Polish from the Riga spoils that ended up there were, for example, the *O naśladowaniu Pana Christysa* by Thomas a Kempis and printed in Kraków in 1603;[31] the *Okulary na zwierciadło nabożeństwa chrześciańskiego w Polszcze* by Marcin Łaszcz, printed in Vilnius in 1594;[32] the *Żołnierskie nabożeństwo* by Piotr Skarga, printed in Kraków in 1606; and Diego Álvarez de Paz's *O żywocie zakonnym*, printed in Kraków in 1613.[33]

Next to the Polish section there were two others on the lower floor where, according to the headings, language was the main criterion of classification. These sections contained books in Italian and in German. In fact, however, most of the titles in these sections had Catholic authors who wrote in these languages. In the Italian section, we find books from Riga such as the *Meditationi sopra tutti gli evangeli del'anno*, by the Jesuit Andreu Capella, printed in Brescia in 1601;[34] the *Dispregio della vanita del mondo* by the Franciscan Diego de

---

25  CRJCBC 174 (USTC 616654); UUB Bibl. arkiv K3, p. 5; UUB U271, p. 2 or 4 [?].
26  CRJCBC 41 (USTC 743347); UUB Bibl. arkiv K3, p. 5; UUB U271, p. 2.
27  CRJCBC 168 (USTC 616569); UUB Bibl. arkiv K3, p. 5; UUB U271, p. 5.
28  CRJCBC 180 (USTC 243000); UUB Bibl. arkiv K3, p. 5; UUB U271, p. 2 or 4 [?].
29  CRJCBC 167 (USTC 616568); UUB Bibl. arkiv K3, p. 37; UUB U271, p. 5 [?].
30  CRJCBC 176 (USTC 678685); UUB Bibl. arkiv K2, p. 113; UUB U271, p. 7.
31  CRJCBC 763 (USTC 250113); UUB U271, p. 16.
32  CRJCBC 499 (USTC 250347); UUB U271, p. 11.
33  CRJCBC 722 (USTC –), and 104 (USTC –); UUB Bibl. arkiv K2, pp. 114–115. In the inventory of Bothvidi there are several entries just stating *liber Polonicus*, not specifying the exact title. This of course makes an absolute identification impossible.
34  CRJCBC 234 (USTC 4036246); UUB Bibl. arkiv K2, p. 117; UUB U271, [?].

Estella, printed in Venice in 1604;[35] and *Effetti mirabili de la limosina*, printed in Rome in 1581 by Giulio Folco.[36] In the German section, we find books such as *Triumph der Warheit* by the Jesuit Georg Scherer, printed in Ingolstadt in 1587 and 1588;[37] the *Anatomiae Lutheri*, printed in Köln in 1595 and edited by the Catholic physician Johann Pistorius the Younger;[38] the *Apologia und gründliche Verthetigung eines kleinen Büchleins*, by the Jesuit Jan Uber, printed in Braniewo in 1606;[39] as well as the German *Postilla catholica evangeliorum de tempore totius anni*, by Johann Eck, printed in Ingolstadt 1583.[40] Common to all books in these three sections on the lower floor, however, is the fact that content had been more decisive for their location than language. We can still find a few books in Polish and Italian, and rather many in German, on the upper floor in the collection arranged according to the four faculties.

## 5   Bible Commentaries and Dogmatic Literature

Moving to Bible commentaries, we can find a section on the lower floor especially reserved for commentaries by Catholic authors (*Commentatores Catholici*), arranged according to size (from folio to duodecimo), while on the upper floor, useful commentaries by both Lutheran and Catholic authors are found in one of the theology sections.[41] According to the University constitutions dating from 1626, one of the four professors of theology had to teach the Old Testament and one professor the New Testament. The third had to teach theological polemics, or the Old and New Testament alternately, while the fourth had to teach the articles of faith or dogmatics.[42] In addition, in the philosophical faculty, the professor of Hebrew had to teach grammar and its usage based on the biblical texts and on the explanation of more obscure and controversial passages, while the professor of Greek had to teach grammar and its usage based on the New Testament, the Church Fathers and the ancient

---

35   CRJCBC 368 (USTC 641277); UUB Bibl. arkiv K2, p. 116; UUB U271, p. 8.
36   CRJCBC 393 (USTC 671394); UUB Bibl. arkiv K2, p. 117; not identified in UUB U271.
37   CRJCBC 708 (USTC 855533), and 709 (USTC –); UUB Bibl. arkiv K2, p. 109; UUB U271, p. 10.
38   CRJCBC 533 (USTC 625157); UUB Bibl. arkiv K2, p. 108; UUB U271, p. 6.
39   CRJCBC 783 (USTC 240336); UUB Bibl. arkiv K2, p. 109; UUB U271, p. 9.
40   CRJCBC 348 (USTC 182850); UUB Bibl. arkiv K2, p. 107; UUB U271, p. 3.
41   Only the heading for 4:o in this section has the explicit *Commentatores Catholici*. However, the label is true for all formats in this section, which all only contain Catholic authors.
42   'Ex Theologis primus veteris testamenti libros auditoribus proponat, alter libros novi testamenti: tertius controversias tractet, aut veteris aut novi testamenti scripta alterne; quartus locos sive articulos fidei'. Cited from Claes Annerstedt, *Upsala universitets historia*, Bihang 1: Handlingar 1477–1654 (Uppsala: Uppsala universitet, 1877), p. 249.

authors.[43] The strong emphasis on biblical studies, including more difficult and debated biblical passages, can explain the considerable presence of Bible commentaries by both Catholic and Protestant authors on the upper floor. We should not, however, confuse this with tolerance. There was a reason why the third professor had to be concerned with Bible studies or controversial theology. With the support of the Bible, the Catholics needed to be proven wrong. The majority of the Catholic authors of Bible commentaries were also kept on the lower floor. Accordingly, we notice, for instance, that the commentary on the Book of Revelations by the Franciscan Francisco de Ribera, printed in Lyon in 1593, a copy of which was also part of the booty from Braniewo, was located on the lower floor.[44] The commentary on the twelve prophets by Pablo de Palacio, printed in Cologne in 1583, was likewise located in the Catholic section on the lower floor.[45] Another example of a title placed there is the commentary on the letters of Paul by Saint Bruno of Cologne, printed in Paris in 1509, which was part of the spoils.[46] On the other hand, a title such as the *Notae in evangelicas lectiones*, printed in Freiburg in 1591 by the Jesuit Petrus Canisius, could be found on both the upper and the lower floors.[47] In addition it should be noted that no titles by Protestant authors can be found under the heading 'Bible commentaries' on the lower floor.

Dogmatic literature, moreover, is a field in which we once more find sections that are labelled as purely Catholic in the lower library, under the heading *Controvertistae Catholici* and divided according to format ranging from folio to duodecimo.[48] Just as in the case of the Bible commentaries, it was also true that some Catholic dogmatic literature could be found among the useful books on the upper floor, where it stood together with and among its Lutheran counterparts. As mentioned, one of the professorial chairs at Uppsala was concerned with polemic theology, and one with the articles of faith; in other words, the arguments of the religious enemies, whether Catholic or Calvinist, had to be scrutinized and defeated.[49] Under *Controvertistae Catholici*, for

43  'Hebreae linguae professor ... juventuti tradat; grammaticam et ejus usum ex textu biblico et obscuriorum ac controversorum locorum explicatione. Graecae linguae professor similiter grammaticam et usum ex novi testamenti libris, ex patrum et veterum auctorum scriptis'. Cited from Annerstedt, *Upsala universitets historia*, Bihang 1, p. 250.
44  CRJCBC 679 (USTC 2105211); UUB Bibl. arkiv K2, p. 13; UUB U271, p. 10.
45  CRJCBC 618 (USTC 250351); UUB Bibl. arkiv K2, p. 15; UUB U271, p. 12.
46  CRJCBC 209 (USTC 143448); UUB Bibl. arkiv K2, p. 14; UUB U271, p. 10.
47  CRJCBC 229 (USTC 678317); UUB Bibl. arkiv K3, p. 18; UUB Bibl. arkiv K2, p. 41; UUB U271, p. 7 and 8.
48  Only the 2:o has the explicit *Catholici* in the heading in this section, but the designation is true for the other formats as well.
49  See further Sjökvist, 'Literary Spoils of War in Uppsala in Practice'.

instance, we find works by the main Catholic antagonist of the Lutherans, Robert Bellarmine (1542–1621), which were part of the spoils from Riga, Braniewo and later Poznań. Bellarmine was the focus of several dissertations in polemic theology at Uppsala at the end of the 1620s and in the 1630s, after both the Riga and Braniewo spoils had arrived. Most books by Bellarmine were located on the lower floor, but occasionally titles by him can also be found on the upper. An example is his *Apologia ... pro responsione sua ad librum Iacobi Magnae Britanniae regis* printed in Vilnius in 1610.[50] Other titles from the Riga spoils to be found among the controversial literature on the lower floor are, for instance, the *Contra universos Catholicae fidei adversarios*, by Catholic bishop Friedrich Nausea (1496–1552), printed in Magdeburg in 1529;[51] the *Pro Catholicae fidei antiquitate et veritate*, Vincent de Lérins, a Gallic monk of Late Antiquity, printed in Cologne in 1569 by;[52] and the *De expresso Dei verbo*, by the Warmian bishop Stanisław Hozjusz (1504–1579), printed in Leuven in 1559.[53] The case of the *Adversus omnes haereses libri quatuordecim*, printed in Lyon 1555 by the Franciscan Alfonso de Castro (1495–1558), is interesting. The book was part of the spoils from both Riga and Braniewo, but in different editions. One copy was thus kept on the upper floor under the heading *Scripta patrum*, while the other was kept in the purely Catholic section on the ground floor.[54] In the 1640s, however, the copy on the upper floor was obviously moved to the lower, as can be seen in a later catalogue.[55] A group of books mainly consisting of Catholic literature were then transported downstairs, presumably in order to make room for new acquisitions.

Worth stressing again is the fact that not a single work by an author of the Lutheran confession has been found on the lower floor. Several books of this kind, however, were part of the spoils from Riga, and they are all to be found on the upper floor, despite sometimes even being in duplicate. Duplicates were not a problem if the books were by Lutheran authors. Among a large number of works by Philipp Melanchthon (1497–1560), Martin Luther (1483–1546), Lucas Osiander (1534–1604), et cetera, we thus find examples from Riga such as the *Catechesis* and *Regulae vitae* by David Chytraeus, printed in Rostock and Bautzen in 1572 and 1571 and bound in the same volume;[56] the *Theologiae*

---

50  CRJCBC 153 (USTC 250272); UUB Bibl. arkiv K3, p. 36; UUB U271, p. 27.
51  CRJCBC 593 (USTC 844515); UUB Bibl. arkiv K2, p. 20; UUB U271, p. 8.
52  CRJCBC 804 (USTC 626152); UUB Bibl. arkiv K2, p. 28; UUB U271, p. 29.
53  CRJCBC 454 (USTC 663913); UUB Bibl. arkiv K2, p. 26; UUB U271, p. 18.
54  CRJCBC 242 (USTC 204802); UUB Bibl. arkiv K3, p. 12; UUB Bibl. arkiv K2, p. 28; UUB U271, p. 13.
55  UUB Bibl. arkiv K4, p. 193.
56  CRJCBC 253 (USTC 400698), and 254 (USTC –); UUB Bibl. arkiv K3, p. 42. UUB U271, p. 21.

*Jesuitarum praecipua capita* by Martin Chemnitz, printed in Leipzig in 1563;[57] the *Husspostilla* in Saxon German by Martin Luther, printed in Wittenberg in 1550;[58] as well as the *Margarita theologica* by Johann Spangenberg (1484–1550), printed in Leipzig in 1542.[59]

Near the section containing Catholic controversial theologians on the lower floor is a smaller section containing catechisms and theological *loci communes*, that is a kind of easily accessible and thematically arranged dogmatic literature directed at Catholic believers. There we find, for instance, books from Riga such as *Piae ac solidae ex Francisco Costero, Petro de Soto, & auctore methodi confessionis catecheses*, printed in Trier in 1590;[60] the *Catholicus catechismus* by Catholic bishop Friedrich Nausea, printed in Antwerp in 1544;[61] and the *Flores R. P. F. Lodoici Granatensis* by the Dominican Luis de Granada, printed in Cologne in 1588.[62]

## 6  Devotional Literature and Sermons

The next section on the lower floor is a purely Catholic one as well, having the heading *Lib. precat et meditat.* ('Books for praying and meditation'). In it can be found such books as the two copies of *De frequenti communione libellus* by the same Dominican Luis de Granada, printed in Cologne in 1586 and 1591;[63] as well as his *Memoriale vitae Christianae*, printed in Cologne in 1589;[64] his *Dux peccatorum*, printed in Cologne in 1590;[65] and his *De devotione, excellentia, utilitate, et necessitate orationis*, printed in Cologne in 1592.[66] Several copies of Thomas de Kempis' *De imitatione Christi* can also be found here, the Riga copy, printed in Vilnius in 1585, among others.[67] But this book can also be found in several places on the upper floor. We also find from Riga on the lower floor the *De vita et laudibus Deiparae Mariae virginis* by the Jesuit Francis Coster, printed in Cologne in 1587.[68]

---

57  CRJCBC 249 (USTC 635973); UUB Bibl. arkiv K3, p. 38; not identified in UUB U271.
58  CRJCBC 539–540 (USTC 664380 and 404719); UUB Bibl. arkiv K3, p. 44; UUB U271, p. 12.
59  CRJCBC 731 (USTC 675067); UUB Bibl. arkiv K3, p. 45; UUB U271, p. 18.
60  CRJCBC 633 (USTC 848195); UUB Bibl. arkiv K2, p. 29; UUB U271, p. 17.
61  CRJCBC 592 (USTC 658307); UUB Bibl. arkiv K2, p. 29; UUB U271, p. 15.
62  CRJCBC 518 (USTC 838970); UUB Bibl. arkiv K2, p. 31; UUB U271, p. 24.
63  CRJCBC 525 (USTC 689706), and 526 (USTC 689712); UUB Bibl. arkiv K2, p. 34; UUB U271, p. 25.
64  CRJCBC 520 (USTC 675677); UUB Bibl. arkiv K2, p. 34; UUB U271, p. 24.
65  CRJCBC 516 (USTC 641804); UUB Bibl. arkiv K2, p. 34; UUB U271, p. 24.
66  CRJCBC 527 (USTC 137096); UUB Bibl. arkiv K2, p. 34; UUB U271, p. 23[?].
67  CRJCBC 762 (USTC 696752); UUB Bibl. arkiv K2, p. 34; UUB U271, p. 23.
68  CRJCBC 295 (USTC 406780); UUB Bibl. arkiv K2, p. 35; UUB U271, p. 24.

Sermons by Catholic authors were mostly to be found on the lower floor also. From the Riga booty we there find, for instance, the *Sermones sive enarrationes in evangelia et epistolas quadragesimales*, by the Dominican Pierre La Palud, printed in Antwerp in 1572;[69] several volumes by the Dominican Gilles vanden Prieele, *Conciones in evangelia et epistolas*, printed in Antwerp in 1574;[70] the *Homiliae in evangelia dominicalia* by the Franciscan Heinrich Helm, printed in Cologne in 1550;[71] the *Sermones de sanctis* by Jacobus de Voragine, printed in Venice in 1580;[72] as well as the *Quadragesimale* by Johannes Gritsch, printed in Nürnberg in 1481.[73]

Catholic devotional literature and sermons are probably the kind of books that we would expect to find among the least useful books in a Lutheran university library. All other theological subjects mentioned had connections with some of the professorial chairs in theology, while the devotional and sermon categories speak rather to the private inner religious life. Being a Catholic in Sweden was forbidden by law at the time and could after 1617 be punished with death. Although this did not happen very often, a few persons were in fact executed for this reason.[74]

In the adjacent sections on the lower floor we can also find one with the heading *Theologi scholastici*, containing mainly duplicate titles by authors who can also be found on the upper floor: medieval writers such as Thomas Aquinas, Jean Gerson, William of Ockham, Peter Lombard and Bonaventure.[75] In the middle room of the lower floor were gathered Catholic manuscripts in a variety of fields, with the exception of law.[76] The case is the same here, however, as with the printed materials. Useful manuscripts were usually found on the upper floor, together and among the printed books. No discrimination was made between a manuscript and a printed copy as long as the book was useful.

Being Catholic confessional literature and duplicates were, as we have seen, the main reasons why some books ended up on the lower floor of the library. It is nevertheless true that we also see some Catholic titles and duplicates on the upper floor. If we focus on the categories there, it will be even more evident how the floors differ from each other in content.

---

69 CRJCBC 631 (USTC –); UUB Bibl. arkiv K2, p. 43; UUB U271, p. 12 or 20[?].
70 CRJCBC 773 (USTC 695126); UUB Bibl. arkiv K2, p. 43; UUB U271, p. 13.
71 CRJCBC 443 (USTC 626440); UUB Bibl. arkiv K2, p. 37; UUB U271, p. 5[?].
72 CRJCBC 458 (USTC 144137); UUB U271, p. 16.
73 CRJCBC 54 (USTC 745407); UUB Bibl. arkiv K2, p. 37; UUB U271, p. 2.
74 See Magnus Nyman, *Förlorarnas historia: Katolskt liv i Sverige från Gustav Vasa till drottning Kristina* (Stockholm: Katolska bokförlaget, 1997), pp. 229–235.
75 UUB Bibl. arkiv K2, pp. 47–56.
76 UUB Bibl. arkiv K2, pp. 75–91.

## 7   Classical Authors, History and Church Fathers

Classical authors are of course unproblematic and valuable in all libraries, thus we find them on the upper floor, in different sections. The works of Cicero, for instance, that were part of the spoils from Riga are mostly located under the heading *Oratores*, corresponding to the professorial chair of rhetoric. We find there the three volumes of his speeches edited by Caelius Curio and printed in Basle in 1592, as well as a copy of the second volume of the Basle edition of 1585;[77] Cicero's *De Officiis*, printed in Cologne in 1612;[78] his *Epistulae familiares* of Lyon and Paris from 1505;[79] and the *Orationes Philippicae*, printed in Cologne. in 1522.[80] Similarly, the upper floor has a copy of the works of Quintilian with commentary, printed in Venice in 1506.[81]

Books by authors writing about history are also kept on the upper floor. This corresponded to the chair in history, which was meant to teach *historia universalis*, according to the university constitutions.[82] Examples were the *Rapsodiae historiarum Enneadum* by Marco Antonio Sabellico, printed in Paris in 1516 and 1517;[83] the *De moribus et ritibus gentium* by Alessandro Sardi, printed in Mainz in 1577;[84] as well as Livy's *Ab urbe condita*, printed in Basle in 1549.[85] The same is the case with books in the field of Church history, which are located separately from those in secular history, regardless of the confession of the author, with yet a separate section for them on the upper floor. We find there from the Riga booty, for instance, the *Ecclesiasticae historiae libri decem* by Nikephoros Kallistos Xanthopoulos of Constantinople, printed in Frankfurt in 1588;[86] the *Catalogus sanctorum et gestorum eorum* by Petrus de Natalibus, printed in Lyon in 1519;[87] the *Historia scholastica* by Petrus Comestor, printed in Strasbourg in 1500;[88] as well as the *De vita Ignatii Loiola* by the Jesuit Giovanni Pietro Maffei, printed in Cologne in 1585.[89]

---

77   CRJCBC 264–265 (USTC 147676), 266 (USTC –), 267 (USTC 674202); UUB Bibl. arkiv K3, p. 114; UUB U271, p. 16[?].
78   CRJCBC 260 (USTC 674530); UUB Bibl. arkiv K3, p. 115; UUB U271, p. 12[?].
79   CRJCBC 255 (USTC 690482); UUB Bibl. arkiv K3, p. 110; Not identified in UUB U271.
80   CRJCBC 262 (USTC 241767); UUB Bibl. arkiv K3, p. 113; UUB U271, p. 11.
81   CRJCBC 666 (USTC –); UUB Bibl. arkiv K3, p. 110; Not identified in UUB U271.
82   Annerstedt, *Upsala universitets historia*, Bihang 1, p. 250.
83   CRJCBC 696–697 (USTC 684065 and 2014962); UUB Bibl. arkiv K3, p. 92; UUB U271, p. 3 or 5[?].
84   CRJCBC 704 (USTC 628858); UUB U271, p. 12.
85   CRJCBC 508 (USTC 673499); UUB Bibl. arkiv K3, p. 94; UUB U271, p. 4.
86   CRJCBC 596 (USTC –); UUB Bibl. arkiv K3, p. 48; UUB U271, p. 1.
87   CRJCBC 628 (USTC 411667); UUB Bibl. arkiv K3, p. 49; UUB U271, p. 2.
88   CRJCBC 69 (USTC 748032): UUB Bibl. arkiv K3, p. 51; UUB U271, p. 5.
89   CRJCBC 545 (USTC 6901200); UUB Bibl. arkiv K3, p. 55; UUB U271, p. 16[?].

The Church Fathers had their own section on the upper floor, and there we also find several books from the Riga booty. In fact, books of very different kinds have been gathered on these particular shelves. The heading *scripta patrum* covers authors from all periods, from the Church fathers of Late Antiquity such as Jerome, Tertullian and Augustine to such medieval theologians as Thomas Aquinas, Denis the Carthusian and Jean Gerson, to post-Reformation authors such as the Franciscan Frans Titelmans and the Jesuits Peter Canisius and Robert Bellarmine, as well as some Protestant authors. The complete works of Augustine, printed in Antwerp in 1576 and 1577[90] can be found there, and also his commentary on the letters of Paul, printed in Paris in 1499.[91] There are also volumes three and four of Origen's works, printed in Paris in 1512.[92] Several other titles by the authors of Late Antiquity resided mainly at the beginning of the section. As mentioned earlier, the works of the Church fathers were used not only by the professors of theology, but also especially by the professor of Greek.

## 8 Medicine, Mathematics and Law

Typical of useful books are those belonging to the faculty of medicine, which had its own section on the upper floor. There we find, for instance, the *Universa medicina* by Jean Fernel, printed in Frankfurt in 1592;[93] the *Methodus curandorum omnium morborum corporis humani* by Guillaume Rondelet, printed in Lyon in 1575;[94] the *De materia medica* by Pedanius Dioscorides, printed in Paris in 1537;[95] the *Opuscula medica* by Girolamo Cardano, printed in Basle in 1559;[96] and the *Judicia urinarum* by Jodocus Willich, printed in Wittenberg in 1562.[97] Under the heading of mathematics on the upper floor, and corresponding to the professorial chairs in this subject, we meet titles from the Riga booty such as Pliny the Younger's *De mundi historia*, printed in Frankfurt in

---

90   CRJCBC 126 (USTC 686497), 129–136 (USTC 686497, 443372, 452634, 452637, 443370, 452636, 452635, 452639); UUB Bibl. arkiv K3, p. 8; UUB U271, p. 3[?].
91   CRJCBC 36 (USTC 739970); UUB Bibl. arkiv K3, p. 8; UUB U271, p. 1. Medicine, Mathematics, and Law.
92   CRJCBC 606–607 (USTC 662789 and 689671); UUB Bibl. arkiv K3, p. 9; UUB U271, p. 3.
93   CRJCBC 376 (USTC 628436); UUB Bibl. arkiv K3, p. 76; UUB U271, p. 3 or 4[?].
94   CRJCBC 684 (USTC 250318); UUB Bibl. arkiv K3, p. 84; UUB U271, p. 20.
95   CRJCBC 338 (USTC 691783); UUB Bibl. arkiv K3, p. 83; UUB U271, p. 12.
96   CRJCBC 237 (USTC 601641); UUB Bibl. arkiv K3, p. 78; UUB U271, p. 2.
97   CRJCBC 816 (USTC –); UUB Bibl. arkiv K3, p. 85; Not identified in UUB U271.

1543;[98] the *Ephemerides* by Luca Gaurico, printed in Venice in 1533;[99] and the *De sphaera* by Johannes de Sacro Bosco, printed in Cologne in 1500.[100]

Finally, the Faculty of Law was of course represented with its own section on the upper floor, but there were also a smaller number of books located under that heading on the lower. In both sections there were many works on Canon law. The difference between the two seems to have had to do with the age of the book. The books on the lower floor were mostly older, while copies from all ages could be found on the upper. The first shelf on the lower floor even held a number of manuscripts, although there were several manuscripts to be found among the printed items as well. From the Riga spoils, which admittedly were not very rich in literature on law, we find on the upper floor, for instance, the three volumes of the *Ex miscellaneorum scriptoribus digestorum, codicis, & institutionum Iuris Ciuilis interpretatio collecta* by Martin Antonio Delrio, printed in Paris in 1580;[101] as well as the *Decretales* of Gregory IX, printed in Paris in 1511.[102] According to the university constitutions of 1626 there were to be two professors of law at Uppsala. One was to lecture on Swedish law and compare it to the Roman, and the other was to lecture on Roman law and moral philosophy.[103]

## 9   Conclusions

Together with previous studies on the arrangement of the first university library building at Uppsala as background, the present study has sought to follow a group of books from the Riga Jesuit college library to their relocation in their new environment, using the new catalogue of Laura Kreigere-Liepiņa and Renāte Berga as well as the early register of Johannes Bothvidi and the first library catalogues at Uppsala from 1638–1641. The books from Riga were initially placed on the upper floor of the building, but the collection was soon broken up, scattered among other collections, and arranged according to subject. Accordingly, we find books from Riga remaining on the upper floor, which contained the actual university library and was arranged according to the four faculties. The lower floor was more of a storage area for less useful Catholic literature, with the arrangement of theological literature seemingly

---

98   CRJCBC 646 (USTC 695641); UUB Bibl. arkiv K3, p. 89; UUB U271, p. 6.
99   CRJCBC 410 (USTC 689050); UUB Bibl. arkiv K3, p. 89; UUB U271, p. 9.
100  CRJCBC 60 (USTC 746365); UUB Bibl. arkiv K3, p. 91; UUB U271, p. 16.
101  CRJCBC 320 (USTC 6901057); UUB Bibl. arkiv K3, p. 70; UUB U271, p. 7[?].
102  CRJCBC 422 (USTC 640406); UUB Bibl. arkiv K3, p. 70; UUB U271, p. 5[?].
103  Annerstedt, *Upsala universitets historia*, Bihang 1, p. 249.

still following the system from the Braniewo Jesuit College library. Lutheran books, for instance, were always in the 'useful' category, and not a single title by a Lutheran author can, in fact, be found in the registers for the lower floor of the library. These have been the main organizing principles for dealing with the Riga library that entered into the Uppsala collections in the seventeenth century. We do not find that parts of the Riga collection were kept together to the same degree as the books from Braniewo.

The primary reason why the Riga library was scattered among the collections to a greater degree was that it had first been located on the upper floor, in the active university library where books were rearranged more often than in the lower. The Riga Jesuit library was also considerably smaller than the one from Braniewo, being only about one third of its size. At the end of the seventeenth century, a librarian at Uppsala even wondered whether it had really arrived there or not. Among the useful books from Riga we find German and Dutch Bibles; Bible commentaries, including such Catholic authors as Petrus Canisius; books on theological polemics, including such Catholic authors as Alfonso de Castro (although his work was revaluated after a while); of course, books by Protestant authors such as David Chytraeus, Martin Luther and Philipp Melanchthon; the Church fathers, even including Catholic authors of the time; books in Church history by both Protestants and Catholics; and also devotional literature such as the *De imitatione Christi* of Thomas de Kempis. Books from Riga in secular subjects were less problematic, and usually were to be found on the upper floor. We find there classical authors such as Cicero, Quintilian and Livy, alongside with works in history, medicine, mathematics and law. Admittedly, the latter also contains titles on canon law.

Somewhat paradoxically, the Catholic books that were of less use in Lutheran Uppsala seemed still to be valued. In the abovementioned poem on the new university library from the end of the 1620s, Jonas Columbus related how a stranger comes to Uppsala and admired the great number of books kept there.[104] For a poor university in a poor state foreign book collections were bound to increase domestic cultural capital considerably, regardless of the content that met the eyes of the reader who at a certain point decided to open the books themselves.[105]

---

104 'Et quoties aliquis veniens novus advena spectat,/ Ah quantus, clamat, librorum accrevit acervus!' Jonas Columbus, manuscript at Linköping Diocese Library, W 28. Apograph at UUB, R 383.
105 See further Peter Sjökvist and Krister Östlund, 'Bokliga krigsbyten som kulturtransfer?', in Peter Sjökvist (ed.), *Kulturarvsperspektiv: Texter från en seminarieserie om specialsamlingar i Sverige* (Uppsala: Uppsala universitetsbibliotek, 2018), pp. 141–149.

CHAPTER 10

# Battles of Books in Denmark from the Reformation to the Great Northern War

*Anders Toftgaard*

Books have been lost through history for many reasons, and some of the most important causes are use, neglect, discarding, censorship, fire and war.[1] Libraries play a key role in the survival of individual books. In an important contribution to the study of lost books, Andrew Pettegree reminded us that 'Most early printed books that survive, particularly those that survive in many copies, do so because they were collected and preserved close to the date of publication'.[2] Libraries have been an important precondition for books to survive. Not only books, however, but also libraries have their individual fate. Discarding, fire and war can lead to (partial or complete) destruction, dispersal, or removal of libraries.

The two only Danish libraries mentioned in the book *Traité des plus belles bibliothèques de l'Europe*, published in 1680, were eventually lost.[3] The author, Pierre Le Gallois, stated that the two most considerable libraries in Copenhagen were the library of the University and the library of Heinrich Rantzau.[4] The

---

1 Flavia Bruni and Andrew Pettegree (eds.), *Lost Books: Reconstructing the Print World of Pre-Industrial Europe* (Leiden: Brill, 2016).
2 Andrew Pettegree, 'The Legion of the Lost: Recovering the Lost Books of Early Modern Europe', in Bruni and Pettegree, *Lost Books*, pp. 1–27, p. 23.
3 The author of *Traité des plus belles bibliothèques de l'Europe*, 'sieur de Gallois' was identified as Pierre Le Gallois by Alexandre Cioranescu, *Bibliographie de la littérature française du dix-septième siècle* (3 vols., Paris: Centre National de la Recherche Scientifique, 1965), 2, p. 1240, n. 41.755. For further information on the author, see Claude Jolly et al. (eds.), *Histoire des bibliothèques françaises* (Paris: Éditions du Cercle de la librairie, 1988); J. Rouvière, 'Le Gallois (Pierre)', in Jules Balteau et al. (eds.), *Dictionnaire de biographie française* (22 vols., Paris: Librairie Letouzey et Ané, 2011), 20, p. 879.
4 'Le Dannemarc a aussi quelques Bibliotheques fort considerables dans Coppenhague: Il y a eu premierement celle de Henry de Rantzau Gentilhomme Danois ... Il y a encore dans l'Université de Coppenhague une tres-belle Bibliothèque, qui doit une partie de ce qu'elle est à plusieurs autres Bibliotheques, qui y ont esté reunies par la liberalité de quelques particuliers.' (Denmark also has some considerable libraries in Copenhagen: First of all there was the library of the Danish nobleman Heinrich Rantzau ... There is still in the university of Copenhagen a very beautiful library, which owes part of what it is to several other libraries

library of Heinrich Rantzau (1526–1598) was located not in Copenhagen, but in the Duchies of Schleswig and Holstein, and it had been dissolved many years before the treatise was published, as early as 1627 during the Thirty Years' War. The library of the University of Copenhagen had been founded together with the university itself in 1482 and it held rich collections. In 1652 the collections had been moved to the Trinity Church, but they were annihilated by the fire of Copenhagen in 1728, except for one manuscript which is today in the Royal Danish Library.[5]

Pierre Le Gallois based the entry on Denmark on previous works, as, for instance, the more detailed description in *Traicté des plus belles bibliothèques publiques et particulières qui ont été et qui sont à présent dans le monde* by Louis Jacob de Saint-Charles, and what he wrote was also going to be used by successors.[6] Thus, in spite of the fact that the two libraries had ceased to exist in 1728, the author of the long entry on libraries in the *Encyclopédie*, published in 1752, copied the text about these two Danish libraries from *Traité des plus belles bibliothèques de l'Europe*.[7] It may not be surprising that what the *Encyclopédie* wrote about libraries in Denmark (and in Sweden) was based on copying; but the result is surprising, since the description is very far from the contemporary reality that it seeks to describe. The authors of the *Encyclopédie*, the 'Plundering Philosophers', explicitly admitted borrowing from other authors, but the fact that what was stated as a fact was so far from reality, shows how remote from the Parisian centre of learning the peripheral kingdom of Denmark-Norway could be in the eighteenth century.[8]

---

which have been integrated into it thanks to the generosity of some private persons.) Pierre Le Gallois, *Traité des plus belles bibliothèques de l'Europe* (Paris, Estienne Michallet, 1680), pp. 119–120.

5   Shelf mark GKS 1813 4to.
6   Louis Jacob de Saint-Charles, *Traicté des plus belles bibliothèques publiques et particulières qui ont été et qui sont à présent dans le monde* (Paris: Rolet le Duc, 1644), USTC 6035314, pp. 237–242.
7   'De ce nombre ['les plus considérables'] sont à Copenhague la *bibliotheque* de l'université, & celle qu'y a fondée Henri Rantzau, gentilhomme Danois.' (The most important [...] in Copenhagen are the library of the University, and the one which was founded there by Henry Rantzau, a Danish nobleman.) Anon., 'Bibliothèque', in Denis Diderot and Jean le Rond d'Alembert (eds.) *Encyclopédie, ou Dictionnaire Raisonné des Sciences, des Arts et des Métiers par une Société de Gens de Lettres* (36 vols., Paris: Chez Samuel Faulche & Compagnie, 1751), 2, p. 234.
8   Timothy Allen et al., 'Plundering Philosophers: Identifying Sources of the Encyclopédie', *Journal of the Association for History and Computing*, 13:1 (2010).

The entry in *Traité des plus belles bibliothèques de l'Europe* from 1680 alerts us to the fact that present-day Denmark is different from seventeenth century Denmark. In *What is the History of the Book?* James Raven addresses the 'framing and division of much European and Western bibliographical and book history by nation-states' and argues that in so many ways 'the nation is a misleading geographical unit for such research'.[9] It is indeed difficult to escape the danger of inherent, methodological nationalism, when writing the history of Danish libraries. The extension of Denmark in the sixteenth and seventeenth centuries was different from the extension of present-day Denmark. The Kalmar Union between Denmark, Sweden and Norway (including Iceland and Greenland) had existed from 1397, but from 1464 only Denmark and Norway were united in a personal union. After Gustav I Vasa (1496?–1560) became King of Sweden in 1523, the Kalmar Union ceased to exist, and the Danish King was King of Denmark and Norway. He was also Duke of Schleswig and Holstein, since a personal union between Schleswig-Holstein and the Danish King had been created in 1459. The duchy was split for dynastical reasons in 1490, in 1544 and in 1564. The Danish king was thus Duke of parts of Holstein, whereas his relatives were Dukes of other parts. In 1721, following the Great Northern War, the duchies of Schleswig and Holstein were integrated into Denmark as a fief (which was eventually split following the wars in the nineteenth and twentieth centuries). Some of the provinces in present-day Sweden were parts of Denmark-Norway. The Norwegian province of Bohuslän and the Danish provinces Scania, Halland and Blekinge were ceded to Sweden following treaties of 1658 and 1660. The island of Saarema in present-day Estonia (called Ösel in Danish in the period), which was the remnant of the diocese of Saare-Lääne (Ösel-Wieck) acquired in 1560, was ceded to Sweden in 1645 along with Gotland in the Peace of Brömsebro.

The difference in extension has bibliographical implications. The concept of Denmark inherent in the Danish national bibliography printed in the nineteenth century, *Bibliotheca Danica*, is larger than the concept of Denmark in *Dansk Bibliografi 1482–1600*.[10] *Bibliotheca Danica* encompasses the entire United Monarchy, whereas Lauritz Nielsen (1881–1947) did not include books printed in Holstein in his *Dansk Bibliografi 1482–1600*.[11] For this reason, more titles are included in *Bibliotheca Danica* from the period 1482–1600 than in

---

9   James Raven, *What Is the History of the Book?* (Cambridge: Polity Press, 2017), p. 75.
10  Chr. Bruun et al., *Bibliotheca Danica: Systematisk fortegnelse over den danske litteratur fra 1482–1830*. (5 vols., Copenhagen: Gyldendal, 1877–1931, revised edition ed. by Erik Dal: Copenhagen: Rosenkilde og Bagger, 1961–1963).
11  Lauritz Nielsen, *Dansk Bibliografi 1482–1600* (5 vols., Copenhagen: Gyldendal, 1919–1935, revised edition Copenhagen: Det Kgl. Bibliotek & DSL, 1996).

*Dansk Bibliografi 1482–1600*. The difference consists of 625 editions and among these we find books authored by Heinrich Rantzau.

The present study deals with battles of the book in Denmark in the sixteenth and seventeenth centuries. 'Battles of the book' is a metaphor, which combines elements from two contrasting domains, Arms and Letters. Arms and Letters were two different ways of gaining and exercising power in early modern Europe. For good reasons, the invention of the printing press and the invention of gunpowder (modern versions of the pen and the sword) were considered parallel inventions. I will look into books and libraries that were involved in religious battles between different world orders or in military battles between different states. Books and libraries were removed or lost or dispersed. The study will be concerned with elements of continuity and discontinuity in Danish libraries in the sixteenth and seventeenth centuries. It will therefore both touch upon libraries and book collections of religious institutions before and after the Reformation and upon books and libraries as war booties in northern European wars in the seventeenth century.

## 1      The Reformation and Books from the Catholic Past

As in other parts of Northern Europe, the Reformation in Denmark-Norway saw the removal and in some cases destruction of medieval books. The Reformation in Denmark was an ongoing process from the evangelical sermons of Hans Tausen (1494–1561) in Viborg in 1525 to the decapitation of the catholic bishop Jon Arason (1484–1550) in Iceland in 1550. Already in 1528, the Lutheran evangelical Reformation was introduced in the province of Haderslev and Tørning by Duke Christian of Haderslev and Tørning, son of King Frederick I (1471–1533) and future king of Denmark and Norway under the name Christian III (1503–1559). In 1536, following the Count's War from which Christian III came out victorious, Denmark became Lutheran-Evangelical. Norway, which had been an independent kingdom before the Kalmar Union, was reduced to a province of Denmark, and continued to be a vassal state until the dissolution of the union in 1814.

During the Reformation, books were removed or destroyed in local incidents of looting. In the Skiby Chronicle, the Carmelite Paul Helgesen (*c*.1485–1534) gives an example of an individual case of destruction of books. Helgesen recounts how on 27 December 1530 Lutherans intruded into the Church of Our Lady, the cathedral of Copenhagen, and destroyed images of the saints, insulted the priests and went as far as tearing books apart ('cetera omnia sunt prophanata, etiam usque ad librorum dilacerationem', all the rest was violated, going as far as tearing books apart).[12] In this rare case, the books were considered enemy images.

After the Reformation, books were also removed or destroyed at a more systematic level. The new protestant regulations of the society, the church and the university – the Copenhagen Recess (1536), the Church Ordinance (1537/1539) and the Deed of Foundation for University of Copenhagen (1537/1539) – included the regulation of book collections.[13] The king intervened in person in order to collect useful books from the monasteries. In a letter dated 8 September 1537, King Christian III sent the German scholar Jürgen Thornmann (alias Georgius Pylander, active in the years around 1540) to Danish monasteries in order to collect books that could be of use to the university library.[14] Johann Bugenhagen (1485–1558) supervised the outcome and declared at a certain point, that a decent library had been gathered.[15] Again in 1554, Christian III ordered his Court chaplain Heinrich Bruchofen (d. 1576) to remove relevant books from Vor Abbey, a Benedictine abbey near Skanderborg in Jutland, and deliver them to the professors at the university.[16] Books from the 1537 and 1554 transfers formed part of the old library, *Vetus Bibliotheca*, of the University of Copenhagen.[17]

Some books from the monastic libraries were thus preserved. As Birgitte Langkilde argues, 'Evangelical ideas about what a library should contain may have influenced what is extant today and what has been lost'.[18] Some of the preserved books from the monastic libraries were later transferred to private libraries or even princely libraries, wherefrom they were eventually looted.

The monasteries of the mendicant orders almost entirely disappeared with the Reformation, and the text *De expulsione fratrum minorum* describes the

---

12   Poul Helgesen, *Chronicon Skibyense*, (Copenhagen: Danske Sprog- og Litteraturselskab, 1937), p. 120.
13   Birgitte Langkilde, 'Monastic Books in Sixteenth-Century Denmark', in Lars Bisgaard et al. (eds.) *The Dissolution of Monasteries: The Case of Denmark in a Regional Perspective*, (Odense: Syddansk Universitetsforlag, 2019), pp. 357–384, p. 377.
14   Sophus Birket-Smith, *Om Kjøbenhavns Universitetsbibliothek før 1728 især dets Håndskriftsamlinger* (Copenhagen: Gyldendal, 1882), p. 13.
15   Harald Ilsøe, 'Universitetets biblioteker til 1728', in Svend Ellehøj and Leif Grane (eds.), *Københavns Universitet 1479–1979*, 4: Gods, bygninger, biblioteker (Copenhagen: Gad, 1980), pp. 294–295.
16   Holger Fr. Rørdam, 'Bidrag til den danske Reformationshistorie. VIII: Om Reformationen af Herreklostrene', *Ny Kirkehistoriske Samlinger*, 2 (1862), pp. 755–756.
17   Birket-Smith, *Om Kjøbenhavns Universitetsbibliothek før 1728*, p. 13.
18   Langkilde, 'Monastic Books in Sixteenth-Century Denmark', p. 377.

losses of the Franciscan monasteries.[19] Not all monasteries, however, were dissolved. Some of the abbeys were allowed to exist. Both the Copenhagen Recess and the Church Ordinance declared that the monks, friars and nuns were free to leave their monasteries but also free to stay there. If they stayed in the monasteries, they should obey the head of the monastery and attend the sermons of the theological lecturer. The Benedictine Abbey of Saint Canut in Odense existed until 1572, and the principals of the Benedictine Abbey of Ringsted (located centrally in the island of Zealand) were called abbots until 1592.[20] In 1592, the building was given by Lave Beck to Førslev (1530–1607) as a fief, and Lave Beck lived there from 1592 to 1605. Ringsted Abbey continued to be the fief (*embedslen*) of the High Court judge of Seeland for many decades. Convents of nuns existed even longer: the Brigittine Convent in Mariager existed as long as 1588 and the Brigittine Convent in Maribo as long as 1623. Eventually, the abbeys were transformed into secular fiefs.

What was left in the monasteries was not considered worthy of preservation and therefore ceased to be used. Two generations after the Reformation, Christian IV (1577–1648), king of Denmark and Norway (1588–1648), ordered the destruction of medieval books, repurposing them as cartridges in fireworks and weapons. Thus, in 1608, he ordered the destruction of 70 codices from Herrisvad Abbey.[21] Later, at the marriage of his son Christian in 1634, manuscripts in parchment were again transferred from Abbeys to the arsenal, for use as cartridges. The books were referred to spitefully as 'munkebøger' (munks' books).[22] Likewise, the parchment books were used as book bindings for accounts books, and even as book binding of a volume of school essays authored by the king Christian IV as a boy.[23] Some of these bindings have since been removed from the books in order to form separate fragment collections, but their tie to the book for which they previously formed the wrapping has not always been documented.

Books from the Catholic past – the kind of books which we would today from a historicist point of view consider important as 'cultural heritage'

---

19  The main manuscript Royal Danish library, NKS 276 8vo. The Latin text was originally published in: Martin Clarencius Geertz (ed.), *Scriptores minores historiæ Danicæ medii ævi* (2 vols., Copenhagen: Selskabet for Udgivelse af Kilder til dansk Historie, 1917–1922), 2, pp. 325–367.
20  Bjørn Kornerup, *Den danske kirkes historie*, 4: Det lærde tidsrum (Copenhagen: Gyldendal, 1959), pp. 42–43.
21  Otto Blom, 'Middelalderlig Literaturs skæbne', *For ide og virkelighed*, 1 (1869), p. 93.
22  Chr. Bruun, *De illuminerede Haandskrifter i Det store kongelige Bibliothek* (Copenhagen: Gyldendal, 1890), pp. 19–20.
23  Royal Danish library, Schiønning 2 8vo. Bent Christensen and Chr. Gorm Tortzen (eds.), *Liber compositionum: Christian IV's latinske brevstile 1591–1593* (Herning: Systime, 1988).

documenting the Catholic age of Denmark – were considered useless, because they were artifacts from a condemned worldview. These books were waste to be discarded or, since material such as parchment had value, recycled.

## 2   Travels Abroad and Books from the Catholic Present

On the other hand, some books from contemporary Catholic countries were considered useful. In the second half of the sixteenth century many young Danish noblemen travelled to Catholic countries in order to study. Danes travelling to Italy to study went especially to Padua, where (under the motto 'Universa universis patavina libertas') during the Venetian dominion Protestant students were allowed to study after the counterreformation. Thus, from 1536 to 1660 as many as 355 Danish and Norwegian students were enrolled at the University of Padua and 132 in Siena.[24]

Among the most exceptional cases of these travels are those of Jakob Ulfeldt Junior (1567–1630) and Christian Barnekow (1556–1612). Jakob Ulfeldt, who was the son of Chancellor Jakob Ulfeldt Senior (1535–1593), spent thirteen years traveling. Jakob Ulfeldt Junior and Christian Barnekow travelled to the Middle East and subsequently Ulfeldt visited Spain. On their return, they both joined the court and Ulfeldt eventually became chancellor. Jakob Ulfeldt and his wife, Birgitte Lauridsdatter Brockenhuus (1580–1656), had seventeen children, among whom Corfitz Ulfeldt (1606–1664) was one.

In a copy of a Leipzig edition of Melanchthon's *Loci*, 1559, in the Royal Danish Library there is a list of the library of Jakob Ulfeldt Junior, which shows his interest in the classics and contemporary history.[25] Most of the books are printed, but there is also a set of *relationes manuscriptæ*. Jakob Ulfeldt brought home from Italy a collection of these 'manuscript relations', of which six volumes are today kept at the Royal Danish Library and others are at Uppsala University Library.[26] Christian Barnekow's library also shows a keen interest in political history and in the world beyond Europe. Indeed, Federico Zuliani has

---

24   Vello Helk, *Dansk-norske studierejser: Fra reformationen til enevælden 1536–1660* (Odense: Odense universitetsforlag, 1987), pp. 42–43.

25   Ellen Jørgensen, 'En Bogliste fra det 16. Aarhundredes Slutning [Jacob Ulfeldts Bogsamling]', *Danske Magazin*, 6, række 3 (1923), pp. 175–182; Philipp Melanchthon, *Loci præcipui theologici: Nunc denuo cura et diligentia summa recogniti, multisque in locis copiose illustrati; cum appendice disputationis de Coniugio* (Lipsiae: in officina haeredum Valentini Papae, 1559), USTC 673479, Shelf mark 88, 28 00654.

26   Shelfmark: GKS 500–505 folio. An owner's mark in one of the volumes of these relations states that Jakob Ulfeldt had bought them in Padua in 1590: 'Jacobus Ulffelt Patavii 1590'.

claimed that this kind of manuscript was used as a way to study contemporary history, a discipline which was not taught at the universities.[27]

The students who had studied abroad, returned with polite manners, with knowledge of languages and with books acquired abroad. Books were considered to be important material evidence of learning, and in some funeral sermons they are referred to as such. Federico Zuliani quotes Resen's at Christian Barnekow's funeral, where it is stressed that the latter returned with books in many foreign languages.[28]

Some of the books concerning modern history also dealt with the contemporary reality of the Catholic countries. Christian Barnekow's librarian, the Italian humanist Giacomo Castelvetro (1546–1616) travelled in Europe with this kind of books. In exile from Modena, Castelvetro transmitted Italian Renaissance culture to the court of James VI and Queen Anna of Denmark in Edinburgh, to the court of Christian IV in Copenhagen and to Shakespeare's London, while he incessantly collected manuscripts on Italian literature and European contemporary history. Castelvetro also stayed in Denmark from August 1594 to 11 October 1595 and copied a number of texts there, most of which are today in Newberry Library in Chicago.[29] Various manuscripts and books which belonged to Castelvetro are now kept in the Royal Danish Library in Copenhagen.

After Copenhagen, Castelvetro went to Sweden and entered the service of the later King Charles IX. He stayed in Sweden for two years and was there part of the network of informants of Sir Robert Cecil (1563–1612), 1st Earl of Salisbury. In May 1598 Castelvetro began a longer trip to Italy with Venice as

---

27   Federico Zuliani, 'En samling politiske håndskrifter fra slutningen af det 16. århundrede: Giacomo Castelvetro og Christian Barnekows bibliotek', *Fund og Forskning i Det Kongelige Biblioteks Samlinger*, 50 (2011), pp. 229–257.

28   Hans Poulsen Resen, *Herrens Borg: Den XLVI. Kong Davids Psalme, om en sand oc fast Trøst i dette Leffnets Strijd, til visse Seyervinding Offuer Christian Barnekovs til Birkholm, Kgl. May. Befalnings Mand paa Landskrone Slot, hans Lijg i Helsingøer 26. Mart. 1612 ... nognlunde viist oc forklaret* (Copenhagen: Salomon Sartor, 1613), (no USTC number), pp. Diiir–Diiiv.

29   These manuscripts came from the Dietrichstein library to Chicago in the twentieth century. The Dietrichstein library was founded by Baron Adam Dietrichstein (1527–1590) and enlarged by his son Franz (1570–1636), bishop of Olomouc, in Moravia. After the conquest of Nikolsburg by the Swedish army during the Thirty Years' War, in 1645, the entire library was sent to Sweden as war booty, see Otto Walde, *Storhetstidens litterära krigsbyten en kulturhistorisk-bibliografisk studie* (2 vols., Uppsala: Almqvist & Wiksell, 1916–1920), 1, pp. 247–305. Subsequent generations of the Dietrichstein family created a new library and the Castelvetro manuscripts entered this new library. The manuscripts from this Dietrichstein library were sold at an auction in Lucerne in 1933.

final destination. He ended up staying in Venice, where he worked with the printer Giovan Battista Ciotti, for twelve years.

Castelvetro's brother Lelio was burned as a relapsed heretic in nearby Mantua in 1609. In 1611 Castelvetro himself was arrested in Venice at the request of the Roman Inquisition. He was saved from death by the English Ambassador to Venice, Dudley Carleton (1574–1632). Carleton claimed that Castelvetro was in his service and threatened to create a diplomatic scandal. After saving Castelvetro's life, Carleton wrote to Sir Robert Cecil that his intervention had been decisive: if he had not promptly removed the most compromising writings from Castelvetro's residence, he would not have been able to save his life:

> It was my good fortune to recover his books and papers a little before the Officers of the Inquisition went to his lodging to seize them, for I caused them to be brought unto me upon the first news of his apprehension, under cover of some writings of mine which he had in his hands. And this indeed was the poore man's safetie, for if they had made themselves masters of that Magazine, wherein was store and provision of all sorts of pasquins, libels, relations, layde up for many years together against their master the Pope, nothing could have saved him.[30]

These books were dangerous objects for their owner in Venice. Some of these same books ended up in the Royal Danish Library. Among them is a copy of an edition of the two dialogues by Alfonso de Valdés, which Castelvetro had reclaimed from his friend, the friar Fulgenzio Manfredi (c.1560–1610) who went to meet the Inquisition in Rome and never returned, because he was sentenced to death and burnt in Rome's *Campo dei Fiori*.[31]

Books that were perceived as dangerous in Catholic countries were not necessarily perceived as dangerous in Protestant countries. The books which the

---

30   Quoted from Kathleen T.B. Butler, 'Giacomo Castelvetro 1546–1616', *Italian Studies*, 5 (1950), pp. 1–42, here p. 28. Cf. Anders Toftgaard, '"Måske vil vi engang glædes ved at mindes dette": Om Giacomo Castelvetros håndskrifter i Det Kongelige Bibliotek', *Fund og Forskning i Det Kongelige Biblioteks Samlinger*, 50 (2011), p. 195.

31   *Due dialoghi. L'uno di Mercurio et Caronte, nel quale ... si raconta quel, che accade nella guerra dopo l'anno MDXXI: l'altro di Lattantio et di uno archidiacono, nel quale ... si trattano le cose avenute in Roma nell'ano MDXXVII di spagnuolo in italiano con molta acutezza et tradotti, et revisti*, ([s.l.]: [s.n.], [s.a.] [after 1546]), USTC 861673, Edit 16 CNCE 50696, cf. Anders Toftgaard, 'Proverbi italiani nell'Europa del Nord. Il Significato d'alquanti Proverbi dell'italica favella di Giacomo Castelvetro', in Giuseppe Crimi and Franco Pignatti (eds.), *Il Proverbio nella letteratura italiana dal XV al XVII Secolo. Atti delle giornate di studio Università degli Studi Roma Tre – Fondazione Marco Besso Roma 5-6 Dicembre 2012* (Marziana: Vecchiarelli, 2014), pp. 367–393.

English Ambassador had saved from Castelvetro's home in Venice could easily find their way into Denmark.

On the other hand, the Danish legislation also tried to avoid having vicious books coming to Denmark.[32] The Church Ordinance from (1537/1539) stipulated censorship by university professors of all books printed or put on sale in Denmark.[33] After Corfitz Ulfeldt had published his defence of his honor (see below), a decree was issued on 18 September 1652, which prohibited Ulfeldt's publication and the production or dissemination of any kind of lampoon that could dishonour the government or the council.[34] After the introduction of absolutism in 1660, an edict of 1667 introduced the compulsory presence of an imprimatur in approved books.[35] The anonymously published *Apologia nobilitatis danicæ* (1681) by Oluf Rosenkrantz (1623–1685), which contained a criticism of the king and of absolutism, was sentenced for lack of these paratexts. The Danish law, published in 1683, had a separate chapter on books and almanacs that organized the censorship (2-21-1 to 2-21-6), and a chapter on matters of honour forbade pasquils (6-21-8).[36]

## 3  Heinrich Rantzau and His Beloved Books

One of the persons who gave the humanist love of the material book its clearest expression was Heinrich Rantzau (1526–1598). Heinrich's father was the famous Johan Rantzau (1492–1565), who had won the Danish civil war in 1536,

---

32  Øystein Rian, *Sensuren i Danmark-Norge: Vilkårene for offentlige ytringer 1536–1814* (Oslo: Universitetsforlaget, 2014); Jesper Düring Jørgensen, 'Censur og bogundertrykkelse 1500–1849', *Magasin fra Det Kongelige Bibliotek*, 8 (3), (1993), pp. 89–94.

33  Charlotte Appel, *Læsning og bogmarked i 1600-tallets Danmark* (2 vols., Copenhagen, Museum Tusculanum, 2001), 1, pp. 381–383.

34  Corfitz Ulfeldt, *Høytrengende Aeris Forsuar, imod den publiceerde Usandferdig Kiøbenhaffns Beretning, anlangende Dinæ oc Walters Sag, som ved Uordentlig Proces samme stetz bleff udført Anno 1651: Med hosfølgende Aarsager som hafuer nød oc tuungen mig underskrefuen (for en tid) at begifue mig aff mit kiere Fæderneland* ([s.l.]: [s.n.], 1652); *Kong Frederik den Tredies Declaration, dat. Kiøbenh. d. 18. Sept. 1652, ang. Corfitz Ulfelds Høytrengende Aeris Forsvar* ([Copenhagen]: [s.n.], 1652), cf. V.A. Secher, *Corpus constitutionum Daniæ: Forordninger, Recesser og andre kongelige Breve, Danmarks Lovgivning vedkommende 1558–1660*, vol. 6 (Copenhagen: (s.n.), 1887), pp. 107–113.

35  Harald Ilsøe, 'Censur og Approbation: Lidt om bogcensurens administration i 1600-tallet', in John T. Lauridsen and Olaf Olsen (eds.), *Umisteligt. Festskrift til Erland Kolding Nielsen*, (Copenhagen: Det Kongelige Bibliotek, 2007), pp. 119–135.

36  *Kong Christian den Femtis Danske Lov: Ved Justitsministeriets Foranstaltning udg. paa Grundlag af den af V. A. Secher med Kildehenvisninger forsynede Udgave af 1911*, [reprint] (Copenhagen: Gad, 1944).

and had become viceroy in the Duchies; he had also led the war against the peasant republic of the Ditmarshes in 1559.[37] The viceroy, or *produx* in Latin, was the representative of the Danish king in the king's segment of the Duchies.

Heinrich Rantzau was viceroy or governor from 1556 and he owned several castles in Holstein. He wrote numerous books, created a renowned library and acted as a patron for scholars.[38] Of his eighteen castles, Rantzau's main castle was Breitenburg near Itzehoe, north-west of Hamburg, where his library was situated (although he also had books in other castles).

In 1583, thanks to an exchange, Heinrich Rantzau acquired a collection of manuscripts and rare books, mostly incunabula, from the Augustinian Abbey of Segeberg. In 1590, Rantzau had more than 6,300 volumes in his library.[39] Most of them were bound in contemporary bindings of parchment or pigskin and carried his *ex libris*. Some of the books had the printed owner's mark 'Hic liber Henrici est equitis cognomine Rantzou' (This book belongs to the knight Henry with the surname Rantzau). The library was arranged systematically and was decorated with globes and astronomical instruments.[40] On the walls of his library, Rantzau had mounted verses of his own and quotations of classical authors. Among his verses there was also a poem which expressed his love of his books.

The poem was quoted for the first time in a book by Georg Crusius (d. 1619, from Hannover) who worked as the preceptor of Rantzau's son, and later it was quoted in a book by Rantzau's collaborator Peter Lindeberg (1562–1596) about Rantzau's possessions, which was published by various publishers in slightly different editions.[41] The poem, consisting in 32 hendecasyllabic lines, starts with the following four lines that recall Catullian poems: 'Salvete aureoli mei libelli / Meæ deliciæ, mei lepores / Quam vos sæpe oculis juvat videre, Et

---

37   Torben Bramming, *Rantzau: Den hellige kriger*. (Copenhagen: Kristeligt Dagblad, 2016).
38   Peter Zeeberg, *Heinrich Rantzau: A Bibliography* (Copenhagen: Society for Danish Language and Literature, 2004); Dieter Lohmeier, 'Heinrich Rantzau und die Adelskultur der frühen Neuzeit', in Dieter Lohmeier (ed.), *Arte et marte: Studien zur Adelskultur des Barockzeitalters in Schweden, Dänemark und Schleswig-Holstein* (Neumünster: Karl Wachholtz, 1978).
39   Approximately 6,500 according to Lauritz Nielsen, *Danske Privatbiblioteker gennem Tiderne*, 1: Indtil Udgangen af det 17. Aarhundrede (Copenhagen: Gyldendal, 1946), p. 35, and more than 6,000 according to Peter Lindeberg, *Hypotyposis arcivm palatiorvm, librorvm, pyramidvm, obeliscorvm, molarvm, fontivm, monumentorum & epitaphiorum ab ... Henrico Ranzovio, Prorege ... Holsato, conditorum edita & conscripta à Petro Lindebergio.* (Rostock: Muellemann, 1590), USTC 664598, p. 7.
40   Walther Ludwig, 'Der Humanist und das Buch. Heinrich Rantzaus Liebeserklärung an Seine Bücher', *Illinois Classical Studies*, 19 (1994), p. 266.
41   Ludwig, 'Der Humanist und das Buch', p. 266, n. 4.

tritos manibus tenere nostris/' (Welcome, my golden books / my darlings, my charmers / It pleases me to behold you often with my eyes / and to hold your worn volumes in my hands).[42] The poem has often been quoted as an example of bibliophilia, by among others Benjamin Disraeli.

In a general decree concerning the library, Heinrich Rantzau also wrote a malediction of any person who would do harm to or steal books from the library.[43] The decree, which states that his library should also remain in the possession of the Rantzau family, says the following about any person who would do harm to the library:

> Si quis secus fecerit, / Libros, partemve aliquam abstulerit, / Extraxerit, clepserit, rapserit / Concerpserit, corruperit Dolo malo: / Illico maledictus, / Perpetuo execrabilis, / Semper detestabilis, / Esto, maneto.[44]

> If anyone should do evil, and take away the books or any part, draw away, steal, plunder, destroy or ruin by evil intention, he shall immediately become and stay damned, forever execrable, forever detestable.

Rantzau commissioned editions of ancient or medieval texts from manuscripts in his library, and the editions bore the words 'ex bibliotheca Ranzoviana'.[45]

Rantzau published a visual account of Frederick II's reign. He also wrote an account of Niels Kaas's death and he contributed to the visual description of northern Europe in Braun's and Hogenberg's visual renderings of major cities.

It was Heinrich Rantzau who allowed Tycho Brahe when, after the coronation of Christian IV Brahe's good fortune in Denmark turned into adversity, to stay at his castle Wandesburg near Hamburg. In Wandsbeck in 1598, Brahe published the book *Astronomiæ Instauratæ Mechanica*, which contains tributes to Brahe, a scientific autobiography and a detailed descriptions, illustrations of the instruments Brahe had ordered to be constructed and also of the

---

42  'Meæ deliciæ, mei lepores' is a quotation from Catullus 32. According to Walther Ludwig, the poem was written in imitation of the Italian Neo-Latin poet Marcantonio Flaminio (1498–1550), but the imitation is limited to the invocation of the books.
43  Otto Walde, 'Henrik Rantzaus bibliotek och dess öden', *Nordisk tidskrift för bok- och biblioteksväsen*, 1 (1914), pp. 181–192.
44  Peter Lindeberg, *Hypotyposis arcium, palatiorum, librorum, pyramidum, obeliscorum, cipporum, molarum, fontium, monumentorum & epitaphiorum ab ... Henrico Ranzovio ... conditorum ... conscripta et edita à Petro Lindebergio, Rost.* (Frankfurt am Main: apud Ioannem Wechelum, 1592), USTC 664595, pp. 26–27.
45  Zeeberg, *Heinrich Rantzau*, pp. 24–28.

complex of buildings on Hven. The book was dedicated to the Holy Roman Emperor Rudolph II (1552–1612, emperor 1576).[46]

After Heinrich Rantzau's death in 1598, his books were inherited by his son Gert Rantzau (1558–1627), who also became viceroy in the Duchies. Later they were inherited by Gert's son Christian Rantzau (1614–1663). Christian Rantzau was the last Rantzau to own the library. In the Thirty Years' War, after Christian IV's defeat at Lutter am Barenberg (on 27 August 1626), the castle of Breitenburg was looted on 29 September 1627 by troops led by Johann Tserclaes, Count of Tilly (1559–1632) and Albrecht von Wallenstein (1583–1634). Heinrich Rantzau's library was dispersed in its entirety.

Wallenstein sent the greater part of the library to Prague, where he donated it to the Emperor's confessor Wilhelm Lamormain (1570–1648), who in turn gave the books to various Jesuit houses, in particular to the Jesuit college in Saint Nicholas, which had been founded by Wallenstein in 1628. Some of these books were taken as war booty in 1648, when the Swedes, led by Count Hans Christoff von Königsmarck (1600–1663), invaded Prague. Some of these books ended up in German libraries.[47] When the Jesuit Order was suppressed by Pope Clement XIV in 1773, the library was seized and a few years later (1777) donated to the university library of Prague.

Thanks to Scandinavian book historians of the early twentieth century (Isak Collijn, Otto Walde, H.O. Lange) some hundreds of books from Heinrich Rantzau's library have been rediscovered in public libraries – the most important parts of it in Prague – and occasionally books are also found on the market. According to Lauritz Nielsen, some of Rantzau's books at Itzehoe had not been taken by Wallenstein, but by other soldiers who had sold the books in Hamburg. Moreover, Rantzau donated many books as gifts, and therefore books with a connection to Heinrich Rantzau appear in many library collections.[48]

The fact that Heinrich Rantzau's literary production has not become part of our literary canon, far from it, should not lead us to underestimate the value of his library. The library was used by its owner to create his own research centre at his castle. The library was improved by manuscripts from a secularized monastery (Segeberg). The interior decoration of Rantzau's library was part of the owner's self-fashioning, in Stephen Greenblatt's sense of construction of identity and public persona.[49] Since the library was scattered, it does not seem to have contributed much at its various destinations.

---

46  Tycho Brahe, *Tychonis Brahe Astronomiæ instauratæ mechanica*. (Wandsbek: [Tycho Brahe], 1598), USTC 699876.
47  Nielsen, *Danske Privatbiblioteker gennem Tiderne*, 1, p. 38.
48  Peter Zeeberg, 'Patron of the Arts and Bibliophile', *Renæssanceforum*, 15 (2019), p. 18.
49  Stephen Greenblatt, *Renaissance Self-Fashioning: From More to Shakespeare*. (Chicago: University of Chicago Press, 1980).

## 4   The Baltic Battle of the Books

Books were parts of wars in many ways. During the war against the peasant republic of the Ditmarshes in 1559, the chancellor Johan Friis of Hesselager (1494–1570) managed to obtain a contemporary legal manuscript that is today preserved in the Arnamagnean collection (AM 2 4to). Friis asked his servant Klaus Rytter (who was later in his life, 1584–1589, mayor of Copenhagen) to bring it to Denmark.[50]

In the sixteenth century, book battles were part of the conflict between Denmark and Sweden which culminated with The Nordic Seven Years' War (1563–1570). When Olaus Magnus (1490–1557) published Johannes Magnus' (1488–1544) *Historia Gothorum* in Rome in 1554, it was full of vehement criticism of the Danes. Most notably, the text included a speech by the bishop of the diocese of Linköping, Hemming Gadh (c.1450–1520) against the Danes.[51] The rubric explained the content of the speech thus: 'Vehemens contra Danos oratio'.[52] The Danes responded with a treatise, a *refutatio*, by Hans Svaning (1503–1584), which on the title page was falsely attributed to recently deceased Petrus Parvus Rosæfontanus (1500–1559) and retrodated, so that it seemed to have been published in 1560, during the reign of Gustav I Vasa, and not in 1561, during the reign of Erik XIV (1533–1577).[53]

---

50   Klaus Rytter explains on fol. 69v: 'och ther wdj Meldorp feck Johann friss tiil hesselag-ger thene bog och andtuorde hand meg Claws Rytter ther thene bog, som ieg thend tid war sin tienere, att skulle förre same bog hiem', (and there, in Meldorp. Johann Friis to Hesselager got this book and he made me, Klaus Rytter, who was his servant, responsible for bringing this book home), cf. the catalogue record on <handrit.is/manu script/view/en/AM04-0002/>. The entire text written by Klaus Rytter has been published as 'En kort Beretning om Ditmarskens Erobring 1559. Af Klavs Rytter, Kansler Johan Friis's Tjener', in Rørdam Holger Fr., *Monumenta historiæ Danicæ: Historiske Kildeskrifter og Bearbejdelser af dansk Historie, især fra det 16. Aarhundrede* (2 vols., Copenhagen: Gad, 1885) II, 2, pp. 563–570.

51   Johannes Magnus, *Historia Ioannis Magni Gothi Sedis apostolicae legati Svetiae et Gotiae primatis ac archiepiscopi vpsalensis, de omnibvs Gothorvm Sveonvmqve regibvs qvi vnquam ab initio nationis extitere, eorúmque memorabilibus bellis late varieqve per orbem gestis, opera Olai Magni Gothi fratris eiusdem autoris ac etiam archiepiscopi vpsalenlis in lucem* (Rome: Giovanni Maria Viotti, 1554), USTC 839648; *Historia Ioannis Magni*, 753–776.

52   The speech has since been proven to have been most probably a work of Johannes Magnus himself.

53   Petrus Parvus Rosefontanus and Hans Svaning, *Refutatio calumniarvm cuiusdam Ioannis Magni Gothi Upsalensis, quibus in historia sua ac famosa oratione Danicam gentem incessit ... scripta a Petro Parvo Rosefontano ... Huic accessit Chronicon siue Historia Ioannis Regis Daniæ ... unà cum sententia illa iudiciali, quam duorum regnorum Daniæ atque Norvagiæ Patres, Anno 1505 die Julii prima, Calmarniæ, contra Stenonem Sture eiusque complices tulerunt ... Anno 1560* (Copenhagen: Christoph Barth, 1561), USTC 302482.

In Denmark a new edition of the *Rimkrønike* (rhymed chronicle), which had been published for the first time in 1495, and which was the first book to be printed in the Danish language, appeared in 1555.[54] It contained verses directed against Swedish kings, and therefore Gustav I Vasa ordered Peder Andreæ (Svart, d. 1562) to write a rejoinder. Svart's rejoinder was published in Stockholm in 1558 with the title: 'Some pieces of the Danish chronicle, from king Waldemar's age and the following ages, in which the Swedes are rudely and falsely assailed. In addition the just and inevitable response of the Swedes, which they could not at all avoid, but they had to defend their honour and reputation and as consequence were forced and provoked to respond.'[55] As a response, the Danish chancellor Johan Friis in person wrote a lampoon against the Swedish King.[56]

Some contemporary historians considered these slanderous books to be one of the causes of the war, a view championed, for example by the aforementioned historian Hans Svaning. In his notes to a manuscript by Svaning in which Svaning tried to explain the causes of the war, historian Anders Sørensen Vedel (1542–1616) listed the following four main reasons for the war:

I. *3 Coronæ* (the three crowns).
II. *Lifflandia* (Livonia).
III. *Libelli famosi* (slanderous books).
IV. *Occultus belli apparatus et 3 naves abductæ* (The secret preparations for war and the three ships, which were taken away).[57]

Outside the 'slanderous books,' the three other reasons require some contextual information. The Danish king had used the three crowns, an originally Swedish symbol, which had been current during the union of three kingdoms. As to

---

54   *Hær begynner thñ danskæ Krønnickæ well offuerseet och ræth* (Copenhagen: Godfred af Ghemen, 1495), ISTC No. ic00476500, LN 232; *Her Begyndes den Danske Krønicke paa Rim vel offuer seet oc bedre rettet end hun vaar føre* (Copenhagen: Hans Vingaard, 1555), USTC 302343, LN 1401.

55   *Någer stycker aff then danske cröneke, ifrå konung Woldemars tijd och hans effterkommande, ther inne the swenske bliffue fast groffueligen och med osanning antastade: Teslikest the swenskes rätferdelige och oumgångelige genswar, som the ingelunde kunde förbi gå, vthan ther sijn åhre och gode rychte åndeligen förswara moste, ther til the högt äre trengde och förorsakade* (Stockholm: [s.n.], 1558), USTC 271389. Cf. Axel Nelson, 'Peder Swarts gensvar 1558', in *Uppsala universitetsbiblioteks minnesskrift 1621–1921* (Uppsala: Almqvist & Wiksell, 1921), pp. 139–166.

56   Harald Ilsøe, 'Omkring Hans Svanings Refutatio og Chronicon Ioannis', *Historisk Tidsskrift*, 12 (1973), pp. 21–58, here p. 36.

57   GKS 2577 4to: *En retractat eller Forklaring paa den Beretning, som er nyligen udgangen de Svenske til vilge, om alt det, som er skied og forhandlit emellum the Danske oc the Suenske aar 1565.* The text has been published in: Rørdam Holger Fr, *Monumenta historiæ Danicæ = Historiske Kildeskrifter og Bearbejdelser af dansk Historie, især fra det 16. Aarhundrede*, (4 vols., Copenhagen: Gad, 1873–1887), 2, pp. 117–162.

Livonia, Frederick II had bought the bishopric of Saare-Lääne. It comprised the islands Saaremaa (Øsel) and Hiiumaa (Dagø). Frederick II had appointed his brother Magnus (1540–1583), bishop of the diocese. The arrival of Magnus had interfered with the power struggle between the Swedish princes Erik and his brother Johan. The secret preparations for war and the three ships, refer to Sweden's negotiations with Hessel, and the so-called Battle of Bornholm in 1563, which was the first naval battle in the Seven Years' War (1563–1570).

The battle of the books or the literary feud was thus part of the causes of the war, and therefore it was also part of the peace treaty after the war. In the Treaty of Stettin, which was signed on 13 December 1570, one of the clauses (22) declared a ban on any kind of lampoon ('schand- und schmeheschrifte') in Denmark and Sweden.[58] Some later books in Latin do however seem to have eschewed the ban.[59]

The battle of books was among the reasons for the war. But the material books themselves were also part of the Seven Years' War. During the war, the Danish army seized books and manuscripts at the castle of Älvsborg between Danish Halland and Norwegian Bohuslän, near present-day Gothenburg and the only Swedish port to the Kattegat.[60] The Danish army seized a manuscript containing a Swedish translation of Hemming Gadh's oration. This particular manuscript, which does not seem to have survived, is mentioned in a list of documents given to the Danish peace negotiators (Otte Krumpen, Jørgen Ottesen Rosenkrantz, Heinrich Rantzau and the secretary Joachim Hincke) who were to bargain peace in Rostock in 1564.[61]

A copy of an edition, printed in Venice, of the memorable deeds and sayings of Valerius Maximus was seized at the castle of Älvsborg on 1 September 1563. King Frederick II gave the book to Holger Ottosen Rosenkrantz (1517–1575), who wrote a lengthy note on the flyleaf at the end of the book on 8 January 1564. The inscription celebrated the victory as a memorable deed and explained that the inscription had been written in order for such deeds to be remembered:

> Ut autem hæ res gestæ in perpetuam manaret memoria, huic libro digne adscriptum est, quod tunc Helsburgiæe, et post illis deditionem inve[n]tum & à Sere:[-nissima] R.[egia] M.[aiestate] Holgero Rose[n]kra[n]tz Ottonis filio, Capitaneo in Schanderburg. & Buholm, hæreditarius in

---

58 Laurs Rasmus Laursen, *Danmark-Norges Traktater 1523–1750: Med dertil hørende Aktstykker* (11 vols., Copenhagen: Gad, 1912–1949), 2, pp. 254–255.
59 Karen Skovgaard-Petersen, 'Margaretica: Et bidrag til den dansk-svenske pennefejde i det 16. århundrede', *Historisk Tidsskrift*, 87 (1987), pp. 209–236.
60 Harald Ilsøe, 'Bog- og bibliotekshistoriske notitser', *Fund og Forskning i Det Kongelige Biblioteks Samlinger*, 21 (1974), pp. 165–166.
61 Additamenta 127 folio 1, 1 ('kk' on the list).

Bolwern & RosenWaldt, dono datum est. qui eum in hunc locum reponi curavit. / Anno à nato Chr[ist]o M.D. LXIIII VIII Januarii.

In order for these deeds to remain in perpetual memory, it was added in writing in this book, which was found in Älvsborg after its capitulation and was given as a gift by his Royal Majesty to Holger Rosenkrantz, Otto's son, governor of Scanderburg and Bygholm [near Horsens], Lord of Boller & Rosenvold, who then saw to having it written down in this place. In the year 1564 after Christ's birth on 8 January.[62]

The inscription was written in the humanist hand and recorded the names of the most important Danes in the battle. The Roman historian's work was the proper place for recording the memorable deeds at Älvsborg. This particular book served as a kind of monument.

Marginalia and owners' marks also allow us to link books to battles. During the same war, King Frederick II recorded in his copy of an edition of the Bible in Luther's German translation, that he was reading the Bible during the war with the Swedes.[63] He noted the fact twice during the war, in 1566 and in 1567.

The ship master Jens Munk (1579–1628), who served Frederick II's son, Christian IV, and who was later going to try to find the northwest passage, participated in capturing a pirate named Mendoza off the Norwegian coast. He noted on the pastedown of a Spanish book on the art of navigation that he had seized it from Mendoza on his ship in June 1615: 'Dene Bog Eier Jenß Munk vdj sin tid och hafuer ieg den bekomet Vnder Kandeneß i Kapten Mendoses skieb den tid wie blef hanom Megtig den 26 Junj Anno 1615.' (This book is owned by Jens Munk in his time and I obtained it off Kanin-nes [Kanin Nos in present-day Russia] on the ship of Captain Mendoza, when we defeated him on 26 June Anno 1615.)[64]

---

62  Handwritten note on the flyleaf of a copy of Valerius Maximus, *Factorum ac dictorum memorabilium*. (Venezia: arte & impensis Ioannes Forliviensi Gregorique fratrum [de Gregoriis], March 8. 1487), ISTC No. iv00036000, Shelf mark: Inc. Haun 4063 in the Royal Danish Library in Copenhagen.

63  *Biblia, das ist, Die gantze heilige Schrifft Deutsch Auffs new zugericht Doct. Mart. Luther.* (Wittenberg: Hans Lufft, 1550–1551), USTC 616664, VD16 B 2729. Cf. Rolf Hardy Christensen, *Om Frederiksborg-Bibelen og en række af Frederik 2. udgivne eller understøttede værker* (Herlev: Eget Forlag, 2021).

64  Ilsøe, 'Bog- og bibliotekshistoriske notitser'. Ilsøe was the first to mention this book: Zamorano Rodrigo, *Compendio del arte de navegar* (Sevilla: Ioan de Leon, 1588), USTC 342533. Shelfmark: 53, 33.

## 5   Jørgen Seefeld's Library

Heinrich Rantzau's library was one of the Danish libraries that were lost during the Thirty Years' War. Two other important libraries were lost in the First Northern War (1655–1660): the libraries of Otte Krag (1611–1666, member of the Council of the Realm) at Egeskov and Jørgen Seefeld (1594–1662) at Ringsted Abbey. Some manuscripts written by Otte Krag have been preserved in the Royal Danish Library, and some of his books in The National Library of Sweden.[65] In the present study, I will focus on the library of Jørgen Seefeld, which was the most impressive of the two, and hence also the one which has been most thoroughly described.

Jørgen Seefeld (1594–1662) was the owner of one of the richest libraries in Denmark-Norway in the seventeenth century. He was the son of Christopher Lauritzen Seefeld of Refsnæs (near Aalborg in Northern Jutland) and Else Nielsdatter of Kvotrup and Tustrup. Jørgen Seefeld had been educated at the cathedral school in Viborg and had travelled for years (1610–1618) abroad, in Wittenberg, Leipzig, France, England and the Netherlands.[66]

In 1630 Seefeld was appointed High Court judge of Seeland and given the fief of Ringsted Abbey. In 1640 he became a member of the Council of the Realm (*Rigsrådet*) together with Hannibal Sehested (1609–1666). Seefeld lived in Ringsted Abbey from 1630 to 1664 and it was there that he kept his library. He considered selling his collection of books to King Frederick III, who was founding his own library in those years but resolved not to do so.[67]

Seefeld had a number of librarians taking care of his books.[68] Peder Villadsen (1610–1673, later bishop in Viborg) worked there from 1635 to 1636; Werner Meyer, former librarian of Holger Rosenkrantz worked there in 1642, and Zacharias Lund (1608–1667), former head of Herlufsholm and later

---

65   William Christensen, 'Om den gamle Adels historiske Interesse', in *Festskrift til Kristian Erslev den 28. decbr. 1927 fra danske Historikere* (Copenhagen: Hagerups Boghandel, 1927), pp. 326–329; Walde, *Storhetstidens litterära krigsbyten*, 2, pp. 404–406.

66   Arctander Niels Lauridsen, Petrafontanus Johannes Martini and Jensen Paaske, *Mora Dei: Om Guds Dwælelse oc hvad Sager der ere til, at hand i vor Nød, under tiden tøffuer met sin Hielp oc Bønhørelse ... En nyttig Forklaring udi ... Christopher Lauritzsøns Seefelds, til Reffsnis, begraffuelse, i Nørkongsleff Kircke, den 16. Martij, Anno 1612 predictet* (Copenhagen: Henrich Waldkirch, 1614), No USTC, p. C2r; C.O. Bøggild-Andersen, 'Jørgen Seefeld, 7.3.1594-28.2.1662', in *Dansk biografisk leksikon*, ed. Svend Cedergreen Bech et al., third edition (Copenhagen: Gyldendal, 1979).

67   E.C. Werlauff, 'Jørgen Seefeldt og hans Bibliothek', *Historisk Tidsskrift*, 2 (1856), p. 227.

68   Christian Kaaber, 'Viden og fyrstepragt 1660–1728', in Nan Dahlkild and Steen Bille Larsen (eds.), *Dansk bibliotekshistorie* (2 vols., Aarhus: Aarhus Universitetsforlag, 2021), 1, pp. 86–87.

secretary in the Danish Chancellery worked there from 1654 until the dispersal of the library. The Icelander Paul Hallsen worked there also, most probably with the Icelandic manuscripts.[69]

The poet Zacharias Lund, who wrote his poetry in in Latin, was one of the renowned scholars who worked as librarian for Jørgen Seefeld, and it was he who created a manuscript description of the collection that was published and shaped all subsequent descriptions of the library, including the present one.[70] According to Lund, the library consisted of 26,000 items, and contained many rare and old manuscripts pertaining to Danish, Norwegian, Icelandic and Swedish history. The Icelandic manuscripts Seefeld had received from bishop Brynjólfur Sveinsson.[71] Seefeld returned some of these manuscripts to Sveinsson, but kept at least one, which is today preserved in Stockholm.[72] A medieval Danish manuscript is the prayer book of Marine Jespersdatter, which is today part of the Arnamagnean collection, after having been in the nineteenth century part of the manuscript collection of the University Library.[73] Arne Magnusson bought the prayer book at the auction of Frederik Rostgaard's library in 1726.[74] The book contains the following note: 'Reliqiæ ex bibliothecis Nobilissimi Domini Georgij Sefellt.'[75]

Seefeld's library also held manuscripts of the professor from the academy of Sorø, Johannes Meursius.[76] Moreover, it contained an *Herbarium* in 32 volumes, which is today in Uppsala, and which was used by Linné (Linnæus). There were also 204 bible editions, among them the polyglot Bible published 1569–1572

---

69  Nielsen, *Danske Privatbiblioteker gennem Tiderne* , 1, p. 87.
70  Zacharias Lund, 'Jørgen Seefelds Bibliotek. (Af en gammel Copiebog)', in Peter Frederik Suhm (ed.), *Samlinger til den danske Historie*, (2 vols., Copenhagen: Gyldendals Forlag, 1782), 2, pp. 185–187. According to Werlauff, 'Jørgen Seefeldt og hans Bibliothek', p. 222, there is another copy of the text in Klevenfelds samlinger in the Danish National Archives.
71  Nielsen, *Danske Privatbiblioteker gennem Tiderne*, 1, p. 86.
72  Kristian Kålund, 'Den Nordiske (Norrøne) Oldlitteraturs Samling og Bevaring', in *Katalog over de Oldnorsk-Islandske Håndskrifter* (Copenhagen: Gyldendal, 1900), p. XXIV.
73  It is referred to as Additamenta 421 oktav in Werlauff, 'Jørgen Seefeldt Og Hans Bibliothek.' and in Christian Walther Bruun, 'Danske Privatbiblioteker i 17.–18. Aarhundrede', Royal Danish Library, NKS 3680 4to, vol. 1, p. 13. In 1884, manuscripts from the additamenta collection, which had been originally bought by Arne Magnusson, were transferred to the Arnemagnean collection, cf. Kålund, 'Den Nordiske (Norrøne) Oldlitteraturs Samling og Bevaring.', p. LII and Carl S. Petersen, *Det kongelige Biblioteks Haandskriftsamling* (Copenhagen: Munksgaard, 1943), p. 47.
74  Anne Mette Hansen, 'Marine Jespersdatters Bønnebog', www.handrit.is/manuscript/view/da/AM12-0421 (last accessed 14 January 2022).
75  Hansen, 'Marine Jespersdatters Bønnebog'.
76  Holger Fr. Rørdam, *Historiske Samlinger og Studier vedrørende danske Forhold og Personligheder især i det 17. Aarhundrede* (4 vols., Kjøbenhavn: G. E. C. Gad, 1891), I, p. 278.

by Christopher Plantin, and the polyglot Bible published in Paris 1628–1645. According to Zacharias Lund, there were rarities, which could be found neither in Oxford nor in the Vatican Library. The library also contained a handwritten manuscript by Jørgen Seefeld about the life of King Frederick II; and manuscripts on armories and genealogy, which were inherited by the descendants of Erik Krag, and of which some volumes, according to the well-informed Tycho de Hoffman, were in the library of Otto Thott.[77]

Seefeld also had parchment and cardboard stored for future bindings of his books, this material having the value of 1,200 *rigsdaler*. These stores were seized by the Swedish army, which used them for the cartridges at the siege of Copenhagen in 1658–1659.[78] According to Lund, Seefeld wanted to make a catalogue of his library that was like the catalogue of Gesner's library, but only after the library had reached perfection. That was a dangerous goal, and as a consequence no catalogue was ever published.

The professor at Sorø Academy Heinrich Ernst (1603–1665) dedicated his description of the Laurentine library to Seefeld.[79] The library of Seefeld was praised by Louis Jacob de Saint-Charles and its tragic history was mentioned in Johannes Buno's notes to Philipp Cluver's *Introductio in Universam Geographiam* (1697): 'Nostro seculo hunc locum instructissima sua Bibliotheca illustraverat Georges Seefeld regni Senator verum illa per belli calamitatem postea direpta est.' (In our century Jørgen Seefeld, a member of the Council of the Realm, rendered this place famous by his extremely well-furnished library, but it was later plundered during the calamity of war.)[80]

Seefeld lost his library to the brother-in-law of the Danish king Frederick III, Corfitz Ulfeldt. Ulfeldt is the most prominent of the seventeen children of Jakob Ulfeldt and one of the most colourful characters in Danish history. In 1637, Ulfeldt married Leonora Christina, one of the daughters of Christian IV and his second wife, Kirsten Munk; and after an impressive career he died in exile near Geneva, having been executed in effigy for high treason in Denmark, where his wife spent twenty-two years in prison. Steffen Heiberg has argued that Ulfeldt probably saw himself as a great minister, as a Danish Mazarin or

---

77  Tycho de Hofman, *Portraits historiques des hommes illustres de Dannemark: Remarquables par leur mérite, leurs charges & leur noblesse : avec leurs tables généalogiques*, 5 (Hague: [s.n.], 1746), p. 67.
78  Walde, *Storhetstidens litterära krigsbyten*, 2, p. 396.
79  Ernst, Heinrich, *Catalogvs librorum refertissimae Bibliothecae Miceae, quae asservatur Florentiae in coenobio D. Laurentii* (Amsterdam: apud Joannem Janssonivm, 1641), USTC 1030745, pp. 3–8.
80  Philipp Clüver, *Introductio in universam geographiam tam veterem quam novam tabulas geographicis XLVI*, (Amsterdam: apud Joannem Wolters, 1697), p. 229.

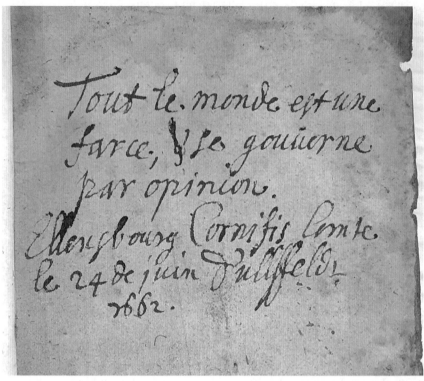

FIGURE 10.1    'Tout le monde est une farce, et se gouverne par opinion.' Corfitz Ulfeldt's motto in a copy of Martin Rinckart, *Circulorum memoriæ decas* (Leipzig: Elia Rehfeld und Joh. Grossen 1629)

Oxenstierna.[81] Corfitz Ulfeldt's motto was 'Tout le monde est une farce, et se gouverne par opinion', which can be seen in the owner's mark on one of his books in the Royal Danish Library, and in his entry in the album amicorum of bishop Erik Pontoppidan (1616–1678).[82]

After the death of Christian IV in 1648, Corfitz Ulfeldt and Leonora Christina soon came to be on bad terms with the new king, Frederick III. Following accusations concerning his administration as Seneschal, Ulfeldt and Leonora Christina fled from Denmark in 1651 to the Netherlands, and soon thereafter Ulfeldt's former protegé, Joachim Gersdorff, was appointed as the new Seneschal. From the Netherlands Corfitz Ulfeldt and his wife arrived at Queen

---

81  Steffen Heiberg, *Enhjørningen Corfitz Ulfeldt* (Copenhagen: Gyldendal, 2003), p. 95.
82  Erik Pontoppidan's album: Royal Danish Library, Acc. 2020/96. Martin Rinckart, *Circulorum memoriæ decas* (Leipzig: Elia Rehfeld und Joh. Grossen 1629), USTC 2135360, VD17 23:275856C cf. Heiberg, *Enhjørningen Corfitz Ulfeldt*, p. 211.

Christina's court in Stockholm. After Christina's abdication in 1654, Ulfeldt sought to help and eventually swore allegiance to her successor, King Charles X Gustav, who accepted his service. After the Danish declaration of war in 1657, Ulfeldt participated in the invasion of Denmark. Ulfeldt used the invasion to take revenge on enemies, and he received Charles X Gustav's permission to seize the libraries of the Councillor of the Realm Otte Krag at Egeskov castle (of which he had only been in possession since 1656) and of Jørgen Seefeld.[83] Thus, after the Swedish troops reached Seeland in February 1658, Ulfeldt let his son Christian transport these libraries to his nearby manor house in Bavelse. At a later point in time, he shipped the books he had seized from Otte Krag and from Jørgen Seefeld to his house in Malmö. Books from Seefeld's library formed an important part of Ulfeldt's library.

Ulfeldt used the books from Seefeld's library as a weapon of revenge and as an interior decoration. According to what Seefeld himself wrote in a letter to Peter Julius Coyet from Bruges in May 1663, Corfitz Ulfeldt's library probably consisted of 700 volumes, and Seefeld claimed that most of them were rarities.[84] Otto Walde, however, does not see any reason to believe that Ulfeldt's library in itself differed from the libraries of his noble contemporaries.

Jørgen Seefeld tried to get his library back but never succeeded in doing so. According to the French diplomat Hugues de Terlon, a person in high esteem asked Terlon to save Seefeld's library. Ulfeldt offered to sell Seefeld his library at the price of 6,000 *rigsdaler*, but Seefeld did not want to pay for his rightful possession (even though it was, according to Terlon, worth 50,000 *rigsdaler*).[85]

With the peace treaty signed in Roskilde 26 February 1658, Denmark had to make huge territorial concessions to Sweden. Denmark lost the provinces Scania, Halland and Blekinge and the island of Bornholm, as well as the Norwegian provinces of Bohuslän and Trøndelag. War broke out again already six months later, and in the Treaty of Copenhagen (1660), Denmark regained the island of Bornholm in the Baltic Sea and the province of Trøndelag in Norway.

When Ulfeldt was eventually sentenced and escaped from Sweden in 1660, his library was seized and transported to the royal library in Stockholm. A major part of the library was thus lost in the fire of 1697. Nevertheless, parts of it had been given to the Antiquities Archive before the fire, and some

---

83 Heiberg, *Enhjørningen Corfitz Ulfeldt*, p. 154.
84 Bengt Bergius, David Ståhl and Jöns Lind, *Nytt Förråd af äldre och nyare handlingar rörande nordiska historien* (Stockholm: Jacob Merckell, 1753), p. 209 cf. Walde, *Storhetstidens litterära krigsbyten*, 2, pp. 395, 401–402.
85 Hugues de Terlon, *Mémoires du chevalier de Terlon: Pour rendre compte au Roy de ses Négociations, depuis l'année 1656 jusqu'en 1661* (Paris: chez la Veuve Louis Billaine, 1681), pp. 175–176.

volumes had been given to Emund Gripenhielm (1622–1675), who was the head of the royal library and received duplicates. After his death, the Bibliotheca Gripenhielmiana was given to Lund University Library.[86] After the dissolution of the Antiquities Archive in 1780, books were transferred to the royal library in Stockholm. Therefore, some books from Ulfeldt's library have survived in Stockholm and Lund.

Ulfeldt had not taken all of Seefeld's books, however. According to Zacharias Lund, Seefeld kept 4,000 books and soon acquired new ones. When war broke out again between Sweden and Denmark in August 1658, Peter Julius Coyet (1618–1667) obtained the permission to take possession of the rest of the library. These books were brought to Stockholm, and then to Coyet's manor Ljungbygaard (present-day Trolle-Ljungby) in Scania. Coyet, who was one of the Swedish delegates at the peace negotiation in Roskilde in 1658, had received the manor in 1662.[87] He donated some of the manuscripts to the Antiquities Archives in Uppsala, and decades after his death, his son, Wilhelm Julius Coyet (1649–1709), sold most of his fathers' remaining books at auctions in Stockholm and Uppsala during the years 1700–1701.

Some decades later, in 1710 during the Great Northern War, the Danish troops in Scania seized both the library and the archive of Ljungbygaard as war booty.[88] The manuscripts and archival material from Ljungbygaard were handed over to the Danish Royal Library, and the rest of the books were sold at an auction at which the Royal Library also acquired some of them. Some parts of the archival material were given to the Danish National Archives and other parts were exchanged with Sweden in 1929.[89] Thus, a number of books and manuscripts from the Coyet family are today in the Royal Danish Library and to some extent in other Danish collections. Among these items we can find some books and manuscripts from Jørgen Seefeld's library.

Thanks to his thorough research, Otto Walde was able to show that books from Seefeld's library originally from Ulfeldt's library can be found in the National Library of Sweden, in the Lund University Library, in the National Archives and in private collections.[90] Jørgen Seefeld had a characteristic *ex libris* with his family blason with three hearts on the shield, but he used it for

---

86  Jakob H. Grønbæk and Wolfgang Undorf, 'Dänemark und Schweden', in Bernhard Fabian et al. (eds.), *Handbuch deutscher historischer Buchbestände in Europa: Eine Übersicht über Sammlungen in ausgewählten Bibliotheken* (Hildesheim: Olms-Weidmann, 1998).
87  Dan H. Andersen, *Store Nordiske Krig* (Copenhagen: Politiken, 2021), p. 449.
88  Andersen, *Store Nordiske Krig*, p. 449.
89  Harald Ilsøe, *Det kongelige Bibliotek i støbeskeen: Studier og samlinger til bestandens historie indtil ca. 1780* (2 vols., Copenhagen: Det Kongelige Bibliotek & Museum Tusculanum Press, 1999), I, pp. 289–312.
90  Walde, *Storhetstidens litterära krigsbyten*, 2, pp. 396–397.

only few of his books.[91] Apparently, he did not as a rule write his name or other owner's marks in his books. In some of the manuscripts there is however an 'FS' on the binding.

In 2020 the Royal Danish Library acquired a book which, according to a previous owner, came from Seefeld's library: a copy of *Sjællandske Lov*, 1505.[92] On a flyleaf, the book contains the following proverbial spell that is also known from medieval manuscripts:

> Sorte Supernorum Scriptor libri potiatur
> Morte malignorum raptor libri moriatur.[93]

> The writer of a book obtains a celestial fate
> The robber of a book dies the death of the malignant.

Since the proverbial saying is dated 1632, it could be in Seefeld's handwriting, but this still remains to be tested by paleographical analysis. If it were written by Seefeld, it would have been a powerful prophecy of Ulfeldt's death.

## 6 A Danish War Booty: the Gottorp Library

In the present study, I have described various incidents involving libraries taken as war booty from Danish libraries. There is, however, also an important case of an entire library being taken by Danish troops as war booty: the Gottorp Library. During the seventeenth century the dukes at Gottorp Castle in Schleswig brought together a splendid library. The library (which drew upon previous possessions of the dukes) was founded as an institution in 1606 by Duke Johann Adolf (1575–1616) and was continued by his successors. It was particularly famous for its approximately 350 medieval manuscripts, but it also contained more than 10,000 printed books. Several of the medieval manuscripts and the incunabula came from the monasteries of Bordesholm and Cismar, which had been secularized after the Reformation.

---

91  See reproduction in Nielsen, *Danske Privatbiblioteker gennem Tiderne*, 1, p. 93.
92  *Sjællandske Lov* (Copenhagen: Gotfred af Ghemen, 1505), USTC 302266. Shelf mark: LN 133 copy 5.
93  Bénédictins du Bouveret, *Colophons de manuscrits occidentaux des origines au XVIe siècle*, 6: Anonymes, Spicilegii Friburgensis subsidia 2 (Fribourg: Ed. universitaires, 1982), p. 515 (no. 23589); Hans Walther, *Proverbia sententiaeque Latinitatis medii aevi. Lateinische Sprichwörter und Sentenzen des Mittelalters in alphabetischer Anordnung*, 5 (Göttingen: Vandenhoeck & Ruprecht, 1963), no. 30085, with bibliographical references.

In February 1713, during the Great Northern War (1700–1721), Gottorp Castle was taken by Danish troops, and the library became Danish booty of war. Between 1735 and 1749 the library was transferred (together with other cultural treasures which were incorporated into the royal collections) to the Royal Library. From Gottorp castle come the Royal Danish Library's copy of the Gutenberg bible, and many of its medieval manuscripts. The fragment of Lucretius *De rerum natura*, (GKS 211 folio, often referred to as *Schedae Gottorpienses*), which is one of the oldest manuscripts in the Royal Library, also comes from the Gottorp collection. The fragment was well known and was studied by scholars while it was still in Gottorp Castle. Substantial amounts of research have been done in recent years concerning provenances of the books from the library of Gottorp Castle.[94]

Not only the Royal Library but also the Royal Treasury collection benefited from the booty of war.[95] One object was not transferred to Copenhagen. The celebrated celestial globe, constructed in the years 1655–1657, was presented as a gift from King Frederick IV to Peter the Great and transferred to Saint Petersburg, where it was installed in the tower of the newly founded Kunstkamera in 1717.[96]

## 7  Dispersal and Collection

Dispersal and collection are to a certain extent two faces of the same coin. The dispersal of book collections often benefit other book collectors, in a manner that can be described with the old proverb 'unus colligit, alius collecta dispergit', (one collects, and the other one scatters what has been collected).[97]

---

[94] Erik Petersen, 'Bibliotheca Gottorpiensis Manuscripta: The Inventories of the Manuscripts of Gottorp', *Auskunft: Zeitschrift für Bibliothek, Archiv und Information in Norddeutschland*, 28:1 (2008), pp. 117–128; Karen Skovgaard-Petersen, 'Gottorp Books in the Royal Library of Copenhagen', pp. 131–147, and Ivan Boserup, 'Some New Ways to Identify Prints with a Gottorp Provenance in the Royal Library, Copenhagen', pp. 149–168, both in *Virtual Visits To Lost Libraries: Reconstruction of and Access To Dispersed Collections* (London: Consortium of European Research Libraries, 2011); Dieter Lohmeier, 'Die Gottorfer Bibliothek', in *Gottorf im Glanz des Barock, Kunst und Kultur am Schleswiger Hof, 1544–1713: Kataloge der Austellung zum 50-jährigen Bestehen des Schleswig-Holsteinischen Landesmuseum auf Schloss Gottorf und zum 400. Geburtstag Herzog Friedrichs III* (Schleswig: Holsteinisches Landesmuseum, 1997), pp. 325–348.

[95] Mogens Bencard and Jørgen Hein, *Krigsbytte fra Gottorp* (Copenhagen: Rosenborg, 1997).

[96] Andersen, *Store Nordiske Krig*, pp. 200–201.

[97] Andrew Pettegree and Arthur der Weduwen, *The Library: A Fragile History* (New York: Basic Books, 2021), p. 100.

Danish book collectors have profited from calamities in the rest of Europe. When Frederick III was creating the Royal Library after having ascended to the throne in 1648, the Danish book collector and public official Joachim Gersdorff tried to make Villum Lange buy books for the Royal Library at the auction of Mazarin's library (sold as a result of *La Fronde*), but Villum Lange arrived in Paris too late, long after the auction.[98] Queen Christina of Sweden (1626–1689) also aspired to buy books from the Mazarin library, but apparently the books remained in Paris, and she sold them back to Mazarin when he returned to power.[99]

Some Danish book collectors benefited indirectly from the Swedish war booty from the seventeenth century. In the eighteenth century, many of the most important Danish book collectors were present at the auction of the Strängnäs cathedral library in Stockholm in November and December 1763, and some of their purchases eventually ended up in public collections in Copenhagen. Victor Madsen identified 103 incunabula from that sale in the holdings of the Royal Library in Copenhagen, of which 52 had been bought by Otto Thott (1703–1785).[100] Many of the books from the Strängnäs cathedral library were Swedish war booty from the Thirty Years' War.

Some private libraries, such as the libraries of Heinrich Rantzau and the library of Jørgen Seefeld, benefited from books that were taken by force from ecclesiastical institutions. During the Thirty Years' War some of these private libraries were taken as war booty. This led to their dispersal as smaller book collections. The libraries as such were lost, but a small amount of books from these libraries survived. Many such printed books and manuscripts were on the move until some of them came to be preserved more permanently in public libraries.

The existence of libraries has been an important precondition for books to survive. But not even great public libraries are necessarily permanent locations for all books. Books in libraries also risk dispersal or removal, and perhaps more so now than just a few decades ago. Digitisation, which makes possible the ubiquitous presence of a simulacrum of one copy of an edition, has led to

---

98   As stated in a letter from Lange to Gersdorff written in Paris in the middle of 1652, cf. Carl S. Petersen, 'Marcus Meibom og Villum Lange: Et bidrag til Det Kongelige Biblioteks historie', *Fund og Forskning i Det Kongelige Biblioteks Samlinger*, 1 (1954), pp. 1–39.
99   Alfred Franklin, *Histoire de la Bibliothèque Mazarine et du Palais de l'Institut*, 2. éd. (Paris: Welter, 1901), pp. 100–101.
100  Victor Madsen, 'Strängnäs-dubletter i Det kongelige Bibliotek i København', *Nordisk tidskrift för bok- och biblioteksväsen*, 11 (1924), pp. 89–111; Otto Walde, 'Strängnäsdupletter m.m. i danska och norska bibliotek', *Nordisk tidskrift för bok- och biblioteksväsen*, 31 (1944), pp. 59–80.

the idea that one copy of an edition is sufficient and other copies of the same edition redundant. As a consequence, some public libraries are being dissolved and other public libraries are discarding historical collections. For instance, in Denmark, the Navy's Library, which was founded in 1765, was merged in 2010 with other libraries into a new entity called the Library of the Armed Forces (Forsvarets bibliotek), and some of its old manuscripts seem to have been sold in the process.[101]

In the first wave of digitisation, it was believed that this procedure could become a means to share cultural heritage through digital repatriation.[102] But digital repatriation was an oxymoron and would seem to remain a wishful metaphor. Digital reproduction could not completely replace the aura and the material significance of the physical object. In the Baltic area, there have been cases involving physical 'repatriations' of manuscripts on a small scale in recent years. In 2011, the Royal Danish Library received what was believed to be the earliest manuscript of the law of Jutland, Codex Holmiensis C37 (C 37), a manuscript in the Kungliga Biblioteket in Stockholm, in exchange for a manuscript of the Swedish provincial law, Södermannalagen (NKS 2237 4to).[103] There had been considerable pressure from the national conservative party Dansk Folkeparti (Danish People's Party) in favour of returning the manuscript, but, as the late head of the Royal Library, Erland Kolding Nielsen (1947–2017) observed, it was precisely the fact that the manuscript was not war-booty, that made the exchange possible.[104] In 2019, the government of Iceland created a task force for planning negotiations with Denmark about having more Icelandic manuscripts transported from Copenhagen to Iceland than had been delivered in the period 1971–1997, following an agreement from 1965.[105] Instead, in 2021, a Danish-Icelandic Working Group on Old Icelandic Manuscripts was created. The group would 'focus on ways to strengthen and

---

101   In 2021 the Royal Danish Library bought three manuscript copies of the Danish translation by Barthold Johan Lodde of J.B. d'Apres de Mannevillette, *Mémoire sur la navigation de France aux Indes* (1768), *Efterretning om Seilatsen fra Frankrig til Indien*. The three manuscripts used to be part of the collection of the Navy's Library and were mentioned as such in 1987 by Erik Gøbel, 'Asiatisk Kompagnis sejlads på Indien 1732–1772 (The Danish Asiatic Company's Voyages to India 1732–1772)', *Handels- og Søfartsmuseets Årbog*, 46 (1987), pp. 22–86, here p. 81.
102   Ivan Boserup, 'The Manuscript and the Internet: Digital Repatriation of Cultural Heritage', *IFLA Journal*, 31:2 (2005), pp. 169–173.
103   The signature in the Royal Danish Library is Acc. 2011/157.
104   Erland Kolding Nielsen, 'Jyske Lov som krigsbytte: En mytes opståen, udnyttelse og fald', *Fund og Forskning i Det Kongelige Biblioteks Samlinger*, 49 (2010), pp. 437–510, here p. 505.
105   Linda Corfitz Jensen and Morten Mikkelsen, 'Island beder Danmark udlevere flere verdensarv-håndskrifter'. *Kristeligt Dagblad*, 4 September 2019.

promote research regarding the manuscripts and the dissemination of the research'.[106] In 2021, the National Library of Norway requested medieval manuscripts from the Royal Danish library and from the Arnamagnæan Manuscript Collection at the University of Copenhagen for a permanent exhibition, but only the manuscripts from the Royal Danish Library were made available as temporary loans.[107] In spite of the fact that 2022 witnessed the outbreak of war in Europe, book battles in Scandinavia are not related to military conflict but rather to peaceful political negotiations concerning cultural heritage, a heritage which has been shaped by battles of the past and which is not stable but always under negotiation.

---

106 'Danish-Icelandic Working Group on Old Icelandic Manuscripts – memo April 2021', ufm .dk/aktuelt/nyheder/2021/filer/danish-icelandic-working-group-on-old-icelandic-manu scripts-memo-april-2021 (last accessed 17 March 2022).
107 Thomas Westergaard, 'Københavns Universitet afviser udlån af historiske dokumenter til Norge', www.dr.dk, 23 December 2021, www.dr.dk/nyheder/kultur/koebenhavns-univer sitet-afviser-udlaan-af-historiske-dokumenter-til-norge (last accessed 17 October 2022).

CHAPTER 11

# 'An Ornament for the Church and the Gymnasium'
## The War Booty in Strängnäs Cathedral and Its Relation to the School

*Elin Andersson*

Strängnäs cathedral library, located in the northwest corner of the church, is unique to Sweden as a church library of considerable size still housed within the cathedral premises.[1] Despite its having been diminished in the past by theft, fire and auction, the collection still consists of about two thousand volumes from the late middle ages to the 1750s.[2] Above all, the collection is defined by the large amount of war booty books (for example from Olomouc, Prague and Mikulov) that considerably enlarged the collection in the days of Johannes Matthiae, bishop of Strängnäs 1643–1664 and once teacher to the young Queen Christina (1626–1689).

The history of the cathedral library has been thoroughly studied on many occasions; in the early twentieth century, the historian and librarian Isak Fehr (1850–1929) successfully searched Swedish archives and libraries for source material regarding the history of the ancient Strängnäs collections kept in the

---

1  It may be added here that in recent years there has been an increased interest and focus on ancient books kept in Swedish parish churches; see for example Martin Kjellgren, 'Upp ur glömskan: Om antikvariska inventeringar av kyrkliga boksamlingar', *Biblis: Kvartalstidskrift för bokvänner*, 91 (2020), pp. 12–21. Of particular interest is a collection of Jesuit war booty books from Poland (Bydgoszcz, Toruń, Ostroh and Lutsk), donated by Schering Rosenhane (1609–1663) to the parish churches of Bärbo and Husby-Oppunda (Strängnäs diocese) in 1661. A small number of war booty books from Toruń and Lutsk donated to Bärbo are today kept in the parish house in nearby Stigtomta; the collection at Husby-Oppunda contains 97 war booty volumes and is still kept in the church, in a cabinet with the inscription *Bibliotheca Theologica*. Rosenhane wished for the library to be available for the parish priests *Nordisk tidskrift för bok- och biblioteksväsen*, 4 (1917), p. 240; Otto Walde, *Storhetstidens litterära krigsbyten: En kulturhistorisk-bibliografisk studie* (2 vols., Uppsala: Almqvist & Wiksell, 1916–1920), 2, pp. 153–155; Bengt-Ingmar Kilström, 'Husby-Oppunda kyrka', *Sörmländska kyrkor*, 67 (1996), p. 74; Björn Fröberg, *"Aller nådigste Herre": Familjen Rosenhane – en sörmländsk släktsaga under svensk stormaktstid* (Bettna: Rosenhanska sällskapet, 2008), pp. 190–193.
2  For a comprehensive history of Strängnäs cathedral library, see Ragnhild Lundgren, *Strängnäs domkyrkobibliotek: Systematisk katalog över tryckta böcker* (2 vols., Skellefteå: Artos, 2017), 1, pp. 19–28 (in English). The most in-depth account of the ancient Strängnäs libraries is found in [Isak Fehr], 'Strängnäs stift', in *Betänkande och förslag angående läroverks- och landsbibliotek* (Stockholm: Ecklesiastikdepartementet, 1924), pp. 171–218.

© ELIN ANDERSSON, 2023 | DOI:10.1163/9789004441217_013
This is an open access chapter distributed under the terms of the CC BY-NC-ND 4.0 license.

cathedral and the nearby Strängnäs gymnasium (upper secondary school).[3] It has often been stressed that the libraries of these two institutions have always belonged to different units, the cathedral and the school, while cathedral libraries in other Swedish cities (such as Växjö, Linköping or Västerås) have long since merged with the school libraries, and later with the municipal libraries.[4] However, although Strängnäs cathedral library has always had its own catalogue and for most of the time has been physically separated from the school library, the history of both collections is intertwined. In the present study, I aim to give a few examples of how the war booty placed in the cathedral library was used or regarded by the gymnasium. While it was originally intended to be a useful resource for the school, in reality, it did not take many decades for the cathedral library to become a static and closed collection that was hardly ever

FIGURE 11.1    Strängnäs Cathedral and Rogge Castle (*Collegium*, school house) from Erik Dahlbergh's *Suecia antiqua et hodierna*

---

3    On Isak Fehr, see Bengt Löw, 'Isak Nikolaus Fehr', in *Svenskt biografiskt lexikon*, 15 (Stockholm: Samfundet för svenskt biografiskt lexikons utgivande, 1956), p. 478.
4    The Strängnäs gymnasium library is since 1968 a part of the National Library of Sweden, under the name Roggebiblioteket (the Rogge library).

used, except in order to provide the economical means to enlarge the library of the gymnasium.

## 1 Strängnäs in the Seventeenth Century

In the seventeenth century, Strängnäs went through major changes: the gymnasium was founded in 1626, and a printing office was established about the same time. In 1648, Queen Christina granted tax relief for Strängnäs for a period of five years. The town now had the economic means to construct a new town hall in stone and establish a regulated street system.[5] This period of stability, expansion and modernization coincided with the time of service of Bishop Johannes Matthiae (1593–1670), whom the Queen favoured with titles, wealth and several estates.[6] In Strängnäs, Johannes Matthiae founded an orphanage as well as village schools for young children, initiated the roofing of Strängnäs cathedral with copper, and at the end of the 1640s constructed the bishop's palace, since then the home of his successors.[7] The medieval choirs in the Cathedral were transformed into crypts for prominent families during the course of the seventeenth century; the north-west choir of the church was claimed by Johannes Matthiae himself.[8] Here, the bishop organised his *selectior bibliotheca* (see below) as well as the war booty books the cathedral received from Queen Christina, and, presumably, the older (late medieval) parts of the cathedral library as well. Johannes Matthiae's family crypt is located underneath the floor of the cathedral library, which further connects his person to this very part of the building and the books kept there.

To summarise, the cathedral library we see today consists of several collections put together over time: the 'medieval' library with manuscripts and printed books donated in the fifteenth and sixteenth centuries by bishops, priest and lay persons; the war booty books that arrived after the Thirty Years' War; a few additional volumes added in the seventeenth and eighteenth centuries, and finally, Johannes Matthiae's own section in the library. After a fire

---

5  Sigurd Wallin, 'Stadsbilden' in Hans Jägerstad (ed.), *Strängnäs stads historia* (Strängnäs: Oskar Erikssons bokhandel, 1959), pp. 137–270, here p. 202.
6  For example, the manor Janslunda on the island Selaön near Strängnäs is named after Johannes Matthiae.
7  Hans Cnattingius, 'Biskoppssäte, domkyrka och kloster: Tiden 1563 till våra dagar', in *Strängnäs stads historia*, pp. 546–580, here p. 561.
8  Isak Fehr, *Strängnäs. Det forna och det nuvarande* (Strängnäs: Oskar Erikssons bokhandel, 1910), p. 21.

that severely damaged the cathedral library in 1864, at the time kept in the old printing office next to the church, hundreds of books were repaired and given the similar covers that today give the library a uniform appearance. Johannes Matthiae's books stand out for the visitor as they are kept in a separate bookshelf and are marked 'J. Matthiae,' followed by a serial number.

## 2    The Arrival of War Booty Books in Strängnäs: the Cathedral and the School

Strängnäs gymnasium (upper secondary school) was established in 1626 by royal mandate from King Gustavus Adolphus, with Strängnäs bishop Laurentius Paulinus Gothus (1565–1646) as the driving force.[9] From the very beginning, the school was in need of books. In a letter to Axel Oxenstierna dated 1 August 1634, Laurentius Paulinus explicitly asked for books taken as war booty to enrich the collections in his diocese. In Paulinus' words, God himself by His grace had helped the Swedes to capture the enemies' 'famous collegia and beautiful libraries, which they misuse in order to suppress true religion, but here [in Strängnäs] they may come to proper use.'[10] The question of *useful books* (or sometimes the opposite) became associated with the cathedral library on many occasions; however, when the war booty books arrived in Strängnäs, they were not placed in the school, but in the cathedral. The close relation between Johannes Matthiae and Queen Christina was most likely one important reason for this. A practical reason might also have been accessibility: the schoolhouse was partly occupied by the local printing office, and space

---

9    On the history of Strängnäs gymnasium, see Albert Falk (ed.), *Regium Gustavianum Gymnasium Strengnense MDCXXVI–MCMXXVI* (Strängnäs: Strängnäs läroverkskollegium, 1926), pp. 1–16. See also Erland Sellberg, 'Humanist Learning and the Reformation on the Bookshelves', in Lundgren, *Strängnäs domkyrkobibliotek*, 1, pp. 39–49; for an account of the Swedish education system in the seventeenth and eighteenth centuries, see Axel Hörstedt, *Latin Dissertations and Disputations in the Early Modern Swedish Gymnasium: A Study of Latin School Tradition c.1620–c.1820* (PhD, dissertation, University of Gothenburg, 2018), pp. 25–32.

10   Herman Lundström, *Laurentius Paulinus Gothus: Hans lif och verksamhet* (Uppsala: Almqvist & Wiksell, 1893), pp. 230–231; Sellberg, 'Humanist Learning', pp. 41–42; the concept of 'proper use' has been discussed by Emma Hagström Molin, 'The Materiality of War Booty Books: The case of Strängnäs cathedral library', in Anna Källén (ed.), *Making cultural history: New perspectives on Western Heritage* (Lund: Nordic Academic Press, 2013), pp. 131–140, p. 131.

was limited (of which more below).[11] Perhaps it was also a question of continuity; the school library was still very small, while the cathedral library had a long history to build on.

The discrepancy between the cathedral library and the school library when it comes to war booty books is striking: while there are hundreds of war booty volumes in the cathedral, very few are to be found in the school library (today's *Roggebiblioteket*), and most of them seem to have been incorporated into the school library via donations in the eighteenth and nineteenth centuries.[12] Below is a table of books in today's *Roggebiblioteket* with war booty provenance.

TABLE 11.1   Books in Roggebiblioteket with war booty provenance

| War booty provenance | Title | Later provenance; USTC number |
|---|---|---|
| Jesuit college, Olomouc | Lonicer, *Graece grammaticae methodus* (Basle, 1536) | Blue nineteenth-century covers, possibly purchased by the school around that time.[a] USTC 660206. |
| Dietrichstein library, Mikulov (Nikolsburg) | Tertullianus' *Opera* (Paris, 1580) | Part of a large donation to the school library by the Latin professor and priest Carl Johan Lundvall (1775–1858).[b] USTC 170530. |
| Julius Echter von Mespelbrunn, prince bishop of Würzburg | Theofylaktos, *Hermeneia eis ta tessara euaggelia* (Rome, 1542) | Owner's notes by Ingemund Bröms (1669–1722), professor in Pärnu and Turku, lecturer at Strängnäs gymnasium around 1700.[c] USTC 858975. |

a   Per-Olof Samuelsson, *Inkunabler och 1500-talstryck ("vaggtryck" och "koltålderstryck") i Roggebiblioteket* (Strängnäs: Roggebiblioteket, 2009), p. 44; accessible online via www.kb.se/besok-och-anvand/roggebibliioteket.html (last accessed 15 March 2022).
b   Fehr, 'Strängnäs stift', p. 210; www.krigsbyte.lib.cas.cz (last accessed 22 November 2022); record number DK 418; Samuelsson, *Inkunabler och 1500-talstryck*, p. 19.
c   Samuelsson, *Inkunabler och 1500-talstryck*, p. 17.

11   Vårdprogram Roggeborgen (unpublished: Statens fastighetsverk, 2008).
12   See also Fehr, 'Strängnäs stift', pp. 212–213. The school library grew considerably through donations from private persons in the eighteenth and nineteenth centuries; for an overview of the history of the school library, see Elin Andersson, 'Inledning', in Elin Andersson and Emil Stenback, *Böckerna i borgen: Ett halvsekel i Roggebiblioteket* (Stockholm: Kungliga biblioteket, 2018), pp. 9–27.

TABLE 11.1    Books in Roggebiblioteket with war booty provenance (cont.)

| War booty provenance | Title | Later provenance; USTC number |
|---|---|---|
| Julius Echter von Mespelbrunn, prince bishop of Würzburg | Antonius Musa Brasavolus, *De medicamentis ... catharticis* (Venice, 1552) | Owner's notes from 1634 mentioning a certain Erich Larson.[d] USTC 816781. |
| St Kilian's seminar in Würzburg.[e] | Josephus Flavius, *Opera* (Frankfurt, 1580) | Provenance from Samuel Aurelius (1669–1742) and M. Abrahamus Nagelius Gamundianus ('from Gmünd'). On the cover: M A N 1583.[f] USTC 679627. |
| Jesuit college, Braniewo | Lukianos, *Meros proton Luciani Samosatensis pars prima* (Hagenau, 1535) | Included in a large donation from Strängnäs bishop Johan Adam Tingstadius (1748–1827).[g] USTC 673665. |
| Jesuit college, Toruń | Alexander Scot, *Apparatus latinae locutionis* (Geneva, 1612) | No information on later provenance available. Not registered in USTC. |
| Jesuit college, Poznán | Filon of Alexandria, *Opera* [Φίλωνος Ιουδαίου εις τα του Μωσεως – *Philonis Ivdæi in libros Mosis*], (Paris, 1552) | Cover exlibris of Gabriel Szadkovius (professor in Cracow around 1560). Donated to the school library by the heirs of Strängnäs bishop Daniel Lundius (1666–1747).[h] USTC 151178. |
| Dominican convent, Poznán | Sante Pagnini, *Thesaurus linguae sanctae* (Lyon, 1577) | Posthumous donation to the school library by Johan Kumblaeus (1714–60), priest in Torshälla (diocese of Strängnäs).[i] USTC 141471. |

d   Samuelsson, *Inkunabler och 1500-talstryck*, p. 58.
e   The volume is not listed by Walde, who only mentions one volume from Saint Kilian's seminar in Swedish collections: Pius II, *Epistolae familiares* (Cologne, 1478) kept at Uppsala university library; Otto Walde, *Storhetstidens litterära krigsbyten*, 1, p. 125; Fehr, 'Strängnäs stift', p. 212.
f   Samuelsson, *Inkunabler och 1500-talstryck*, p. 18.
g   Samuelsson, *Inkunabler och 1500-talstryck*, p. 48. On Tingstadius, see Fehr, 'Strängnäs stift', p. 209.
h   Samuelsson, *Inkunabler och 1500-talstryck*, p. 25; 107.
i   Samuelsson, *Inkunabler och 1500-talstryck*, p. 23.

TABLE 11.1  Books in Roggebiblioteket with war booty provenance (*cont.*)

| War booty provenance | Title | Later provenance; USTC number |
| --- | --- | --- |
| Sigismund III (1566–1632)? | Claude de Sainctes, *De rebus eucharistiae controversis* (Paris, 1576) | Donated to the school library in 1751 by a certain Johan Hallman Samuelsson.[j] A note in the volume, 'Ex Ill[mi] principis', led Isak Fehr to the conclusion that the volume had previously belonged to Sigismund III. USTC 170309. |
| Sigismund III (1566–1632) | Augustinus, *Opera* I–II (Basle, 1569) | With the note 'Ex libris Serenissimi regis Sigismundi'. Owner's notes from Erik Castovius (1655–1703), professor in philosophy at Uppsala university. The volume was included in a donation from Strängnäs bishop Thure Annerstedt (1806–1881).[k] USTC 686573. |
| Sigismund II August (1520–72) | Hesiodos, *Opera* (Basle, 1544). | A donation from Strängnäs teacher and dean Isak Samuel Widebeck (1801–1863).[l] Provenance note from Georg Stiernhielm (1598–1672). USTC 662387. |
| Sigismund II August (1520–72) | Alexander ab Alexadro, *Dies geniales* (Cologne, 1539) | In the library section containing books donated in the 1720s by the rector Josef Thun (1661–1721).[m] Shelfmark 2:25. Previously owned by Gustavus Esberni Maræus (d. 1678), priest and teacher in the diocese of Strängnäs.[n] Not registered in USTC. |

j  Fehr, 'Strängnäs stift', p. 213 (footnote 3); Samuelsson, *Inkunabler och 1500-talstryck*, p. 21.
k  Samuelsson, *Inkunabler och 1500-talstryck*, p. 18.
l  Samuelsson, *Inkunabler och 1500-talstryck*, p. 47; 117.
m  Per-Olof Samuelsson, *Bibliotheca Thuniana: Katalog över Roggebibliotekets äldsta bokdonation* (Strängnäs: Roggebiblioteket, 2009), accessible online via www.kb.se/besok-och-anvand/roggebiblioteket.html (last accessed 15 March 2022). Josef Thun's library is considered to be the first major book donation to the school; Ruth Lundström, 'Josef Thun och Bibliotheca Thuniana: Anteckningar vid inventeringen av Roggebibliotekets första donation', in Ruth Lundström (ed.), *Från biskop Rogge till Roggebiblioteket* (Stockholm: Kungliga biblioteket, 1976), p. 112; Johanna Akujärvi, 'Greek Occasional Poetry from the Swedish Empire: The Case of Josef Thun', in Arne Jönson et al. (eds.), *Att dikta för livet, döden och evigheten: Tillfällesdiktning under tidigmodern tid* (Göteborg: Makadam, 2020), pp. 61–86.
n  Samuelsson, *Bibliotheca Thuniana* p. 9; Samuelsson, *Inkunabler och 1500-talstryck*, p. 108.

TABLE 11.1  Books in Roggebiblioteket with war booty provenance (cont.)

| War booty provenance | Title | Later provenance; USTC number |
|---|---|---|
| Rosenberg library, Prague | Arrianos, *De Epicteti ... dissertationibus* (Basle, 1554) | Josef Thun's donation (shelfmark 4:16).[o] USTC 613168. |
| Jesuit College, Riga | Cornelis Jansen, *Commentarii in suam concordiam* (Lyon, 1577) | Josef Thun' donation (shelfmark 2:13; purchased in Uppsala, 1701). The book originally belonged to the Jesuit college in Vilnius.[p] USTC 141438. |
| Jesuit college in Bydgoszcz (Bromberg) | Dio Cassius, *Romaïka* (Hannover, 1606) | Josef Thun's donation (shelfmark 2:7), via Conrad Ribbing (1671–1736) and Johan Scheringsson Rosenhane (1672–1710).[q] USTC 2027386. |
| Jesuit college in Bydgoszcz (Bromberg) | Christophorus Clavius, *In sphaeram Ioannis de Sacro Bosco commentarius* (Saint-Gervais, 1608) | To the school library via Ioannes Polanski; Sven Gabriel Hedin; Samuel Widebeck; lector Lindman 1864. USTC 6810827. |
| Jakob Conrad Praetorius von Perlenberg, Mikulov (Nikolsburg)[r] | Vergilius, *Opera* (Paris, 1512) | Josef Thun's donation (shelfmark 2:22). Cover exlibris: D. Iacobvs Conrad Prætorivs.[s] USTC 203048. |
| Jesuit college, Lutsk (Łuck) | Horatius, *Opera*[t] = *Dionysii lambini monstroliensis regii professoris, in q. Horatium flaccum commentariis auctis, atque amplificatis, illustratum* (Frankfurt, 1596). | The words 'Collegij Luceorien[sis] Soc. Jesu' have been crossed out. The volume was a posthumous donation to the school library from Daniel Magnus Ahlgren (1727–1817), lecturer in Strängnäs and doctor in theology.[u] UTSC 637645. |

o   Samuelsson, *Bibliotheca Thuniana* p. 12; www.krigsbyte.lib.cas.cz (last accessed 20 November 2022), record number: RK 622.
p   *Catalogue of the Riga Jesuit College Book Collection (1583–1621): History and Reconstruction of the Collection*, eds. Gustavs Strenga and Andris Levāns (Riga: Latvijas Nacionālā bibliotēka, 2021), pp. 378–379.
q   Samuelsson, *Bibliotheca Thuniana*, p. 5.
r   Walde, *Storhetstidens litterära krigsbyten*, 1, p. 249; www.krigsbyte.lib.cas.cz (last accessed 20 November 2022), record number: DK 731.
s   Samuelsson, *Bibliotheca Thuniana*, p. 8.
t   The title used in Samuelsson's catalogue.
u   Fehr, 'Strängnäs stift', p. 213, footnote 2; Samuelsson, *Inkunabler och 1500-talstryck*, p. 50.

## 3   The Systematically Organised Library and Johannes Matthiae's *Selectior Bibliotheca*

When it comes to the arrival of the war booty books to the cathedral library around 1650, an early eyewitness account is the diary of the priest Petrus Gyllenius (1622–1675). In an entry dated 21 June 1652, Gyllenius mentions a visit to Strängnäs cathedral, where he admired 'the great library' (*thet stoora Librijt*).[13] This is one of the earliest descriptions of the war booty books put on public display in the cathedral. Unfortunately, much of the source material regarding the arrival of the war booty books has since long been lost. The earliest extant catalogue is a bound manuscript volume produced by Laurentz Fredrik Peringer (d. 1686) in 1674.[14] This catalogue largely follows the classification system drawn up by Christina's cataloguer, Isaac Vossius, which must have been put in use in Strängnäs at an early stage.[15] Seventeenth century sources also mention a number of other catalogues, for example, one dated 1649, but none of these volumes have survived.[16]

The oldest extant catalogue, dated 1674, does not include manuscripts from the 'old' library. Some pages have been cut out, and it is possible that those volumes were one listed there. The catalogue ends with a list of books from Johannes Matthiae's section in the library entitled *Selectior bibliotheca ex liberalitate doctoris Johannis Matthiae episcopi boni, optimi, in hujus monumenti templique ornamentum sue apposita*. In preserved acts from the 1660s, Johannes Matthiae maintained that most of the books in this part of the library were bought at his own expense. They were most likely always meant to make up a separate part of the collection, but since all documentation about Johannes Matthiae's library has been lost, it is impossible to outline the conditions of its earliest origins.[17] Furthermore, there are no writings or notes

---

13   Reinhold Hansen (ed.), *Diarium Gyllenianum* (Helsinki: Finska statsarkivet, 1882), p. 182.
14   Fehr, 'Strängnäs stift', p. 189.
15   On Vossius and his catalogue, see Christian Callmer, *Königin Christina, ihre Bibliothekare und ihre Handschriften* (Stockholm: Kungliga biblioteket, 1977); Eva Nilsson Nylander, *The Mild Boredom of Order: A Study in the History of the Manuscript Collection of Queen Christina of Sweden* (Lund: Lund University, 2011), pp. 94–104; Christian Callmer (ed.), *Catalogus codicum manu scriptorum bibliothecae regiae Holmiensis c. annum MXCL ductu et auspicio Isaac Vossii conscriptus* (Stockholm: Norstedts, 1971); on Vossius' classification system transferred to Strängnäs, see Otto Walde, 'Strängnäsdupletter m.m. i danska och norska bibliotek', *Nordisk tidskrift för bok- och biblioteksväsen*, 31 (1944), pp. 60–61; Molin, 'The Materiality of War Booty Books', pp. 135–136.
16   Fehr, 'Strängnäs stift', pp. 182–183; Lundgren, *Strängnäs domkyrkobibliotek*, 1, pp. 21–22.
17   Fehr, 'Strängnäs stift', pp. 180; 184–185. For a discussion on the contents of Johannes Matthiae's library, see Erland Sellberg, 'Humanist Learning', pp. 39–60, pp. 39–49.

in Johannes Matthiae's hand in the part of the library that bears his name.[18] There are also books in his *selectior bibiotheca* that originally did not belong to this section at all, such as the *Scriptores rei rusticae* (JM 51 fol), a beautifully decorated volume printed in Venice in 1472. It was previously owned by Reinhold Ragvaldsson (d. 1599), dean of Strängnäs cathedral, and donated to the cathedral library by his son-in-law. In some cases, books have moved in the opposite direction: a copy of the *Missale Upsalense* (Basle, 1513) once belonged to Johannes Matthiae's section, according to the 1674 catalogue, but the only copy in the library today is located together with other missals in the part of the library that follows Vossius' system (A–X).[19] It may also be added that there are very few war booty books in Johannes Matthiae's section, which perhaps further confirms his own statement that he himself had purchased most of the books in this section.[20]

Two volumes stand out in Johannes Matthiae's bookshelf and are instantly recognizable: the *Missale Moguntinum* (JM 35 fol; Mainz, 1602)[21] and a Bible in Finnish (JM 34 fol; Stockholm, 1642).[22] They are both bound in red velvet covers, a fact already noted in the 1674 catalogue.[23] The nineteenth-century cataloguer Henrik Aminson supposed (a conjecture most likely based on the red velvet binding) that the missal had once been given to Queen Christina, and presumably that it at some point became a personal gift from her to Johannes Matthiae; the assumption is repeated in Ragnhild Lundgren's systematic catalogue of printed works (2017).[24] Cathedral librarian and theologian Carl-Gösta Frithz (1932–1995) argued that the volume was originally a war booty, taken when the Swedes ransacked Mainz in 1631.[25] On this occasion, Johannes Matthiae was present as field chaplain, personally assigned by the king to search the libraries in Mainz for books. Frithz therefore argues that the volume either was given to the bishop by Queen Christina, together with

---

18   Fehr, 'Strängnäs stift', p. 187.
19   Fehr, 'Strängnäs stift', p. 201. On the different parts of the library and how they have been intertwined, see also Emma Hagström Molin, 'The Materiality of War Booty Books', pp. 136–137.
20   Fehr, 'Strängnäs stift', p. 184.
21   USTC 2078607.
22   USTC 2178828.
23   The 1674 catalogue notes them as 'Biblia Finnonica holoserico involuta [bound in silk]' and 'Missale Romanum Moguntinum holoser. involutum'.
24   Henrik Aminson, *Bibliotheca templi cathedralis Strengnesensis* (Stockholm: Isaac Marcus, 1863–1864), *Supplementum*, p. cxxii: 'Si conjicere licet, hoc exemplar ita mutilatum Christinae Reginae traditum est.' Lundgren, *Strängnäs domkyrkobibliotek*, 1, no. 3624.
25   Carl-Gösta Frithz, 'Ett märkligt Missale Moguntinum', *Kyrkohistorisk årsskrift* (1981), pp. 52–61.

other war booty books, or, more likely, that Johannes Matthiae acquired it for himself in Mainz 1631. Since the first flyleaves show a watermark from the archbishopric of Mainz, Frithz considers the binding to be original; however, he does not include the Finnish Bible, with exactly the same type of binding, in the discussion.[26] Since the volumes appear in similar velvet covers and have been kept next to each other since the very beginning, it is likely that they arrived in Strängnäs together. At any rate, the Mainz missal is the only volume that cataloguers have associated with Queen Christina because of its outward appearance.

The war booty in Strängnäs cathedral library has been subject to thorough research and cataloguing efforts.[27] Still, the collection holds many items with uncertain provenances. One interesting case is the volume *Horae: ad usum Romanum* (signum U 575 oct.), a remarkably beautiful and extremely rare book of hours, printed in Naples by Conradus Guldenmund in 1477 (see figure 11.2, p. 340).

According to book historian Isak Collijn, this volume may have belonged to the war booty given to the library by Queen Christina. Since the book was badly damaged in the 1864 fire, any previous notes on provenance have disappeared.[28] Collijn bases this assumption upon hand-written additions of feast days in the volume's calendar that can be linked to the diocese of Salzburg, and argues that the volume first belonged to a community in said diocese, whence it at some point made its way to Olomouc, perhaps to the Franciscan convent, from which there are about 30 titles in Strängnäs cathedral library.[29]

---

26  One of the flyleaves in the Finnish Bible has a water mark from the nineteenth-century Forssa paper mill, which shows that it has been repaired at a much later stage, most likely after the fire in 1864.

27  See for example the database on the Czech war booty (*The Swedish Booty of Books from Bohemia and Moravia 1646–1648*) by Lenka Veselá (as well as her chapter in the present volume): www.knizni-korist.cz/ (last accessed 15 March 2022); Maria Juda, Ewa Teodorowicz-Hellman, Ragnhild Lundgren, *Polonika w bibliotece katedralnej w Strängnäs* [= *The Polonica in the Library of Strängnäs Cathedral*] (Stockholm: Stockholm University, Department of Slavic Languages and Literatures, 2011).

28  'Non v'ha dubbio che il piccolo volume ... faccia pure parte dei libri donati alla Cattedrale di Strängnäs dalla Regina Cristina', Isak Collijn, 'La prima impressione di Corrado Guldenmund a Napoli', *La Bibliofilia*, 27 (1926), pp. 3–7, here p. 5. Aminson's catalogue, printed shortly before the fire, does not give any information on provenance for this volume.

29  34 titles, according to the database of war booty from the Czech lands; www.krigsbyte.lib.cas.cz/ (last accessed 27 January 2022). Among the feast days added by hand, we find Saint Rupert of Salzburg (27 March and 24 September); Sigismundus rex (2 May, patron saint of Bohemia); Stanislaus of Szczepanów (7 May); Saint Virgil of Salzburg (27 November); Collijn, 'La prima impressione', pp. 6–7.

'AN ORNAMENT FOR THE CHURCH AND THE GYMNASIUM' 253

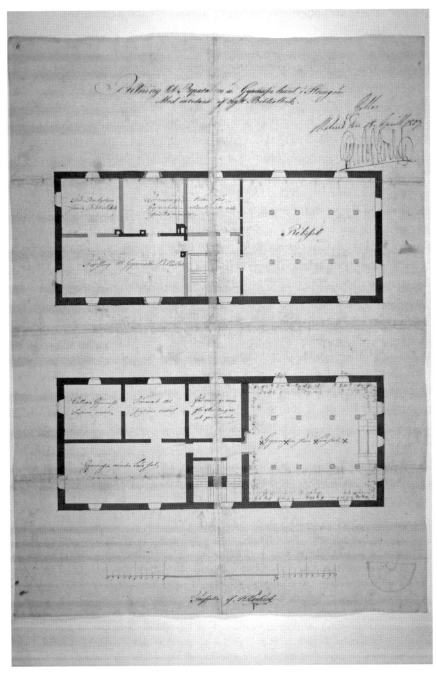

FIGURE 11.3  A prospect for the disposition of rooms in Strängnäs Gymnasium 1807. Landsarkivet, Uppsala. Note that the cathedral library is to be kept separately in one of the smaller rooms (*För Domkyrkans Gamla Bibliothek*, 'For the Old Library of the Cathedral.')

## 4 Strängnäs Volumes in Vossius' Catalogue – and a Retrieved Manuscript

Isaac Vossius' catalogue of the royal library was produced 1650–1651 and encompassed the manuscripts in the royal library, as well as the printed works A–F. Two volumes of the books listed in Vossius' catalogue are pointed out by Christian Callmer as being part of Strängnäs cathedral library today. One of the books (shelfmark F 74 Q a) is a collection of printed works, containing, for example, Adam Francisci Carnovius (1540–1593), *Hortulus Filii Dei*, printed in Wittenberg in 1566.[30] The volume has owner's notes from one Georg Wilisch, whom I have not been able to identify. The other book is a small manuscript, *Iglaviensium compactatorum expositio* (MS 21).[31] This manuscript contains the so-called 'Jihlava compact', an agreement between the Catholic Church and the Bohemian Hussites promulgated in Jihlava in 1436, and was copied by the Humanist author Matthaeus Collinus (1516–1566).[32] Beda Dudík studied this manuscript during his visit to Strängnäs in 1850; in contemporary Czech research, the manuscript is considered to have been lost in the Strängnäs town fire of 1871.[33] In fact, the 1871 fire did not affect the library at all; as mentioned above, the fire that damaged or destroyed the books in the cathedral library took place in December 1864 and was limited to the library building where the collection was kept at the time.[34] However, the manuscript seems to have been misplaced for some time afterwards, perhaps as a result of the relocation of the library in 1910. A note attached to the manuscript, written by the priest

---

30   Christian Callmer (ed.), *Catalogus codicum manu scriptorum bibliothecae regiae Holmiensis c. annum MXCL ductu et auspicio Isaac Vossii conscriptus* (Stockholm: Norstedts, 1971), p. 203.

31   Strängnäs Cathedral Library MS 21; Callmer, *Catalogus*, p. 203; Callmer, *Königin Christina*, p. 121.

32   On the cover of the manuscript are written the following words: *Scripsit hanc compactatorum expositionem propria manu clarissimus vir, dominus Math. Collinus Pragae*. On Collinus, see Lucie Storchová, 'Collinus, Matthaeus', in Lucie Storchová (ed.), *Companion to Central and Eastern European Humanism*, 2: The Czech Lands (Berlin: De Gruyter, 2020), pp. 298–316; on the authorship of *De Compactatis*, see p. 314.

33   On Dudík's travels in Sweden and Rome, see Emma Hagström Molin, 'Skattjakten: Beda Dudíks sökande efter Mährens historia i Stockholm och Rom 1851–1853', *Biblis: Kvartalstidskrift för bokvänner*, 77 (2017), pp. 2–11; on the manuscript, Adam Palka, *Super responso Pii pape: Martina Lupáče jako historický pramen* (Master's thesis, Masaryk University, 2014), p. 43; I wish to express my gratitude to Lenka Veselá, who provided me with the information on this source.

34   A police report after the fire, issued 22 December 1864, is kept at Landsarkivet, Uppsala (Strängnäs rådhusrätt och magistrat); see below.

and cathedral librarian Mats Åmark (1882–1973), informs us that he found the Jihlava manuscript among 'catalogue fragments' in 1930.

5    The Proceedings Against Johannes Matthiae and the Concept of 'Useful Books'

Following religious controversies that we will not dwell on here, Johannes Matthiae was forced to resign as bishop in 1664.[35] Documents from the proceedings against him are preserved in Uppsala University Library and give many interesting insights regarding the cathedral library and how it was used at the time, when about fifteen years had passed since the war booty books first arrived in Strängnäs.[36] Teachers (in the acts referred to as *consistoriales*) from the gymnasium were interrogated on many occasions by the committee. As pointed out by Fehr, their statements are filled with contradictions. For example, Petrus Grubb (d. 1686), lecturer at the gymnasium, referred to the war booty books as 'the library from Ulm' (in the margin noted as a probable mistake for Olomouc). The teachers furthermore accused the bishop for keeping the library in bad order, and it was remarked that although the collection was large, there were not many *useful* books to be found on the shelves. Johannes Matthiae, in turn, refuted these remarks by pointing out that the library, intended as an 'ornament for the church and the gymnasium', was kept in good order in a bright, beautiful choir, and that the catalogue was placed on the table, accessible for everyone. The teachers, on the other hand, had borrowed books from the library on many occasions, and kept them for years.[37] If the books were so useless, why did the schoolteachers (with obvious sarcasm referred to as *homines litterati* by the bishop) keep books from the library without returning them?

As mentioned above, the crypt of Johannes Matthiae and his family is located under the library choir in the north-west corner of the church. After Johannes Matthiae's death, the responsibility for the library was transferred to family members, who neglected the task and left the library in disarray. In addition, Johannes Matthiae's bitter enemy, Erik Emporagius (1606–1674), succeeded him as bishop, and he seems to have been primarily interested in the

---

35   See further Sellberg, 'Humanist Learning'.
36   Uppsala University Library, X 276 (*Acta in caussa Reverendissimi Domini Episcopi Strengnensis Doct. Johannis Matthiae, anno 1663*); Fehr, 'Strängnäs stift', pp. 180–185. Note that Fehr gives the wrong shelfmark (X 267).
37   Notably, Mercator's *Atlas* is mentioned (JM 1).

'old' part of the library (the medieval manuscripts and early prints donated to the library in the fifteenth and sixteenth century).[38] The 'medieval' library seems to have moved back and forth to the Upper Sacristy at the turn of the century, and it was probably during this period that the different parts of the library first became mixed up.[39] It may also be noted that new acquisitions were made around this time: an addendum in the 1674 catalogue lists books that were added to the collection in 1706, among which we find works like Johannes Messenius' *Scondia illustrata* (1700) and Johannes Loccenius' *Sveciae leges civiles in linguam latinam traductae* (1672). All works on the list are printed in Stockholm; many of the titles added in 1706 are still to be found in the collection.[40]

## 6  The 1704 Theft

Teachers obviously borrowed and used books from the cathedral in Johannes Matthiae's time, but how known was the collection to the students? An interesting episode in the history of Strängnäs cathedral library and its relation to the school and its students occurred in 1704, when three pupils broke into the library on a number of occasions and stole dozens of books in various formats and sizes. According to the subsequent investigation by the town magistrate, 96 books were stolen.[41] Above all, the students seem to have seized books in smaller formats, simply because they were easier to carry. The lengthy acts dealing with the process give the impression that, first and foremost, the theft was an impulsive act of youthful curiosity: the students probably had no idea what they were after. This fact was also underlined by the court, which stated that the three students had wanted 'to see and to read all kinds of foreign books

---

38  Fehr, 'Strängnäs stift', pp. 188. It may be briefly noted here that Johannes Matthiae's family crypt was in a very poor state when it was reopened in 1909: several coffins were broken, and the bones of various individuals were scattered over the floor; Robert Bennett and Erik Bohrn, *Strängnäs domkyrka: Gravminnen* (Stockholm: Almqvist & Wiksell, 1974), p. 61.
39  Fehr, 'Strängnäs stift', pp. 189–190.
40  Johannes Messenius, Johan Hadorph, *Twå gambla svenske rijm-krönikor* (Stockholm: Niclas Wankijf, 1674–76), shelfmark K 267 q and Johannes Sleidanus (translated by Johannes Sylvius), *Historie-book* (Stockholm: Niclas Wankijf, 1675), K 405 fol.; Johannes Messenius, *Scondia illustrata* (Stockholm: Olaus Enaeus, 1700–1703), K 402 fol., Johannes Cochlaeus, *Vita Theoderici* (Stockholm: Olaus Enaeus, 1699), K 270 q.
41  Landsarkivet, Uppsala, Strängnäs rådhusrätt och magistrat 1704 ('wahrandes till antalet uti åskilliga formater 96').

that they did not know anything about.'[42] For example, one of the students had previously pawned a pair of trousers to a fellow classmate, but was now able to get his clothes back in exchange for one of the stolen volumes.[43]

Only a few works were described in the investigation: 'a Finnish Bible' that one of the boys threw into the water after a failed attempt to sell it in Stockholm, maps torn from Mercator's *Atlas*,[44] 'German calendars', parchment leaves, a volume containing works by Roberto Bellarmino and 'a Jesuit book in folio, *De virgine deipara*'.[45] Unfortunately, 'the Jesuit book' was destroyed by one of the students, since he believed that it would be difficult to sell.

The proceedings against the three young boys were lengthy and emotional; the youngest of the three was only 15 years old. Although the thieves claimed that they had planned to return the books to the library, the court found them guilty of having stolen and destroyed Church property, a most serious crime, and they were all sentenced to death (later changed to prison terms).[46] The aftermath of the sad events in 1704 at least had a fruitful outcome: the librarian was now given the task to oversee the collection, including the old cathedral library, by that time kept in the Upper Sacristy.[47]

At the same time, the school library was still quite small. The local printing office supplied the students with literature needed for their lessons and a large number of such books were stored in the schoolhouse, but they were not regarded as part of the school library *per se*.[48] In 1704, the cathedral library was by far the larger library of the two, but the nature of the books kept there seems to have been quite unknown to the students. The statement by the court mentioned above underlines the fact that the cathedral library was regarded primarily as church property and not part of the school.

---

42   Landsarkivet, Uppsala, Strängnäs rådhusrätt och magistrat 1704 ('att see och läsa allehanda främmande Böcker som dem alldrig bekante wahrit').
43   Sune Cairén, 'Bokstölden i domkyrkan', in *Bland borgmästare och stadsbönder: Strängnäs Gilles skriftserie*, 25 (1990), pp. 43–50, p. 48.
44   Still kept in Johannes Matthiae's 'private' section with the shelfmark JM 1. A note in the 1674 catalogue, added after the theft, remarks that the volume has been mistreated 'by thieving hands' (*furtivis manibus*).
45   On the importance of Bellarmino as a polemist, see Sellberg, 'Humanist Learning', pp. 43–44.
46   Joakim Åkerman, 'Blev de verkligen avrättade, djäknarna som stal böcker i Strängnäs domkyrka?', *Strängnäs Gilles årsskrift*, 30 (1995–1996), pp. 17–20; Landsarkivet, Uppsala, Strängnäs rådhusrätt och magistrat 1704 ('att de derigenom kyrckians egentelige ägendom och skrudh spolierat').
47   Landsarkivet, Uppsala: Strängnäs domkapitel, 14 September 1704.
48   Fehr, 'Strängnäs stift', p. 203.

## 7 The Eighteenth-Century Decline

While the eighteenth century saw the rise and growth of the gymnasium and its library, the narrative regarding the cathedral library was mostly negative and referred to a collection in disarray, the situation at one point even described as 'barbaric'.[49] In the 1750s, the censor regius Niklas von Oelreich (1699–1770) was given the task of bringing order to the library. He clearly regarded the library as consisting of two parts: books taken as war booty during the 'German war' and later donated by Queen Christina, and books given to the church by Johannes Matthiae.[50]

Oelreich's efforts were highlighted by the priest Lars Hallman (d. 1762), author of the encyclopedic *Thet gamla och nya Strengnes* ('The old and new Strängnäs'). He provided the following eyewitness account of the cathedral library in the 1750s:

> The walls are covered with books, mostly well bound. There is no doubt that this collection has its origins in the papacy, and it looks as though the books were brought here as war booty, taken from some monastery abroad, but it has since been enlarged. In 1597, the royal secretary Sven Elofsson[51] donated a fair amount of books. During the German War, Queen Christina donated a large collection, above all from Olmütz in Moravia, and finally the books from Johannes Matthiae were put here after his death. Now there are over 4,500 books here, most of them in folio. All kinds of sciences are discussed in these books, but most works concern theology, law and history. Many are printed in the fifteenth century, when the art of printing first originated. This library has been in great disarray since the fire of 1723, but thanks to chancellor Oelreich, it is now in good order under the care of lector Wetter.[52]

It may be noted that Olomouc is explicitly mentioned on a number of occasions: in the 1660s proceedings against Johannes Matthiae (confused with Ulm), by Oelrecih and by Hallman. This is perhaps not surprising, since the greatest number by far of war booty books in Strängnäs came from Moravia,

---

49  1750; see Fehr, 'Strängnäs stift', pp. 190–192.
50  Fehr, 'Strängnäs stift', p. 192.
51  120 books; on this donation, see Fehr, 'Strängnäs stift', pp. 178–179.
52  Lars Hallman, *Det gamla och nya Strängnäs*, ed. Kerstin Pettersson (Eskilstuna: Lokalhistoria sällskapet, 2005), p. 99.

especially Olomouc; in the public memory, Olomouc thus became the *pars pro toto* for all of the war booty kept in Strängnäs cathedral library.

In 1765, an infamous auction of duplicates and 'superfluous' volumes took place under the auspices of bishop Jacob Serenius. It has been argued that the auction can be seen as a step towards greater control and organization of a neglected library.[53] To this argumentation, I would like to add economic motives and the recurrent wish to obtain 'useful books' for the school. Such arguments were probably as strong as any wish to bring order to the collection; in fact, in a 1764 protocol from the chapter, Bishop Serenius requested that the 'good and useful' (*goda och dugliga*) books in the cathedral library were to be spared, and that the school should buy 'other useful books' (*andra brukliga böcker*) using the auction profits.[54] In reality, the profits were mainly used for repair of the school building. Since the establishment of the gymnasium in 1626, the schoolhouse next to the church had been in a poor state and had undergone a number of repairs: the top floor of the building was in the eighteenth century neglected and empty.[55] The school actually occupied only one floor in the whole building; the school library was limited to one small room and in need of new acquisitions. As shown above, it was explicitly stated by bishop Jacob Serenius in the acts preceding the auction that the goal was to dispose of 'useless' books and duplicates in the cathedral library, and to use the profits in order to obtain books that were otherwise too expensive for teachers and pupils.[56] At this time, the cathedral library, including the war booty books, were regarded as a means of supporting the school financially. Likewise, it was natural for the rector Josef Thun to place his own collection in the cathedral and not in the schoolhouse.[57]

---

53  Hagström Molin, 'The materiality of war booty books', p. 137. For an in-depth analysis of the auction, see Lenka Veselá, 'Czech Books in the 1765 Auction of the Strängnäs Cathedral Library', *Knihy a dějiny*, 29 (2022), pp. 6–42.

54  Uppsala Landsarkiv, Strängnäs domkapitels protokoll, 7 March 1764.

55  Vårdprogram Roggeborgen, pp. 10–12.

56  Fehr, 'Strängnäs stift', p. 194; As has previously been pointed out by Lenka Veselá, the title of the catalogue reads Catalogus librorum ab antiquis bibliothecis, Pragensi et Olomuciensi, quibus olim Regium Gymnasium Gustavianum Strengnesense donaverat gl. m. Regina Christina – 'A catalogue of books from ancient libraries in Prague and Olomouc, that Queen Christina once bestowed upon the Royal Gustavian Gymnasium in Strängnäs'. The cathedral is not mentioned at all. See Lenka Veselá, 'Užitečné, či nepotřebné? Knihy z Čech a Moravy jako dar královny Kristiny švédským vzdělávacím institucím v polovině 17. století', in Lucie Heilandová and Jindra Pavelková (eds.), *Knihovny a jejich majitelé: Odraz zájmu a touhy po poznání* (Brno: Moravská zemská knihovna v Brne, 2018), p. 67, 71.

57  The will of Josef Thun (d. 1721) expresses a wish to have his books arranged in the cathedral, 'accessible for all students', but for various reasons, the collection was placed in the schoolhouse after his death; Lundström, 'Josef Thun', p. 105.

## 8 The Relocated Cathedral Library

In 1775, the cathedral library was moved from the church to the schoolhouse, once again on the initiative of bishop Jacob Serenius. By royal mandate, the two libraries were kept in separate rooms and with separate catalogues. The first printed catalogue of the cathedral library was published in 1776; it follows the same structure as the 1674 catalogue, with printed works, manuscripts (not included in the 1674 catalogue) and Johannes Matthiae's library.[58] A plan of the rooms from 1807 shows that the cathedral library, here labelled 'The old cathedral library' (*Domkyrkans Gamla Bibliothek*) was separated from the school library and kept in a small room on the top floor.

Gustaf Wilhelm Gumaelius (1789–1877), rector of Strängnäs gymnasium around 1830, has given an assessment of the school library and the cathedral library in an 1831 discourse. In the 1830s, both libraries were placed in the auditorium on the top floor ('Rikssalen'), which was now renovated and put to use again after centuries of neglect (this had actually already been suggested by Niklas von Oelreich about 80 years earlier). According to Gumaelius, the cathedral library was now the property of the school ('it used to belong to the cathedral'), but the school library was decidedly the more useful of the two: the cathedral library, he remarked, was indeed luxorious, but of interest mainly to bibliophiles; though it contained many treasures, it was poorly catalogued.[59]

Likewise, in an 1835 dissertation about a medieval manuscript in the cathedral library, the author praised bishop Jacob Serenius for having had the books removed from the church, where they were kept 'in shameful disarray' (*ubi turpi paulatim situ corrumpebantur*) and relocated to a 'more convenient' place in the schoolhouse (*ubi etiamnum commode servantur*).[60] The thesis was written around the time when both the school library and the cathedral library had been moved to the newly renovated great auditorium on the top floor of the school house, as mentioned above, arguably a more accessible location.

---

58  Carl Gustaf Barkman, *Catalogus bibliothecae templi cathedralis Strengnesensis* (Strängnäs, Arvid Collin, 1776).
59  Fehr, 'Strängnäs stift', pp. 207–208. It may be pointed out that as opposed to the school library by this time, the cathedral library actually had a printed catalogue. The school library catalogues from the time only exist as manuscripts.
60  Pehr Erik Thyselius (praeses), Sem Johannes Franzén, *Historiolam, quae inscribitur Constantinopolitane urbis expugnacio* (Uppsala: Regiae Academiae typographi, 1835), p. 1.

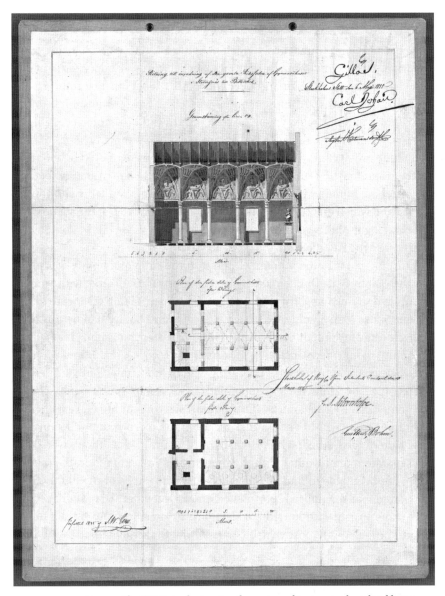

FIGURE 11.4　Prospect by J.W. Geiss for turning the main auditorium in the school house into a library, 1835
PHOTO: NATIONAL LIBRARY OF SWEDEN

## 9 From Cabinet of Curiosities to a Well of Knowledge

Some decades after Gumaelius' time, Jonas Otto Pontén (1813–1887), the town physician, teacher and librarian, simply labelled the war booty parts of the cathedral library 'the German collection' (most likely an association with the Thirty Years' War). At one point, he wanted to have it transferred to the royal library in Stockholm, where he believed it would be more accessible to scholars.[61] Pontén was obviously less interested in the war booty books than in the unique Swedish prints in the Strängnäs collections requested by the royal library around 1870.[62] Pontén's interests as a librarian were primarily focused on the school library, which was used daily by teachers, students and townspeople, and which grew considerably during his long service at the school. The 1860s catalogue of the cathedral library was therefore made not by Pontén, but by his colleague Henrik Aminson (1814–1885).

A turning point in the scholarly interest in the cathedral library was probably the visit by Beda Dudík in the 1850s. In Strängnäs, Dudík met with Pontén, whom he described as 'a friendly, open-minded man' taking great care of the ancient books.[63] As mentioned above, the cathedral library had by this time been relocated to the auditorium on the top floor of the gymnasium ('Rikssalen'), a beautiful room where Gustav Vasa (according to the local tradition) was said to have been elected king in 1523, a setting which Dudík found both impressive and moving. The 'Moravian and Bohemian books', using Dudík's words, were at this point organised separately. His visit took place about fifteen years before both libraries moved to yet another location: the old printing office on the other side of the Cathedral hill. Here, parts of the cathedral library were kept in a separate room together with the numismatic collection from the school. I have not been able to find any drawings or photographs of the library from this period, but the police report issued on 22 December 1864 (after the fire) gives some insight into how the collection was organised. According to the report, the 'older and most valuable parts of the Cathedral Library' were kept

---

61　Lars Sellberg, 'Jonas Otto Pontén, läkaren och botanisten i biblioteket', *Sörmlandsbygden* (2002), pp. 111–130, here pp. 121–122.

62　Sellberg, 'Jonas Otto Pontén', p. 122; article in *Aftonbladet*, 22 March 1870. Preserved letters in the cathedral library show that the Royal Library's head librarian Gustaf Edvard Klemming (1823–1893) in vain tried to borrow the cathedral's unique copy of *Missale Strengnense* (Stockholm, 1487), and that Pontén refused to let the volume leave Strängnäs, even for a limited period of time.

63　Beda Dudík, *Forschungen in Schweden* (Brünn: Carl Winiker, 1852), p. 344.

in a separate room together with the numismatic collection from the school. For safety, the door and the windows of this room had been fortified with iron. Likewise, the many accounts and bills from the local book-binders repairing the volumes after the fire leave the impression that the cathedral library was regarded as a collection worth saving.[64]

Finally, in 1910, the cathedral library was transferred back to the church, as a part of major restoration works on the building as a whole. Here, scholars such as Isak Collijn and Isak Fehr continued the research initiated by Dudík; as shown in the photo, Polish researchers, including the philologist Jan Łoś (1860–1928), visited the library shortly after the collection's relocation back to the church. This is probably the earliest photo of international scholars studying the collection.

FIGURE 11.5    From Jan Łoś, 'Fotografier från den polska kommissionens besök i Sverige sommaren 1911' (Photographs from the Polish Commission's visit to Sweden in the summer of 1911), album kept at the National Library of Sweden

64   Landsarkivet, Uppsala, Strängnäs domkapitels protokoll, 1865–1867.

## 10   Conclusions

While the cathedral library moved back to the church in 1910, the school library remained in the old printing house until 1968. About thirty years earlier, the upper secondary school had left the Rogge castle next to the cathedral and been relocated to modern buildings. Around that time, the school library also entered into a new stage: books that were regarded as useful for students and teachers were sorted out for the modern school library; the rest of the collections remained in the printing house until 1968, when the old gymnasium library became part of the National Library and moved back to the Rogge Castle. It is tempting to make a comparison with the situation for the cathedral library in the eighteenth century: dozens of newspaper articles from the mid-twentieth century lament the sad and neglected state of the school library, and the librarian's diary bluntly states (in 1934) that the collection at this point had become a static 'book museum'.[65]

Johannes Matthiae, and before him Laurentius Paulinus, wished for the war booty books to come to 'proper use' for the school and its students. In reality, the war booty in the cathedral library became neglected soon after Johannes Matthiae's death, and was rarely used or studied until the nineteenth and twentieth centuries. In relation to the school library, the cathedral library seems for a long time to have been regarded as a fascinating and somewhat mysterious phenomenon. In retrospect, it is perhaps not surprising that the teachers and students in the early modern gymnasium did not find the time or reason to put the war booty books in the cathedral library to frequent use. In all probability, much of the literature taken as war booty, large quantities of which were made up by Catholic theology and patristics, would not easily have fit into the curriculum, with its strong focus on written and oral proficiency in Latin through the study of classical authors as well as on the preparation of the schoolboys for future positions as Lutheran priests.[66]

---

65   Andersson, 'Inledning', pp. 17–21.
66   Hörstedt, *Latin Dissertations*, p. 25. A very useful schematic overview of the subjects covered in the Strängnäs war booty is found in Veselá, 'Užitečné, či nepotřebné?', p. 70.

# PART 3

## *Reconstructing Libraries*

CHAPTER 12

# The Fragment of the Personal Library of Johannes Poliander in the National Library of Poland

*Fryderyk Rozen*

Johannes Poliander (Johann Gramann or Graumann, 1487–1541) was a famous pastor in sixteenth-century Königsberg and in the Lutheran community. Luther counted him among the 'apostles of Prussia'.[1] Although Poliander's work has been described many times, not all aspects of his personal library have yet been examined.[2] First of all, a detailed bibliographical description, provenance evidence and a depiction of bindings is lacking. The dissipation and partial destruction of libraries in Königsberg during Second World War for a time inhibits the study of the Poliander private library. The stock of libraries relocated after World War II from Königsberg to other cities is object of growing scholarly interest. The postwar studies create a possibility of new research on the Poliander's book collection in the context of the book culture in the sixteenth century Duchy of Prussia. Surely the personal library of such an influential intellectual as Johannes Poliander is worth of examination. The main purpose of this paper is to present the results of the identification of the copies from Poliander's collection in the National Library of Poland where some of the Königsberg's books are located nowadays. Firstly, a state of knowledge on the Poliander library and the book culture in Königsberg in the sixteenth century will be presented. Then various methods of identification of Poliander's volumes will be discussed. Finally, conclusions resulting from the study of the volumes will be described. Additionally, the records of Poliander's books will be attached.

---

1 Janusz Tondel and Arkadiusz Wagner, *The Silver Library of Duke Albrecht of Prussia and his Wife Anna Maria* (Wien: LIT Verlag, 2019), pp. 15–16.
2 Lately Poliander's book collection was described by Christian Krollmann in the first chapter of his monograph on the subject of the Public Library in Königsberg. Krollmann also edited the catalogue of Poliander library described by Heinrich Zell in 1560. Christian Krollmann, *Geschichte der Stadtbibliothek zu Königsberg* (Königsberg: Magistrats-Druckerei, 1929).

## 1 Poliander and Book Culture in Königsberg

Poliander hailed from Neustadt an der Aisch (Bavaria).[3] In 1503, he began studies at Leipzig University and received a Doctor of Theology degree. In 1516, he became a teacher, afterwards a rector of the Saint Thomas School in Leipzig. During the disputation between the representative of papacy Johann von Eck (1486–1543) and Martin Luther and other evangelical theologians in Leipzig in 1519 he was Johann von Eck's secretary. At that time, he followed the ideas of the Reformation. Then he worked as a canon of a collegiate church in Neumünster and a preacher in Würzburg Cathedral, where he unsuccessfully criticized a veneration of saints. In 1525, he became a rector of Saint Clara parish in Nuremberg. The year 1526 brought a watershed moment in Poliander's life. Duke Albrecht Hohenzollern (reigned 1525–1568) invited him to Königsberg, the capital of the newly established Duchy of Prussia with 9 to 10,000 inhabitants. Poliander assumed the office of pastor in Altstadt Church. Alongside serving in the parish, he founded the school and counseled Duke Albrecht on the subject of education. He was Albrecht's close collaborator and, with others, he had an impact on the formation of the second ducal library in 1529 (so-called *Nova Bibliotheca*).[4]

When Poliander assumed a new role as pastor in the Altstadt Church, Königsberg was an area of significant transition. The Lutheran Duchy of Prussia was newly established in place of the recently secularized State of the Teutonic Order. Duke Albrecht was conducting intense activity in the field of culture. His goal was to create a Renaissance court and community in the capital. There were not enough humanists and scholars in the Duchy of Prussia immediately after the secularization of the State of the Teutonic Order. In spite of the difficulties (Königsberg was reported to be an unattractive town, *civitas incognita*), Albrecht successfully brought them to the Duchy. Reorganization of the Church according to the Reformation principles involved the necessities of the development of education and Christian literature in the vernacular (Prussian, Lithuanian, Polish and German). Initially Albrecht ordered books from other countries, for example he commissioned from Lucas Cranach the Elder (1472–1553) 400 copies of Luther's sermons. Later the import of books was taken over by booksellers, who were backed by Albrecht. The first printing

---

3 *Deutsche Biographische Enzyklopädie* (München: K. G. Saur Verlag, 2007), p. 13; *Biographisch-Bibliographisches Kirchenlexikon* (44 vols., Hamm: Verlag Traugott Bautz, 1990), 2, p. 285.
4 Janusz Tondel, *Biblioteka Zamkowa (1529–1568) księcia Albrechta Pruskiego w Królewcu* (Toruń: Wydaw. UMK, 1992), p. 11.

house was established in Prussia in 1523/24 by Hans Weinreich (?–1560), who was brought from Gdańsk (Danzig) to Königsberg by Albrecht. He printed mainly religious works in German. Later this direction of printing development was maintained. In 1549 an affiliated branch of Hans Lufft (1495–1584), Martin Luther's famous printer in Wittenberg, opened in Königsberg. In the same year, Aleksander Augezdecki's (?–1577) printing house was founded in 1549.[5] Moreover, Albrecht made a huge contribution to the growth of book binding. On the basis of the ducal financial books, it is known that Albrecht was paying the bookbinders (starting from Mats/Mattis from 1531/32 and Michel Pundtschreiber 1537/38).[6] Mats made many bindings for the books of the holdings of the castle library, today in the University Library in Toruń.[7] Also working in Königsberg was Kaspar Angler (fl. 1539–1565), one of the most famous bookbinders in contemporary Germany.[8]

The duke was personally involved in the expansion of the libraries' collections, for instance by the purchase of whole book collections (for example the collection of chancellor Frederick Fischer, who died in 1529).[9] Presumably after the death of Bishop of Kwidzyń (Marienwerder) Paul Speratus (1484–1551), his large book collection was incorporated into the duke's library.[10] Albrecht's desire was to collect all of the works of Martin Luther.[11] He owned two libraries: the Chamber Library (*Kammerbibliothek*) and the Castle Library (*Schloßbibliothek*). Both were used by the duke's court and also by ministers and scholars from the city. The Castle Library was opened for users in 1540, when its holdings numbered around 1,000 volumes from many European printing houses. At the end of Albrecht's life, there were around 3,000 volumes in the Castle Library. The library was under the care of librarians employed by the duke. The first of them was Felix König (*c.*1500–1549), who wrote an alphabetical shelf catalogue.[12] This library was a basic library for scholars and students, likewise the library of the elector of Saxony in Wittenberg, therefore the university in Königsberg owned only a very small

---

5   Tondel, *Silver library*, pp. 18–20.
6   Ernst Kuhnert, *Geschichte der Staats- und Universitäts-Bibliothek zu Königsberg* (Leipzig: Karl W. Hiersemann, 1926), pp. 252–253.
7   Tondel, *The Silver Library*, p. 43.
8   Tondel, *The Silver Library*, p. 21.
9   Tondel, *Biblioteka zamkowa*, p. 78.
10  Alicja Kurkowa, 'Mało znany ekslibris Pawła Speratusa', *Libri Gedanenses*, VIII (1976), p. 163.
11  Tondel, *The Silver Library*, p. 27.
12  Tondel, *The Silver Library*, pp. 37–38.

collection of books.[13] Two of Albrecht's wives, Dorothea of Denmark and Anna Maria of Brunswick-Calenberg-Göttingen (1532–1568), owned the private book collections.[14] The latter of them owned 89 volumes.[15]

Beyond the castle, various private libraries arose thanks to the Albrecht's patronage.[16] The largest of them (300 books) belonged to Professor of Albertina University Urban Störmer, the duke's doctor Andreas Aurifaber (a part of his collection was bought by Albrecht in 1561), Johannes Poliander, and Abraomas Kulvietis (who owned at least 85 books).[17] The smaller collections were gathered by other pastors, students, clerks and townsmen of Königsberg.

Poliander gave his books collection to the Altstadt-Königsberg in his last will. After his death the books were put in the church (*Altstaedtische Kirche*). It was the beginning of the Königsberg Public Library (*Stadtbibliothek Königsberg*). The Urban Council of Königsberg commissioned Heinrich Zell the task of creating an inventory of the collection.[18] He was an important person among local scholars. His life and work is well investigated subject in scholarly literature. He belonged to a family of printers in Cologne. Before getting to Königsberg, he studied at universities in his home town and in Wittenberg. Thereafter he engaged in printing and worked as a teacher in Strasbourg. He taught geography, history and astronomy. He gained recognition for the map *Descriptio Prusiae* printed in Nuremberg in 1542. In 1555, he joined to the emergent University of Königsberg, and in tandem began service in Duke Albrecht's court. Two years later, the duke appointed Zell his librarian.[19] Zell organized the collection, compiled the catalogue and wrote the call numbers on the books.[20] During the work on Poliander's books, Zell compiled a catalogue of

---

13   Tondel, *Bibliotek zamkowa*, pp. 29–30.
14   Tondel, *The Silver Library*, pp. 45–51.
15   Tondel, *The Silver Library*, pp. 86–88.
16   Tondel, *The Silver Library*, p. 22.
17   Urban Störmer: Tondel, *Biblioteka zamkowa*, p. 162; Andreas Aurifaber: Janusz Tondel, *Książka w dawnym Królewcu Pruskim* (Toruń: Wydawnictwo UMK, 2001), p. 88; Johannes Poliander: Tondel, *Książka w dawnym Królewcu*, p. 93; Abraomas Kulvietis: Tondel, *Biblioteka zamkowa*, p. 164.
18   Tondel, *Biblioteka zamkowa*, p. 71.
19   Karl Heinz Burmeister, 'Der Kartograph Heinrich Zell (1518–1564)' in Erna Hilfstein et al. (eds.), *Science and history. Studies in honor of Edward Rosen* (Wrocław: Zakład Narodowy im. Ossolińskich – Wydaw. Polskiej Akademii Nauk 1978).
20   Janusz Tondel, *Katalog Poloników Kammerbibliothek i Nova Bibliotheca księcia Albrechta Pruskiego zachowanych w zbiorach Biblioteki Uniwersyteckiej w Toruniu* (Toruń: Wydawnictwo UMK, 1991), p. IV; Krzysztof Nierzwicki, 'Królewiecki egzemplarz De humani corporis fabrica Andreasa Vesaliusa (Bazylea 1555) w zbiorach Biblioteki Wyższego Seminarium Duchownego Metropolii Warmińskiej Hosianum w Olsztynie', *Z Badań nad Książką i Księgozbiorami Historycznymi*, 15:1 (2021), p. 37.

the collection and noted the numbers on the books.[21] The *Catalogus* includes around 430 volumes and 342 unbound books. Items are put in order according to their formats (folio, quarto, octavo). Zell specified authors and noted, but not accurately, the titles, and in some cases he described the themes of the books. The volumes were numbered using Arabic or Roman numerals. After Zell's work, the collection was not made available to the public until the beginning of the seventeenth century. Before that, access was restricted to a select number of scholars and bibliophiles.[22]

Gradually the Public Library of Königsberg, following the acquisition of the Poliander collection, was further enriched by other personal collections, among which the biggest was the library of Johann Lomoller (1490–c.1560).[23] The library changed location several times over the years. It was eventually located in the old campus of the University of Königsberg. World War II ended the library's existence and the holdings were dispersed.[24] In 1944, Germans removed the Municipal Library's holdings from Königsberg and abandoned them near Mohrungen (today Morąg).

## 2  Previous Works on the Poliander's Library

In Autumn 1946, the first part of books evacuated from Königsberg were moved to the newly established Nicolaus Copernicus University Library in Toruń. More books were moved in 1947.[25] Another portion of the Municipal

---

21  'Catalogus librorum qui conseruantur in Bibliotheca Ecclesiae parochialis veteris urbis Regiomontanae ex Testamente Reuerend. D. Joannis Poliandri vel Grauman, anno 1560, conscriptus ab illustriss. principis Alberti Borussorum ducis bibliothecario Heinricho Zellio Agrippinate.' Printed in *Geschichte der Stadtbibliothek zu Königsberg* (cf. note 2).
22  Tondel, *Biblioteka zamkowa*, p. 177.
23  Krollmann, *Geschichte der Stadtbibliothek*, pp. 21–25.
24  It is worth mentioning that, before World War II, Prof. Otto Günther located books from Poliander's library in the Municipal Library in Gdańsk: Otto Günther, 'Lateinische Gedichte des Johannes Poliander', *Zeitschrift des Westpreussischen Geschichtsvereins*, 49 (1907), pp. 351–381; Otto Günther, *Katalog der Handschriften der Danziger Stadtbibliothek* (Danzig: Kommissions-Verlag der L. Saunierschen Buch- und Kunsthandlung, 1909), 3, p. 296 (Ms. 2436).
25  Henryk Baranowski, *Zbiory biblioteki Uniwersyteckiej w Toruniu, ich rozwój i kierunki przyszłego kształtowania* in B. Ryszewski (ed.), *Studia o działalności i zbiorach Biblioteki Uniwersytetu Mikołaja Kopernika*, cz. 5, (Toruń: Uniwersytet Mikołaja Kopernika w Toruniu, Biblioteka Uniwersytecka, 1990) p. 28. For more information about the collections from Königsberg in University Library in Toruń, see: Maria Strutyńska, 'Alte Drucke Königsberger Provenienz in den Beständen der Universitätsbibliothek Toruń' in Axel Walter (ed.), *Königsberger Buch- und Bibliotheksgeschichte* (Köln: Böhlau Verlag, 2004).

Library's holdings were taken to the National Library of Poland: 8,900 volumes, including: 12 incunabula, 1,100 sixteenth-century volumes, 2,700 seventeenth-century volumes, 4,100 eighteenth-century volumes and 1,000 volumes of periodicals.[26] After the Second World War, collecting information about the surviving books from Königsberg and their new locations became a challenging new task for librarians and historians. These works were undertaken initially by the German researchers.[27] On a large scale, work on collecting information about the scattered books from Königsberg was conducted by Klaus Garber. In Poland, research on the history of the libraries in Königsberg was conducted at the Nicolaus Copernicus University in Toruń and in that university's library, because after the war it came into possession of some books from Königsberg.[28] Moreover, the books from Königsberg (Castle Library, Königliche Deutsche Gesellschaft and Stadtbibliothek Königsberg) were described in the catalogue of sixteenth-century early printed books at the University of Warsaw Library.[29] The valuable books from the ducal library are located in the Kórnik Library.[30] Furthermore, eleven incunabula from the Public Library in Königsberg were described in the *Catalogue of Incunabula*

---

26   Spandowski, *Catalogue of Incunabula*, 1, p. 19; Bernhard Fabian et al. (eds.), *Handbuch Deutscher Historischer Buchbestände in Europa*, (Hildesheim: Olms-Weidmann, 1999), 6, p. 57. Klaus Garber, 'Königsberger Bücher in Polen, Litauen und Rußland', *Zeitschrift für Regionalgeschichte*, 4 (1995), p. 33.

27   Walther Hubatsch, 'Königsberger Frühdrucke in westdeutschen und ausländischen Bibliotheken', in *Acta Prussica: Abhandlungen zur Geschichte Ost- und Westpreußens* (Würzburg: Holzner-Verlag, 1968); Walther Hubatsch, 'Königsberger Frühdrucke in Bibliotheken des Ostens', *Preußenland*, 9 (1971), pp. 1–11; Manfred Komorowski, 'Das Schicksal der Staats- und Universitätsbibliothek Königsberg', *Bibliothek Forschung und Praxis*, 4:2 (1980).

28   Fifty incunabula from Königsberg, in most cases from Königsberg State and University Library, are described in: Maria Strutyńska, *Katalog inkunabułów Biblioteki Uniwersyteckiej w Toruniu* (Toruń: Wydawnictwo UMK, 1995). Sixty-six medieval codices from Königsberg State and University Library are described in: Marta Czyżak with collaboration from Monika Jakubek-Raczkowska and Arkadiusz Wagner, *Katalog rękopisów średniowiecznych Biblioteki Uniwersyteckiej w Toruniu* (Toruń: Wydawnictwo Naukowe Uniwersytetu Mikołaja Kopernika, 2016).

29   Maria Cubrzyńska-Leonarczyk (ed.), *Katalog druków XV i l wieku w zbiorach Biblioteki Uniwersyteckiej w Warszawie: Zbiorczy indeks proweniencyjny* (8 vols., Warszawa, Wydawnictwa Uniwersytetu Warszawskiego, 2018), 8.

30   Arkadiusz Wagner, 'Z dedykacją dla książęcego syna: O renesansowej oprawie królewieckiej Kaspra Anglera w zbiorach Biblioteki Kórnickiej', *Pamiętnik Biblioteki Kórnickiej*, 37 (2020), p. 65.

*in the National Library of Poland*.[31] Among them, three volumes come from the Poliander collection. The sixteenth-century books bound with Poliander's incunabula were only shortly briefly indicated. There are no manuscripts from Poliander's library in the National Library of Poland according to the manuscripts inventory published in 2012.[32]

The catalogue compiled in 1560 by Zell lists 824 volumes of printed books. In 1939, Christian Krollmann identified in the Königsberg Public Library one third of the volumes described three centuries earlier by Zell. Thus, in the National Library of Poland there is only a small part of the collection of the pastor from Königsberg. Nevertheless, it is worth describing. The descriptions from 1560, although they provide an orientation on the subject of the books, do not contain exact bibliographic data. The titles are sometimes distorted and the descriptions lack information about the place and time of printing. For example, Zell described the volume No. XLIV, as follows: '*Verwarnung der vonn Straßburg ann die Eydtgenossen wieder Conrrad Treger*'. Only by examination of the preserved volume (SD XVI.Qu.1153 adl.) can it be established that this description concerns the book by Wolfgang Capito (1478–1541), *Verwarnung der diener des worts vnd der brüder zu Strassburg*, printed in Strasbourg (VD16 C 842) by Wolfgang Köpfel and not in Augsburg by Philipp Ulhart (VD16 C 840). There are many more similar cases in the Sammelbände-containing booklet, especially the works of Martin Luther, which had many editions. Moreover, the Zell catalogue and also the edition prepared by Christian Krollmann do not provide information on binding and handwritten notes. This information can be obtained by describing the preserved copies.

## 3 The Identification of Poliander's Books

Sixteen volumes from Poliander's collection can be recognized today by his inscriptions written on the title pages. He usually used the phrase *Omnis legendi labor legendo superatur Jo. Grauman sibi et amicis comparabat* (The difficulty of reading is overcome by reading. Johann Graumann for himself and his

---

31  Michał Spandowski in collaboration with Sławomir Szyller, descriptions of bookbindings prepared by Maria Brynda, *Catalogue of Incunabula in the National Library of Poland* (2 vols., Warszawa: Biblioteka Narodowa, 2020).

32  There are no manuscripts from Poliander's library in the National Library of Poland described in: Jerzy Kaliszuk, Sławomir Szyller, *Inwentarz rękopisów do połowy XVI wieku w zbiorach Biblioteki Narodowej* (Warszawa: Biblioteka Narodowa, 2012).

friends collected). This sentence is found in 16 volumes.[33] Similar maxims were used by another prominent humanist in Prussia, Bishop Paul Speratus who also organized his library in Prussia according to the Renaissance principle *sibi et amicis* and used a bookplate with the following text: *Me sibi Speratus proprio ere, suisque parauit, Ast vsum voluit, cuilibet esse bono* ...[34] Ownership inscriptions stating that the book was for use of friends were particularly common in the sixteenth century.[35] Apart from the inscription *Omnis legend* ..., Poliander noted a purchase price on most of the books. It was indicated mostly it in groschen, but in one case the book's price was one florin.

Identification of another three of Poliander's volumes is possible based on the numbers written down by Zell on the title pages. In three cases, there is the same number on the title page of a book and in the catalogue. The titles of these books are consistent with Zell's descriptions.[36] Also, the Public Library's call numbers visible on the spine labels of these three books are the same as written down by Christian Krollmann. In one case, an eighteenth-century note on the endpapers indicates Poliander as the owner of the volume: *Possesor ejus qui videtur esse Joh. Poliander alias Graumann* (its owner which seem to be Poliander otherwise Graumann).[37] The book has traces of water damage which could have washed off Zell's number.

Apart from the books belonging to the Poliander collection in the National Library of Poland is one volume donated by Poliander to another person, according to the writing on the title page: "*Hunc libellu[m] plano aureum dono accepi a d. Joanne Polyandro anno 1539*" (I got this small fine book as a unconditional gift from Joannes Poliander in the year 1539).[38] On the top of the same title page is a second phrase by the same hand: *Sum Christophori Langnerii*. Perhaps this Christophor Langner is the same *Christophorus Langer ex valle Joachima* who studied at the university in Wittenberg in 1533.[39] The

---

33  Inc.1344–1346 adl., Inc.F.1337–1338 adl., Inc.F.1357–1358 adl., XVI.F.2136–2137 adl., XVI.F.2151 a–c adl., XVI.F.2159 adl., XVI.F.2195–2196 adl., XVI.F.2209–2213 adl., XVI.F.2223–2224 adl., XVI.F.2287–2288 adl. XVI.Qu.1179–1180 adl., XVI.Qu.1994–1999 adl., XVI.Qu.6018–6023 adl., XVI.O.2926–2928 adl., XVI.O.3103; XVI.F.2372–2373.
34  Tondel, *The Silver Library*, p. 23.
35  David Pearson, *Provenance Research in Book History* (Oxford: Bodleian Library, 2019), pp. 37–39.
36  254 = SD XVI.F.317–318 adl.; 146 = XVI.O.1124–1137 adl.; XLIV = SD XVI.Qu.1145–1178 adl.
37  SD XVI.F.2160 – Zell, Catalogus, *Libri non compacti* α.
38  SD XVI.O.1117–1123 adl.
39  Carolus Eduardus Foerstemann (ed.), *Album Academiae Vitebergensis ab a. Ch. MDII usque ad a. MDLX ex autographo*, (Leipzig: Karl Tauchnitz,1841), p. 150. Vallis Joachima is the latin name for Jáchymov in Czechia or Joachimsthal in Brandenburg. In the National

book which bears these inscriptions is the first part of a Sammelband consisting of seven prints in octavo. In the volume there are theological works by reformational authors: Philipp Melanchthon, Antonius Corvinus, Heinrich VIII, Urbanus Rhegius and Caspar Cruciger.[40] The volume is bound in vellum over cardboard. It has a handwritten shelf mark of the Königsberg Public Library on the front flyleaf: Ca.142 II and 8.b.23 and on the rear flyleaf: 10.14.23 [cross out] and 235.16.

## 4  Bibliographic Data of Books in the Poliander Library

Most books were printed before Poliander's arrival in Königsberg in 1525. The oldest edition is probably Quintus Asconius Pedianus, *Commentarii in orationes Ciceronis*, printed in Venice by Christophorus de Pensis, circa 1496.[41] Two other incunabula were printed in 1500.[42] Other books printed before 1525 originated as follows: 1501–1510, 20 titles; 1511–1520, 17 titles; and 1521–1525, 32 titles (most of them in one Sammelband). After 1525, 14 books were printed (12 in one Sammelband). Among them, two were printed in 1529, and the others originated in the 1530s. The latest editions are from 1537.

The books collected by Poliander and stored today in the National Library of Poland were printed mostly in Germany (70 books), Italy (15), France (6) and Switzerland (3). The majority of the books originated from prominent

---

   Library of Poland is a second early printed book that belonged to Langer: *Iunii Iuvenalis et a Persii Flacci Satyrae*, (Basileae: Froben & Episcopius, 1551), VD16 J 1240; call number: SD XVI.F.327.

40  Philipp Melanchthon, *De ecclesiae authoritate et de veterum scriptis libellis* (Wittenberg: Klug, 1539), VD16 M 3080; Philipp Melanchthon, *Sententiae ex sacris scripturis collectae, quae docent praecipuum cultum Dei esse, promovere Evangelium* (Wittenberg: Klug, 1539), USTC 693323; Antonius Corvinus, *Quatenus expediat aeditam recens Erasmi de sarcienda ecclesiae concordia rationem sequi, tantisper dum adparatur synodus, iuditium* (Wittenberg, Schirlentz, 1534) USTC 689386; Heinrich VIII, *Epistola de Synodo Vincentina* (Vitebergae: Seitz, 1539), USTC 693512; Heinrich VIII, *Illustrissimi ac potentissimi regis, senatus, populique Angliae sententia et de eo Concilio, quod Paulus episc. Romanus Mantuae futurum simulavit et de ea bulla, quae ad Calendas Novembres id prorogarit* (Witemberg: Lufft, 1537), USTC 665110; Urbanus Rhegius, *Cur et quomodo christianum concilium debeat esse liberum* (Vitebergae, Klug, 1537), VD16 R 1755; Caspar Cruciger, *Enarratio symboli Niceni* (Wittenberg, Lufft, 1550), USTC 650060.

41  Inc.F.1345 adl. GW 2740.

42  Appianus, *Historia Romana*, (Venezia: Ch. de Pensis, 1500), GW 2291, Inc.F.1337 adl. and Eusebius Caesariensis, *De evangelica praeparatione* (Venezia: [Bartholomaeus de Zanis], 1500), GW 9445, Inc.F.1358 adl.

centres of printing like Venice (11), Milan (2) and Rome (1) in Italy; Basel in Switzerland; Paris (4) and Lyon (2) in France; and Augsburg (10), Strasbourg (14), Leipzig (8), Cologne (2), Nuremberg (4) and Wittenberg (16) in Germany. One book represents the Johann Weinrich printing house in Königsberg.[43] This book has no imprint, but the printer can be established based on typographical design elements such as the woodcut with lion that was used by Johann Weinrich. This edition is not described in VD16.

A clear difference in the subject area is visible between Poliander's books from Germany and other countries. In most cases, the German books have predominantly religious content, whereas the Italian, French and Swiss books concern secular subjects. Such origins of the books paint Poliander as a man of extensive interests in the field of humanism and reformation. The printing houses of Italy, France and Switzerland provided him mainly with editions of renaissance literature; books printed in the Lutheran cities of Germany supplied his needs in the matter of religion.

The presence of a large number of books printed in Wittenberg in a relatively small fragment of the Poliander collection shows his extremely strong bond with the centre of the Lutheran Reformation, Wittenberg. His collection includes both books printed in Wittenberg before and after his move to Königsberg. The part of his book collection described in this article includes books from eight different printing houses in Wittenberg. Among them are three books by Johann Rhau-Grunenberg (fl. 1507–1527), the first printer to publish Luther's works,[44] and two books printed by Melchior Lotter (c.1470–1549), an excellent printer brought by Luther to Wittenberg. One book was published by Hans Lufft (1495–1584), who was the first to print Luther's translation of the Bible. Other Wittenberg printers whose books Poliander possessed were: Nickel Schirlentz (fl. 1521–1547), Peter Seitz (?–1548), Georg Rhau (1488–1548), Joseph Klug (?–1552) and Wolfgang Stöckel (c.1473–c.1541). Poliander's close ties with Luther explain the presence of many Wittenberg books in the Poliander collection.

---

43 SD XVI.O.1135 adl.
44 The relations of Luther with printers in Wittenberg was recently described by Andrew Pettegree, *Marka Luter: Rok 1517; Druk i początki Reformacji* (Warszawa: Wydawnictwo Krytyki Politycznej, 2017), pp. 58–60, 136–142, 312–315.

## 5 The Description of Copies

Most of Poliander's books show traces of being read: glosses and underlinings. In a few volumes, besides glosses and underlinings, much longer handwritten notation can be found. The glosses and notes written by Poliander (other than *Omnis legendi labor* ... and the prices of the books) are few and short.[45] The more expanded notes were made by previous and subsequent readers. The long notes about the content of the books were written in several volumes. One of them was made at the beginning of the sixteenth century,[46] three were made in the second half of the same century.[47] The tables of contents were written in two Sammelbände.[48] These notes indicate that the books from Poliander personal library was used by many readers in the sixteenth century. The notes about the prices indicate that some of the copies had passed from hand to hand before they were bought by Poliander. In two cases the copies had at least two previous owners.[49] One of the notes specifies the cost of the Sammelbände (the price of the first copy, the price of the second copy, the price of the binding).[50]

Almost all volumes have the Zell catalogue numbers and the shortened titles written on the fore-edge.[51] The numbers and titles are written in different ink. Perhaps the short titles were written by Poliander and the number by Heinrich Zell during the cataloguing of the collection.

All of Poliander's books have sixteenth-century bindings.[52] Fifteen of the bindings are blind-stamped half pigskin over wooden boards. The remaining five volumes have different kinds of bindings (one blind-stamped pigskin over wooden boards, one blind-stamped pigskin over cardboard, one blind-stamped brown calf over wooden boards, and one pigskin over cardboard). In the *Catalogue of Incunabula in the National Library of Poland*, the bookbinding workshops that made the bindings of the incunabula were identified. Two of the bindings were produced in Königsberg (Inc. 1344–1346 adl.

---

45  SD XVI.F.317–318 adl.; SD XVI.F.2195–2196 adl.; SD XVI.F.2209; SD XVI.F.2151; SD XVI.F.2372; SD XVI.F.2287; SD XVI.F.2287; XVI.F.2224 adl. and Inc.F.1345 adl.
46  Inc.F.1344–1346 adl.
47  SD XVI.F. 317–318 adl., SD XVI.F.2287–2288 adl.; SD XVI.F.2195–2196 adl.
48  SD XVI.Qu.1145–1178 adl. and SD XVI.O.1124–1137 adl.
49  Inc.F.1337–1338 adl.; SD XVI.F.2136–2137 adl.
50  SD XVI.F.2223–2224 adl.
51  The exceptions are SD XVI.F.2160 and SD XVI.O.1117–1123 adl. The volume SD XVI.F.2195 has unreadable Zell number.
52  SD XVI.F.2223–2224.

and Inc. F.1357–1358 adl.).⁵³ The binding of the third incunable was made in Leipzig at the Blüte frei ornamental I workshop.⁵⁴ It is worth noting that parts of the four bindings consist of fragments of medieval manuscripts.⁵⁵

## 6   The Posterior Owners of Poliander's Volumes

All books from the Poliander collection that are identified today in the National Library of Poland belonged before 1945 to the Königsberg Public Library and have the typical stamps and call numbers of that library. The older stamp has Königsberg's coat of arms and the text: *Ex Bibliotheca Veteris Oppidi Regiomont*[*ani*]. It was glued into the books after 1607 when the holdings were deallocated from the church to a specially prepared and furnished room in the town hall. Meanwhile the books were refurbished, cleaned, and volumes without bindings were bound.⁵⁶ At the back is the 19th century octagonal stamp with writing "Stadtbibliothek Koenigsberg" placed on the title pages. In the Sammelbände, both stamps are placed only in the first books bound in the volume. Books of the Königsberg Public Library have two kinds of call numbers. The older call numbers are numerals inscribed in black ink on the upper and lower endpapers. The newer call numbers are written down in pencil and are also located on the printed labels pasted on the book's spine.⁵⁷ Two volumes from Poliander's collection have a special call number applied at the Königsberg Public Library to books from the collection of Theodor Gottlieb von Hippel (1776–1843).⁵⁸ At the beginning of such call numbers is the abbreviation H.B., meaning H[ippelsche] B[ibliothek]. This collection of books (2010 volumes) was moved from Hippel's mansion in Lisnowo (*Groß Leistenau*)

---

53   Spandowski, *Catalogue of Incunabula*, no. 96 and 330. One of the Poliander's sixteenth-century volumes has the same blind stamps SD XVI.F.2223–2224.
54   Spandowski, *Catalogue of Incunabula*, no. 73.
55   Fragment of fourteenth-century missal, feria 4 post Dom. 4 Quadragesimae SD XVI.Qu.1994–1999 adl., Thomas Aquinas, *In libros Physicorum*, fifteenth century (?) SD XVI.Qu.6018–6023 adl., and probably fourteenth-century manuscript SD XVI.O.2926–2928 adl. Identification mas made by Sławomir Szyller, Polish Academy of Science.
56   Krollman, *Geschichte der Stadtbibliothek*, pp. 26–27.
57   Maria Strutyńska, *Struktura proweniencyjna zbioru starych druków Biblioteki Uniwersyteckiej w Toruniu* (Toruń: Wydawnictwo Uniwersytetu Mikołaja Kopernika, 1999), p. 16.
58   Anke Lindemann-Stark and Werner Stark, 'Beobachtungen und Funde zu Königsberger Beständen des 18. Jahrhunderts', *Nordost Archiv*, 4:1 (1995), p. 69. SD.Qu.1179–1180 adl. = LXV = H.B. Ph.4.4°; SD XVI.Qu.1994–1999 adl. = LXXV = H.B. Ph.3.4°. SD.Qu.1179–1180 adl. = LXV = H.B. Ph.; SD XVI.Qu.1994–1999 adl. = LXXV = H.B. Ph.

to the Public Library in 1840.[59] Both volumes are included in Zell's catalogue (numbers LXV and LXXV), therefore they must have been taken from the Municipal Library after 1560. The current circumstances in which these books were moved out from the Public Library are unknown. Both volumes lack the seventeenth-century Municipal Library bookplate, which may indicate that they were not in the library before the rest of the books got the bookplate. But it is also probable the books were sold by Michael Lilienthal (1686–1750) who managed the library in 1728–1744 and sold many books because of the library's financial difficulties and lack of space for the holdings in the cramped rooms of Altstädtischen Pauperhaus.[60]

## 7 Conclusions

The postwar research on the book culture in Königsberg confirms the importance of the Poliander collection as one of the largest libraries in the Duchy of Prussia. Prussia being in the sixteenth century a place of serious cultural change, makes his library even more fascinating. In 1560 there were 824 books in the Poliander library. However, in 1929 Christian Krollmann found only around 240 of them in the Königsberg Public Library. Up to today, 18 volumes (in large part Sammelbände) from Poliander's collection have been found in the National Library of Poland. The study of these copies shows the bibliographic data of the books in Poliander's collection. As these volumes are preserved in a very good condition, it was possible to describe their historical bindings and notes. These features show how Poliander and other readers dealt with the books. The subsequent call-numbers and stamps show the history of the Poliander books from sixteenth century to today. The Königsberg Public Library was the institution which stored this collection almost to the end of the Second World War. Thereafter this task was taken over by the National Library of Poland. Presumably some of Poliander's books are located in other libraries. Perhaps the above description of this fragment of Poliander's library will be helpfslaces. The reconstruction of this personal collection appears as a valuable task for the future research on the book history in the Baltic area.[61]

---

59  Krollmann, *Geschichte der Stadtbibliothek*, p. 80.
60  Krollmann, *Geschichte der Stadtbibliothek*, p. 53.
61  The excellent example of a historic library reconstruction would be *Catalogue of the Riga Jesuit College Book Collection (1583–1621): History and reconstruction of the collection*, eds. Andris Levāns and Gustavs Strenga (Rīga: Latvijas Nacionālā bibliotēka, 2021), pp. 215–560, catalogue compiled by Renāte Berga and Laura Kreigere-Liepiņa, and *Bibliotheca Rediviva (16th Century Prints from Former Stargard Libraries)*, compiled by Michał Spandowski and

## The Incunabula and Early Printed Books from Johannes Poliander Personal Library in the National Library of Poland

Inc.F.1344–1346 adl.
Provenance:
1. v gr[ossi]s (beginning of the 16th century).
2. Omnis legendi labor legendo superatur Io. Grauman sibi et amic[is] comparabat. Constat tot[us] liber 44 gr[ossi]s.
3. 12 (former shelfmark on spine)
4. 9 (numbering by H. Zell); Stadtbibliothek Koenigsberg (stamp); 63.13; 98.9; 418,10 (former shelfmark); Bb 55 2° (shelfmark); Bb 55 (shelfmark label on spine).

Binding: blind-stamped half pigskin over wooden boards.
Poliander's notes, annotations in two other hands (beginning of the 16th century). Single glosses (16th century, leaf a3a).

Cicero, Marcus Tullius
*De officiis, De amicitia, De senectute necnon Paradoxa.*
Venice: Giovanni Tacuino, 1514. 2°.
USTC 822111.                                                                                    Inc.F.1344 adl.

Asconius Pedianuss, Quintus
*Commentarii in orationes Ciceronis.*
[Venice: Cristoforo de' Pensi, ca. 1496–1500]. 2°.
GW 2740. Spandowski 96 copy a. IBP 581.                                Inc.F.1345 adl.

Philostratus, Flavius
*Eis ton Apollonion tu Tyaneos bion biblia okto. De vita Apollonii Tyanei libri octo.*
Venice: Manuzio, Aldo Pio, 1504. 2°.
Inc.F.1346 adl.

Inc.F.1337–1338 adl.
Provenance:
1. Emi p[ro] f[loreno?] (15th/16th century).
2. Constat 19 g[rossis] (beginning of the 16th century).
3. [Con]stat 15 gr[ossis] (beginning of the 16th century).

---

Agata Michalska (Szczecin: The Pomerian Library in Szczecin, 2021). The history of libraries in Stargard after Second World War was similar to the history of libraires in Königsberg. The collections were moved to several other cities; *Bibliotheca Rediviva*, pp. 67–69.

4. Omnis legendi labor legendo superatur Jo. Grauman sibi et amic[is] comp[ar]auit.
5. 253 (numbering by H. Zell); Ex Bibliotheca Veteris Oppidi Regiomont. (stamp); Stadtbibliothek Koenigsberg (stamp); 59.13; 90.22 (?); 420,1 (former shelfmarks); Bb 69 (shelfmark).

Glosses in several hands, including Johannes Poliander's? (16th century).
Binding: Blind-stamped pigskin over wooden boards.

Appianus, Alexandrinus
*Historia Romana.*
Venice: Cristoforo de' Pensi, 1500. 2°.
GW 2291. IBP 447. Spandowski 73.                                  Inc.F.1337 adl.

Platina, Bartholomaeus
*Hystoria de vitis pontificum periucunda diligenter recognita.*
Venice: Filippo I Pinzi, 1504. 2°.
USTC 836145.                                                      Inc.F.1338 adl.

Inc.F.1357–1358 adl.
Provenance:
1. x gr[ossis] (beginning of the 16th century).
2. Omnis legendi labor legendo superat[ur] Joannes Grauman sibi et amicis comparabat. Constat XVIj gr[ossis].
3. 255 (numbering by H. Zell); Ex Bibliotheca Veteris Oppidi Regiomont. (stamp); Stadtbibliothek Koegnigsberg (stamp); 163.13, 60.10[?], 331.13 (former shelfmark); Oe 12 (shelfmark).
4. (Shelfmark?:) 352.

Glosses in several hands (beginning of the 16th century).
Binding: blind-stamped half pigskin over wooden boards.

Petrus de Natalibus
*Catalogus sanctorum et gestorum eorum ex diversis voluminibus collectus.*
[Strasbourg: Martin Flach, 1513]. 2°.
USTC 619721. VD16 P-1881                                          Inc.F.1357 adl.

Eusebius Caesariensis
*De evangelica praeparatione.*
Venice: [Bartolomeo Zani], 10 XI 1500.
GW 9445. IBP 2100. Spandowski 330. USTC 995894                    Inc.F.1358 adl.

**SD XVI.F.317–318 adl.**
Provenance:
1. [Johannes Poliander, handwritten notes].
2. 254 (numbering by H. Zell); Ex Bibliotheca Veteris Oppidi Regiomont. (stamp); Stadtbibliothek Koegnigsberg (stamp); 161.24, 58.19 (former shelfmark crossed out); 559, 331.14 (former shelfmark); CC α 19 2° (shelfmark); CC α 19 (shelfmark label on spine).

Glosses and underlinings in two hands (16th century).
Binding: blind-stamped half pigskin over wooden boards with two clasps.

Eusebius Caesariensis, Rufinus Aquileiensis
*Autores historiae ecclesiasticae.*
[Basel: Johann Froben, 1523]. 2°.
USTC 613980. VD16 E-4273. SD XVI.F.317 adl.

Otto, Frisingensis
*Rerum ab origine mundi ad ipsius usque tempora gestarum libri octo.*
Strasbourg: ex aedibvs Matthiae Schurerii, 1515. 2°.
Not in USTC. VD16 O-1434. SD XVI.F.318 adl.

**XVI.F.2136–2137 adl.**
Provenance:
1. Constat 16 gr[ossis]
2. Metamor. [con]stant 8 gr[ossi]s. anno d[omi]ni xvc viij [1508].
3. Omnis legendi labor legendo superatur Joannes Grauman sibi et a[m]ic[is]. Constat m[arca] 9 gr[ossi]s.
4. 43 (numbering by H. Zell); Ex Bibliotheca Veteris Oppidi Regiomont. (stamp); Stadtbibliothek Koegnigsberg (stamp); 153.30, 61.27, 99.18 (former shelfmark crossed out) 73.13, 420.21 (former shelfmark); Bb 86 (shelfmark label on spine).

Notes in various hands on the upper endpaper and title page. Interlinear and marginal glosses (16th century).
Binding: black half leather binding, stamped in blind over wooden boards, two clasps. Manuscript leaf (14th century) used as hinge reinforcement.

Ovidius Naso, Publius
*Quindecim metamorphoseos libri diligentius recogniti.*
Lyon and Paris: Nicolas Wolf, Jacques Huguetan, 1501. 4°.
USTC 142770. SD XVI.F.2136 adl.

Ovidius Naso, Publius
*De arte amandi et de remedio amoris.*
Lyon: Jacques Huguetan, Claude Davost (Paris and Lyon), 1504. 2°.
SD XVI.F.2137 adl.

**SD XVI.F.2151 a–c adl.**
Provenance:
1. Omnis legendi labor legendo superatur Joannes Grauman sibi et amicis co[m]parabat.
2. 197 (numbering by H. Zell); Ex Bibliotheca Veteris Oppidi Regiomont. (stamp); Stadtbibliothek Koegnigsberg (stamp); 3.19, 349.25 (former shelfmark crossed out); 138.17, 355.18 (former shelfmark); CC α 45 (shelfmark label on spine).

Notes on the upper endpaper and title page (16th century).
Binding: blind-stamped half pigskin over wooden boards, two clasps wainting.

Cyrillus Alexandrinus
*Praeclarum opus, quod thesaurus nuncupatur, quatuordecim libros complectens.*
Paris: Wolfgang Hopyl, 1514. 2°.
USTC 181488.                                                    SD XVI.F.2151 a adl.

Cyrillus Alexandrinus
*Opus insigne in evangelium Joannis.*
Paris: Wolfgang Hopyl, impensis Jean Petit et Thielman Kerver, 1508. 2°.
USTC 143407.                                                    SD XVI.F.2151b adl.

Cyrillus Alexandrinus
*Commentarii in Leviticum sexdecim libris digesti.*
Paris: Wolfgang Hopyl, 1514. 2°.
USTC 181461.                                                    SD XVI.F.2151 c adl.

**SD XVI.F.2159**
Provenance:
1. Omnis legendi labor legendo superatur Joannes Grauman sibi et a[m]ic[is]. Constat m[arca] 15 gr[ossi]s.
2. L (numbering by H. Zell) Ex Bibliotheca Veteris Oppidi Regiomont. (stamp); Stadtbibliothek Koegnigsberg (stamp); 61.16, 106.8 (former shelfmark crossed out); 153.26, 199.2 (former shelfmark); Ca 78 (shelfmark label on spine); Ca 78 2° (shelfmark).

Notes in one hand on the upper endpaper, occasional glosses and underlinings (16th century).
Binding: blind-stamped half pigskin over wooden boards with two clasps.

Pico della Mirandola, Giovanni Francesco
*De rerum praenotione libri novem.*
[Strasbourg: Johann Knobloch, 1506–1507]. 2°.
USTC 667780. VD16 P-2636. SD XVI.F.2159

SD XVI.F.2160
Provenance:
1. Auctor Sebaldus Munsterus e Norimberga misit.
2. [Johannes Poliander] (18th century note: possessor eius qui videtur esse Joh. Poliander alias Grammann).
3. α (numbering by H. Zell); Stadtbibliothek Koegnigsberg (stamp); 356.2 (former shelfmark); 22.28, 272.1 (former shelfmark crossed out); remains of label on the spine.

Few underlinings. Marks of water damage.
Binding: pigskin over cardboard.

*Pentateuchus, Liber Iosue, Liber Iudicum, Libri Regum, Novum Testamentum.*
Wittenberg: Nickel Schirlentz, 1529. 2°.
Not in USTC. VD16 Z-1534. SD XVI.F.2160

SD XVI.F.2195–2196 adl.
Provenance:
1. Constat j fl[oreno]
2. Omnis legendi labor legendo superatur Jo[annes] Grauman sibi et amicis comparabat.
3. Stadtbibliothek Koegnigsberg (stamp); 3.17, C.8, 316.13 (former shelfmark crossed out); 46.4, 403.11 (former shelfmark); Ba 22 (shelfmark label on spine).

Notes in various hands on the upper endpaper and title pages, occasional glosses in several hands (16th century).
Binding: blind-stamped half pigskin over wooden boards with two clasps.

Reuchlin, Johannes
*Principium libri.*
[Pforzheim: Thomas Anshelm, 1506]. 2°.
USTC 686605. VD16 R-1252. SD XVI.F.2195 adl.

Reuchlin, Johannes
*Liber de verbo mirifico.*
[Tübingen: Thomas Anshelm, 1514]. 2°.
USTC 667860. VD16 R-1301.                                SD XVI.F.2196 adl.

SD XVI.F.2209–2213 adl.
Provenance:
1. Constat iiij gr[ossis]
2. 5 gr[ossis] constat
3. Omnis legendi labor legendo superatur Jo[annes] Grauman sibi et amicis comparabat. Constat 20 gr[ossis].
4. 41 (numbering by H. Zell); Ex Bibliotheca Veteris Oppidi Regiomont. (stamp); Stadtbibliothek Koegnisberg (stamp); 153.12, 61.2, 99.7 (former shelfmark crossed out); 72.12, 420.10 (former shelfmark); Bb 77 (shelfmark label on spine).

Occasional interlinear glosses and notes in various hands. Underlinings in red (16th century).
Binding: blind-stamped half pigskin over wooden boards with two clasps. 14th century manuscript leaf used as hinge reinforcement.

Tritonius, Petrus
*Melopoiae sive Harmoniae tetracenticae super XXII genera carminum.*
Augsburg: Erhard Oeglin, Johann Rynmann, 1507. 2°.
Not in USTC. VD16 M-4465.                                SD XVI.F.2209 adl.

Iuvenalis, Decimus Iunius
*Iuuenalis nuperrime editus cum commentariis Ioannis Britannnici.*
Milan: Leonard Vegius, 1511. 2°.
Not in USTC.                                             SD XVI.F.2210 adl.

Claudianus, Claudius
*Proserpinae raptus cum Iani Parrhasii commentariis.*
Milan: Giovanni Giacomo da Legnano, Johannes Angelus Scinzenzeler, 1505. 2°.
USTC 822852.                                             SD XVI.F.2211 adl.

Poliziano, Angelo
*Sylva cui titulus est Rusticus.*
[Paris]: Josse Bade, [1519]. 2°.
USTC 145155 [4°].                                        SD XVI.F.2212 adl.

Pico della Mirandola, Giovanni Francesco
*Hymni heroici tres, ad Sanctissimam Trinitatem, ad Christum, et ad virginem Mariam, una cum commentariis luculentiss.*
[Strasbourg: Matthias Schürer, 1511]. 2°.
USTC 667781. VD16 P-2644. SD XVI.F.2213 adl.

**SD XVI F.2223–2224 adl.**
Provenance:
1. vij gr[ossis] et al[ter] li[ber] vii gr[ossis] ligator 3 gr[ossis] sum[m]a xvi gr[ossis]
2. Omnis legendi labor legendo superatur Jo[annes] Grauman sibi et amicis comparabat.
3. 253 (numbering by H. Zell); Ex Bibliotheca Veteris Oppidi Regiomont. (stamp); Stadtbibliothek Koegnigsberg (stamp); 135.22, 163.22, 59.19, 46.14; 122.22 (former shelfmark crossed out); 60.23, 67.4 (former shelfmark); Ob 62 (shelfmark label on spine).

Notes in two hands on the upper endpaper. Notes in various hand on the title page of *Antiquitatum variorum* ... and occasional glosses in one hand (16th century).
Binding: blind-stamped half pigskin over wooden boards.

Boccaccio, Giovanni
*Genealogia deorum gentilium.*
Paris: Louis Hornken and Denis Roce, 1511. 2°.
USTC 143802. SD XVI F 2223 adl.

Nanni, Giovanni
*Antiquitatum variarum volumina XVII.*
[Paris]: Josse Bade and Jean Petit, 1512. 2°.
USTC 187212
SD XVI F 2224 adl.

**SD XVI.F.2287–2288 adl.**
Provenance:
1. Omnis legendi labor legendo superatur Joannes Grauman sibi et amicis co[m]parabat. Constat 38 gr[ossis].
2. 12 (numbering by H. Zell); Ex Bibliotheca Veteris Oppidi Regiomont. (stamp); Stadtbibliothek Koegnigsberg (stamp); 90.19, 122.25, (former shelfmark crossed out); 418.20, 73.2 (former shelfmark); Bb 65 2° (shelfmark); Bb 65 (shelfmark label on spine).

Notes in two hands on the endpaper and title page. Occasional glosses and underlinings (16th century).
Binding: blind-stamped half pigskin over wooden boards with two clasps.

Seneca, Lucius Annaeus
*Lucubrationes omnes ... Erasmi Roterodami cura, si non ab omnibus, certe ab innumeris mendis repurgatae.*
Basel, [Johann Froben], 1515. 2°.
USTC 667432. VD16 S-5758.                                  SD XVI.F.2287 adl.

Tyrius, Maximus
*Sermones e Graeca in Latinam linguam versi Cosmo Paccio interprete.*
Rome: Giacomo Mazzocchi, 1517. 2°.
USTC 841641.                                               SD XVI.F.2288 adl.

SD XVI.F.2372–2373 adl.
Provenance:
1. Omnis legendi labor legendo superatur Joannes Gramman sibi et amicis comparabat. Constat 30 gr[ossis].
2. 18 (numbering by H. Zell); Ex Bibliotheca Veteris Oppidi Regiomont. (stamp); Stadtbibliothek Koegnigsberg (stamp); 151.16, 108.7, 58.18 (former shelfmark crossed out); 55.4, 199.11 (former shelfmark); T 11 (shelfmark label on spine).

Notes on the upper endpaper and occasional glosses in several hands (16th century).
Binding: blind-stamped half pigskin over wooden boards with two clasps.

Pico della Mirandola, Giovanni (1463–1494)
*Omnia opera.*
Reggio Emilia: Lodovico Mazzali, 1506. 2°.
USTC 848409.                                               SD XVI.F.2372 adl.

Bellanti, Lucio
*Defensio astrologiae contra Ioannem Picum Mirandulam.*
Venice: Bernardino Vitali, 1502. 2°.
USTC 813182.                                               SD XVI.F. 2373 adl.

**SD XVI.Qu.1145–1178 adl.**
Provenance:
1. XLIV (numbering by H. Zell); Ex Bibliotheca Veteris Oppidi Regiomont. (stamp); Stadtbibliothek Koegnigsberg (stamp); 49.13 (former shelfmark crossed out); 144.11, 377.10 (former shelfmark); T 78; 2 (shelfmark label on spine); T 78/II (shelfmark).
Handwritten list of the books in the volume (16th century).
Binding: blind-stamped half pigskin over wooden boards with two clasps.

Zwick, Johannes
*Underrichtug warumb die Ee uß menschlichem gsatz in vyl grad verbottrn sey und das die vereeungrn Goettlich geschehen und aber von dem menschen ungoettlich zertrent widerumb soellind bestaetiget warden.*
[Basel: Valentin Curio, ca. 1524]. 4°.
USTC 701651. VD16 Z-736.                    SD XVI.Qu.1145 adl.

*Die Messe von den priesterlichen Hochzeiten.*
[Augsburg: Sigmund Grimm and Marx Wirsung, 1522]. 4°.
USTC 636949. VD16 M-5492.                    SD XVI.Qu.1146 adl.

Firn, Anton
*Supplication des Pfarrhers unnd der pfarrkinder zu Sant Thomam eim ersamen Rath zu Straßburg am. XII. Decembr. überantwurt. Anno MDXXIII.*
[Strasbourg: Wolfgang Köpfel, 1524]. 4°.
USTC 695038. VD16 F-1124.                    SD XVI.Qu.1147 adl.

Zell, Matthäus
*Ein Collation auff die einfürug M. Anthonij Pfarrherrs zu S. Thomas zu Stassburg unnd Katherine seines eelichen gemallhels.*
[Strasbourg: Wolfgang Köpfel, 1523]. 4°.
USTC 643144. VD16 Z-354.                    SD XVI.Qu.1148 adl.

Bucer, Martin
*Nit vrteylen vor der zeyt. Verantwortung M. Butzers vff das jm seine widerwertigen, ein theil mit der worheit, ein theil mit lügen, zum aergsten zumessen.*
[Strasbourg: Johann Schott, 1523]. 4°.
USTC 678152. VD16 B-8931.                    SD XVI.Qu.1149 adl.

Capito, Wolfgang
*An den hochwürdigen Fürsten und Herren Wilhelm, Bischof von Straßburg und Landgraf zu Elsass.*
[Strasbourg: Wolfgang Köpfel, 1523]. 4°.
USTC 632472. VD16 C-813.                                    SD XVI.Qu.1150 adl.

Capito, Wolfgang
*Dass die Pfaffheit schuldig sei bürgerlichen Eid zu tun ohne Verletzung ihrer Ehre.*
[Augsburg: Philipp Ulhart], 1525. 4°.
USTC 627088. VD16 C-821.                                    SD XVI.Qu.1151 adl.

Stifel, Michael
*Antwort Michel Styfels uff Doctor Thoman Murnars murnarrische phantasey so er wider yn erdichtet hat.*
[Strasbourg: Johann Knobloch, 1523]. 4°.
USTC 612162. VD16 S-9005.                                   SD XVI.Qu.1152 adl.

Capito, Wolfgang
*Verwarnung der Diener des Worts und der Brüder zu Straßburg. An die Brüder von Landen und Stetten gemeiner Eidgnoßschafft. Wider die gotslesterige Disputation Bruder Conradts, Augustiner ordens Provincial.*
[Strasbourg: Wolfgang Köpfel], 1524. 4°.
USTC 700911. VD16 C-842.                                    SD XVI.Qu.1153 adl.

Bucer, Martin
*Ein kurtzer warhafftiger bericht von disputationen und gantzen handel so zwischen cunrat treger provincial der Augustiner und den predigern des Evangelii zu Straßburg sich begeben hat. Sein des tregers sendtbrieff an den Bischoff zu Losan und hundert paradoxa vom gewalt der schrifft Kirchen unnd Concilien*
[Strasbourg: Johann Schott, 1524]. 4°.
USTC 644558. VD16 B-8897.
SD XVI.Qu.1154 adl.

Regius, Philadelphus
*Von Lutherischen wunderzaychenn.*
[Augsburg?: Ramminger?, 1524?]. 4°.
Not in USTC.                                                VD16 R-608?
SD XVI.Qu.1155 adl.

Kettenbach, Heinrich von
*Ein New Apologia und Verantworttung Martini Luthers wider der Papisten.*
[Bamberg: Georg Erlinger], 1523. 4°.
USTC 644869. VD16 K-799. SD XVI.Qu.1156 adl.

Apell, Nikolaus
*Ingolstadii XI Aprilis anni praesentis vicesimiquarti, publica disputatione per Sacrae theologiae professores, examinabuntur.*
[Ingolstadt: Andreas Lutz, 1524]. 4°.
USTC 666602. VD16 I-193. SD XVI.Qu.1157 adl.

Probst, Jakob
*Epistola ad auditores suos antwerpienses fratris Jacobi praepositi Augustiniani quondam prioris antuuerpiensis historia utriusque captivitatis propter verbum Dei.*
[Wittenberg: Johann Rhau-Grunenberg], 1522. 4°.
USTC 658206. VD16 P-4914. SD XVI.Qu.1158 adl.

Blarer, Ambrosius
*Wahrhafte Verantwortung Ambrosii einen ehrsamen weisen Konstanz anzeigend warum aus wiederum hineinbegeben wolle.*
[Augsburg: Sigmund Grimm, 1523]. 4°.
USTC 704916. VD16 B-5700. SD XVI.Qu.1159 adl.

Blarer, Ambrosius
*Ir gwalt ist veracht ir kunst wirt verlacht.*
[Augsburg: Philipp Ulhart], 1524. 4°.
Not in USTC. VD16 B-5684. SD XVI.Qu.1160 adl.

Briesmann, Johannes
*Unterricht und Ermanung an die Christlich gemeyn zu Cottbus.*
[Wittenberg: Johann Rhau-Grunenberg], 1523. 4°.
USTC 70000. VD16 B-8307. SD XVI.Qu.1161 adl.

Billicanus, Theobald
*Allen Christen zu Erfurt samt den Predigern und diener Gnade und Friede in Christo Jesu an die christelich Kirch versamlung ainem ersamen Radt und Gemain der Stat Weyl.*
[Augsburg: Melchior Ramminger], 1522. 4°.
USTC 636524. VD16 G-1552. SD XVI.Qu.1162 adl.

Hutten, Ulrich
*Ein demütige Ermanung an ein gemeyne statt Wormbß.*
[Speyer: Jakob Schmidt, 1522]. 4°.
USTC 643156. VD16 H-6318.                           SD XVI.Qu.1163 adl.

Cronberg, Hartmuth von
*Brief an Franciscus von Sickingen, seinen vetter des edeln und ehrnvhesten Hartmudts von Cronberg tzwen brieff eyner an Romische Kayserliche Majestat und der ander an Franciscus von Sickingen seinen vettern dergotlichen und Evangelischen ler und warheit zu furderung geschrieben.*
[Wittenberg: Melchior Lotter, 1521]. 4°.
USTC 635098. VD16 C-5911.                           SD XVI.Qu.1164 adl.

Cronberg, Hartmuth von
*Drey Christliche schrift des Edlen von Ernuesten Hartmudts vonn Cronenberg.*
Wittenberg: Melchior Lotter, 1522. 4°.
USTC 641329. VD16 C-5924.                           SD XVI.Qu.1165 adl.

Cronberg, Hartmuth von
*Ein Schrift und Christlich vermanung an die Strengen vesten Ersamen unnd weisen Meister unnd Rath zu Straßburgk.*
[Strasbourg: Johann Schott], 1523. 4°.
USTC 646733. VD16 C-5932.                           SD XVI.Qu.1166 adl.

Cronberg, Hartmuth von
*Schrifften wider Doctor Peter Meyer Pfarrher zu Franckfurt sein verblendt verstockt unnd Unchristlich leer betreffendt. Sampt zweyer gegenantworten des selben Pfarrher. Zwei gegenantworten.*
[Strasbourg: Johann Schott, 1522]. 4°.
USTC 692519. VD16 C-5933.                           SD XVI.Qu.1167 adl.

Cronberg, Hartmuth von
*Ein treüwe vermanung an alle ständ unnd geschickten auff dem Reichßtag yetzund zu Nürenburg von einem armen veriagten vom adel mit beger solliche vermanung und treüwen radt zu hoeren bedencken und anzunemen von aller edlen wegen die keinen standt im Reich haben.*
[Augsburg: Sigmund Grimm, 1523]. 4°.
USTC 647191. VD16 C-5939.                           SD XVI.Qu.1168 adl.

Sickingen, Franz von
*Ein send brieff so der edel und ernuest Franciscus von Sickingen seynem schweher dem edlen juncker Diethem von Henschuchßheim zu underrichtung etzlicher artickel Christliches glaubens zugeschickt hadt.*
[Bamberg or Coburg: Georg Erlinger or Aegidius Fellenfürst, 1522]. 4°.
USTC 645687. VD16 S-6311.　　　　　　　　　　　　SD XVI.Qu.1169 adl.

Cronberg, Hartmuth von
*Eyn sendbrieff an Bapst Adrianum: daryn mit Christlichem warhafftigen grund angetzeigt wurd eyn sicherer heylsamer weg zu ausreuttung aller kettzereyen: und zu heylsamer rettung gantzer Christenheyt von des Turcken tyranney.*
Wittenberg: [Lukas Cranach I, Christian Döring], 1523. 4°.
USTC 656444. VD16 C-5937.　　　　　　　　　　　　SD XVI.Qu.1170 adl.

Rhegius, Urbanus
*Ein bannbrieff des Bapsts und gantzen Endtchristischen Reichs. Darbey ein gnadenbrieff des Goettlichen und Himmelschen Ablaß allen christglaeubigen troestlich.*
[Nuremberg: Hans Hergot, 1524]. 4°.
USTC 642478. VD16 ZV-1022.　　　　　　　　　　　SD XVI.Qu.1171 adl.

Bugenhagen, Johannes
*Ain Christlicher sendprieff an frauw Anna geborne Hertzogin von Stetin in Pomern summa der seligkait auß der Hailigen Schrifft.*
[Augsburg: Simprecht Ruff, 1525]. 4°.
USTC 609760. VD16 B-9292.　　　　　　　　　　　　SD XVI.Qu.1172 adl.

Peringer, Diepold
*Des Christlichen pawern getrewer rath. Wie die christglawbig seel ain gesprech mit dem menschlichen flaysch taeglich halten und betrachten soll.*
[Nuremberg: Hieronymus Höltzel, 1524]. 4°.
USTC 634956. VD16 P-1387.　　　　　　　　　　　　SD XVI.Qu.1173 adl.

Osiander, Andreas
*Eyn sendbrieff an eyn Christlich gemayn nützlich zulesen.*
Nuremberg: [Hieronymus Höltzel], 1523. 4°.
USTC 656436. VD16 O-1101.　　　　　　　　　　　　SD XVI.Qu.1174 adl.

Schwarzenberg, Johann
*Ein schöner sendtbrief des wolgepornen und edeln Herrn Johannsen Herrn zu Schwartzenberg an Bischoff zu Bamberg außgangen darinn er treffenliche und Christenliche ursachen anzeigt wie und waruemb er sein tochter auß dem Closter daselbst zum heyligen grab genant hinweg gefuert.*
Nuremberg: [Friedrich Peypus], 1524. 4°.
USTC 646670. VD16 S-4736. SD XVI.Qu.1175 adl.

Langenwalde, Hans Magnus von
*Ein Christliche Ermanung zu furdern das wortt Gottis ahn den Hernn Bischoff von Breslaw.*
[Wrocław, Kaspar Libisch, 1524]. 4°.
USTC 642797. VD16 L-367. SD XVI.Qu.1176 adl.

Ulrich von Württemberg
*Des durchleuchtigen hochgebornen Fürsten und Herrn Hern Ulrich Hertzog zu Wirtenberg unnd Teck Grave zu Mümpelgart .&c. Missive an die gubernator der stat bisantz in der ein Christlicher handel zu Mümpelgart verloffen mit grüntlicher warheit angezeigt würt.*
[Basel: Andreas Cratander, 1524]. 4°.
USTC 635069. VD16 W-4449. SD XVI.Qu.1177 adl.

*Apologia inclyti senatus populique Vratislaviensis pro novi pastoris nova electione.*
[Wrocław: Kaspar Libisch, 1523]. 4°.
USTC 612474. VD16 B-8005. SD XVI.Qu.1178 adl.

SD XVI.Qu.1179–1180 adl.
Provenance:
1. Omnis legendi labor legendo superatur Joannes Grauman sibi et a[m]ic[is] comp[ar]abat. Constat 14 gr[ossis].
2. LXV (numbering by H. Zell, Public Library Königsberg).
3. [Hippel Theodor Gottlieb von].
4. Stadtbibliothek Koegnigsberg (stamp); 16o.b.8 (former shelfmark crossed out); 74.15, 73.9 (former shelfmark); H[ippelsche] B[ibliothek] Ph 4 (shelfmark label on spine); H.B. Ph 4 quarto (shelfmark).

Handwritten notes on the title pages and endpapers and glosses in several hands (16th century).
Binding: blind-stamped half pigskin over wooden boards with two clasps.

Beroaldo, Filippo
*Opuscula quae in hoc volumine continentur haec sunt. Declamatio Philippi Beroaldi libellus de optimo statu & principe. Oratio proverbiorum condita a Philippo Beroaldo.Qua doctrina remotior continetur. Declamatio Philippi Beroaldi contra scortatorem & de ebrioso Aleatorem. Philippi Beroaldi heptalogos sive septem sapientes*
[Venice: Giorgio Rusconi, 1508]. 4°.
USTC 814189. SD XVI.Qu.1179 adl.

Marschalk, Nikolaus
*Enchiridion poetarum clarissimorum.*
[Erfurt: Nikolaus Marschalk, 1502]. 4°.
USTC 650387. VD16 ZV-10418. SD XVI.Qu.1180 adl.

**SD XVI.Qu.1994–1999 adl.**
Provenance:
1. Co[n]stat xv gr[ossi]s
2. Omnis legendi labor legendo superatur Jooannes Grauman sibi et amic[is] co[m]pa[ra]bat.
3. LXXV (numbering by H. Zell, Public Library Königsberg).
4. [Hippel Theodor Gottlieb von].
5. Stadtbibliothek Koegnigsberg (stamp); [?].23 (former shelfmark crossed out and partly smudgy); 90.8, 62.5 (former shelfmark); H[ippelsche] B[ibliothek] Ph 3(shelfmark label on spine); H.B. Ph 3 (shelfmark).
Interlinear glosses, notes on the title pages in several hands (16th century).
Binding: Blind-stamped pigskin over wooden boards with two clasps wainting.
Manuscript leaf (Missale, feria 4 post Dom. 4 Quadragesimae, 14th century) used as hinge reinforcement

Baptista, Mantuanus
*Poete nostro tempore prestantissimi Baptiste Mantuani Egloge.*
Leipzig: Wolfgang Stöckel, 1505. 4°.
VD16 S-7173. ??? SD XVI.Qu.1994 adl.

Baptista, Mantuanus
*Celebrandi patris Baptiste Mantuani carmelite theologi parthenices prime liber primus.*
[Wittenberg: Wolfgang Stöckel, 1504]. 4°.
USTC 620878. VD16 S-7318. SD XVI.Qu.1995 adl.

Baptista, Mantuanus
*Divinum secundem parthenices opus sanctissime vginis Catharine passionem heroico carmine complectens non minus cultum qua pium.*
[Leipzig: Wolfgang Stöckel, 1503]. 4°.
USTC 615193. VD16 S-7335. SD XVI.Qu.1996 adl.

Baptista, Mantuanus
*Fratris Baptiste Mantuani carmelite theologi et poete prestantissimi parthenice tertia divarum. Margarite agathes lucie et apolonie agonas continens.*
[Leipzig: Wolfgang Stöckel, 1505]. 4°.
USTC 658202. VD16 S-7354. SD XVI.Qu.1997 adl.

Sedulius Caelius
*Opus paschale, oratione soluta conscriptum iuxta seriem totius Evangelii metrice congestum atque Paschale carmen prenotatum.*
Leipzig: Jakob Thanner, 1502. 4°.
USTC 2212432. VD16 S-5241. SD XVI.Qu.1998 adl.

Petrarca, Francesco
*Opusculum remediorum adverse fortue ex Francisco Petrarcha oratore et poeta sane clarissimo ut si de re qua piam doleas: remedium tibi respondendo affert: dolore ne nimio conficiaris.*
[Leipzig: Jakob Thanner, 1504]. 4°.
USTC 679829. VD16 P-1732. SD XVI.Qu.1999 adl.

SD XVI.Qu.6018–6023 adl.
Provenance:
1. Co[n]stat 11 gr[ossis]. (16th century).
2. Omnis legendi labor legendo superatur Jooannes Grauman sibi et amic[is] co[m]pa[ra]bat.
3. LXXVII (numbering by H. Zell); Ex Bibliotheca Veteris Oppidi Regiomont. (stamp); Stadtbibliothek Koegnigsberg (stamp); 62.14 (former shelfmark crossed out); 56.32, 193.33 (former shelfmark); T 32 (shelfmark label on spine). Binding: blind-stamped half pigskin over wooden boards with two clasps. Manuscript leaf (Thomas de Aquino, In libros Physicorum, 15th century?) used as hinge reinforcement.

Hessus, Helius Eobanus
*Heroidum Christianarum epistolae.*
[Leipzig: Melchior Lotter, 1514]. 4°.
USTC 661904. VD16 E-1506. SD XVI.Qu.6018 adl.

*Busche, Hermann von dem*
*Sermo Colonie in celebri synodo ad clerum dictus.*
[Cologne: Heinrich Quentel (heirs of), 1509]. 4°.
USTC 662124. VD16 B 9946. SD XVI.Qu.6019 adl.

Lobkowitz von Hassenstein, Bohuslaw
*Opuscula.*
[Leipzig: Melchior Lotter d. Ä., 1509]. 4°.
USTC 679790. VD16 L-2176. SD XVI.Qu.6020 adl.

Emser, Hieronymus
*Dialogismus Hieronymi Emser de origine propinandi vulgo compotandi: et an sit toleranda compotatio in rep. Bene instituta nec ne.*
[Leipzig: Jakob Thanner, 1513]. 4°.
USTC 635917. VD16 E-1113. SD XVI.Qu.6021 adl.

Ausonius, Decimus Magnus
*Libellus de ludo septem sapientum. Thilonini philymni choleamynterium in felliflvum philymnomastigiam hercinefurdensem.*
[Wittenberg: Johann Rhau-Grunenberg, 1515]. 4°.
USTC 631966. VD16 A-4397. SD XVI.Qu.6022 adl.

Kitscher, Johann von
*Virtutis et fortune dissidentium certamen. Leonis pontificis arbitri sententia: discussum. Joannis de kiczscher doctoris j.u. Prepositi Aldenburgeñ. etc. Dialogus.*
Leipzig: [Melchior Lotter I], 1515. 4°.
USTC 701399. VD16 K-1101. SD XVI.Qu.6023 adl.

SD XVI.O.1124–1137 adl.
Provenance:
1. Omnis legendi labor legendo sup[er]atur Joannes Grauman sibi et a[m]ic[is] comp[ar]abat. Constat 10 gr[ossis].
2. 146 (numbering by H. Zell); Ex Bibliotheca Veteris Oppidi Regiomont. (stamp); Stadtbibliothek Koegnigsberg (stamp); 17.23, 18.1.23 (former shelfmark crossed out); 22.10, 1.235.15 (former shelfmark); Ca 142 (shelfmark label on spine); Ca 142 8° (shelfmark).

Handwritten list of the books in the volume (16th century).
Binding: blind stamped brown calf over wooden boards with two clasps.

Luther, Martin
*Tessaradecas consolatoria pro laborantibus et onerantibus.*
Wittenberg: [Josef Klug], 1535/1536. 8°.
USTC 696197. VD16 L-6739                               SD XVI.O.1124 adl.

Rhegius, Urbanus
*Disputatio de restitutione regni Israelitici contra omnes omnium seculorum Chiliastas*
[Augsburg: Heinrich von Augsburg Steiner], 1536. 8°.
USTC 631299. VD16 R-1877.                              SD XVI.O.1125 adl.

Breydenbach, Bernhard von
*Peregrinatio ad terram sanctam.*
Wittenberg: [Nickel Schirlentz], 1536. 8°.
USTC 683408. VD16 B-8260.                              SD XVI.O.1126 adl.

Melanchthon, Philipp
*Catechismus puerilis, id est, institutio puerorum in sacris.*
Wittenberg: [Georg Rhau], 1536. 8°.
USTC 620224. VD16 M-4423.                              SD XVI.O.1127 adl.

Corvinus, Antonius
*Loci in evangelia cum dominicalia tum de sanctis, ut vocant, ita adnotati, ut vel commentarii vice esse possint.*
[Wittenberg: Peter Seitz], 1536. 8°.
USTC 673159. VD16 C-5408.                              SD XVI.O.1128 adl.

Luther, Martin
*Conciunculae quaedam Martini Lutheri amico cuidam praescriptae.*
Wittenberg: [Nickel Schirlentz], 1537. 8°.
USTC 622948 [4°]. VD16 L-4232.                         SD XVI.O.1129 adl.

Hus, Jan
*Epistolae quaedam piissimae et eruditissimae Johannis Hus, quae solae satis declarant papistarum pietates, esse satanae furias.*
Wittenberg: Hans Lufft, 1537. 8°.
USTC 651655. VD16 H-6165.                              SD XVI.O.1130 adl.

Hus, Jan
*Disputatio Joannis Hus, quam absoluit dum ageret Constantiae, priusqua in carcerem coniiceretur.*
Wittenberg: [Nickel Schirlentz], 1537. 8°.
USTC 638713. VD16 H-6164.                              SD XVI.O.1131 adl.

*Pasquilli de concilio Mantuano Iudicium.*
Rom in Porta Angelorum [Wittenberg, Nickel Schirlentz], 1537. 8°.
USTC 802801. VD16 P-830.                               SD XVI.O.1132 adl.

Melanchthon, Philipp
*Oratio de ingratitudine cuculi.*
Wittenberg: [s. n.], 1537. 8°.
Not in USTC. VD16 B-2054.                              SD XVI.O.1133 adl.

Alberus, Erasmus
*Utilissima praecepta morum, ex variis autoribus collecta, et Germanicis rythmis reddita.*
Haguenau: Valentin Kobian, 1537. 8°.
USTC 2216743. VD16 ZV-32027.                           SD XVI.O.1134 adl.

*Ein Sermon vom Abendmal des Herrn geprediget zu Königssberg yn Preussen anno 1536.*
Königsberg: Hans Weinreich, [1536]. 8°.
Not in USTC. Not in VD16                               SD XVI.O.1135 adl.

Rhegius, Urbanus
*Ein Sendbrieff an das gantz Convent des Jungfrawen-Closters Wynhusen, wider das unchristliche gesang Salve Regina.*
Wittenberg: Joseph Klug, 1537. 8°.
USTC 646815. VD16 R-1962.                              SD XVI.O.1136 adl.

Luther, Martin
*Methodus, quid in evangeliis quaerendum et expectandum sit.*
[Strasbourg: Johannes Herwagen, 1525]. 4°.
USTC 674884. VD16 L-3948.                              SD XVI.O.1137 adl.

SD XVI.O.2926–2928 adl.
Provenance:
1. 4 gr[ossis]
2. Omnis legendi labor legendo sup[er]atur Joannes Grauman sibi et a[m]ic[is] comp[ar]abat. Constat 10 gr[ossis].
3. 96 (numbering by H. Zell); Ex Bibliotheca Veteris Oppidi Regiomont. (stamp); Stadtbibliothek Koegnigsberg (stamp); 149.236, 43.11 (former shelfmark crossed out); 53.22, 235.4 (former shelfmark); Cb 33 (shelfmark label on spine); Cb 33 octavo (shelfmark).

Binding: blind-stamped pigskin over cardboard, remnants of leather ties. Manuscript leaf (14th century?) used as hinge reinforcement.

Marulić, Marko
*Quinquaginta parabole.*
Venice: Peter Liechtenstein, Francesco Consorti, 1517. 8°.
USTC 841261.                                                        SD XVI.O.2926 adl.

*Exorcismi contra demoniacos diversorum sanctorum approbati, cum benedictionibus necessariis, ac cum cathecumino et baptism.*
Venice: Simone da Lovere, 1513. 8°.
USTC 800292.                                                        SD XVI.O.2927 adl.

Reuchlin, Johannes
*In septem psalmos poenitentiales hebraicos interpretatio.*
Tübingen: Thomas Anshelm, 1512. 8°.
USTC 667859. VD16 B-3406                                            SD XVI.O.2928 adl.

SD XVI.O.3103
1. Omnis legendi labor legendo sup[er]atur Joannes Grauman sibi et a[m]ic[is] comp[ar]abat constat 9 gr[ossis].
2. 101 (numbering by H. Zell); Ex Bibliotheca Veteris Oppidi Regiomont. (stamp); Stadtbibliothek Koegnigsberg (stamp); 145.a.17, 43.4 (former shelfmark crossed out); 16.b, 235.3 (former shelfmark); Ca 137 (shelfmark); Ca 137 (shelfmark label on spine).

Binding: blind-stamped half pigskin over wooden boards with two clasps.

Marulić, Marko
*De institutione benevivendi per exempla sanctorum.*
Venice: Francesco Consorti, Bernardino Vitali, 1506. 8°.
USTC 841258.

CHAPTER 13

# The Fate of the Riga Jesuit College Library (1583–1621)
Aspects of Research into a Historic and Unique Book Collection in the Digital Age

*Laura Kreigere-Liepiņa*

In 2018, the National Library of Latvia launched a project to reconstruct the former Riga Jesuit college library (1583–1621), nowadays held mainly in the Uppsala University Library (*Uppsala universitetsbibliotek*).[1] The Riga Jesuit college book collection, which was looted and transferred to Sweden, has been well preserved for four centuries. The book collection attracted the interest of scholars during the twentieth century, but has not been researched extensively until the twenty-first. Our project's goal was to compile a catalogue that included bibliographic information about the identified and extant copies of the book collection that was once the Riga Jesuit college's property. The assistance of librarians in Sweden and other European countries made this project possible, and the virtual reconstruction of the Riga Jesuit college book collection promoted research in a little-known topic in Latvia's book history and culture, namely, the literary spoils of war.

Who were the former owners of Riga Jesuit college library's books? What is the significance of the Riga Jesuit college heritage in Latvia's cultural history? What was the fate of the Riga Jesuit college book collection? The results of the bibliographic research I will present will reveal the difficulties of identifying books and provenances in the Riga Jesuit college book collection. In this study, I will show the complicated historical circumstances in which the book collection was formed and which affected its ultimate fate.

---

1   This publication is funded by *Latvia's Heritage and Future Challenges for the Sustainability of the State* national research programme project *The Significance of Documentary Heritage in Creating Synergies between Research and Society* (Project No. VPP-IZM-2018/1-0022).

© LAURA KREIGERE-LIEPIŅA, 2023 | DOI:10.1163/9789004441217_015
This is an open access chapter distributed under the terms of the CC BY-NC-ND 4.0 license.

## 1  The Riga Jesuit College Library and Its Historical Background

As the Polish-Lithuanian Commonwealth prevailed in the Livonian War (1558–1583) and acquired most of Livonia, the Catholic Church, with the support of king Stephen Bathory (1533–1586), had the opportunity of embarking on a mission in the conquered territories that had become Protestant after the Reformation. The Riga Jesuit college (*Collegium Rigense Societatis Jesu*), founded in 1583, significantly changed the cultural life of the city during its forty years of existence. The king's plans were to open two Jesuit colleges, in Riga and Tartu (Dorpat), and establish a residence in Cēsis (Wenden).[2] The papal legate, Antonio Possevino (1533–1611), also played an important role in strengthening the influence of the Catholic Church and promoting the Counter-Reformation in Livonia. The seminary Possevino founded in Tartu (*Seminarium Interpretum Derpatense s.j.*) became an influential centre for the implementation of the Jesuit mission on the Baltic coast, in conjunction with the Riga Jesuit college.[3]

The activities of the Jesuits in Riga (cooperation with the Riga City Council and interaction with the townspeople of Riga) are most accurately reflected in the written testimonies they themselves left, printed Jesuit literature and their book collection, the library. The Jesuit books and other objects that belonged to them were taken as war booty to Stockholm and Uppsala in 1621, after the city was conquered by the Swedish troops under the command of King Gustavus Adolphus of Sweden (1594–1632).[4] Today, the books of the Riga Jesuit college library (1583–1621) form one of the oldest book collections in the Uppsala University Library. Valuable copies from the Riga collection attracted the attention of monarchs in the seventeenth century, the interest of bibliophiles as early as in the 17th and 18th centuries, while the twentieth century has seen various aspects of the Riga collection studied in depth.[5] In order to comprehend and reconstruct this historical and diverse book collection,

---

2  Vello Helk, *Die Jesuiten in Dorpat 1583–1625: Ein Vorposten der Gegenreformation in Nordosteuropa* (Odense: Odense Universitet, 1977), p. 13.

3  Oskar Garstein, *Rome and the Counter-Reformation in Scandinavia: Until the Establishment of the S. Congregatio de Propaganda in Fide in 1622* (Oslo: Universitetsforlaget, 1980), p. 32.

4  Otto Walde, *Storhetstidens litterära krigsbyten: En kulturhistorisk-bibliografisk studie* (2 vols., Uppsala: Almqvist & Wiksell, 1916), 1, pp. 43–45; Oskar Garstein, *Rome and the Counter-Reformation in Scandinavia: The Age of Gustavus Adolphus and Queen Christina of Sweden, 1622–1656* (Leiden: Brill, 1992), p. 63.

5  The Riga collection, a term Swedish researchers use to refer to the Riga Jesuit college book collection.

researchers and bibliographers of the National Library of Latvia set out to identify all the books, manuscripts from the Riga Jesuit college library and the artefacts now known to have belonged to the college. Consequently, copies from the Riga collection were not only sought in Sweden, but also in other countries where, historically, Jesuit books could have been taken.

Four centuries after the transfer of the library, the Riga Jesuit college book collection has been reconstructed. The catalogue of the collection contains information about 832 titles, possibly part of the Riga Jesuit college library.[6] Information about items in this collection can also be accessed from an electronic database.[7] Many copies have been lost over the centuries, but others may yet be identified in the future.

The aim of the present study is to describe the content of the book collection taken to Sweden and to discuss its unique publications and copies in local, Latvian, and regional, Northern European, contexts. The study will also provide information about the Riga Jesuit books in Sweden and other countries, in an attempt to reconstruct the names of former book owners and the ways in which the books have been used.[8]

King Stephen Bathory of Poland considered the re-Catholicization of Livonia to be one of his main tasks and gave the Catholics complete religious freedom.[9] When the King arrived in Riga in 1582, there were Jesuits in his entourage. Two of them played a key role in setting up the college. One was the papal legate Antonio Possevino, who had far-reaching strategic plans for spreading the Roman Catholic faith in the former Livonia and in northern Europe

---

6   The catalogue has been compiled by Laura Kreigere-Liepiņa and Renāte Berga, see *Catalogue of the Riga Jesuit College Book Collection (1583–1621): Collection History and Reconstruction = Rīgas Jezuītu kolēģijas grāmatu krājuma (1583–1621) katalogs: Krājuma vēsture un rekonstrukcija*, eds. Gustavs Strenga and Andris Levāns (Riga: Latvijas Nacionālā bibliotēka, 2021), pp. 215–555, hereafter CRJCBC. The catalogue includes 43 incunabula, 33 manuscripts and 756 sixteenth- and seventeenth-century printed works.
7   The Catalogue of the Riga Jesuit College Book Collection 1583–1621. Virtual Reconstruction: www.kopkatalogs.lv/F/?&func=find-b-0&local_base=nba03 (last accessed 4 November 2021).
8   For the compilation of the catalogue and the bibliographic reconstruction of the library, see Laura Kreigere-Liepiņa, 'Bibliographic Reconstruction of the Book Collection of the Riga Jesuit College: Layout of the Volume and Organising Principles of Descriptions', in *Catalogue of the Riga Jesuit College's Book Collection (1583–1621)*, pp. 50–69. During the college's operation, books were exchanged and moved between colleges or when Jesuits went on missions. This explains the fact that today a number of copies can be found in libraries geographically close to Latvia.
9   The activities of the Jesuits in Riga and Livonia were recorded and summarised by the Jesuit Father of Dutch descent, Jean Chretien Josef Kleijntjens (1876–1950): *Latvijas vēstures avoti jezuītu ordeņa arhīvos: Fontes historiae Latviae societatis Jesu* (Riga: Latvijas Vēstures Institūta Apgādiens, 1941), (hereafter: *Fontes SJ* 2), p. VII [7].

in general.[10] Possevino promoted the publication of the Catholic Catechism in Latvian and Church Slavic, which is one of the most valuable printed works in the Riga Jesuit book collection.[11] The other Jesuit was Piotr Skarga (1536–1612), rector of the Vilnius Jesuit college, who preached in the Saint James church to strengthen the position of the Catholic faith in Protestant Riga even before the opening of the college.[12] The Riga Jesuit book collection includes four books with their religious content compiled Skarga.[13]

King Stephen Bathory founded the Riga Jesuit college on 29 June 1583, granting the Jesuits privileges and placing the Cistercian Order's Saint Mary Magdalene nunnery, church, and all buildings under their charge.[14] The Polish King also demanded that the Riga City Council turn over to the Jesuits Saint James church, which had become Riga's non-German (Latvian) Lutheran Church after the Reformation.[15]

The Riga Jesuit college library was probably established in 1583 together with the college itself. This is evidenced by those surviving copies with an

---

10  Garstein, *Rome and the Counter-Reformation in Scandinavia: Until ... 1622*, pp. 24–25.
11  He also organised the publication of the Catechism in Estonian: Helk, *Die Jesuiten in Dorpat 1583–1625*, p. 65; Possevino distributed the Catechism with the help of the clergy and of Riga Jesuit college students: Valdis Trufanovs (Valdis Francisks Plenne), 'Jēzus Biedrības darbība izglītības veicināšanā Latvijas teritorijā (16. gs. beigās–19. gs. sākumā)', *Latvijas Arhīvi*, 1 (2002), pp. 24–36, here pp. 29–30.
12  Ludwik Grzebień, *Encyklopedia wiedzy o jezuitach na ziemiach Polski i Litwy 1564–1995* (Kraków: Wydzial filozoficzny towarzystwa Jezusowego, 1996), p. 619; Garstein, *Rome and the Counter-Reformation in Scandinavia: Until ... 1622*, p. 30; Kleijntjens, *Fontes* SJ 2, pp. XII–XIII [12–13].
13  Piotr Skarga, *Artes duodecim sacramentariorum seu Zvingliocalvinistarum* (Vilnius: Mikołaj Krzysztof Radziwiłł, 1582), USTC 240333, Uppsala University Library (hereafter UUB) Riga 249 (UUB 66:168), CRJCBC, no. 719; Piotr Skarga, *Artes duodecim sacramentariorum seu Zvingliocalvinistarum* (Vilnius: Mikołaj Krzysztof Radziwiłł, 1582), USTC 240333, National Archives of Sweden, Härnösand, Cdd Arkivet, CRJCBC, no. 720; Piotr Skarga, *Vpominanie do ewanyelikow, y do wszystkich spolem nie Kátholikow* (Kraków: Drukarnia Łazarzowa, 1592), USTC 242909, Riga 294 (UUB 68:72), CRJCBC, no. 721; Piotr Skarga, *Zolnierskie nabozenstwo* (Kraków: Jakub Siebeneicher, widow, 1606), Riga 285 (UUB 67:175), CRJCBC, no. 722.
14  Copies of Riga Jesuit college accounting and legal documents, as well as the College's founding documents and privileges granted by monarchs: *Liber privilegiorum Collegii Societatis Jesu Rigensis* [1255–1600], Academic Library of the University of Latvia, MS 61, R2800, fol. 10r.
15  In 1923, the church was returned to the Catholics and is the seat of the archbishop of Riga, Vita Banga and Marina Levina, *Rīgas dievnami* (Riga: Zinātne, 2007), p. 298. For more about the buildings allotted to the Jesuit College: Garstein, *Rome and the Counter-Reformation in Scandinavia: Until ... 1622*, pp. 26–27.

ownership record of the Riga college, dated with the year 1583.[16] The presence of books was important in the implementation of the Jesuit mission in the Riga college from the very beginning of the college's existence.

As already mentioned, the Jesuits' library was later confiscated and brought to Sweden. As was the practice of the time, the victorious Swedish troops confiscated all the assets owned by their ideological opponent, the Catholic Church, in the conquered territories, but spared Protestant institutions.[17] Swedish troops and officials acted in Riga as they later did elsewhere in Central Europe, confiscating valuable book collections from Catholic institutions in the occupied cities of Germany, Poland, Prussia and Bohemia and transferring them to Sweden during the Thirty Years' War. In the majority of cases, these books ended up in the Uppsala University Library collection.[18]

Even before King Gustavus Adolphus donated the Riga Jesuit college library to Uppsala University, its library had already received books from the Franciscan convent in Stockholm, as well as valuable medieval manuscripts from Bridgettine Abbey in Vadstena and a large number of books from the personal collection of the Swedish baron Hogenskild Bilke (1538–1605). Shortly afterwards, books from the Braniewo (Braunsberg) Jesuit college in Frombork (Frauenburg), including some books once owned by Nicolaus Copernicus (1473–1543), reached Uppsala University. In 1636, the Würzburg Bishopric Library was transferred to Uppsala.[19] When the Swedish army occupied Poznań in 1655, significant book collections from Catholic institutions were confiscated. The most important collection belonged to the Poznań Jesuit college, founded in 1572. Many of the copies from the Poznań college Library reached the Uppsala University Library thanks to the literary interests of the Swedish nobleman Clas Rålamb (1622–1698).[20]

---

16   Historical evidence of the library's economic activity dates back to 1592 according to the Jesuit accounting ledgers: Collegium Rigense Societatis Jesu. *Libri Duo Rationum Collegij Rigensis, In quorum primo Accepta In secundo vero Expensa Continentur*, (Riga: 1592–1621), National Archives of Sweden, Stockholm, Livonica I, vol. 45.

17   Garstein, *Rome and the Counter-Reformation in Scandinavia: The Age of Gustavus Adolphus ...*, pp. 62–63; Peter Sjökvist, 'Books from Poznań at the Uppsala University Library', in Jacek Puchalski, et al. (eds.), *Z badań nad książką i księgozbiorami historycznymi: Polonika w zbiorach obcych* (Warszawa: Bractwo Kawalerów Gutenberga, 2017), pp. 319–327, p. 319.

18   Sten Lindroth, *A History of Uppsala University 1477–1977* (Uppsala: Uppsala universitet, 1976), p. 51; Sjökvist, 'Books from Poznań at the Uppsala University Library', p. 319.

19   Lindroth, *A History of Uppsala University 1477–1977*, p. 51.

20   Sjökvist, 'Books from Poznan at the Uppsala University Library', p. 320.

## 2  The Research into the Riga Jesuit College Book Collection and Its Reconstruction in the Twentieth Century

Evidence has survived about the manner in which Riga Jesuit college books were transferred to Sweden. The first list of plundered items could have been made in Riga, when all assets belonging to the Riga Jesuit college, including books and valuables, were confiscated under the leadership of the governor of Swedish-occupied Riga Jesper Mattson Kruus (1576–1622).[21] Johannes Bothvidi (1575–1635), the chaplain of the Swedish court, is said to have compiled a list of the Riga Jesuit college library and handed it to the rector of Uppsala University, Lars Vallius (1588–1638).[22] However, the inventory list known to us today at the Uppsala University Library is most likely a later copy of a document that has not survived.[23]

In the inventory list, which bears the signature U271, the books transferred to Sweden are arranged by format, and unbound materials are mentioned separately. The titles of the library copies are given in Latin or in their original language. Bibliographic entries often include the author's name, abbreviated and/or descriptive titles, and the number of copies. About half of the copies on the list can no longer be located or have not yet been identified in Swedish libraries.

The book register concludes with a list, in Swedish, of *Hußgerådh* items transferred to Sweden.[24] Among the household items and church artefacts,

---

21   Walde, *Storhetstidens litterära krigsbyten*, 1, p. 44; Antoaneta Granberg, 'Carolina Redivivas samling från Jesuitkollegiets bibliotek i Riga och Isak Collijns arkiv', in Per Ambrosiani et al. (eds.), *Да веселитса Новъградъ: Må Novgorod fröjda sig; Hyllningsskrift till Elisabeth Löfstrand* (Stockholm: Stockholms universitet, 2016), pp. 77–94, p. 80; Peter Sjökvist, 'Useful Literary Spoils of War from Riga at Uppsala University Library' in this volume.

22   Inventarium över Jesuitkollegiets i Riga bibliotek, uppgjort av hovpredikanten, sedermera biskopen i Linköping Johannes Bothvidi, (s. l.: [1683]), UUB, U271.

23   *Thenne Cathalogus på böcker, Kåppar, messing, then, som then här i bokstafwen finnes, besannar sig af original Slåttzkÿrkiobokenz ifron Stockholm folio 161, hwarest annoterat star en Berättelse om the böcker som kommo 1622 ifron Rÿga ... Collationerat i Ups. Den 3 Novemb A °. 1683*, ('This catalogue, which lists books, copper, brass, and tin paraphernalia, refers to the Stockholm Inventory List's *Folio 161*, which reflects the books transferred from Riga', followed by this quotation in another hand: 'Compared at Uppsala in November 1683'); Inventarium, p. 31; Granberg, 'Carolina Redivivas samling från Jesuitkollegiets bibliotek i Riga och Isak Collijns arkiv', p. 80; more about the inventory itself: Walde, *Storhetstidens litterära krigsbyten*, 1, pp. 49–50; Sjökvist, 'Useful Literary Spoils of War from Riga at Uppsala University Library' in this volume.

24   Inventarium, pp. 30–31; Claes Annerstedt, *Upsala universitetsbiblioteks historia intill år 1702* (Stockholm: Norstedts, 1894), pp. 82–84; Detailed description of icons and other items mentioned in the inventory list: Renāte Berga, 'Rara et cara: Collection of Rare Books and

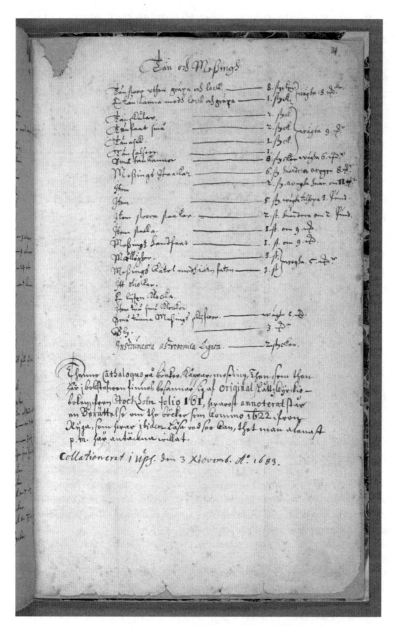

FIGURE 13.1   'Inventarium över Jesuitkollegiets i Riga bibliotek, uppgjort av hovpredikanten, sedermera biskopen i Linköping Johannes Bothvidi' (s. l.: [1683]), Uppsala University Library, U271, page 31. The last page of the inventory gives information about the church and household items listed in Swedish. Annotations about the origin and the date of the document below

four of the five listed icons have been identified in the Uppsala University's Gustavianum Museum.[25] Three icons featuring Saint Nicholas the Wonderworker and one with Our Lady of Vladimir, two of which (U 749, U 750) have text, probably in Old Slavic, written on wood on the back, were probably brought from Riga together with the Jesuit College Library (see figure 13.2, p. 341).

The Swedish bibliographer Isak Collijn (1875–1949), who had intended to compile and publish a catalogue of the Riga Jesuit's library, made a significant contribution to the research and reconstruction of the Riga Jesuit college book collection.[26] Collijn devoted many years to researching the history of the Riga college and created a manuscript of the library catalogue; however, his work has remained unpublished and is rarely cited in research literature. To date, this has been the only such comprehensive study of the Riga Jesuit college book collection in Uppsala University Library.[27] The most complete description of his work with this collection can be found in the archive materials entitled *Riga Jesuit Library. A contribution to its history. The inventory of 1622 and an attempt to reconstruct the library*.[28] As the title suggests, Collijn tried to reconstruct the former library collection in accordance with the inventory list of 1622. According to Collijn, the list attributed to Bothvidi reflects only a part of the Riga collection and is possibly the oldest surviving source of information about the books transferred from Riga to Sweden in 1621.[29]

The fact that the details of copies in the list were inaccurate, without an exact place and year of publication, with descriptive titles only, made it difficult to

---

Books of Cultural and Historical Significance in the Riga Jesuit college', in *The Catalogue of the Riga Jesuit College's Book Collection (1583–1621)*, pp. 134–149, here pp. 147–149.

25 *Uppsala universitetsmuseum Gustavianum*, Uppsala, UU 749–752; There are five Russian icons on the inventory list, but only four Russian icons are listed later in the lists of objects held by Uppsala University: Ture Arne, 'Några ryska helgonbilder i svenska samlingar', *Fornvännen*, 10 (1915), pp. 117–148, here pp. 121–122; Granberg, 'Carolina Redivivas samling från Jesuitkollegiets bibliotek i Riga och Isak Collijns arkiv', p. 79.

26 He informed the Riga City Library librarian, Nikolaus Busch (1864–1933) about this in a 1926 letter: Isak Collijn to N. Busch, UL Academic Library, Rk 2487,4; more about Isak Collijn in *Svenskt biografiskt lexikon*: www.sok.riksarkivet.se/sbl/Presentation.aspx?id=14922 (last accessed 15 September 2021).

27 Granberg, 'Carolina Redivivas samling från Jesuitkollegiets bibliotek i Riga och Isak Collijns arkiv', p. 82.

28 In Swedish: *Jesuitkollegiets i Riga bibliotek: Bidrag till dess historia. 1622 års inventarium och försök till bibliotekets rekonstruktion*.

29 Isak Collijn: Isak Collijns samling. Diverse. Biblioteksmöte i Sthlm IFLA 1930; Corr. Inbunden, incunabler, manus., (S. l.: s. d.), UUB, 475 D: 2, fol. [6]r; more about Collijn's archive and his library reconstruction see Granberg, 'Carolina Redivivas samling från Jesuitkollegiets bibliotek i Riga och Isak Collijns arkiv', pp. 82–85; Kreigere-Liepiṇa, 'Bibliographic Reconstruction of the Book Collection of the Riga Jesuit College', pp. 54–57.

identify the books within our project. However, the inventory of Bothvidi has not been the only source in the complex process of identifying copies. Collijn used information from older library catalogues.[30] They are referenced next to the book titles in the manuscript, with, for example, K2, K3 or the abbreviation HA, which is a reference to the catalogues compiled by the librarian Haquinus (Haquinus, Andreae Granaeus, ca 1640), Collijn also recorded the number of copies for the respective edition mentioned in the catalogues.[31] It is clear that Collijn had carried out comparative research on copies in the oldest Uppsala University Library collections, as well as studied the book collection brought from Braniewo, which had suffered the same fate as the Riga Jesuit college library.[32] To identify books from the Riga collection, he studied library holdings both in Sweden and outside it. As a result of this work, precise bibliographic descriptions of the copies recorded in the aforementioned list were recorded, with notes on the number of copies, affiliation with the collection, duplicates in the list, and signatures from the Uppsala University Library or other Swedish libraries. Collijn established that some copies had been sold at auction or had perished.[33] Books that have survived and have been identified as belonging to the Riga Jesuit college are designated with an asterisk in Collijn's archive materials.

Collijn noted that some copies in the Riga Jesuit college book collection had bindings that, in his opinion, indicated their belonging to the Riga Jesuit college library.[34] It is not known which features of the bindings led him to assume the books were from Riga, but some of his observations have helped to identify Riga college books in the Uppsala University Library that do not have a college ownership record, but do have bindings that show visual and textual similarities in the rendition of symbols and ornamentation.[35] One of the most tell-tale Riga college book bindings is one decorated with the keys and coat of arms of Riga. Some bindings in the Uppsala University Library and one copy in the

30   Designated Bibl. Arkiv. K2, Bibl. Arkiv. K3.
31   Designated Bibl. Arkiv. K4 and Bibl. Arkiv. K5, which is also how they are designated in Collijn's materials, in parallel with the abbreviation HA.
32   Garstein, *Rome and the Counter-Reformation in Scandinavia: The Age of Gustavus Adolphus* ..., p. 70; the Braniewo College Library catalogues were brought to Uppsala along with the library itself, one of them, MS U 274 also the College's expenditure ledger MS H 169.
33   Isak Collijns samling, UUB, 475 D: 2, fol. [6]v; for more about Uppsala University Library catalogues and copies: Annerstedt, *Upsala universitetsbiblioteks historia intill år 1702*.
34   Kreigere-Liepiņa, 'Bibliographic Reconstruction of the Book Collection of the Riga Jesuit College', p. 52.
35   Isak Collijns samling, UUB, 475 D: 2, fols. [7]r–[8]r.

Tallinn University Academic Library feature the monogram *D G* next to the Riga symbols, which indicate the binding's affiliation with Riga.[36]

## 3 Number of Copies in the Riga Jesuit College Library and Protestant Literature

In the Riga college, most of the books were recorded in the library's book catalogue, but this inventory has probably not survived.[37] In 1622, the inventory list registered 893 works and 61 unbound editions (Swedish: *oinbundna materier*) as having been brought from Riga.[38] Collijn pointed out that the list of books from the Riga college mentions 849 volumes, of which some convolutes (bound volumes with many separate items) contain as many as 26 publications, and 61 are unbound. He had identified at least 450 volumes, including incunabula and manuscripts, with ownership records of the Riga Jesuit college or of Catholic clerics who had been active in Riga.[39]

---

36   Some of them: Pedro da Fonseca, *Commentariorum Petri Fonsecae D.* (Rome: Bartolomeo Tosi, Francesco Zanetti, 1577), USTC 830216, Riga 356 (UUB 71:42), CRJCBC, no. 396; Aristoteles, *D. Francisci Toleti Societatis Iesv commentaria* (Cologne: Arnold Birckmann, heirs, 1583), USTC 626425, Riga 357 (UUB 71:56), CRJCBC, no. 117; Noël Taillepied, *Summarische Historia Vnd Warhafftig Geschicht Von dem Leben* (Ingolstadt: Wolfgang Eder, Officina Weissenhorniana, 1582), USTC 694956, Tallinn University Academic Library, I–851, CRJCBC, no. 747. To date, nine bindings with the monogram *D G* and eight bindings with the Riga keys symbol have been identified. In nine cases, the Riga coat of arms and the monogram *D G* are depicted on a book binding. *Katalog der Rigaschen culturhistorischen Ausstellung veranstaltet von der Gesellschaft für Geschichte und Alterthumskunde der Ostseeprovinzen Russlands* (Riga: Müllersche Buchdrukerei, 1883) mentions that two books with the Riga coat of arms and the monogram *D G* were displayed in the exhibition. One with the provenance of Riga City Physician, Johann Bavarus (no 99), the other, a Riga City Land Register, bound in brown leather, adorned with an imprint of the year *1597* and the Riga coat of arms (no 110), pp. 14–15.

37   Inscriptions in at least 35 titles in the college catalogue attest to this.

38   Annerstedt, *Upsala universitetsbibliotheks historia intill år 1702*, p. 9; Walde, *Storhetstidens litterära krigsbyten*, 1, p. 48.

39   Isak Collijn, '"Storhetstidens litterära krigsbyten: En kulturhistoriskbibliografisk studie", Af O. Walde', review in *Nordisk tidskrift för bok- och biblioteksväsen*, 3 (1916), pp. 294–320, here p. 298; a study of the books from the Riga Cistercian Convent of Saint Mary Magdalene in the Uppsala University Library: Andris Levāns and Gustavs Strenga, 'Medieval Manuscripts in the Riga Jesuit College Book Collection: Manuscripts of the Riga St. Mary Magdalene Cistercian Nunnery and Their Tradition', in *The Catalogue of the Riga Jesuit College's Book Collection (1583–1621)*, pp. 166–186; a review of the manuscripts of the Riga Jesuit college: Berga, 'Rara et cara', p. 139.

The 2021 reconstruction of the Riga Jesuit college book collection includes, first of all, not only the copies in the Uppsala University Library and other Swedish libraries, but also books located in other countries. Secondly, every copy has been bibliographed, rather than just bindings, and consequently the printed catalogue includes 832 copies that belonged to the Riga college, of which 772 are in the Uppsala University Library.[40]

When compiling the book catalogue, the bibliographic information provided by Collijn was meticulously evaluated, but for the majority of the books, the issue of provenance continued to be unclear. In 1621, was it only the Riga college books that were transferred from Riga to Stockholm? There are no reports of any other libraries in Riga, outside the Jesuit College Library, being confiscated and transferred to Sweden. It is possible that the Jesuit household items also included books that did not belong to anyone.[41] As the college's historical book catalogue has disappeared and there are few documents about the collection transferred to Sweden, it is impossible to give an exact answer about the number of copies in the Riga Jesuit college library at that time, but it can be assumed that all the books on the inventory list of 1622 were brought from the Riga Jesuit college.

The inventory of Bothvidi includes some books that are Protestant literature. One example is the unbound material *Der Bapst is der Antichrist*, recorded as 44 copies, none of which have survived.[42] We see that in the inventory list books by the Lutheran reformers Martin Luther (1483–1546) and Philip Melanchthon (1497–1560) also included.[43] It is significant that the Protestant books in this collection often contain ownership records of Riga citizens, which suggests that the books were donated to the college. The presence of Protestant literature in a Catholic institution was not uncommon. It provided an opportunity to learn about Martin Luther's 'false doctrine'.[44] The proportion of Protestant literature could also be explained by the preponderance of Lutherans among Riga's population, whose books could have reached the college in various ways.[45] Ludwik Grzebień mentions Riga as a Protestant city

---

40   More about these copies: CRJCBC.
41   Walde, *Storhetstidens litterära krigsbyten*, 1, p. 46.
42   Walde, *Storhetstidens litterära krigsbyten*, 1, p. 48; Inventarium, UUB U271, p. 27.
43   At least 29 copies authored or co-authored by Luther and 14 copies authored or co-authored by Melanchthon are included in the catalogue.
44   Garstein, *Rome and the Counter-Reformation in Scandinavia: Until ... 1622*, p. 31.
45   13% of 717 titles have a Protestant connection, in the form of a Protestant author or editor: Peter Sjökvist 'Protestant Books in Jesuit Libraries from Riga, Braniewo and Poznań: Catholic Post-Publication Censorship in Practice', (forthcoming).

where it was possible to obtain 'forbidden' books that were also of interest to Jesuits in other colleges.[46]

## 4 Cultural Valuables of the Riga Jesuit College Book Collection

Items that are significant in the context of Latvian culture and history are also a part of the Riga Jesuit college book collection. Within the Riga Jesuit college library project rare and valuable copies, examples of medieval literature and sacred music in Livonia are highlighted in many scholarly publications and reports. Several of these valuable artifacts have been uncovered and researched in the twentieth century.

A unique handwritten book, the parish register of Saint James church (1582–1621), is one such rare material/form in Riga's church history that has survived into the present. The parish register of Saint James church arrived in Sweden along with the Riga Jesuit college library.[47] In the inventory list, this copy was designated by the Latin name *Nomina eorum qui Rigae matrimonij benedictionem acceperunt* (Names of citizens married in Riga).[48] The second part of the handwritten book contains baptismal records, the names of baptised children, and the names of their parents and godparents.[49]

Another important document on the activities of the Riga Jesuit college is its accounting ledgers (*Libri Duo Rationum Collegij Rigensis*).[50] The ledgers, like the other college books, were most likely war booty, but so far it has

---

46   Ludwik Grzebień, *Organizacja bibliotek jezuickich w Polsce od XVI do XVIII wieku* (Kraków: Wydawnictwo WAM, 2013), p. 175.
47   Collegium Rigense Societatis Jesu. St. Jakobs i Riga kyrkobok, Riga, 1582–1621 (Church Book of St. James church in Riga), UUB H 145.
48   Inventarium, UUB U271, p. 7.
49   Haralds Biezais (ed.), *Das Kirchenbuch der St. Jakobskirche in Riga, 1582–1621* (Uppsala: Lundequist, 1957), p. 24; Biezais has tried to identify Riga College copies in the Uppsala University Library and describe them, mostly books with religious content. His notes about them are in his personal archive: Haralds Biezais, *Rīgas Jezuītu kolēģijas bibliotēkas materiāli Upsalas Universitātes bibliotēkas krājumā: Izraksti un H. Biezā piezīmes* (Uppsala: 195–?), National Library of Latvia, Rare Book and Manuscript collection, RXA263, N327.
50   This manuscript *Jesuitkollegiets i Riga räkenskapsbok*, code E/RA/2401/B/45, is held in the Livonica I collection of the National Archives of Sweden. H. Biezais' personal archive in the National Library of Latvia Rare Book and Manuscript collection has a partial transcript of the manuscript with the author's corrections and notes (RXA263, 264–267). The Latvian State Historical Archive holds photocopies of the manuscript made in 1960 (LVVA, 4060. f., 2. apr., 108. l.). The original has been digitised as part of the Riga Jesuit college library project: dom.lndb.lv/data/obj/895069.html and (last accessed 4 May 2023).

not been possible to determine how this manuscript arrived in the Swedish National Archives (*Riksarkivet Stockholm*). The ledgers record the college's revenue (*Accepta*) and expenditure (*Expensa*) for the period 1592 to 1621. There is information about the Jesuit college's economic situation, for example, about Jesuit rural properties outside Riga and their managers and tenants, and about craftsmen employed by the college.[51] Special mention is made of donors to the college, among them notable historical figures of the time: college founder King Stephen Bathory of Poland, King Sigismund III Vasa (1566–1632), the Polish Great Hetman Jan Zamoyski (1542–1605), the bishop of Wenden Otto Schenking (1554–1637), the Lithuanian ambassador Jan Karol Chodkiewicz (1570/1571–1621) and other donors.[52] The nuns of the Convent of Saint Mary Magdalene are also mentioned at the beginning of the list.

Information about Riga Jesuit books is contained in both the revenue and expenditure sections. In the expenses' section, expenditure for the Jesuit library is entered in a special column *Library*, sorted by date.[53] In December 1592, 15 guilders were paid for the transport of books from Vilnius.[54] In December 1614, the college purchased a variety of books for 11 florins and 19 guilders, without adding more precise bibliographic information about specific copies.[55] Although the expenditure records, including those for the purchase and binding of books, are mostly descriptive, which could mean that more precise information was recorded in other college documents, these records have nevertheless facilitated the identification of certain copies in the Uppsala University Library.[56]

There is one book in the collection brought from Riga to Uppsala that has a great relevance for Latvian cultural history. The collection holds Petrus Canisius (1521–1597) Catholic Catechism in Latvian, printed in Vilnius in 1585. Collijn believed that this could be the book called *Catechismus catholicus* in the inventory of Bothvidi, although the copy in the Uppsala University Library does not have a Riga college ownership record.[57]

---

51   *Libri Duo Rationum Collegij Rigensis*, Livonica I, vol. 45, fols. 1r–282r; a broader overview of Riga Jesuit properties in the vicinity of Riga: Vasilijs Dorošenko, *Myza i rynok: Chozjajstvo Rižskoj iezuitskoj kollegii na rubeže XVI i XVIII vv* (Riga: Zinātne, 1973), pp. 26–44.
52   *Libri Duo Rationum Collegij Rigensis*, Livonica I, vol. 45, fol. 1r.
53   Dorošenko, *Myza i rynok*, pp. 116–117.
54   'Pro vectura librorum Vilna, Libri Duo Rationum Collegij Rigensis', Livonica I, vol. 45, fol. 310v; Dorošenko, *Myza i rynok*, pp. 116–117.
55   'Libri varij [et incertu [m] cui ...] empti, Libri Duo Rationum Collegij Rigensis', Livonica I, vol. 45, fol. 613v.
56   Isak Collijns samling, UUB, 475 D: 2, fol. [7]r; Dorošenko, *Myza i rynok*, p. 17.
57   Inventarium, UUB U271, p. 25; Isak Collijn, 'Det äldsta lettiska trycket', *Nordisk tidskrift för bok- och biblioteksvänen*, 8 (1921), pp. 39–40, here p. 39.

In total, 1,002 copies of the Catechism were published, which is a relatively large print run for the end of the sixteenth century.[58] However, only three copies have survived. The one in the Uppsala University Library is the only complete copy of this publication in the world and the Canisius Catechism is known as the oldest printed book in Latvian.[59] Two other copies, which are only fragments, are in the University of Warsaw Library (*Biblioteka Uniwersytecka w Warszawie*) and the National Library of Poland (*Biblioteka Narodowa*).[60]

Another significant book in the Riga collection and in Latvia's cultural history is the Catholic *Agenda* published in Leipzig in 1507, which, according to the ownership record on the title page, was located in the Riga Jesuit college from 1584.[61] The ownership of this specific copy prior to 1584 can be deduced from other entries in the book: the title page is decorated with an entry by the Catholic priest Nicolaus Gisbert: *Hic liber pertinet d[omi]no Nicolao Guzbert et hui [us] est possessor [15]48*.[62] For the Latvian cultural history this book is significant since it contains the first four lines of the Lord's Prayer on the back (*verso*) of the title page, these lines being considered to be one of the oldest datable handwritten texts in Latvian.[63] Notes on phrases used in baptismal ceremonies, in Latvian, have been found on the margins of the book's pages, which, along with the Lord's Prayer, are considered to be the oldest liturgical

---

58   Māra Grudule 'Lasīšanas vēsture no reformācijas līdz zviedru ienākšanai Vidzemē 1629. gadā', in *Lasīšanas pandēmija: Esejas par lasīšanas vēsturi Latvijā = The reading pandemic: Essays on the history of reading in Latvia* (Rīga, Latvijas Nacionālā bibliotēka, 2020), pp. 40–51, here p. 48.

59   Petrus Canisius, *Catechismvs Catholicorum* (Vilnius: Daniel z Lęczycy, 1585), USTC 6911452, Utl. Rar. 174, CRJCBC, no. 226; more about the copy of the Canisius Catechism in the Uppsala University Library: Berga, 'Rara et cara', pp. 140–141.

60   Petrus Canisius, *Catechismvs Catholicorum* (Vilnius: Daniel z Lęczycy, 1585), USTC 6911452, University of Warsaw Library, Sd.618.211, CRJCBC, no. 227; Petrus Canisius, *Catechismvs Catholicorum* (Vilnius: Daniel z Lęczycy, 1585), USTC 6911452, National Library of Poland, SD XVI.O.6350, CRJCBC, no. 228; More information about the publication, see Renāte Berga, 'Sv. Pētera Kanīzija "Catechismus catholicorum" (Viļņa, 1585) – senākā līdz mūsdienām saglabājusies grāmata latviešu valodā', in Viesturs Zanders (ed.), *Grāmata Latvijai ārpus Latvijas: Kolektīvā monogrāfija* (Riga: Latvijas Nacionālā bibliotēka, 2021), pp. 55–82.

61   *Liber Collegij Societatis IESV Riga [e] anno 1584 – Agenda sive benedictionale commune* (Leipzig: Melchior Lotter, (sen.), 1507), Riga 160 (UUB 64:79), CRJCBC, no. 87, USTC 609610.

62   Biezais on the problem of identifying Nicholas Gisbert's and other inscriptions: Haralds Biezais, *Beiträge zur lettischen Kultur- und Sprachgeschichte* (Åbo: Åbo akademi, 1973), pp. 11–12.

63   Gustavs Strenga and Andris Levāns (eds.), *Luther: The Turn; Catalogue of the Exhibition, National Library of Latvia, Riga, 01.11.2017–04.02.2018* (Riga: Latvijas Nacionālā bibliotēka, 2017), pp. 156–157.

texts in Latvian. Haralds Biezais dates these manuscripts to the first half of the sixteenth century, but it is not known whether the *Agenda* was also used for the needs of the Riga Jesuit college. Recent research on the entries on the *Agenda* suggests that they may have been made between 1529 and 1534.[64]

A significant number of the books that were once held by the Library had previously belonged to the Livonian priest Reinold Gemekow (?–after 1593).[65] Entries in the books help to reconstruct his biography, as little information about this person has survived.[66] How this private collection of books and handwritten text could end up in the Riga Jesuit college? Gemekow's books probably arrived at the Riga Jesuit college together with donations from other Livonian priests.[67]

Books came to the Riga Jesuit college in various ways: they were purchased, exchanged, bequeathed, and specially printed for the college's requirements. An in-depth study of the Riga Jesuit college books leads to the conclusion that a large part of them were compiled at the college in accordance with *Ratio studiorum* requirements. The Library's corpus did not lack classical literature, theological literature and philosophical works, which were the main subjects in Jesuit educational institutions.[68] Copies featuring written testimonies, exercises in Latin and Greek grammar, alphabetic notes and quotations in Latin have survived, indicating the process of educating students, possibly at the Riga Jesuit school or another Jesuit school.[69] One book, owned by the Catholic

---

64   Biezais, *Beiträge zur lettischen Kultur- und Sprachgeschichte*, pp. 12–17; Gustavs Strenga, 'Meklējot lasītājus [klausītājus]: Pārdomas par lasīšanas vēsturi Latvijas teritorijā no 12. gadsimta beigām līdz 16. gadsimta sākumam', in *Lasīšanas pandēmija*, pp. 28–39, here p. 39.

65   More about Gemekow's books: Reinis Norkārkls, 'The Riga Jesuit College and its Book Collection' in *Catalogue of the Riga Jesuit College's Book Collection (1583–1621)*, pp. 90–111, here p. 104.

66   Records of provenance show that he was a priest in Tartu (Dorpat), Saaremaa (Oesel) and Tczew (Dersovia): *Reinoldi Gemekow Anno* [15]40 *Terpaten, Reinoldj Gemekow R[everendissim]j D[omin]j Ep[iscop]j Ozilien[sis] Arensburgae aulicj co[n]cionatoris, donatio[n]e uero R[evere]ndj D[omi]nj Henricj a Lhaer paroecj in Karmel possidet A[nn]o &c.* [15]58, *Reinoldj Gemekow Decanj [et] Paroecj Dersouien[sis] 1574*.

67   At least twenty-five copies, including thirteen *incunabula*, may have belonged to him. More about the specific copies: CRJCBC.

68   The content of the Riga Jesuit college book collection is set out by subject group, Sjökvist, 'Useful Literary Spoils of War from Riga at Uppsala University Library' in this volume; more about the nature of the collection's content: Berga, 'Rara et cara'; Trufanovs, 'Jēzus Biedrības darbība izglītības veicināšanā Latvijas teritorijā (16. gs. beigās–19. gs. sākumā)', p. 30.

69   More about the Riga Jesuit School, Norkārkls, 'The Riga Jesuit College and its Book Collection', pp. 96–98.

priest Gemekow, shows exercises in grammatical cases (the pronouns *hic*, *haec*, *hoc* with declensions of the proper noun *Reinold*).[70] Another book contains grammar exercises and reading notes.[71] A book owned by the Jesuit Theodor Meidel (1564–1588) of the Braniewo School, which may have been used in the Riga college, also contains notes on the meaning of the book, including notes of a legal nature and references to Cicero's works.[72] One of the books, which contains the Latin aphorisms typical of Jesuit books, also features a motto and a hand-drawn stylised Jesuit emblem on the title page.[73]

## 5   Identification of Copies from the Riga Jesuit College Book Collection and Their Fate in Sweden

The bibliographic reconstruction of the Riga Jesuit college book collection was started in 2018 and resulted in the reunification of collection in one room in the Uppsala University Library (the Book Hall), as well as in a catalogue and in electronic database formats. Over several years, at least a thousand items potentially from the Riga Jesuit college library were evaluated, and the collection was thoroughly researched. Thanks to the valuable information on the inventory list of 1622 and Collijn's working materials, it was possible to start compiling bibliographies of the book collection transferred to Sweden, where most of the collection has historically been stored.

The catalogue includes items with ownership records from the Riga college and others, mentioned on the inventory list, that have been identified in other Swedish book repositories. Collijn has written that he had also found twenty or more Riga college books, about which there is no information in the list.[74] One such example could be the *Agenda* mentioned above, with the oldest dated handwritten text in Latvian.[75] There is also a Latin transcript, also

---

70   Giovanni Battista Spagnoli, *Fratris Baptiste Mantuani Carmelite Theologi de contemnenda Morte Carmen* (Deventer: Albert Pafraet, 1514), Riga 10 (UUB Kk:85), CRJCBC, no. 730, USTC 420459.
71   Johannes Brenz, *Catechismvs Johannis Brentij Deudsch* (Leipzig: Jakob Bärwald, 1553), Riga 82 (UUB 49:531), CRJCBC, no. 192, USTC 620251.
72   David Chyträus, *Catechesis Davidis Chytraei* (Rostock: Andreas Gutterwitz, Hans Stockelmann, 1572), Riga 68 (UUB 49:338), CRJCBC, no. 254; David Chyträus, *Regvlae vitae* (Bautzen: Johann Wolrab, 1571), USTC 690482, Riga 68 (UUB 49:338), CRJCBC, no. 255.
73   Paolo Manuzio, *Epistolarvm Pavli Manvtii libri V* (Venetia: Paolo Manuzio, 1561), USTC 840479, Riga 148 (UUB 60: 568), CRJCBC, no. 552.
74   Isak Collijns samling, UUB, 475 D: 2, fol. [6]r.
75   *Agenda sive benedictionale commune* (Leipzig: Melchior Lotter, (sen.), 1507), USTC 609610, Riga 160 (UUB 64:79), CRJCBC, no. 87.

written in the fifteenth century, of the Benedictine Rule intended for use in a female convent. Its title page has a Riga college ownership record, but the book cannot be found in the inventory list.[76] This manuscript has been included in the catalogue along with other books from the Cistercian nunnery of Saint Mary Magdalene, which became the property of the Riga Jesuits when all the nuns had died.[77] The majority of these items do not have a Riga Jesuit college ownership record, and they cannot be found in the inventory of Bothvidi or in the Collijn archive. This leads me to conclude that the Cistercian books were transferred to the Uppsala University Library separately from the entire Riga Jesuit college collection, or were located somewhere else at the time the inventory of Bothvidi was compiled. Consequently, many were not registered in the list.[78]

Since the Riga Jesuit college collection in 1621 was first taken to Stockholm, it is possible that part of the collection never arrived in Uppsala, the most valuable items in the Riga collection having been added to the royal library of Stockholm immediately after arriving in Sweden.[79] Many of the books on the inventory list were not found by Collijn during the reconstruction of the library, which fact can be explained by the books being sold as duplicates at auctions organised by the Uppsala University Library, or having been destroyed or lost.[80]

The Riga college books ended up not only in major libraries, but also became objects of interest to bibliophiles.[81] Among these is a volume in the Östersund Library (*Östersunds bibliotek*) that is part of the Library's oldest collection, namely, in the personal collection of Carl Zetterström (1767–1829), a former Uppsala University medical professor. This is now known as the *Zetterströmska*

---

76   David de Augusta, *De exterioris and interioris hominis compositione* (Riga: 15th century), UUB C 802, CRJCBC, no. 12; Nicolaus Busch, *Nachgelassene Schriften von Dr. phil. h.c. Nicolaus Busch, Stadtbibliothekar zu Riga* (2 vols., Riga: Rigaer Stadtvervaltung, 1937), 2, p. 95; Levāns and Strenga, 'Medieval Manuscripts in the Riga Jesuit College Book Collection', p. 185.

77   Levāns and Strenga, 'Medieval Manuscripts in the Riga Jesuit College Book Collection', p. 172.

78   These manuscripts were included in the catalogue on the basis of a study carried out during the compilation of a manuscript catalogue for Uppsala University Library: Margarete Andersson-Schmitt et al., *Mittelalterliche Handschriften der Universitätsbibliothek Uppsala: Katalog über die C-Sammlung*. (8 vols., Stockholm: Almqvist & Wiksell, 1988–1995).

79   Isak Collijns samling, UUB, 475 D: 2, fol. [6]v.

80   Walde, *Storhetstidens litterära krigsbyten*, 1, pp. 50–51; Collijn, 'Storhetstidens litterära krigsbyten', p. 298.

81   Some copies belonging to the Riga College were later found in the collections of the Swedish National Library, Lund University Library and other Swedish libraries; for more see CRJCBC.

*biblioteket*.[82] Inscriptions in the volume indicate that the Uppsala University Library sold this rare copy as a duplicate. At the same time, it is not known what happened to the second identical volume mentioned in Isak Collijn's archive.[83]

Thanks to the interest of Uppsala University librarian Erik Benzelius the Younger (1675–1743), books with Riga college provenance came into his personal collection.[84] One copy from his personal collection was probably included in the Gothenburg High School collections at the time, when Benzelius became bishop of Gothenburg (1726–1731), although there is no clear evidence of this.[85] Among other things, Benzelius was probably the designer of a *supralibros* for the Uppsala University Library, called $Ιατρεῖον\ Ψυχῆς$ (*Iatreion psyches*, Healing Place of the Soul), which has also been embossed in gold on some of the rare Riga college bindings.[86]

Several books brought from Riga were included in the personal collections of prominent Swedish officials and never reached the Uppsala University Library.[87] Specific examples have not been identified, so the exact number of Riga Jesuit books held in personal collections is unknown. My observations attest that several copies from personal collections later ended up in smaller Swedish libraries.[88]

## 6   The Riga Jesuit College Legacy Outside Swedish Libraries

A search for copies of books from the former Riga college was also conducted in the Lithuanian capital, which was an important centre of Catholic culture

---

82   Martin Luther, *Der Euangelische Wetter Han* (Braniewo: Johann Sachse, 1590), USTC 633259, Östersund Municipal Library, Östersund, Zetterström 6160, CRJCBC, no. 536.

83   Isak Collijns samling, UUB, 475 D: 2, p. 157 (*576).

84   Classical philologist, orientalist, expert on Greco-Jewish philosophy, researcher of Swedish medieval history and the Gothic texts of the Silver Bible, he helped the library to thrive with his active efforts. He compiled new catalogues, participated in book auctions and collaborated with bibliophiles, Lindroth, *A history of Uppsala University 1477–1977*, p. 63.

85   Granberg, 'Carolina Redivivas samling från Jesuitkollegiets bibliotek i Riga och Isak Collijns arkiv', p. 82.

86   Gustaf Rudbeck, *Uppsala universitetsbiblioteks exlibris* (Uppsala: Almqvist & Wiksell, 1921), p. 395; bindings with this supralibros are depicted in CRJCBC: no 174, 463, 679, 691.

87   Granberg, 'Carolina Redivivas samling från Jesuitkollegiets bibliotek i Riga och Isak Collijns arkiv', p. 81.

88   Kreigere-Liepiņa, 'Bibliographic Reconstruction of the Book Collection of the Riga Jesuit College', pp. 58–60.

in the region for several centuries. Compilation of the catalogue revealed that several books intended for the Riga college were printed in the printing house of the Vilnius Jesuit Academy (*Officina Academiae Vilnensis Societatis Iesu*), which suggests there was close cooperation between the two institutions.[89] The Vilnius Jesuit college existed long before the Riga college was founded, and the Vilnius Academy (*Academia Vilnensis*) was the only Jesuit university in the Polish-Lithuanian Commonwealth.[90] All this made Vilnius an useful place for printing Jesuit literature during the existence of the Riga college and a favourable place for the continuation of Jesuit missions after the closing of the Riga college.

When, in 1621, the Swedish crown ordered the confiscation of Jesuit property and the Jesuits themselves were expelled from Riga, they headed for Lithuania and the Vilnius Jesuit college. Some Jesuits even fled there with college property before Riga was occupied.[91] Frisius (1572–1638), then Rector of the Riga college, and others of the Catholic elite fled to Vilnius, taking the most valuable liturgical objects with them.[92] Two of these objects (a silver cup and a ciborium) have survived to this day and are currently held by the Vilnius Church Heritage Museum.[93] It is very likely that the Jesuits also took some of the college's valuable books to Vilnius to save them from the Swedish army. Every surviving copy with a Riga college ownership record in Vilnius library collections is of great value, all the more so because the collection of rare books owned by Vilnius Academy Jesuits, which probably contained volumes from Riga, suffered a number of fires during several wars and was moved from one country to another.[94]

To date, a total of twenty-three books and one manuscript with a Riga college ownership record have been identified in Vilnius libraries: the National Library of Lithuania, the Vilnius University Library and the Wroblewski Library of the Lithuanian Academy of Sciences. Six of these had been transferred to

---

89  In total, twenty-six copies published by this printing house are included in the CRJCBC.
90  Jakub Niedźwiedź, 'Jesuit Education in the Polish-Lithuanian Commonwealth', *Journal of Jesuit Studies 5* (2018), pp. 441–455, here p. 451.
91  Walde, *Storhetstidens litterära krigsbyten*, 1, p. 44.
92  Kleijntjens, *Fontes SJ*, p. XXI [21]. For Frisius see: Grzebień, *Encyklopedia wiedzy o jezuitach na ziemiach Polski i Litwy 1564–1995*, p. 169.
93  Inv. no BPM BP-15; BPM BP-1100; Dalia Vasiliūnienė, Martynas Jakulis, Liudas Jovaiša, *Dangaus miestas: Vilniaus vienuolynų palikimas Bažnytinio paveldo muziejuje* [City of Heaven: The Heritage of Vilnius Monasteries at the Museum of Church Heritage] (Vilnius: Bažnytinio paveldo muziejus, 2020), p. 106; Berga, 'Rara et cara', pp. 148–149.
94  *Vetera Reducta: Exhibition catalogue 15 November 2012–15 June 2013* (Vilnius: Vilniaus universiteto leidykla, 2012), pp. 15–16.

Vilnius from the Daugavpils residence or college.[95] With the collapse of the Polish-Lithuanian Commonwealth, books from Lithuania were systematically transferred to Russian libraries. In this way, in the nineteenth century, several Riga college copies ended up in the Library of the Saint Petersburg Imperial Roman Catholic Theological Academy, later the Russian Academy of Sciences.[96] Other Riga Jesuit college copies reached the library of Kyiv's Saint Vladimir University, from where, thanks to a project led by Vilnius University professor Levas Vladimirovas (1912–1999), they were returned to Vilnius in the middle of the twentieth century, together with a large number of books from the historic Vilnius University.[97] One Riga Jesuit college copy was also in the private *Bibliotheca Sapiehana* collection for some time, which Kazimierz Leon Sapieha (1609–1656), a statesman of the Grand Duchy of Lithuania, bequeathed to the Vilnius Jesuit Academy on 20 July 1655.[98] These items and thirteen other Vilnius University books contain the inscription *Bibliothecae Magnae*, which was used to label the most valuable books in the Vilnius Jesuit College Library.[99]

The different names Vilnius University has had in its long history allow us to date roughly the inclusion of copies in the library's collection. Also helpful is the likelihood that the books may have been purchased from the Riga Jesuit college, as evidenced by the price tag in florins on the title pages of at least nine books. Collijn pointed out that Riga college purchased books from Vilnius college, which is also confirmed by entries in accounting ledgers.[100] In addition, a few copies were purchased from the Vilnius Jesuit Novitiate.[101]

The Riga Jesuit college library has preserved several publications printed in one of the oldest printing houses in Vilnius that belonged to the Karcan family. Preliminary research revealed that this number includes a breviary convolute,

---

95 Bibliographic information about *Riga Jesuit College Library* copies in Vilnius libraries can be obtained from the CRJCBC, as well as from electronic library reference catalogues.
96 *Vetera Reducta*, pp. 36–37, 73.
97 *Vetera Reducta*, pp. 16, 33–34, 121.
98 Michael von Isselt, *Mercurii Gallobelgici ... Nuntii, tomus secundus* (Cologne: Gottfried von Kempen, 1597) USTC 675710, Vilnius University Library, BAV 40.9.33b/2, CRJCBC, no. 469; Michael von Isselt, *Mercurii Gallobelgici ... Nuntii, tomus tertius* (Cologne: Gottfried von Kempen, 1596) USTC 675715, Vilnius University Library, BAV 40.9.33b/3, CRJCBC, no. 470; Alma Braziūnienė and Aušra Rinkūnaitė, *Bibliotheca Sapiehana: Vilniaus Universiteto bibliotekos rinkinys: katalogas* (Vilnius: Lietuvių literaturos ir tautosakos institutas, 2010), pp. 408–409.
99 Braziūnienė, Rinkūnaitė, *Bibliotheca Sapiehana*, p. XXXVIII.
100 Isak Collijns samling, UUB, 475 D: 2, fol. [8]r; Collijn, 'Storhetstidens litterära krigsbyten', p. 299.
101 Luca Pinelli, *Odoskonalosci zakonney, Księgi czwore* (Kraków: Mikołaj Lob, 1607), USTC 2154909, Riga 182 (UUB 65:43), CRJCBC, no. 636; Girolamo Piatti, *Dobra dvchowne stanv zakonnego* (Kalisz: Wojciech Gedeliusz, 1606), Riga 241 (UUB 66:99), CRJCBC, no. 632.

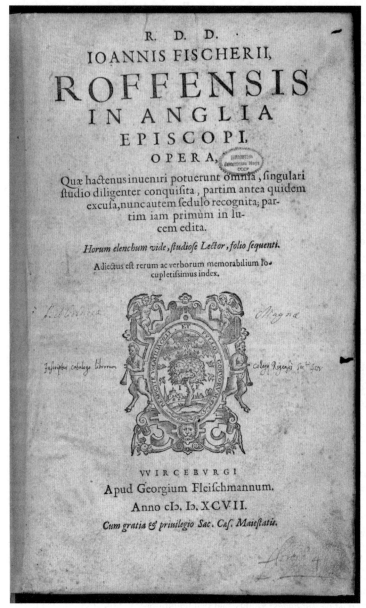

FIGURE 13.3  A title page of the Riga Jesuit college library's book bearing provenance inscription Bibliothecae Magnae of the former institution, Vilnius Jesuit college library, and a stamp of the Russian Academy of Sciences. John Fisher, *Opera, quae hactenus inveniri potuerunt omnia ...*, (Würzburg: Georg Fleischmann, 1597), Vilnius University Library, BAV 7.2.10., CRJCBC, no. 392, USTC 689682

valuable in the context of Jesuit heritage. The breviary came from the Jesuit notable Laurentius Nicolai Norvegus (called Kloster Lasse, 1538–1622), who worked at the Riga college from 1610 to 1612, and then also resided in Vilnius until the end of his life. He donated it to Sebastian Kromer († 1605), Canon of Warmia.[102] The number also includes a publication printed in Vilnius but not identified elsewhere in the bibliography, together with two other Antwerp publications.[103] The Riga Jesuit Library collection includes two other Vilnius editions produced at the Karcan printing house, a Catechism and its appendix in Polish, but these have not yet been identified in the bibliography.[104]

During the reconstruction project a book with a college ownership inscription in Estonia was also identified. This is a treatise on the teachings and lives of Luther and Jean Calvin (1509–1564) in German, currently held by the Tallinn University Academic Library.[105] This item can be linked to another in the Uppsala University Library collection, namely, the book by the Portuguese Jesuit and theologian Pedro da Fonseca (1527–1599): a commentary on Aristotle's work *Metaphysics*.[106] During the preliminary research on the Riga Jesuit college copy, it was established that there are at least nine books bound with the unifying features of the 'Riga binding'. The elements tooled in the binding of the Tallinn copy – the monogram *D G* and the Riga city symbol: crossed keys – indicate that the books may have been bound in Riga, or was bound on order from Riga's Jesuits. It is also possible that this copy was already mentioned in the 1660 inventory of Saint Olav's Church in Tallinn (Reval), and

---

102 Norwegian Jesuit priest Laurentius Nicolai Norvegus after an unsuccessful Swedish mission *Missio Suetica* came to Livonia most likely with books that in 1621 were taken back to Stockholm. For more on the Jesuit *Norvegus* see Helk, *Die Jesuiten in Dorpat 1583–1625*, pp. 20–21, 156; Grzebień, *Encyklopedia wiedzy o jezuitach na ziemiach Polski i Litwy 1564–1995*, p. 454.

103 *Officium S. Angeli Custodis* (Vilnius: Juozapas Karcanas, 1612), USTC 250293, Riga 162 (UUB 64:86), CRJCBC, no. 600; Daiva Narbutienė, *Lietuvos Didžiosios Kunigaikštijos lotyniškoji knyga XV–XVII a.* (Vilnius: Lietuvių literatūros ir tautosakos institutas, 2004), p. 124; Józef Trypućko, *Polonica vetera Upsaliensia* (Uppsala: Almqvist & Wiksell, 1958), p. 186.

104 *Katechism álbo krotkie wiáry y powinnośći* (Vilnius: Jan Karcan, 1594), Riga 214 (UUB 65:232), CRJCBC, no. 487; *Forma Albo* (Vilnius: Jan Karcan, 1594), Riga 214 (UUB 65:232), CRJCBC, no. 398.

105 Noël Taillepied, *Summarische Historia Vnd Warhafftig Geschicht Von dem Leben* (Ingolstadt: Wolfgang Eder, Officina Weissenhorniana, 1582), USTC 694956, Tallinn University Academic Library, I-851, CRJCBC, no. 747; see reference 36.

106 Pedro da Fonseca, *Commentariorum Petri Fonsecae D.* (Rome: Bartolomeo Tosi, Francesco Zanetti, 1577), USTC 830216, Riga 356 (UUB 71:42), CRJCBC, no. 396; Estonian researcher Kaspar Kolk has pointed out the copies' links with the Riga Jesuit college.

described as 'ein Gottloses Buch', but there is no direct information on how the book reached Tallinn from the Riga Jesuit college[107] (see figure 13.4, p. 342).

The problem of books with Tartu Jesuit college (1583–1625) ownership inscriptions in the reconstructed Riga college collection has not yet been fully resolved. They were included on the basis of the inventory list of 1622 and, most likely, the Tartu books arrived in Sweden at the same time as the Riga Jesuit college library.[108]

The fates of the Riga and Tartu colleges differed. The Tartu college had suffered more during the Polish-Swedish War and endured two lootings. At the beginning of the seventeenth century and in 1625, Swedish troops overran Tartu and seized the Jesuit college's property.[109] It is most likely that the majority of the books were destroyed, with the most valuable copies ending up in the libraries of other colleges. Helk believes that the Tartu Jesuits regularly visited neighbouring colleges, including the Riga college.[110] This suggests that such visits allowed book exchanges books or the presentation of books to other colleges as gifts. Two copies belonging to the Tartu college also bear the name of the Riga college, but in an atypical manner. That is, the Tartu college inscription was deleted and corrected to the Riga college entry in the book *Nowy Ray Duszny*; for its part, the copy of *De re militari* which later reached Poland, has the inscription on its inside front cover.[111] Most of the Riga college inscriptions are on the title pages of books. These inscriptions and information in the Jesuit accounting ledgers attest to the connection between the two colleges at a time

---

107 Verzeichnüs derer Bücher, so von der alten Revalschen Bibliothec, sent Ao. 1552. überblieben, und jetzo, in S. Olai Kirche, annoch vorhanden sind: www.etera.ee/zoom/21901/view ?page=32&p=separate&tool=info&view=0,1269,3191,3539 (last accessed 5 May 2023).

108 In the CRJCBC, bibliographic records have been produced for a total of seventeen independent works and possible alligates that belonged to the Tartu college; The Tartu college books were transferred together with the Riga Jesuit Library and their titles can be found in the inventory list of 1622; Walde, *Storhetstidens litterära krigsbyten*, 1, pp. 50–51; Collijn, 'Storhetstidens litterära krigsbyten', pp. 298–299.

109 Helk, *Die Jesuiten in Dorpat 1583–1625*, pp. 128–130; Klaus Garber, *Schatzhäuser des Geistes: Alte Bibliotheken und Büchersammlungen im Baltikum* (Köln: Böhlau, 2007), p. 134.

110 Helk, *Die Jesuiten in Dorpat 1583–1625*, p. 156.

111 *Pro Coll [egio] [Derpatensi]* (changed to *Rigensi Soc. Jesu*) – Jan Buys, *Nowy Ray Duszny* ... (Kraków: Mikołaj Lob, 1608), Riga 176 (UUB 64:314), CRJCBC, no. 216; *[Insc]riptus [Catalogueo] Rigensi Anno 1597* – Giovanni Antonio Valtrinus, *De re militari* (Cologne: Arnold Mylius, Arnold Birckmann, heirs, 1597), USTC 667441, University of Warsaw Library, Sd. 608.4477, CRJCBC, no. 793; for more about the possible fate of the book see: Izabella Wiencek-Sielska, 'Atbrīvoti no iesējuma – par Varšavā glabātajiem "Catechismus catholicorum" (Viļņa, 1585) eksemplāriem', in *Grāmata Latvijai ārpus Latvijas*, pp. 85–117.

when they were active bases for the promulgation of Catholicism in Livonia.[112] It cannot be said, however, that all the books with Tartu college inscriptions were at some time also used in the Riga college, but the few surviving copies in Swedish libraries suggest that they were spoils of war, similar to the Riga Jesuit college book collection removed to Sweden.[113]

Although the greater part of the college library was transported to Sweden, at least six books remained in Latvia and ended up in the Riga City Library.[114] Today, the oldest copies from this library, including the two Riga Jesuit college copies, form the rare book collection of the University of Latvia Academic Library.[115] It is difficult to say what happened to the other four books. They may have simply disappeared or perished in a 1941 fire that destroyed the historic catalogues and more than 400,000 of the City Library's books, mostly early prints, including many occasional writings.[116]

A previously unidentified college book was accidentally found during the closing stages of the reconstruction project, namely, a work by the Spanish Jesuit Alvarez de Páz, with a Riga Jesuit college ownership inscription. The volume is now in the collection of the National History Museum of Latvia.[117] This find is an important addition to the information about the Riga Jesuit books that remained in Latvia, and it is possible other books that once belonged to the Jesuits may be found in the collections of Latvian memory institutions in the future.

---

112   In November 1594, the College received 12 florins and 15 guilders from Tartu for the binding of books: *Compactori a libris Terpatensis, Libri Duo Rationum Collegij Rigensis*, Livonica I, vol. 45, fols. 346v–347r; on the College's cooperation with Tartu: Garstein, *Rome and the Counter-Reformation in Scandinavia: Until ... 1622*, p. 24.

113   For more information on the *Tartu college Library* copies, see Helk, *Die Jesuiten in Dorpat 1583–1625*, pp. 254–255.

114   Busch, *Nachgelassene Schriften*, p. 97.

115   Orazio Torsellini, *Horatii Tursellini Romani e Societate Iesu Lauretanae historiae* (Mainz: Balthasar Lipp, Arnold Mylius, 1599), USTC 664128, UL Academic Library, F12/1 inv. 1116, CRJCBC, no. 781; Saint Johannes Chrysostomus, *D. Ioan. Chrysostomi Constantinopolitani episcopi, Commentarium in Acta Apostolorum, Desiderio Erasmo Roterodamo interprete* (Antwerp: Joannes Steelsius, 1542), USTC 400698, UL Academic Library, R H2/6, CRJCBC, no. 253.

116   Garber, *Schatzhäuser des Geistes*, p. 210.

117   Diego Álvarez de Paz, *De exterminatione mali, [et] Promotione boni, Libri quinque ... Tomus secundus* (Mainz: Balthasar Lipp, Anton Hierat, (sen.), 1614), VD 17: 12:106270S, Latvian National Museum of History, CVVM 277521, CRJCBC, no. 831*.

7    Conclusions

Research into and reconstruction of the Riga Jesuit college library began in 2018, when, with cooperation between bibliographers and researchers at the Uppsala University Library and National Library of Latvia, attention came to be focused on copies from the former Jesuit library, with the intention of compiling a catalogue of the book collection. In parallel with the creation of bibliographic descriptions for the catalogue and research concerning each specific item, the catalogue compilers undertook a number of studies of and read lectures about the Riga Jesuit college book collection.

Interest in this collection, however, dates back to the seventeenth and eighteenth centuries, when the collection became available to Swedish researchers and bibliophiles. As one of the spoils of the seventeenth-century Swedish War, the Riga Jesuit books had already been studied in depth in the monograph *Storhetstidens litterära krigsbyten (1916–20)* by Otto Walde (1879–1963), a book historian. At the beginning of the twentieth century, the bibliographer Isak Collijn tried to reconstruct the Riga Jesuit college book collection. These important studies on Riga Jesuit books in Swedish libraries were the most widely known scholarship until the twenty-first century, when the current project was launched. Building on the earlier studies and using information from them, the Riga Jesuit college library has been reconstructed and has now taken its rightful place in the context of Northern European libraries of the Counter-Reformation period.

By comparison with other libraries removed by Sweden as spoils of war, the Riga Jesuit college book collection is relatively small.[118] Of the approximately 1,000 books registered on the inventory list of 1622, about half are still in Swedish library repositories. During the current project, dozens of books belonging to the college were also identified in other countries, which attests to the cooperation of Jesuit colleges in neighbouring countries.

When the Jesuits were travelling during missions and visits, books went to neighbouring colleges as gifts or loans. At times, book inscriptions serve as guideposts to the Jesuit journeys on the map of sixteenth and seventeenth century Europe or to the places where Jesuit books were purchased.

---

118   The Braniewo Jesuit College Library has information compiled on 3,274 books and manuscripts: Józef Trypućko, *The Catalogue of the Book Collection of the Jesuit College in Braniewo held in the University Library in Uppsala = Katalog księgozbioru Kolegium Jezuitów w Braniewie zachowanego w Bibliotece Uniwersyteckiej w Uppsali*, eds. Michał Spandowski, Sławomir Szyller (3 vols., Warszawa: Biblioteka Narodowa, 2007); the Poznań College Library may have had around 2,000 or more books transferred to Sweden: Sjökvist, 'Books from Poznan at the Uppsala University Library', p. 322.

What types of evidence have the books of the Riga Jesuit college left us? From this collection, it is clear that the Jesuit library was not lacking in books of religious content for Catholic teaching purposes, but also included Protestant literature. The books were assembled in accordance with the standards of the Jesuit college education system, *Ratio studiorum*. Most of them were the works of classical authors and early medieval theologians that were read at the college. In terms of content, the collection is heterogeneous and multicultural. The books were printed in several languages, though most are in Latin. A Jesuit library cannot be imagined without Biblical texts, which are also preserved in this collection, moreover in several languages.

The reconstruction process highlighted the most valuable items that had already been widely reviewed in the literature, as well as books that had previously remained unknown. One of the benefits of reconstructing the book collection was the partial digitisation of the collection, providing researchers with the incentive to closely study the Riga Jesuit college copies.[119]

Many of the books transferred to the Uppsala University Library are not only well preserved but appear to never have been read at all. Those which have been used often, however, reveal much about the book's former owner or owners. According to provenance inscriptions, which often include people's names and years, as well as by reference to the inscription's language, books were recognised and included in the Riga Jesuit college book collection brought to Sweden in 1621 as a war booty. Most of the Riga Jesuit college library consisted of books used in the college and ones that belonged to clergy or Riga townspeople connected with the college.

Information about and research on the Riga Jesuit college book collection is an original contribution to Latvia's cultural and publishing history. Particular emphasis should be placed on the registering of hitherto unidentified copies, the study of Riga bindings and, above all, on the compilation of a bibliographic catalogue, reuniting this historical collection digitally and in printed form. Today's digital means of communication and efficient reference services have enabled books from antiquity to be read and viewed anywhere in the world.

---

119  Digitisation has facilitated work on one of the College's copies, which has been translated into Lithuanian: Darius Antanavičius, *Basilius Hyacinthius Vilnensis, Panegyricus in excidium polocence (1580)* = *Bazilijus Hiacintijus iš Vilniaus, Panegirika Polocko sugriovimo proga (1580)* (Vilnius: Lietuvos istorijos institutas, [2021]).

CHAPTER 14

# Dissonance and Consonance in the Early Modern Battle of Books

*A Personal Reading*

*Janis Kreslins*

Book culture in early modern Europe is mired in paradox. Intertwined with seemingly endless military conflicts and upheavals, it seems, at first glance, to manifest itself in the agitated and convulsive interplay between cultural paradigms and historical events. The more pronounced the external stimuli that incite aggression and foster anxiety, the more unsettled the intellectual and cultural environments. We are wont to assume that this turbulence not only leaves an indelible impact on print culture, but also profoundly influences other forms of cultural expression.

This current volume demonstrates that the early modern period, if viewed through the lens of media culture especially in its print form, projects a completely different view. Before our eyes there unfolds a tapestry, the *individual threads of which* display discrepancy and dissonance; the *patterns* formed in the embroidery as a whole, however, seem to possess a surprising degree of consonance, unity and coherence. The modern Europe that takes form in the throes of the Thirty Years' War projects a surprisingly composite image.

Consequently, it is only fitting to ask whether the purported *battle of books*, the term chosen as the title of this volume, truly presages and sets in motion broader changes and lasting shifts in cultural values. Do these changes indisputably reflect more than just random fluctuations? How should we apprehend cultural phenomena against the background of institutional transformations and the reconfiguration of power structures in the European North? How are we to reassess the transition from medieval paradigms to more modern ones? To what extent does the development of technical platforms and production methods interplay with ideological notions and perceptions?

These questions compel the authors of this volume to calibrate the porosity and receptiveness of this region, at times broadly, at others, in minute detail. Battles usually promulgate and enforce clear borders and divisions, many of which tend to be less visible and less tangible before the actual commencement of hostilities. They also frequently take place without marked aesthetic impact. Books, regardless of their ideological colouration, resemble works of art. At times, users of very different persuasions can view them and find

© JANIS KRESLINS, 2023 | DOI:10.1163/9789004441217_016
This is an open access chapter distributed under the terms of the CC BY-NC-ND 4.0 license.

meaning and purpose in them. They can also be viewed and not necessarily perused. Very portable, even when transported in bulk, they can change their character with a change of environment. They can make spectacular entries, only to disappear from public view just as quickly. They unravel microcosms and allude to macrocosms.

One circumscribed microcosm is at the centre of Matthias Lundberg's exposition on the interplay between market interests and ecclesiastical idiosyncrasies. He demonstrates how missals, often regarded as crown jewels in the history of early modern printing, seem to live in a world of their own. There seems to be an insatiable appetite for large format publications that display technical brilliance and virtuosity. The ink had hardly dried before dioceses demonstrated their command of the media market by launching new large-scale follow-up editions. The turnarounds were quick and effective.

Against the mirror of these showy editions, Lundberg engages the question whether it is viable to regard the Baltic as a region from the perspective of book production. The fissure between larger centres with resources and those without the infrastructure for conceiving large print projects was striking. This dichotomy allows us, hundreds of years later, to discern how disinterested the producers and printers themselves were in ecclesiastical matters. Lundberg also underscores how infatuated church circles could be with the size of individual print editions.

Book production, however, does not always follow strict market criteria. In her contribution, Lenka Veselá points to the importance of underscoring narrow indicators at the expense of more comprehensive approaches. Detail is all-important, despite the magnitude of her source material! Her contribution returns repeatedly to the question of why some libraries were very coveted, while others not at all. She advocates opening the question of the functionality of books in motion and provides a rather stunning excursus on the bold efforts of the Bishop Mathiae of Strängnäs to open the transferred collections to a broader public upon their arrival at their final destination.

At times, the volume expands time perspectives by concentrating on a limited physical territory. Fryderyk Rozen not only draws attention to the importance of private libraries in early modern Europe, but also on the vagaries of territorial jurisdictions and disappearing histories. Underlying his entire presentation is the notion or erasure. Not only have we lost our appreciation of the differences between Royal and Ducal Prussia, but encounter almost insurmountable barriers in our attempts to focus on the disappearance of a regional cultural tradition in the aftermath of the Second World War.

Reconfigured geography figures in a meaningful way also in Anders Toftgaard's chapter on Holstein and Denmark. To this day, this area provides a telling example of the, at times, complicated interplay between political and cultural borders. Toftgaard calls into question how the identities of book collectors can raise questions and concerns in trying to devise fault-proof models of cultural interaction. Of particular interest, is the role that the language used in books can be used as a weapon, most often provocatively in dealings with one's neighbours and rivals. Also insightful is Toftgaard's observation on the role that book sales can have in reconfiguring cultural identity and literacy. A book auction in Strängnäs in central Sweden provided an opportunity for Danes to shore up and enhance their competitive positioning in a cultural landscape beset with contradictions and turmoil. This can even have repercussions in dealing with issues of heritage in contemporary settings.

Laine Tabora enables us to pause for a moment and view the role that manuscript editing can have on printed cultural values long after any emendations are made. The battle for Tabora can be discerned already in handwritten books of hours, as seemingly minor alterations enabled religious orders to sustain liturgical traditions and practices. New meanings could be created by the seemingly innocuous shift from the singular to the plural in certain passages.

Jonas Nordin raises the interesting question as to how items confiscated or taken as booty differ from those imported through usual channels. What happens once they have found their new homes in their new settings? The entire volume contains a plethora of examples where staking claim to material resources is no guarantee for preferential treatment or enhanced legacy. Propriety does not appear to be influenced by the process by which ownership and control is transferred. Without stating it explicitly, he intimates that the practice of conspicuous consumption does not follow the same patterns when physical objects contain intellectual capital. How are we to assess intellectual value upon its assimilation in a new environment? This question should garner more attention, since selection and curatorship was not necessarily performed by specialists or enthusiasts, but by secretaries of the field chancellery or other clerks of various sorts. Extremely titillating is Nordin's claim that the movement of intellectual property may have a direct correlation with the rise of censorship and control.

This line of thought leads well into Kathleen M. Comerford's reflection as to why certain books have appeal and others not. Closely related with that is the question of how books are used, especially after shifts in ownership. Comerford provides us with a glimpse into this world of how *regulae*, indices, and prescriptive guidelines such as the Jesuit *Ratio Studiorum*, provided guidance for those faced with challenge of weeding in the early modern world-wide-web. This volume insightfully documents a very central shift in this world – from one in which libraries were not yet *selecta* in more modern sense of the word to one in which the organic growth and shrinkage of collections developed into a *habitus*. This *habitus* endured for centuries and was fractured and fissured significantly for the first time in a significant way with the onset of the digital world. The confiscation of books contributed to the development of a practice of selection – one is tempted to claim that the early modern period teaches us that disappropriation is an indispensable part or collection development.

Curatorship is the activity that enables us to deconstruct these processes. Elin Andersson in her presentation on an early modern academic gymnasium directs our attention to the notion of curatorship. Anderson concentrates more on the concept of curatorship than on individual curators, the more common approach. A library connected to an educational institution must address the question of what exactly is a useful book. Useful books play an elevated role in curriculum development. Curriculums are, and always have, set in motion volatile exchange. All through history, discussions about them have drawn battle lines and allegiances.

Hanna Matzheika, in turn, reminds us that books do not instigate battles on their own. They need their instigators. Not always was content the most important issue. In Poland-Lithuania, a Calvinist-Protestant Commonwealth, book cultures could coexist. This was especially true of poetry. This coexistence manifested itself even materially. Sustainability could manifest itself in use, re-use and repair. A Cistercian parchment could seemingly effortlessly be reinvented as a part of a Jesuit flyleaf!

Religious orders played a significant role in early modern book culture in North-eastern Europe. A common misconception is that religious orders thrived in isolated settings. Andris Levāns and Gustavs Strenga unfold a rapturous tale of the role that mendicant orders played in urban settings. There arose allegiances that left visible footprints in book culture. But even within particular orders, internal reform could disrupt social networks. Religious orders could ally themselves, at times, with the nobility, at others with merchants, with very different outcomes. In these settings, private book collections could interact with collective ones in astounding ways, thus forming multi-level book cultures in which women played leading roles, not only as stewards and custodians, but also as patrons and benefactors. The most active engagement with books not infrequently took place in the most unexpected environs. Books could thrive not only in seemingly unnoticed and secluded hideaways, but also in the crossfire of cultural social and political forces.

Some of the most effective weapons in battle could be catalogues that served as windows to that which the native eye not always could perceive. The key to a material's imperishableness and renewability lay frequently in the infrequency of its use. The confluence of these two phenomena, placement and catalogues, comes to the fore very vividly in the contributions of Peter Sjökvist and Laura Kreigere-Liepiņa.

## 1   The Practical and Symbolic Use of Books as Objects, Aids and Collections

A question that remains unanswered in almost every contribution in this volume is whether books engaged individually behave differently from those that are parts of collections. Does their individualization and privatization alter patterns of use? This issue unambiguously also demonstrates that books do not necessarily need to be opened and perused to exert influence and partake in societal building processes. This can happen in the following ways:

(1) Books can grant status and prestige by their sheer bulk, artistic quality, and visual impact. This volume manifests repeatedly how the desirability of individual objects and collections is only marginally related to use. Even more surprising perhaps for modern readers, is how neglect and indifference, disregard for subject matter, could set in motion unexpected processes.

(2) This volume also seems to illuminate how early modern books, when not used for devotional ends, were surprisingly often used as encyclopaedic reference tools. This was true of one's engagement with text, as well as with image. Some of the most sought after works incorporated intricate search systems with cross references and other tracking tools.

Early modern society was permeated with an abundance of sources the access to which did *not* present unconquerable hurdles. Source criticism acquired new depths and dimensions through the transformation of cognitive abilities not only in how users construed sources, but also in how the sources themselves were perceived. Books with interesting Windows-like layouts and physical tab-systems frequently show the greatest use. To reach any significant conclusions in these matters it is necessary to peruse collections and physically engage them – a task not made easier by restricted access to storage areas today. The early modern era was a golden age for reference source materials. It took some two hundred years for this force to reappear.

(3) Books also served as financial weapons – a way in which to arrange financial dealings and commercial exchange. This volume illustrates clearly, how war-booty was not only driven by policies to gain access to information, but also to accrue wealth. It provided an alternative system with which to settle accounts, certify balances and, at times, intimidate and fiscally embarrass enemies and opposing players. Books even more than artworks also provided an alternative currency. There are parallels with our contemporary

crypto-currency. They both constitute a financial system that lacks a central regulating authority, thus introducing an element of decentralization. The more mercurial the times, the more effective were dealings not overseen by any governing agency.

(4) This volume also illustrates how books served as an important tool in conflict resolution. The shambles that battlefields leave behind can be rectified and regulated with the help of physical objects be they works of arts or books. The most normative text in this regard was Hugo Grotius's *De iure belli ac pacis* (1625). Almost singlehandedly, this manual, introduced in this volume by Jonas Nordin, spelled out how books could be used in conflict resolution and outlined the hitherto lacking notions of how a law of booty and prize could be formulated.

For most of us, the first association with the concept of *battle* in which books are used as instruments of warfare is with war booty. Hugo Grotius was a true pioneer in this subject area. Grotius demonstrated how ideological warfare could be intermeshed not only with market regulation, but also with a court of justice. More was at stake here than a public show of military or political power intended to peeve an opponent. A stockroom full of artworks did not necessarily improve one's cash flow, but it could solidify one's money reserve – a tool to improve one's line of revolving credit on an international market. It hearkens back to gold credit – important to possess, but difficult to use.

(5) The early modern battle of books coincides with the proliferation and expansion of the Jesuit educational network in the European north. In today's book world, distinctiveness is a highly prized quality that provides added value. The Jesuit collections were in many regards the antithesis of this and left their mark by their number and their likeness. By expropriating one collection, one could claim a limited victory, no matter how spectacular the prize may have been. These small battles created sudden headlines and notoriety. Just as those of today, collections could disappear quickly from sight and collective consciousness.

The Jesuit collections demonstrated how sheer number and spread played an important role in times of political tension and ideological warfare. Neither is the role that glamour and fashion played to be disparaged; comprehensive networks of book collections far outstripped individual items, no matter what symbolic qualities they possessed, no matter their opulence. On the battlefield, uniformity and ubiquity proved to be the most effective weapon in the battle of books. It is no coincidence that Jesuit collections are the subject of interest for a number of the authors of this volume.

(6) The Jesuit predilection for uniformity opens the question of variance and eclecticism. Parallel to the Jesuit 'franchise-form' libraries, we find simultaneously cabinets of curiosities that served as showcases for the

informational/cognitive power of variance. Here the goal was not to assemble as comprehensive a collection of books or works of art that fit into certain stylistic categories, but to create laboratories in which exploration took place communally and multi-medially. Here the battlefield was reconfigured. The outer appearance of books by the early modern period was quite standardized and uniform in appearance. Only opened, did they significantly differ. 'Opening' a painting involved deciphering its iconological confessional perspective. Cabinets of curiosities, on the other hand, constituted a no man's land, geographically broad, but not bound to one location. The viewer was asked to relocate him- or herself.

(7) To outperform one's adversaries in this battle of books it was incumbent upon the participants to demonstrate technical proficiency and creativity. It was necessary not only to create new platforms, but also to reinforce and leverage existing ones. During the early modern period, the appearance of books underwent a profound shift in the way information was produced, viewed, and assessed. Of supreme importance were print techniques that furthered visualization and inquiry. In this battle, the appearance of books could change marginally, but their valence and their firepower could be encased and cloaked in technically advanced production methods and techniques.

## 2   Reconfigurations as Time Capsules

In most circumstances, we associate battles with build-ups and breakdowns, suddenness and unpredictability, and dramatic shift. This volume clearly demonstrates that the great build-ups only infrequently led to real change. These build-ups are frequently much more convulsive than the transfers themselves. Individual books or those that are a part of collections seem to lose their distinctiveness and idiosyncratic quality once they are moved. Puzzling are the circumstances that surround the transfer of books. There are countless contemporary examples of how the effectors of these transfers pursue objects with greater vigour and intensity than the skilled craftsmen and artisans themselves.

This volume also compels us to reconsider the notion that library identities seem to oscillate between two very distinct, though contrapuntal identities – that of the isolated safe haven and that of hubs of intertwined entanglement. From the contributions here it is clear that entanglement and simultaneity are not to be immediately conflated with battlegrounds.

Our contemporary notion of the library is that of a safeguard, albeit one that does not always live up to its call. To understand this role better, we must introduce yet another tension integral to the battle for books, that between suddenness and intransigence. We are apt to regard libraries as only marginally affected by change. A library that is removed from public space, a library the access to which is not used as a tool of political enforcement, is frequently immune to change; their most frequent challenge is to remain relevant and useful for the societal processes in their midst that motivate history and cultural evolution. Physical destruction of libraries takes place, but seldom.

This volume presents a telling example. The confessional battles in Riga in the post-Reformation era do not result in unrestricted iconoclasm; institutions, practices, and attitudes continue to live their lives in varying forms and to varying degrees. Not every institution was worn into submission. Instead of working in the open, books were safeguarded and stored, preserved not for intensive use in the moment, but for an unforeseeable future. Just as a pilot light does not provide enough heat for heat-intensive cooking, so, too, were books placed on a back burner. This explains how many seemingly untenable collections survive. The more irrelevant they are, the greater the chance that their possessions fall out of the spotlight and survive. The convent of Mary Magdalene Riga, we learn, provides such a haven in a turbulent world. And this is not merely a forlorn and distant historical example. Collections have been safeguarded in a similar manner during more recent times – inaccessible and icebound, collections can go into hibernation. Hibernation contributes to the natural ability of items to survive the presence of onslaughts of the most varied kind.

The library world in early modern Europe could be very insular. In many cases, libraries were the last institutions affected by change. Except for a few spectacular, politically motivated media events, they lived rather reclusive lives. Most often private or off-limits, they reflected individual tastes and creativity – not those of society as a whole. Individuality could be collective, as the Jesuit libraries so poignantly demonstrate. This was a franchised individuality, one lacking in medieval settings. Manuscripts fostered vastly diverging forms of devotion more subject to constant appraisal and change.

An almost sacred value for early modern libraries was safeism. Guaranteeing safety became ever more difficult as their invisibility decreased. There is an underlying expectation that collections are fragile and can be disbanded at any moment. Thus, collectors are wont not to flaunt wealth, but to ensure that collections reflect the collectors' good sense of style and taste. This involved making trade-offs demanded by practical and moral concerns.

The greater the emphasis on safety, the more private and secure the collections. Once again, the Jesuit collections stand out, as they were integrated into instruction. Instruction, in turn, unleashed a creativity that extended the walls of the physical collections. There arose a tradition grounded in material elusiveness. A prime example of this is Jesuit drama. Seldom did the plays themselves find their way into the physical book collections. Yet the organizational imperative to record and report led to the rise of rich archival collections outlining the process of production that not only complemented the book collections themselves, but also infused them with energy and life. Thus the key to understanding the inner workings of book collections comes not from the books themselves alone or the occasional catalogue, but from source material, outlining the performances and their production. It is very possible that the most dynamic collections are not book, but ephemeral collections. As frequently is the case, the volatile oral, performative, ephemeral world makes the book world seem stringent and intransigent in comparison. Yet books remain the object of desire. The plays are much more mobile than the books. Books, at times, could be more a liability than an asset.

Idiosyncratic and iconoclastic keepers play major roles in the grand theatre of early modern book collecting. Interestingly enough, they are largely missing in this battle report with the exception of some surreptitious nuns. The names of owners appear to be brandished in this volume, but were early modern books truly without keepers? Did books have cameo roles, supporting roles, or were they at the centre of attention? At times, it appears that they were independent of all human involvement, frozen in time. One could almost draw the conclusion that a book incorporated into a collection lost its dynamic quality if it was not embraced and taken care of by a keeper. The more eccentric the keeper, the more things happened. The keepers were the only ones who viewed the mass of books as an intertwined organic entity with its special identity. They were the ones who systematized and catalogued; they breathed life into the collections. In many regards, the keepers were the catalysts moving books to the front lines.

Since the collections and their keepers conflated, the story of the battle of books cannot be told without paying attention to their contribution. By directing the spotlight at the transfer of collections in bulk, we ignore that books were exchanged and reallocated. It is quite possible that he greatest battle of books took place out of sight – keepers weeding, replacing and exchanging, restocking, physically moving them around as chess pieces, and, in many cases, receiving them as recompense for services and incorporating them unobtrusively into one's own private collections or just losing track of them for no particular reason at all.

Regardless of their form, reconfigurations of collections play an important role in ideological battles. Not always was what you saw that what you got! Material could be excerpted, abridged, and taken out of context, thus muddling the original source. This was a frequent ploy in confessional battles and provided for the opportunity to circumvent censorship. This was the tour de force in controversial questions. There was no purer sense of conquest than using the writing of one's opponent to further one's own polemic intentions. Today, this would be considered as blatant plagiarism – using material without providing their source – but here the ends justified the means. Thus, Jesuit devotional texts could be retooled and rearranged and neatly made to fit in Protestant settings. Books could enter enemy territory without being noticed.

3      Relocating Books from Private to Public Spheres

The early modern age is also a harbinger of a new dichotomy in the world of books. On the one hand, private reading, which previously had been the domain of manuscripts, many frequently copied, written and illuminated on demand, now was closely intertwined with production processes that were determined by market forces of demand and supply. Gaining possession of an individual manuscript involved, in some ways, assuming and appropriating a very specific identity, both of the producer and the user. With the spread of print, the object could be monetized and relegated to a commodity. This involved a redefining of individuality and autonomy in reading. The notion of collectiveness was transformed. It lost some of its performative character. This was replaced by the notion that imaginary collective thinking could be fostered when a wide spectrum of readers were engaging the same text, even though each in his or her own particular way.

A pioneer in this regard was the Swedish polymath Gabriel Sparwenfeld (1655–1727). In Swedish civil service, he understood that the real battle of books did not primarily involve sequestering books in private libraries, but rather transforming them into public space. Moving books and collections would be of the greatest benefit if they contributed to change markedly the essence of societies. He also understood that opening borders, ultimately, would have the most significant lasting effect. The purpose was not to assume a defensive stance and to preserve an ideologically uniformity or to extend cross-jurisdictional conflicts, by emptying the hard-discs of one's enemies, but to promote and enhance movement that would serve constructive ends and not merely political positioning.

The true battle of books for him involved constructing a worldview that was not purely based on bilateralism. This meant not cleansing collections of rival publication, but acquainting oneself with a broader playing field. For Sparwenfeld, this implied traveling extensively and learning languages – a prerequisite for being able to access the riches in this world. He did not believe that this could be done by engaging a linguistic topography in direct view; one also needed to open one's eyes to the rich flora that existed, but may have been outside one's direct scope. His travels took him to places off the beaten track and involved learning languages that provided access to this rich tapestry of cultural expression.

Sparwenfeld was a prophet of the globalism to which we aspire today. Well aware that the greatest danger was ruptures in the chain of memory, he proposed taking intellectually in possession and serious engagement with the unknown by launching the idea of public institutions that would contribute to the notion of stewardship and deflate antagonism. As Wolfgang Undorf so poignantly underscores in his contribution, the whole notion of battles may be undermined by the insight that we have a penchant for misconstruing borders and devaluing market forces. Ironically, one of the most powerful market forces was the Index of Prohibited Books that directly contributed to the 'more modern' commodification and commercialization of books. This volume illustrates that the real war may not have been fought on the battlefield of legitimacy, ideology and vaunting. Its physical dimension may not have been its most important attribute. Its contours were vague, just as those of the then nascent and now ubiquitous modern financial market.

*Colour Illustrations*

FIGURE 3.5   Gilded initial in the second Missale Upsalense, Pforzheim: Basel, 1513

FIGURE 11.2    U 575 oct., possibly a war booty book from the Franciscan convent in Olomouc

ILLUSTRATIONS 341

FIGURE 13.2    Madonna with child ('Our Lady of Vladimir'), sixteenth century, Uppsala University Museum Gustavianum, UU 749. Probably one of the five Russian icons brought from Riga and mentioned on the inventory list, now held by Uppsala University

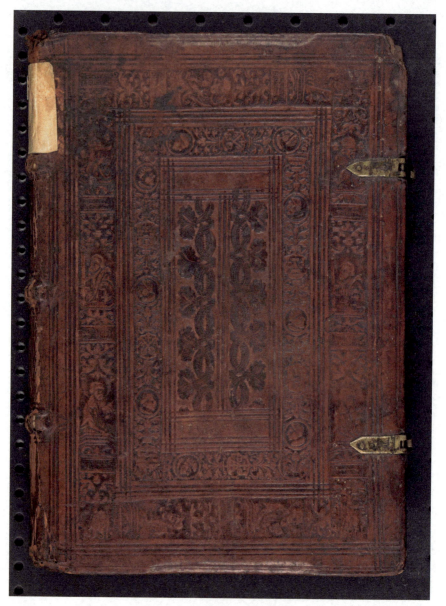

FIGURE 13.4    The book binding representing the monogram D G and Riga city symbol: crossed keys. These features indicate to possibility that the book was bound in Riga or for an order from Riga's Jesuits. Noël Taillepied, *Summarische Historia Vnd Warhafftig Geschicht Von dem Leben* (Ingolstadt: Wolfgang Eder, Officina Weissenhorniana, 1582), Tallinn University Academic Library, I-851, CRJCBC No 747, USTC 694956

# Index

The index includes historical and contemporary people, cities, regions, institutions and select phenomena. The title ascribed to each person is only an indication of their role in this context and is not a comprehensive description of an individual's position or overall importance. Places of printing are normally not included in the index.

Abrecrombie, Patrick, Jesuit   108, 115, 117
Abercrombie, Robert Jesuit   110–111, 119
Abercrombie, Thomas, Jesuit   107, 114
Abercrombie, William, Jesuit   115
Åbo. *See* Turku
Agricola, Michael, theologian   83
Ahldén, Tage, germanist   45
Aidie, Andrew, agent   118–119
Albrecht Hohenzollern, duke of Prussia   268–270
Alexander IV, Pope   17
Alexandria, library of   1–2
Älvsborg Castle   229–230
Åmark, Mats, librarian   255
Aminson, Henrik, librarian   251, 262
Amsterdam   155, 163
Andersson, Elin, librarian   329
Angler, Kaspar, bookbinder   269
Anna Maria of Brunswick-Calenberg-Göttingen, duchess   270
Anna of Denmark, queen of England and Scotland   221
Antwerp   86, 104, 138, 140, 321
Arason, Jon, bishop   217
Ariminiensis, Henricus, printer   169
Aristotle, philosopher   152, 156, 178, 321
Arndes, Stephan, printer   74
Arnamagnean collection   227, 232, 241
Aston, Arthur Jr, soldier   115
Attomes, Thomas, Jesuit   113–114
Augezdecki, Aleksander, printer   269
Augsburg   133, 276
Aurifaber, Andreas, physician   270
Avignon   28, 47

Badin, Jean, printer   86–87
Barcelona, University of   128
Barnekow, Christian, diplomat   220–221
Barthlet, John, author   121–122

Basel   57, 68, 70–73, 82–83, 87, 91, 95, 275
Bavarus, Johann, physician   309
Beck, Lave, nobleman   219
Belli, Pierino, legal scholar   167
Benzelius, Erik the Younger, bishop   317
Berga, Renāte, librarian   199–200, 203, 212
Biblioteka Narodowa. *See* National Library of Poland
Bibliotheca Palatina   9
*Bibliotheca selecta* (Possevino)   130, 135
Bielke, Hogenskild, councillor   93–95, 105, 155, 157, 162, 304
Biezais, Haralds, theologian   314
Billström, Tobias, politician   5
Bodin, Jean, jurist   156, 167
books of hours   14–20 *passim*, 22, 24, 27–31, 34–36, 45, 52–55, 87, 252, 328
Borowy, Wacław, historian   116
Bosgrave, James, Jesuit   110, 123
Bothvidi, Johannes, chaplain/Bothvidi inventory   8, 197–199, 203, 212, 305–306, 308, 310, 312, 316
Brahe, Per the Elder, procurator of the realm   155–156
Brahe, Per the Younger, procurator of the realm   161–162, 171, 174
Brahe, Tycho, astronomer   225
Brandis, Matthaeus, printer   67, 71, 75, 88
Braniewo, Jesuit college of   6–7, 108–109, 113–115, 118–119, 164, 187, 197n, 201–203, 205–207, 213, 304, 308, 315, 324n
Brasiator, Nicolaus, priest   51
Brask, Hans, bishop   72, 87, 89, 92
Breitenburg Castle   224, 226
Bremen   63, 65, 67, 175
Brent, James, Jesuit   112
Brenz, Johannes, theologian   93
breviaries   14, 17–20, 24–25, 27–28, 34–36, 45, 62–77, 87, 108

Bridget, Saint   26–27, 85, 152–153
Bridgettine Order   26–27
Bring, Ove, legal scholar   3
British Library   62
Brook, Adam, Jesuit   110–111
Bruchofen, Heinrich, chaplain   218
Bryncke, Margrete, nun   55
Bugenhagen, Johann, theologian   93
Buno, Johannes, theologian   233
Bureus, Johannes, librarian   203
Buringh, Eltjo, historian   175
Busch, Nicolaus, historian   43, 57
Bussow, Johannes, commissioner   183, 187, 193
Butler, James, colonel   114
Bydgoszcz   242n

cadukes   168
Callmer, Christian, librarian   254
Campion, Edmund, Jesuit   123–124
Canisius, Petrus, Jesuit   312
Carleton, Dudley, diplomat   222
Casimir Jagiellon, prince   107–108
Castelvetro, Giacomo, librarian   221–223
Castelvetro, Lelio, heretic   222
Cecil, Robert, statesman   221–222
Celsius, Magnus, librarian   173
Celsius, Olof, historian   168–169, 171
censorship   106, 127, 129, 131, 176–177, 214, 223, 328, 335
Cēsis   301
Charles IX, king of Sweden   156, 221
Charles X Gustav, king of Sweden   160, 175, 235
   wars of   170–173, 231, 235–236
Charles XI, king of Sweden   171
Charles XII, king of Sweden   160, 172–173
Chodkiewicz, Jan Karol, ambassador   312
Christian II, king of Denmark   90
Christian III, king of Denmark   157, 217–218
Christian IV, king of Denmark   219, 221, 225–226, 230, 233–234
Christian, duke of Haderslev and Tørning   217
Christina, queen of Sweden   158n, 160, 164, 175, 178, 187–191, 193–194, 235, 239, 242, 244–245, 250–252, 258, 259n

Ciotti, Giovan Battista, printer   222
Clement VII, Pope   107
Clement XIV, Pope   226
Cluj   130
Codex Argenteus. See Silver Bible
Codex Gigas. See Devil's Bible
Codex Holmiensis C   37 2, 240
Collijn, Isak, librarian   8, 152–153, 199–200, 226, 252, 263, 307–310, 315–317, 319, 324
Collinus, Matthaeus, humanist   254
Cologne   48, 67, 89, 154, 206–210, 212, 270, 276
Columbus, Jonas, poet   202n, 213
Comerford, Kathleen M., historian   328
Count's War   217
Counter-Reformation   1, 37, 108, 120, 124, 301, 324
Confessionalization, Age of   1
Copenhagen   64, 70, 92, 94–95, 105, 171, 214–215, 217–219, 221, 227, 233, 238–241
   Treaty of   235
Copernicus, Nicolaus   6, 304
Coyet, Peter Julius, envoy   235–236
Coyet, Wilhelm Julius, secretary   236
Cranach, Lucas the Elder, painter   268
Crusius, Georg, author   224
Czaika, Otfried, church historian   91, 96, 103, 153

Dahlbergh, Erik, military   171
Daugavapils   319
De Guibert, Joseph, theologian   143
De la Gardie, Beata, noblewoman   162
De la Gardie, Jakob, councillor   160
De la Gardie, Magnus, chancellor   160–161, 171, 191
Delft   138, 140
Devil's Bible   3–4, 169
Dietrichstein Library   179, 184, 186–188, 221n
Dietz, Ludwig, printer   90
Disraeli, Benjamin, prime minister   225
Ditmarshes   224, 227
Dizos, Joannes Nicolaus, student   107–108
Dorothea of Denmark, duchess   270
Dorpat. See Tartu
Douai   113
Douglas, William, Jesuit   114

INDEX

Dreling, Paul, city councillor  57
Dresden  168
Dudík, Beda, historian  254, 262–263
Duff, Thomas, Jesuit  115
Dulken, Cornelius, friar  50–51, 58–60

Eck, Johann von, theologian  268
Elofsson, Sven, secretary  258
Emporagrius, Erik, bishop  255
*Encyclopédie*, Diderot's  215
Erasmus of Rotterdam, philosopher  156
Erfurt  35, 65, 104, 161
Erik XIV, king of Sweden  155, 157, 227, 229
Ernst, Heinrich, philologist  233
Erskine, Alexander, military  189
European Jesuit Libraries Provenance Project, EJLPP  127–148 *passim*

Fabri, Johannes, printer  68
Farrell, Allan P., historian  144
Faunt, Laurence Arthur, theologian  111
Fehr, Isak, librarian  242, 255, 263
Fischer, Frederick, chancellor  269
Florence  141, 191
Floyd, Griffith, Jesuit  119
Fonseca, Pedro da, Jesuit  321
Forster, Robert, Jesuit  112
Foxe, John, historian  121
Frankfurt am Main  83, 91, 93, 95, 105, 163
Frauenburg. *See* Frombork
Frederick I, king of Denmark  90, 217
Frederick II, king of Denmark  225, 229–230
Frederick III, king of Denmark  231, 233–234, 239
Frederick IV, king of Denmark  238
Freedman, Joseph S., historian  135
Friis, Johan, chancellor  227–228
Frithz, Carl-Gösta, librarian  251
Frombork  6–7, 51, 164, 201–203, 304
Fulke, William, theologian  121

Gadh, Hemming, bishop  227, 229
Garber, Klaus, germanist  272
Garnier, Jean, Jesuit  131
Gdańsk  161
Gemekow, Reinold, priest  58–59, 314–315
Gentili, Alberico, legal scholar  167

345

Georgia Southern University  128
Gersdorff, Joachim, seneschal  234
Ghotan, Bartolomeus, printer  68, 74, 152, 157
Giampetro Ferraris, legal scholar  49
Giessen  162
Gifford, Richard, Jesuit  112
Gisbert, Nicolaus, priest  313
Good, William, Jesuit  111
Gothenburg  317
Gottorp Library  237–238
Graheli, Shanti, literary scholar  73
Graman/Graumann, Johann. *See* Poliander, Johannes
Great Northern War  160, 172–174, 216, 236, 238
Greenblatt, Stephen, literary historian  226
Grickevičius, Arūnas, historian  113
Gripenhielm, Edmund Figrelius, councillor  171, 191, 235–236
Grotius, Hugo, legal scholar  166–168, 331
Grubb, Petrus, lecturer  255
Grzebień, Ludwik, Jesuit  310
Guldenmund, Conradus, printer  252
Gumaelius, Gustaf Wilhelm, rector  260
Gustav I Vasa, king of Sweden  90, 153, 216, 227–228, 262
Gustavus Adolphus, king of Sweden  5–6, 114, 156–160, 162, 164–165, 167–168, 174, 1782, 183n, 197, 199, 201, 301
Gyllenius, Petrus, priest  250

Hallman, Lars, priest  258
Hallsen, Paul, librarian  232
Hamburg  65, 82, 84, 104, 224–226
Hanseatic League  64–65, 83–84
Haquinus, librarian  308
Hathonus, Thomas; Jesuit  114
Hay, John, Jesuit  109–110
Heiberg, Steffen, historian  233
Heidelberg  9
Heiligenstadt  161
Helgesen, Paul, Carmelite  217
Hermelin, Olof, historiographer  173
Hippel, Theodor Gottlieb von, author  278
Hoffman, Tycho de, judge  233
Holstein  158, 215–216, 224, 327

Honsonus, Gwalter, Jesuit   114
Hosius, Stanislaus, cardinal   111, 121–122
Howlett, John, Jeuit   111
Huggut, Henrik Matsson, royal secretary   95
Hussite Wars   180

icons   307, 341
Index of Prohibited Books   129–130, 336

Jacobi, Sveno, bishop   91, 93
Jacob Ulfsson, archbishop   68, 70
Jahn, Michal, superior   182
Jakobsen, Johnny Grandjean Gøgsig, medievalist   41
Jakó, Klára, historian   130
James I/VI, king of England/Scotland   118, 221
Jewel, John, bishop   121
Johan III, king of Sweden   155, 168, 229
Johann Adolf, duke of Holstein   237
John XXII, Pope   47
Jordan, Simon, Jesuit   112
Justinian, emperor   156

Kalmar   174
Kalmar Union   216–217
Kankel, Johann, printer   161
Karcan family and printing house   319, 321
Kaufmann, Thomas, church historian   91
Kinnaird, David Leonard, Jesuit   114
Kleijntjens, Jean Chretien Josef, Jesuit   302$n$
Klug, Joseph, printer   276
Koberger, Anton, printer   50
Koberger, Margarethe, burgher's wife   50
König, Felix, librarian   269
Königsberg   267–273, 275–279, 280$n$
Königsmarck, Hans Christoff von, field marshal   226
Köpfel, Wolfgang, printer   273
Krag, Otte, Councillor   231, 235
Kraye, Jill, historian   135
Kreigere-Liepiṇa, Laura, librarian   199–200, 203, 213, 330
Krollmann, Christian, philologist   267$n$, 273–274, 279
Kromer, Sebastian, canon   321
Kruus, Jesper Mattson, field marshal   305
Kulvietis, Abraomas, legal scholar   270
Kyiv   319

Lambert, William, Jesuit   110–111
Lamormain, Wilhelm, confessor   226
Lange, Hans Ostenfeld, librarian   226
Lange, Villum, county judge   239
Langkilde, Birgitte, librarian   218
Langner, Christophor, student   274
Laurentius Nicolai Norvegus, Jesuit   169, 321
Liège   131$n$, 138, 140–142
Leech, Andrew, Jesuit   117–118
Le Gallois, Pierre, author   214–215
Leiden   183, 195
Leipzig   48, 83, 86, 93–94, 231, 268, 276, 278, 313
Leonora Christina, princess   233–234
Leuven   138, 140
Levāns, Andris, historian   329
Lewkenor, Samuel, Jesuit   109, 114, 117, 125
Linde, Ann, politician   4, 6
Lindeberg, Peter, author   2245
Lindsey, James, Jesuit   114
Linköping   68, 87, 89, 174, 243
Linnæus, Carl, botanist   232
Lipsius, Justus, humanist   127$n$, 131
Lithuanian Academy of Sciences Library   14, 39, 45
Little Free Library   126
Livonian War   301
Loccenius, Johannes, historiographer   256
Lock, Andrew, Jesuit   113
Locke, Edward, Jesuit   115
Lomoller, Johann, diplomat   271
Łoś, Jan, philologist   263
Losman, Arne, historian   163
Lotter, Melchior, printer   276
Lübeck   64, 67–68, 71, 74–75, 81, 82–85, 88–91, 95–96, 101–102, 152
Lufft, Hans, printer   269, 276
Lund   72, 86, 105, 174, 236
Lund, Zacharias, librarian   231–233, 236
Lundberg, Matthias, musicologist   327
Lundgren, Ragnhild, librarian   251
Luther, Martin, theologian   58, 92–93, 104, 268–269, 310
Lutsk   242$n$
Lyon   276

Madsen, Victor, librarian   239
Magalotti, Lorenzo, diplomat   163
Magnus, bishop   229

INDEX

Magnus, Johannes, archbishop   154–155, 227
Magnus, Olaus, archbishop   153–155, 227
Mainz   7, 81, 164, 202n, 210, 251–252
Makowski, Tomasz, librarian   6
Malins, Thomas, Jesuit   112
Malmö   86, 174, 235
Mariager   219
Mariani, Andrea, historian   130
Maribo   219
Matthiae, Johannes Gothus, bishop
    192–194, 242, 244–245, 250–251,
    255–256, 258, 260, 264, 327
Mazheika, Hanna, historian   329
Mazarin, Jules, cardinal   239
Meidel, Theodor, Jesuit   315
Melanchthon, Philipp, theologian   93, 156, 310
Mendoza, pirate   230
Mennander, Carl Fredrik, bishop   178
Mercurian, Everard, Jesuit   108
Messenius, Johannes, historian   256
Meursius, Johannes, philologist   232
Meyer, Werner, librarian   231
Mikulov Castle   179, 184, 186–188, 190, 242
Milan   275
Molin, Emma Hagström, historian   163
Montoya, Diego Ruiz de, Jesuit   135
Moscow   177
Moseley, Humphrey, printer   120
Munich   133, 143
Munk, Jens, ship master   230
Munk, Kirsten, royal spouse   233
musical notation   14–15, 29–33, 35–36,
    63–64, 68

National Archives of Denmark   236
National Archives of Sweden   236, 312
National History Museum of Latvia   323
National Library of Latvia   7–8, 200, 300,
    302, 324
National Library of Lithuania   318
National Library of Norway   241
National Library of Poland   6, 267, 272–273,
    275, 277–279, 313
National Library of Sweden   1–4, 59, 96, 161,
    171, 231, 236, 262, 264
National Library of the Czech Republic   3
natural law   166–167

Naudé, Gabriel, librarian   158n
Neumünster   268
Newberry Library, Chicago   221
Nielsen, Erland Kolding, librarian   240
Nielsen, Lauritz, bibliographer   216, 226
Noetken, Anna, nun   52–54, 60
Nordic Seven Years' War   227, 229
Nordin, Jonas, historian   328
Norkārkls, Reinis, historian   56
Norrköping   174
Nowakowska, Natalia, historian   63
Nuremberg   50, 87, 89, 104, 268, 276
Nyköping   174

Odense   65, 67, 75, 88–89, 105, 219
Oelreich, Niklas von, censor   258, 260
Olmütz. See Olomouc
Olomouc, Jesuit college of   7, 108–109, 169,
    179–196 passim, 221, 242, 252, 255,
    258–259, 340
Östersund   316
Ostroh   242n
Ottosen, Knud, church historian   22
Oxenstierna, Axel, chancellor   163, 165, 168,
    183, 245
Oxenstierna, Gabriel Gustafsson,
    councillor   163

Padua   220
Paris   72, 85–86, 89, 105, 276
Pärnu   173
Paulinus, Laurentius, bishop   164, 264
Paykull, Georg, military commander   182,
    193
Páz, Alvarez de, Jesuit   323
Pedersen, Christian, dean   85, 104–105
Peder Svart, historian   228
Pelinka, Jiři, Jesuit   182
Pensis, Christophorus de, printer   275
Peringer, Laurentz Fredrik, lecturer   250
Pernstein, Friedrich von, archbishop
    46–48, 60
Peter I, Russian czar   177, 238
Petrarch, humanist   156
Petrevius, Joannes   108
Pettegree, Andrew, historian   1, 73, 79–80,
    151, 214
Plantin, Christopher, printer   233

Plettenberg, Wolter von, knight   42
Poliander, Johannes, pastor   267, 270, 273–274, 276–279
Połock/Polotsk   112
Pontén, Jonas Otto, librarian   262
Pontoppidan, Erik, bishop   234
Poplatek, Jan, historian   113–114
Possevino, Antonio, Jesuit scholar   130–131, 301–303
Poznań   170, 187, 197n, 304
Prague   3–4, 7, 133, 142–144, 146, 169, 179, 184, 187–188, 190, 226, 242
Prat, Antoine du, parliamentarian   151

Radziwiłł, Krzysztof, hetman   115
Radziwiłł, Mikołaj, 'the Red', grand chancellor   110
Radziwiłł, Mikołaj Krzysztof, 'the Orphan', voivode   115, 121, 124
Ragvaldsson, Reinhold, dean   251
Rålamb, Claes, councillor   171, 304
Rantzau, Christian, governor   226
Rantzau, Gert, military commander   226
Rantzau, Heinrich, governor   214–215, 217, 223–226, 229, 239
Rantzau, Johan, viceroy   223–224
*Ratio studioum*   131, 139, 144, 314, 325, 328
Ravesteyn, Johannes van, printer   154
Reedtz, Jørgen, nobleman   161
Reval. *See* Tallinn
Rhau, Georg, printer   276
Rhau-Grunenberg, Johann, printer   276
Riga   46–61 *passim*, 164, 174, 197, 333, 342
  Cistercian nunnery of Saint Mary Magdalene   13–40, 42, 45, 52, 56, 60
  Jesuit college of, and spoils from   7–8, 13–14, 38, 54, 56, 59, 187, 198–199, 201, 204, 207, 208–213, 300–325
Ringsted   219, 231
Robinson, Christopher, Jesuit   112
Rogers, John, agent   110
Rogge, Kort, bishop   68
Roggebiblioteket   246–249, 264
Roman Law   168
Rome   42, 78, 80, 82, 104, 111–115, 124, 132, 138, 140, 142, 146, 160, 188, 191, 222, 275
Rosæfontanus, Petrus Parvus, humanist   227
Rosenberg Library   179, 188
Rosenhane, Schering, councillor   171, 242n

Rosenkrantz, Gunde, councillor   161
Rosenkrantz, Holger Ottosen, court marshal   229–231
Rosenkrantz, Oluf, dissident   223
Roskilde   67, 235–236
Rostgaard, Frederik, clerk   232
Rostock   82–85, 90–91, 95–96, 101–102, 152
Royal Danish Library   2, 183n, 215, 220–222, 231, 234, 236–241
Royal Library, Sweden. *See* Stockholm, royal library in (before 1877), National Library of Sweden (from 1878)
Rozen, Fryderyk, librarian   327
Rudnicki, Simon, bishop   119
Rudolph II, emperor   226
Rundle, David, historian   79
Rytter, Klaus, mayor   227

Sahlin, Gunnar, librarian   4
Saint-Charles, Louis Jacob de, author   215, 233
Saint Petersburg   238, 319
Sapieha, Kazimierz Leon, statesman   319
Sapieha, Lew, chancellor   107
Sarbiewski, Maciej Casimir, poet   119
Sarkander, Jan, cleric   189
Sarkander, Mikuláš, cleric   189
Schacklock, Richard, theologian   122
Schefferus, Johannes, historiographer   160
Schenking, Otto, bishop   312
Schirlentz, Nickel, printer   276
Schleswig   65, 67, 74, 158, 215–216, 237
Schroderus, Eric, printer   176
Schwerin   67
Schmid, Toni, historian   25, 28, 45
Second World War   267, 271–272, 279, 280n, 327
Seefeld, Jørgen, councillor   231–233, 235–237, 239
Segeberg   224, 226
Sehested, Hannibal, councillor   231
Seitz, Peter, printer   276
Serenius, Jacob, bishop   259–260
Shepreve, William, priest   124–125
Siena   141
Sigismund (III), king of Sweden and Poland   5, 90, 107, 115–116, 120, 157, 312
Silver Bible   169, 317n
Singleton, Richard, theologian   111

INDEX

Sjökvist, Peter, librarian   190, 330
Skara   68, 83, 91
Skarga, Piotr, Jesuit   120–124, 303
Skokloster Castle   162–163, 171
Skytte, Johan, councillor   158
Smolensk War   115
Snell, Johan, printer   152, 157
Söder, Björn, politician   4–5
Södermannalagen (NKS 2237 4°)   2, 240
Soltrump, Johannes, burgomaster   48–49
Soltrump, Reinhold, priest   44, 48–49, 60
Sørensen, Peder, pastor   93
Sorø   232–233
Sotheron, William, Jesuit   116–117
Sparwenfeld, Gabriel, polymath   335–336
Speratus, Paul, bishop   269, 274
Staatsbibliothek zu Berlin   62
Stade   175
Stapleton, Thomas, theologian   122
Stephanius, Stephanus Johannis, historiographer   161
Stephen Bathory, king of Poland   7, 53, 123, 301–303, 312
Stöckel, Wolfgang, printer   276
Stockholm   3, 38, 65–66, 68, 94–96, 102, 104–105, 152–154, 157, 169, 164, 168–170, 172–174, 187–188, 190–191, 194, 197, 199, 200, 203, 228, 232, 235–236, 239–240, 256–257, 301, 304, 310, 316
  royal library in   3, 59, 169, 164, 171, 173, 177, 188, 191, 194, 235–236, 254, 262, 316
Störmer, Urban, professor   270
Stralsund   175
Strängnäs   68, 174, 191–194, 242–264 passim, 328
Strasbourg   48, 83, 162, 210, 270, 273, 276
Strenga, Gustavs, historian   329
Stuchs, Georg, printer   87
Stuhmsdorf   170
Suerbeer, Albert, archbishop   38
Sunyer, Francisco, Jesuit   120
Svaning, Hans, historian   227–228
Sveinson, Brynjólfur, bishop   232
Szczecin   175, 187

Tabora, Laine, musicologist   328
Taimiņa, Aija, librarian   48
Tallinn   21n, 26, 58, 175, 309, 321–322
Tartu   58–59, 173, 301, 309 314n, 322–323

Tausen, Hans, bishop   217
Terentianus Maurus, grammarian   1
Terlon, Hugues de, diplomat   235
Terserus, Johannes, bishop   170
Thirty Years' War   3, 160, 162, 164, 168, 179, 193, 215, 221n, 226, 231, 234, 244, 262, 304, 326
Thomas Aquinas, theologian   167, 169
Thornmann, Jürgen, scholar   218
Thott, Otto, councillor   233, 239
Thus, Josef, rector   259
Tilly, Johann Tserclaes, field marshal   226
Toftgaard, Anders, librarian   327–328
Torstenson, Lennart, field marshal   162, 165, 179, 193
Toruń   242n, 269, 271–272
Trondheim   64
Trzecieski, Andrzej, poet   110
Turku   63, 68–69, 83, 95, 161, 170–171, 173–174, 178, 192

Ulfeldt, Corfitz, statesman   220, 223, 233–236
Ulfeldt, Jakob Sr, councillor   220
Ulfeldt, Jakob Jr, chancellor   220, 233
Ulhart, Philip, printer   273
Ulm   255
Undorf, Wolfgang, librarian   71, 336
University of Latvia Academic Library   38, 323
Uppsala   72, 82, 204 236
Uppsala University   70, 152, 156–157, 174, 197–198, 205, 207, 212, 307
Uppsala University Library   6–8, 13, 39, 44, 51, 56, 94, 128, 157–158, 161, 164, 167–171, 191n, 192, 194, 197n, 199–203, 212–213, 220, 232, 255, 300–301, 304–305, 307–309, 312–313, 315–317, 321, 324–325
Urne, Hans, dean   88, 105

Vadstena Abbey   44, 89, 152, 169, 304
Vallerius, Harald, librarian   203n
Vallius, Lars, rector   305
Van Zanden, Jan Luiten, historian   175
Varensbeke, Katherina, nun   55
Västerås   64, 71, 74, 82, 89, 174, 191–192, 243
Vatican Apostolic Archive   46
Vatican Library   9, 47, 160
Växjö   243

Vedel, Anders Sørensen, priest   161, 228
Venice   83, 89, 127*n*, 222–223, 275
Veselá, Lenka, book historian   327
Viborg (Denmark)   74, 92, 217, 231
Viborg (Finland)   174
Vienna   185
Villadsen, Peder, bishop   231
Vilnius   13, 34, 38, 107, 112, 123, 170, 312, 319, 321
  Jesuit Academy of   107–119 *passim*, 124–125, 303, 318
Vilnius Cistercian psalter   17, 19, 21–22, 25, 29, 32–33, 35
Visingsö   161, 174
Vladimirovas, Levas, bibliographer   319
Volanus, Andreas, theologian   110
Vossius, Isaac, librarian   191, 250–251, 254

Walde, Otto, librarian   170, 226, 235–236, 324
Wallenstein, Albrecht von, military commander   226
Wallius, Laurentius Olai, vice-chancellor   197, 199
Warsaw   4, 123, 170, 272, 313
Weduwen, Arthur der, book historian   1
Wenssler, Michel, printer   73

Werner, Sarah, book historian   73–74
Westphalian Peace Treaty   169–170, 178
Wilisch, Georg, book owner   254
Wismar   175
Wittenberg   78, 89, 91–93, 95, 104–105, 231, 269–270, 274, 276
Wittenberg, Arvid, general   187
Wojna, Benedykt, bishop   107
Wolff von Pforzheim, Jakob, printer   68, 70–71, 87
World War II. *See* Second World War
Wrangel, Carl Gustaf, field marshal   162–163, 171
Würzburg   7, 164, 202*n*, 268, 304

Zaczkovic, Jakub Pavel, friar   180*n*, 182
Zamoyski, Jan, hetman   312
Zell, Heinrich, printer   270–271, 273–274, 277
Zetterström, Carl, medical scholar   216
Zirckendorfer, Ferdinand Julius, burgher   186
Zuliani, Federico, historian   220–221
Zutshi, Patrick, medievalist   47
Zygmunt III. *See* Sigismund, king of Sweden and Poland